960
+lo

M
blk.st.

Afrocentrism

Afrocentrism

Mythical Pasts and Imagined Homes

STEPHEN HOWE

VERSO

London • New York

First published by Verso 1998
© Stephen Howe 1998
All rights reserved

The right of Stephen Howe to be identified as the author of this work
has been asserted by him in accordance with
the Copyright, Designs and Patents Act 1988

Verso
UK: 6 Meard Street, London W1V 3HR
USA: 180 Varick Street, New York NY 10014–4606

Verso is the imprint of New Left Books

ISBN 1–85984–873–7

British Library Cataloguing in Publication Data
A catalogue record for this book is available from the British Library

Library of Congress Cataloging-in-Publication Data
A catalog record for this book is available from the Library of Congress

Typeset by SetSystems Ltd, Saffron Walden, Essex
Printed by Biddles Ltd, Guildford and King's Lynn

Contents

Acknowledgements   vii

A Note on Language, Terminology and Sources   ix

Introduction   1

PART ONE ANCESTORS AND INFLUENCES

1   Race: What's in a Name?   19

2   Pan-Africanism and *Négritude*   23

3   African Origins and the Claim of Primacy   28

4   Diasporic Images of Africa before Afrocentrism   35

5   The Birth of Afrocentrism   59

6   The Masonic Connection   66

7   Caribbean Currents   73

8   Afro-America as Nation, and as Internal Colony   87

9   African Cultures and the New World   101

PART TWO VISIONS OF HISTORY

10 Hamites, Semites and Statue-Stealers   115

11 The Lure of Egypt   122

12 Nubia and 'Inner Africa': the Ideological Uses of African
    State-Building   138

13 African Unity and African Philosophy   156

14 Cheikh Anta Diop   163

15 Martin Bernal   193

PART THREE AFROCENTRISM IN THE PRESENT

16 Wild Afrocentricity   215

17 Molefi Asante: Godfather of Afrocentrism   230

18 The Network, the School and the Fellow-Travellers   240

19 Afrocentrism and Science   259

20 Psychology, Race and Magic Melanin   265

21 Polemics and Prejudices: Sex, Race, Religion and Afrocentrism   275

Bibliography   287

Index   327

Acknowledgements

My thanks for advice, guidance and/or invaluable criticism of earlier drafts to Kwame Anthony Appiah, Neil Belton, Robin Blackburn, Sebastian Budgen, Michael Francis, Paul Gilroy, Sari Horwitz, Marek Kohn, Shehu Othman, Michael Rosen, Sariel Shalev, John Sutton, Boyd Tonkin, Daphna Vardi, Lindsay Waters, Robert Young. None of them is responsible for my errors of fact, interpretation or judgement.

Thanks also to the staffs of the Bodleian Library, Ashmolean Museum, Radcliffe Science Library, Institute of Anthropology, Nuffield College and Ruskin College libraries, Oxford; the British Library, London; the Schomburg Center for Research in Black Culture and New York Public Library, New York.

A Note on Language,
Terminology and Sources

The preferred terms for various racially defined groups in American society have shifted several times in recent decades – most obviously, the changes from 'Negro' to 'black' (or 'Black'; some people thinking the capitalization important, for rather unclear reasons) to 'African-American' or sometimes 'Afro-American'. I think people should usually be called whatever they prefer to be called, and many of the writers discussed in these pages have a very strong, principled preference for 'African-American'. On the other hand, all else being equal, one syllable is better than seven; and opinion polls have shown clear majorities of African-descended Americans still preferring the older label 'black'. Meanwhile, ironically, even the house magazine of the Afrocentric movement is still called the *Journal of Black Studies*, and its editor has written highly publicized articles in what continued to be entitled the *Journal of Negro Education*. I have used 'black', 'Afro-American' and 'African-American' interchangeably, if only to avoid monotony, while mainly according with the last preference. When discussing earlier writings in which the term 'Negro' is used, I have retained those writers' language: to modernize it would be to distort their contexts and intentions, since the subtle relationships among the terms 'Negro', 'black', 'African' and 'Ethiopian' in many nineteenth-century Afro-American texts, for instance, are important to an understanding of their messages.

Many of the writers discussed here refer to Pharaonic Egypt by the name 'Kemet' or 'Kemit', while Yosef Ben-Jochannen prefers 'Ta-Merry' and Henry Olela 'Sais'; all renderings, supposedly, of ancient Egyptians' own names for their land. There are good reasons for such usages – but those reasons would apply equally to calling modern Egypt 'Misr', Germany 'Deutschland', and so on. (In fact, they would apply at *least* equally, since Ben-Jochannen's and Olela's terms are idiosyncratic to say the least.) In the interests of accessibility, I have kept the name Egypt for both the ancient and the modern states occupying roughly the same geographical area. Amitav Ghosh has argued that use of the name Egypt is particularly inappropriate – he calls it 'almost as much a weapon as a word' (1992: 33) – because of its association with a range of pejorative phrases. The tags he cites, however, are not only long vanished from popular usage, but had nothing to do with the place itself: all derived from sixteenth-century English attitudes to Roma or gypsies, whose association with Egypt was simply a matter of erroneous theories about their origins. To underline how ideologically charged the issue is, it might be noted that allegedly, when ancient historian James Muhly made the same point about use of 'Kemet' that I have just made, at a 1991 Temple University conference on Martin Bernal's *Black Athena*, he was booed by the audience (M. Levine 1992a: 451).

Dating is also potentially controversial. I use what seems the most neutral accessible form: CE (which can, according to taste, stand for 'Christian Era' or 'Common Era') rather than AD, and BCE (Before Christian/Common Era) rather than BC.

Also for reasons of accessibility, I refer almost exclusively, and wherever possible, to works in English – even where, as with the important writings of Cheikh Anta Diop, original publication was in French. I make reference, however, to a handful of particularly important, untranslated, works in French and German. In these cases translations of quoted passages are my own.

Many people prefer to put the term 'race' in scare quotes, denoting the belief that it refers to nothing real but, rather, to an undefinable, artificial and almost always pernicious imaginative construct. I agree with them, but will in these pages be discussing numerous writers who do not. Since I am talking about their ideas, and certainly not proposing a theory of race of my own, I omit the scare quotes. Imagine them if you like.

Introduction

If somebody uses tradition as a way of limiting your choices, in a
way that's as racist as saying you have to sit at the back of the bus.
                              Anthony Davis, quoted in Lock (1988: 1)

Afro-American pianist and composer Davis was thinking primarily of those
critics and music industry moguls – mostly white – who seek to block black
artistic creativity by imposing restrictive, monolithic or romanticized notions
of jazz or blues tradition on African-American music. But his complaint
applies powerfully to important modern currents in Afro-American thought.
For a mystical, essentialist, irrationalist and often, in the end, racist set of
doctrines has arisen, out of the cultural nationalist milieu, to occupy centre
ground of media attention in relation to black American thinking. The self-
ascribed or preferred label for these doctrines is Afrocentricity, or
Afrocentrism.[1]

Afrocentrism may, in its looser sense or more moderate forms, mean little
more than an emphasis on shared African origins among all 'black' people,
taking a pride in those origins and an interest in African history and culture
– or those aspects of New World cultures seen as representing African
'survivals' – and a belief that Eurocentric bias has blocked or distorted
knowledge of Africans and their cultures. In this broad sense, a very great
deal of the cultural and intellectual history of African-descended peoples
throughout the Americas and, indeed, the world could be thought of as
'Afrocentric' – interest in these themes can be documented throughout
those histories. It has had its European impact too – especially, of course,
among communities of Afro-Caribbean descent but also, notably, through
enthusiasm for black diasporic musics among many whites.[2]

But in its stronger versions, which have appeared in recent years to be
ascendant and to have arrogated the 'Afrocentric' label to themselves, a far
more cohesive, dogmatic and essentially irrational ideology becomes evident. It provides a direct analogue to the extreme forms of cultural
nationalism, premised on beliefs about race, which flourished in nineteenth-
century Europe. In this aspect it reproduces all the essential features of what
Walker Connor influentially baptized 'ethnonationalism' (Connor 1994);

1

though there is – as we shall also see below – extreme vagueness over who or what exactly comprises the 'nation' in question. Like nineteenth-century European ethnonationalism, or that evident among some 1930s Germans and 1990s Serbs, 'strong' Afrocentrism is accompanied by a mass of invented traditions, by a mythical vision of the past, and by a body of racial pseudo-science, in this case much of it centred on grotesque ideas about the skin-colouring chemical melanin.

From all this follows extreme intellectual and cultural separatism, involving belief in fundamentally distinct and internally homogeneous 'African' ways of knowing and feeling about the world, ways which only members of the group can possibly understand. Even those who *are* apparently in-group members, by birth, ancestry or pigmentation, can be excluded from it on ideological grounds if they fail to accept the ideology's doctrines; for such failure can be attributed, quite simply, to brainwashing by the dominant Eurocentric culture. Thus the belief system is insulated from the possibility of critique or falsification.

Outside the USA, such views have been gaining increasing salience in Britain, Canada, France, and even in some parts of Africa itself: though it is striking and important that what Americans call Afrocentrism is not especially popular among continental or non-diasporic African intellectuals. It is perhaps more clearly recognized by many of them than it is by some in Europe and North America that Afrocentrism in the contemporary, narrow US sense is largely a deviation or degeneration from the wider tradition of the politics of liberation: perhaps more an index of frustration than of progress.

For the historian, there are at least three clusters of issues here, clearly distinct from one another though also conceptually and, even more, politically related. They are, first, questions about the history of Africa, especially about the degree of cultural unity across the African landmass and the relationship between ancient Egyptian civilization and other states and cultures on the continent. Second, issues around the role of African peoples in the origins and development of diverse ideas, practices and technologies generally recognized as being of global significance: Egypt, and especially its putative influence on ancient Greece, is again central here. Third, controversies about the extent and nature of African influences in what is often now called the 'African diaspora'; controversies which have been especially salient in relation to the United States, have interacted heavily with sensitive issues of current public policy, and involve questions both wide and fundamental about contemporary US politics and culture.

In general terms, relationships among these three sets of issues would be of interest to anyone who is curious about history, anyone who takes pleasure in looking at long-term patterns of historical change and the interaction of cultures, regions and traditions across the great sweep of human development. That curiosity and pleasure are the main motivations for my inquiry here. The story of Afrocentrism and its ancestors is a fascinating chapter in the history of ideas, whatever else it may be. The intrinsic interest of the questions raised compensates, in part, for the depression induced by a more particular, perhaps urgent, more directly political reason for linking the three spheres of concern. This more urgent political reason is that disputes over African history, over the sources of a bundle of attributes labelled 'civilization', and over the character of ethnic cultures in diverse North American and other societies, have all been linked in violent argument around what is now called Afrocentrism.

All these matters have, in the past few years, been raised with especial acuity in the USA. There, they have become central to the storm over multiculturalism and so-called Political Correctness in education, media, government policies, and in the public sphere quite generally. Public controversy has centred particularly around the inroads Afrocentrism has made into school-level education in the USA. By 1991, it was reported, roughly 350 private schools or 'Afrocentric academies' devoted to the approach had been established, educating more than 50,000 children. The number has continued to grow. Numerous public school authorities have also introduced Afrocentric curricula, including wholly 'Afrocentric schools' in predominantly black districts, as Detroit, Baltimore and Milwaukee had done (Marable 1993: 120). Elsewhere, curriculum reform designed to introduce Afrocentric perspectives produced national-level public storms and political battles, as in New York and Washington, DC. A first generation of explicitly Afrocentric school textbooks has begun to appear (e.g. Asante 1995a, b; C. Crawford 1996; Rashidi 1992).[3]

The disputes have given rise to a massive polemical literature, including such bestsellers as Dinesh D'Souza's *Illiberal Education* and *The End of Racism*, Robert Hughes's *Culture of Complaint* and Arthur Schlesinger's *The Disuniting of America*. Yet US debate over everything from Frederick Douglass's autobiographies to rap lyrics has been persistently parochial, mistaking for American phenomena what are actually much wider ones. The 'culture wars' of recent years in the USA have, to a quite astonishing degree, been almost exclusively focused around rival versions of Americanism; even – or perhaps especially – when some protagonists have been proclaiming their 'Africanism'. Advocacy and criticism of educational 'multiculturalism' have rarely been about what schoolchildren and students should know of the world, but about what they should be taught of the histories and beliefs of various social groups in the USA's own population. It is the 'We Are the World' syndrome, with a vengeance.

Necessarily, what follows here focuses heavily on those American disputes – though, unlike almost all the vast outpouring of words in the United States on these questions, I also give substantial attention to related themes in European and, above all, in African controversies. This is, in part, to register a protest and to indicate an alternative. As writers like Robert Farris Thompson and, more recently, Paul Gilroy have shown, the ideas and cultural forms of black communities – like those of other ethnic formations – on all the shores of the Atlantic have composed a single story, an elaborate pattern of call and response. This makes a nonsense of the national

frameworks within which black history and culture are usually discussed.
And that pattern in its turn is far more influentially intertwined with the
central themes of Euro-American modernity than is ordinarily thought:
which means that dominant discourses about Europeanism, Englishness,
Americanism, modernism and postmodernism – with their mirror-image,
currently fashionable 'Afrocentric' theories – also need drastic revision.
Much the same is true of the Mediterranean world, three thousand years
ago as well as today. 'Black Athena' is a slogan just as false to history as is
'White Egypt'.

In what follows, I have tried to show that the views of writers usually
labelled Afrocentric are largely erroneous, in part by comparing them
against the opinions on the same subjects of various other writers. What
matters to me – and, I hope, to almost all readers – is that the writers whose
views I prefer are more expert in their subjects, more careful and coherent
in their arguments, offer more and better evidence and higher standards of
clarity and logic in pursuit of the beliefs they advance, than their opponents.
Some, however, will think that it is more important that those I judge
negatively are mostly – though very far from all – of at least partial African
descent, while those I assess more favourably are often of European or Euro-
American origin: though very many are not, and in some cases I am quite
ignorant and happily uncurious about their ancestry or skin colour. Those
who are fixated on the view that racial or ethnic origin inevitably dictates
intellectual position will no doubt therefore dismiss the ideas of many of
these authors, and will dismiss mine for the same reason. So be it: that
fundamentally racist attitude to intellectual inquiry is, as I shall argue, the
most basic of all the faults in the work I examine, and judge negatively, in
the following pages.

Yet by no means all, or even most, of these charges stick against all the
writers I analyse here. Some of them seem to me to have made genuine and
crucial contributions to knowledge, and to political enlightenment. The
works of Cheikh Anta Diop, St Clair Drake and Martin Bernal, in particular,
have power and importance for their negative critique of European colonial
arrogance and its latter-day legacies. They remain significant for that
necessary debunking function, even if there are grave problems with the
positive cases which these authors offer to replace the views they assail.
Much of the earlier historical writing by African-Americans within what has
been called the 'vindicationist' tradition (Drake 1987: xv–1) can be
defended on similar grounds. Even where the authors made what now
appear quite inaccurate or exaggerated claims about black and African
achievement, they provided an impassioned corrective to Euro-American
and European disparagement. As such, writing like this takes its place in the
long history of intellectual decolonization of which Edward Said has written
movingly in his *Culture and Imperialism* and elsewhere, and of which Said's
own works are among the most distinguished modern examples.

I do not seek to imply that all, or even most, Afrocentric writers are
deliberate intellectual frauds – though I think some certainly are. More,

probably, sincerely believe in the ideas they propound, or think that the political or psychological usefulness of those ideas outweighs their often dubious intrinsic merit, or adopt some mixture of those two stances. The latter – the belief that however questionable the claims about history, culture, collective psychology or science made by Afrocentrists, they have positive confidence-building or identity-affirming functions – would be, if it were true, the strongest defence of the movement. The prominent African-American historian Wilson J. Moses has suggested something of the sort: 'Like most mythologies, it is only half believed and simply represents an attempt on the part of respectable, honest people to create a positive folk mythology' (quoted in G. Thomas 1995: 28). One can certainly accept that more-or-less honest people, in their capacity as political activists, might seek to build a positive folk mythology which encourages those they wish to mobilize – even if they do not wholly believe in the propositions they advance. It is less clear whether honest *intellectuals* can properly behave in such a way, using their university posts, editorships, classroom or media access and the apparatus of scholarship to do so; still less whether such a stance is compatible with the insistent claims of most Afrocentrists that they are recovering the truth of African history from others' mythmaking – that they are pioneering a new scholarly discipline, or even a science.

More importantly, however, I do not think that the faith in the political or psychological benefits of false 'folk mythologies' is justified. It depends on two beliefs: that false and mythicized ideas can – even in principle – be politically capacitating, and that the particular false ideas propounded by Afrocentrists can have positive political consequences under the particular circumstances in which they are propounded. The first, I think, would be true of Afrocentrism only if politics were always and only a zero-sum game (if 'we' win, 'you' must necessarily lose) setting ethnic or racial collectivities against one another. This is not the case, even in the contemporary USA: politics is, at the least, a great deal more complicated than that. Presenting it in terms of such grand simplicities is of advantage only to a few individuals, who can gain influence by claiming to speak for the 'imagined communities' whose leaders they pretend to be. The second is in my view also false, for reasons which will be explained further on, but which come down to the observation that Afro-America's problems are above all problems of economic deprivation, and cannot be remedied by approaches which entirely ignore economics. This is still more true of Africa itself.

I am unconvinced, therefore, by the widely voiced claims that Afrocentrism – perhaps especially at the level of high-school education – is of psychological, cultural or political benefit to African-Americans, providing resources to combat racism and other disabilities under which they labour. Its characteristic emphases seem to me, on the contrary, often to be barriers to or digressions from the development of effective strategies against racism and for social justice. It might, of course, still be thought that Afrocentrism is primarily a cultural or psychological phenomenon rather than an intellectual or pedagogic one. On some levels this is certainly true, notably for such ideas' influence in popular culture (for instance in rap music). However, these aspects are not my main focus here. Whatever else it may be, Afrocentrism is *also* an educational and intellectual movement, whose proponents make very strong claims about the truth-value of their ideas: especially their ideas about history, but also about psychology, anthropology and various natural sciences. Indeed, their characteristic stance, far from asserting that they are putting forward useful or psychologically capacitating myths (as Moses's diagnosis would imply), is to say that their views represent the true historical reality, long suppressed and concealed by European racist misconceptions or lies. As Gerald Early perceptively points out, Afrocentrism resembles many earlier nationalist ideologies in being:

> the orthodoxy of the books . . . an attempt to wed knowledge and ideology. Movements like Afrocentrism, which feels both its mission and its authority hinge on the revelation of a denied and buried truth, promote a fervent scholasticism, a hermeneutical ardor among true believers for compilations of historical minutiae on the one hand, and for grand philosophical tracts on the other. (1995: 34)[4]

It is on that level, the level of the truth-value of Afrocentric claims, that I seek primarily to assess the movement.

In the end, indeed, I believe that most of the arguments about the racialization of scholarship, proposed in recent years from a wide range of perspectives, are an evasion of or a distraction from serious political issues in relation to Africa and its diaspora, as much as for anywhere else. To observe that scholarly perspectives on African and diasporic societies have been massively influenced by racial ideology is one thing, and is obviously true. To analyse those histories of racialized scholarship, and to trace the ways in which writers' own ethnic origins have influenced their views, are important and fascinating tasks. But it is quite another thing to believe that such analyses offer significant aid in solving contemporary political or economic problems – let alone to think that the erection of counter-myths about African racial superiority or a unitary, transhistorical 'black perspective' does so. At the height of the bitter battles in the American African Studies Association (battles which play a walk-on part in the story told here) Pierre L. van den Berghe pointed out – overgeneralizing in his anger, but with, I believe, an essential, powerful truth – that:

> The African peasant does not care one whit whether his oppressor is white or black. Rightly, he does not consider 'race' relevant. It should be a matter of deepest shame to us 'intellectuals' that we still talk as if it were relevant. (1970: 336)[5]

If anything, that is even more true today than it was over twenty-five years ago.

It should hardly be necessary to say that all these traits can be found paralleled in many other parts of the world, and among many US groups other than African-Americans. Indeed, they seem ubiquitous wherever history is pressed into service in ethnic contestation. There is no intention here of seeking to imply that the mostly Afro-American writers analysed are uniquely blameworthy, or that African-American culture is somehow more credulously disposed than any other towards mythicized self-legitimation, racially charged fantasies of origin or mystical pseudo-history.

Every intellectual failing identified in this book has its parallels elsewhere: often parallels that have done or could do vastly greater political damage than those that are popular in some sections of the African-American public sphere. Virtually every European state and ethnic group has drawn on and abused the discipline of archaeology in its search for historical roots, often involving straightforwardly racist ideas about the origins and destiny of itself and its neighbours (see, for example, Diaz-Andreu and Champion 1996). In the cases I know best, those of Britain and Ireland, very long histories of utterly fantastic racial myth and ideas about the national pasts and origins can be traced, involving all the elements of mysticism, claims of racial primacy and superiority, and promiscuous borrowings from esoteric lore and Masonic tradition which we shall observe operating in the African-American case.[6] This was not just the preserve of mystics or irrationalists: central figures of the European Enlightenment held not only racist ideas but ideas which now appear utterly grotesque about racial difference, national character and human origins (see, for example, Eze 1996, 1997). Nor is it merely a matter of the European past, of an intellectual stage now transcended. The immense and gullible appetite of contemporary Euro-peans and Euro-Americans for occult, irrational and fantastic 'histories' is evident from the shelves of almost any bookstore, where such works commonly command far more shelf space and greater sales than works of genuine history. These works frequently revolve around many of the same themes as those popular in romantic Afrocentrism: theories about the lost wisdom of ancient civilizations, especially that of Egypt, bizarre claims about the history of Freemasonry or Theosophism, stories of lost continents, and so on. As we shall see, indeed, these are not only parallel but often interconnected stories, with African-American vindicationists (and fantas-ists) often drawing heavily on various earlier European racial theories and bodies of esoteric thought. Perhaps the worst thing one could say of the more eccentric African-American writers discussed below is (to adapt Mark Twain on the Jews) that they've shown they can be just as bad as everybody else.

Few, if any, of the polemicists who have assaulted Afrocentric and related intellectual trends in the US 'culture wars' of recent years appear to have read much – or even any – of the Afrocentrists' work. Dinesh D'Souza (1991), Arthur Schlesinger (1992), Robert Hughes (1993), Richard Bern-stein (1994) and others refer almost exclusively to newspaper reports on it, rather than the writings themselves. Mass media attention to Afrocentrism and associated beliefs can be said to have started with the polemical writings of D'Souza, a young conservative journalist and researcher at the right-wing think-tank the American Enterprise Institute. (The book which contributed most to beginning the rather artificial controversy over 'political correctness' in academe, Allan Bloom's *Closing of the American Mind* [Bloom 1987], had not specifically targeted Afrocentrism or Black Studies, though it had bemoaned affirmative action programmes and separatist sentiment among students.) Afrocentrism was only one of the targets of D'Souza's freewheeling, often slapdash assault in *Illiberal Education* on multiculturalism, 'political correctness', and left-wing academia. He sneered at the young enthusiasts at Howard University and elsewhere who were, in his terms, 'in search of Black Pharaohs', but he did not look at their ideas either closely or fairly.

Soon thereafter, though, the distinguished historian Arthur M. Schlesinger Jr joined the fray with an equally polemical but more thoughtfully argued book, *The Disuniting of America.* Schlesinger mounted his critique from the standpoint of a New Deal liberal as contrasted with D'Souza's neoconservatism, but he was no less hostile to the 'eruption of ethnicity' (1992: 15) in the worlds of education and public policy. He believed that a resurgent ethnocentrism in cultural politics threatened the all-important traditions of the USA as an integrationist melting-pot, especially in its insistence on teaching history as 'filopietistic commemoration' (ibid. 99). The result was to 'sanction and deepen racial tensions' (69) and threaten equally the academic values of accuracy and objectivity, and the political values of tolerance and liberalism. He placed Afrocentrism more firmly in his sights than did D'Souza, seeing it as representing many of the worst excesses of the general cultural trends he deplored.

The noted art critic Robert Hughes went in, if anything, even harder; though his *Culture of Complaint* (1993) has the merit of assaulting the 'patriotically correct' idiocies of the right as well as the 'politically correct' ones of the left. The Afrocentrists and allied trends, Hughes believes, 'are proposing, not an informed multiculturalism, but a blinkered and wildly polemical separatism' (ibid. 129). Hughes's notion of Afrocentric ideas, like Schlesinger's, is apparently based on an extremely narrow reading. He cites the Senegalese historian Cheikh Anta Diop and the British theorist Martin Bernal, but very few other Afrocentric writers, and may too readily associate Afrocentrism as a whole with the ravings of works favoured by the Nation of Islam and by black anti-Semites, such as *The Iceman Inheritance* and *The Secret Relationship between Blacks and Jews* (137–8, 143–4). In the end, Hughes believes, Afrocentric beliefs 'want to create a separatist history and enforce it on kids who are still too young to dispute it'. They amount to claims for 'purely remedial history' with 'symbolic' functions: 'part of a reaction of despair, frustration and rage', and part of a universal tendency of insurgent nationalisms to fabricate myths about the past (148).

Another left-wing scholar and polemicist, the Afro-American political scientist Manning Marable, has been almost equally harsh in his judgements. Although Afrocentrism aims to provide the basis for an alternative worldview and oppositional consciousness, he feels, it is essentially opposed to pluralism and diversity, blind to issues of gender and social class, and '"freezes" the meaning of culture, reducing the dynamics and multiple currents of interpersonal and group interaction to a rigid set of ahistorical categories' (Marable 1995: 122). Marable is suspicious of the movement's exclusivism, though he notes the irony that it is at least as often white administrators and academics as black separatists who harbour the 'hidden assumption . . . that no one who was not born black would have any reason to cultivate a scholarly interest or the proper dedication for the study of black life and history' (ibid.: 122–3). Above all, Afrocentrism's neglect of economic realities damns it in his eyes:

> It looks to a romantic, mythical reconstruction of yesterday to find some understanding of the cultural basis of today's racial and class challenges. Yet that critical understanding of reality cannot begin with an examination of the lives of Egyptian Pharaohs. It must begin by critiquing the vast structure of power and privilege which characterizes the political economy of post-industrial capitalist America. (1995: 200)

Dinesh D'Souza returned to the fray with *The End of Racism* (1995). Here he (or his research assistants) seemed to have read rather more widely than in his earlier polemic, and the new book included a much more detailed examination of Afrocentrism. His treatment of the theme, however, still seemed dominated by a desire for simple dismissal of Afrocentric ideas rather than tracing their roots or evaluating their claims. The book also expresses disconcertingly sharp prejudice and scorn towards African-American communities. Its treatment of alleged genetic differences between racial groups is especially puzzling. D'Souza gives an extended and sympathetic précis of the views of those who believe there are significant inherited inequalities of intelligence, with African-Americans scoring markedly lower than Europeans and Asians. Not only is his summary sympathetic: he distorts the theories of Sandra Scarr and others to make them seem like clear-cut proponents of such views, which they are not. Equally, he caricatures the arguments of writers on the other side like Stephen Jay Gould, seeking to make them sound merely illogical or inconsistent. But after all this, D'Souza insists that his own view is that cultural and behavioural traits, not genetic ones, determine the myriad failures he discerns in Afro-America. Therefore the whole genetic argument is an irrelevance to his case. Why, then, has he presented it at such length and in such partisan fashion, unless on the old proverbial basis that 'if you throw enough mud, some of it must stick'?[7]

The longest and most detailed assault on Afrocentrism to appear thus far has been Mary Lefkowitz's book *Not Out of Africa* (1996a). This, however, has a far narrower compass than its title would imply. Among the numerous different claims made by Afrocentric writers, Lefkowitz considers only one: Egyptian influence on ancient Greece, primarily in the sphere of philosophy. Her main purpose is, quite simply, to defend the 'integrity' of ancient Greece and of traditional classical scholarship against what she regards as

Afrocentric calumnies. In this respect, she regularly slips into the kind of ethnocentric arguments against which she protests elsewhere. Lefkowitz complains that Afrocentrism 'robs the ancient Greeks and their modern descendants of a heritage that rightly belongs to them' (ibid.: 126). Such 'untruths do injustice, not only to the ancient Greeks who have been falsely maligned, but to their descendants' (168).

Lefkowitz offers an extremely attenuated and in some respects inaccurate account of Afrocentrism's intellectual genealogy: for instance, she regards Marcus Garvey as having originated views which, as we shall see, he had in fact only popularized from varied older sources (130–34). Her explanation of how Masonic ideas fed into Afrocentric writing is equally inadequate: I attempt to provide a more satisfactory account of this odd byway in the history of ideas below. Lefkowitz's book, short as it is, is 'padded' with various digressions – for instance, a seemingly irrelevant excursus on Mozart's *Magic Flute* (56, 118–20) – and much repetition. Some of her arguments are extremely questionable: in her eagerness to disprove Afrocentric claims that Cleopatra was black (on which she is no doubt correct) she insists, far less plausibly, that Shakespeare's *Antony and Cleopatra* does not depict her as being dark-skinned: a view that involves her in quite fanciful readings of passages in the play (38–9). She attacks Afrocentrists for not being properly interested in relations between ancient Egypt and Sub-Saharan Africa (a judgement which only ignorance about the range of Afrocentric writing could sanction); but ironically, her own single, brief reference to that issue is not only inaccurate about African kingship but relies on the same out-of-date authority, Henri Frankfort, whose views underpin some of the wilder claims made by Diop and other Afrocentrists (135).

Lefkowitz proclaims an interest in the sociology of knowledge, and promises more than once to explain *why* Afrocentrism has had such appeal to some students and intellectuals. This, however, she never does. Her discussion of intellectual climates and traditions is brief and crude. She appears to associate Afrocentrism with postmodernist, textualist or relativist approaches to historical study, with the view of 'history as a form of fiction' (xiv) and confusingly describes such stances as 'cultural history' (50) – by which is usually meant the history of culture, but which she uses to mean history written from the viewpoint of cultural particularism – and 'new historicism' (50) – a term normally denoting the approach of such literary scholars as Stephen Greenblatt, but for Lefkowitz apparently meaning 'mythicized history'.

Lefkowitz's Conclusion, moreover, does not attempt to summarize the intellectual balance sheet of Afrocentrism's pseudo-historical claims, but discusses how best to mount a police action against them. It is hard not to suspect that the very particular controversies in which Lefkowitz has been engaged at Wellesley College, around the activities of her colleague Tony Martin (see below, pp. 277–8), provided much of the stimulus for this. Her final pages are, in effect, a call for university faculties and authorities to censor Afrocentric courses, even if she believes that 'the first line of defence should be words and, when appropriate, even ridicule' (171–2).

Perhaps the most serious flaw in Lefkowitz's book, however, is that its analysis of Afrocentric writings is almost as narrowly based as those of Hughes or Schlesinger. She makes fairly brief reference to the work of Yosef Ben-Jochannen, Cheikh Anta Diop, and J.A. Rogers, and has elsewhere (Lefkowitz 1992, 1996b) criticized Martin Bernal's *Black Athena*, but her main target of attack – and the only Afrocentric text she investigates in detail – is George G.M. James's *Stolen Legacy*. James's little book has certainly had an influence, but the metonymic approach of allowing it to stand in for Afrocentrist history as a whole is clearly inadequate. Other writings in the genre, many of them more substantial and coherently argued than James's, have very grave faults; but they are not necessarily the *same* faults as his. *Stolen Legacy* is a work of the utmost intellectual naivety, innocent of even the outward appearances of academic procedure: to assail its inadequacies as a piece of scholarship in the way Lefkowitz does is to use a steamroller to crack a nut. Lefkowitz does not appear to have uncovered any information about James himself, or sought to do so: his motivation (which he discusses in some detail) is not considered. Thus Lefkowitz does not begin to fulfil her promise to explain 'how and why mythic or propagandistic "histories" come to be written' (134). An adequate and thorough investigation of Afrocentric views of history would have to trace their genealogies through a mass of nineteenth- and early-twentieth-century black American writing about Africa, to take detailed note of such major protagonists as Marimba Ani, Molefi Asante, John G. Jackson, Ron Karenga, Ivan Van Sertima and Chancellor Williams, and – perhaps above all – to look closely at the most influential and intellectually substantial of them all, Cheikh Anta Diop. Lefkowitz does none of these things. I attempt them in the pages that follow.

A far more substantial volume, co-edited by Lefkowitz and her Wellesley colleague Guy MacLean Rogers, appeared almost simultaneously with *Not Out of Africa: Black Athena Revisited* (Lefkowitz and Rogers 1996), a collection of responses to Martin Bernal's work, almost all of them highly critical, by various classicists, Egyptologists and others. This too, therefore, has a relatively restricted focus, but includes extremely important contributions by such major scholars as John Baines, Loring Brace, Robert Palter, Frank Snowden and Frank Yurco. Their findings and arguments will be discussed and drawn upon at various points below, especially in the chapter on Martin Bernal (Chapter 15).

One fairly elementary but widespread confusion should be dealt with at the outset. A common rallying cry among many involved in African-American education, writing and politics is the critique of 'universalism'; the same is true in what has become labelled postcolonial studies, and in some branches of feminist thought. Very often, this critique seems to confuse two or all of three rather different issues. First, there is opposition to false or pseudo-universalism: criticism of a European particularism or, indeed, chauvinism which poses as universal, as it has evidently done in a great deal of modern 'Western' thought. Such criticism of historic European or Western pretensions, which were often closely linked with European colonialism, has been a major and important part of the cultural politics of recent decades.

Second, though, is the critique of what one might – albeit guardedly – call genuine universalism: attack on or dismissal of values, practices, techniques which – there are good reasons to think – transcend particular cultures and traditions (or should do so). This second strand defends the local, the particular, the culture-specific, or what it claims to be the traditional. It very readily slides towards nationalist, xenophobic or racist stances. Third – and entirely different again – is the critique of philosophical universalism: the denial, often associated with postmodernist theories, that notions of truth, logic, reason, and so on can be held independently of particular cultures or interpretive communities.

The antithesis or counter to the first 'universalism' is, quite simply, awareness of and respect for cultural difference. The antithesis to the second, however, is particularism, shading into what Edward Said (1993) calls nativism and Samir Amin (1989) provincialism. The antithesis to the third is an extreme relativism. For instance, a person who points out that the male-headed nuclear family is not a 'universal' form of social organization but a culture-specific one (and one that is neither ubiquitous nor in any strong sense traditional within Western Europe itself) is engaged in the first kind of critique. Someone who claims, as the Chinese and some Islamic governments did at recent United Nations human rights summits, that a universal code of human rights conduct is invalid because their countries' cultural traditions dictate different – and apparently much more restrictive – conceptions of such rights, is mounting the second and, in my view, far less creditable sort of critique. And someone who says that the proposition 'If A is greater than B, B cannot be greater than A' is true only in certain cultures, certain traditions of thought, and not in others (not a far-fetched example, as we shall see in relation to some Afrocentric thinkers) is involved in the third line of critique.

In my view, the first kind of 'anti-universalism' is a valuable – indeed, essential – corrective to European cultural pretensions and distortions of history. The second, however, is at best a profoundly uninteresting kind of cultural parochialism, and at worst (as with those repressive governments which used it to defend human rights abuses, or with some Africans' defence of female genital mutilation on grounds of 'tradition') an alibi for inhumane and regressive practices. The third is simply absurd. We shall be seeing all three, often muddled together, in operation in the theories discussed in these pages.[8]

My primary subject here, contemporary American Afrocentrism, is only one broad strand – not the only one, arguably not the most important, certainly not the most coherent or attractive – in the long story of New World appropriations of the image of Africa. As Stuart Hall says, reflecting on cultural identities in the Caribbean:

The political movements in the New World in the twentieth century have had to pass through the re-encounter with Africa. The African diasporas of the New World have been in one way or another incapable of finding a place in modern history without the symbolic return to Africa. It has taken many forms, it has been embodied in many movements both intellectual and popular. (S. Hall 1995: 9)

But further on, Hall issues a warning which applies accurately to many of the ideas discussed in these pages:

Africa is not waiting there in the fifteenth or seventeenth century, waiting for you to roll back across the Atlantic and rediscover it in its tribal purity, waiting there in its prelogical mentality, waiting to be woken from inside by its returning sons and daughters. (ibid.: 11)

Images and stereotypes of Africa may have been a constantly recurring theme in the histories of New World diasporic groups, but real practical engagement with the troubles of contemporary Africa has been a much more uneven story. As we shall see, it was very much a minority phenomenon among Afro-Americans, many of whom rejected the idea of having special ties to the African continent, at least until the 1950s–60s era of decolonization in Africa and Civil Rights in the USA. We shall be tracing aspects of Afro-American responses to Africa and its history – some of them surprisingly perennial, constantly recurring themes of romanticization and ambivalence. We shall not, however, be investigating the important but distinct theme of direct political engagement by African-Americans seeking to aid the continent's liberation; a story which would run from Max Yergan's Council on African Affairs, founded in 1937, through the American Negro Leadership Conference on Africa, the 1960s African Liberation Support Committee and its successors, culminating in the major African-American mobilization against apartheid in the 1980s. Different aspects of this constructive and often impassioned engagement have been analysed by various scholars.[9]

Afrocentrists' contributions to these campaigns, however, appear to have been minimal. Few of the Afro-American cultural nationalists who loudly proclaim their identification with Africa have seemed to evince a close or informed interest in the continent itself, or have played any major or constructive role in the political campaigns against apartheid, let alone against state repression in postcolonial Africa or on behalf of the victims of genocide in Rwanda and famine elsewhere. Their Africa – as Stuart Hall's comment implies, and as many critics have complained – is an imaginary place, without a real human history (as opposed to the mythographies of conquering kings, superheroes, and bucolic bliss which they construct) as well as without a present: not only without hunger, military coups, gender inequality and genocide, but equally without TV stations or traffic jams, human rights movements and contemporary artistic creativity. To my knowledge, no self-proclaimed Afrocentrist in North America has ever yet published a detailed, substantial study of any particular African society, past or present, ancient or modern – with the partial exception, symptomatically, of works about ancient Egypt. The attitude is very well summed up in the story a friend recently told me about a US academic conference a few years back – a story I have no reason to disbelieve. The friend had presented a paper analysing the sharply different stances on both aesthetics and politics of two great current African writers, the Nigerian Wole Soyinka and the Kenyan Ngugi Wa Thiong'o. At the end, the most prominent of all the academic Afrocentrists rose to denounce, in the most bitter terms, what had been said. He had no quarrel with any of the actual arguments put forward; he seemed barely to have heard them. His objection was more fundamental. He thought it simply wrong that a white person should dare to suggest that two Africans disagreed with one another. As an African himself (albeit one born in Georgia) he knew it just could not be: all Africans share the same values. End of argument, so far as he was concerned.

But if the Africa of the Afrocentrists is an imaginary place, then so, arguably, is their America. Their ideas, like cultural nationalism in general, quite simply have nothing at all to say about the most central problem facing Afro-Americans: the conditions of economic marginality, insecurity and underprivilege under which most of them exist. The cultural nationalist stress on ethnicity to the virtual exclusion of all else may have done some good in addressing the handicap of low self-esteem which is a legacy of Euro-racism and perhaps of slavery. Or rather, since the Afrocentrists and cultural nationalists come overwhelmingly from the black middle class, or aspire to it, it addresses problems of self-image – and others' negative perceptions – which most affect *them*.[10] Economic analysis, and programmes for economic reform, are simply absent, unaddressed. As Orlando Patterson lamented over twenty years ago:

> All this, of course, simply plays into the hands of the American establishment, for there is no concerted attack on the economic root cause of the problem – an attack which involves real concessions if it is to be met by means other than repression. Ironically, the cultural and symbolic demands emphasized by most black leaders are all too easily met. It was ridiculously easy for the establishment to respond by changing the color of a few faces in the ads ... by publishing a spate of third-rate books on the greatness of the African tradition, by the glorification of black roots. (Patterson 1977: 155)

Afrocentrism, today, responds to the ever deepening crisis of the black American poor by demanding more of the same.[11]

Notes

1. The label itself is not universally accepted among those usually called Afrocentrists. A few prefer 'Africentrism', which actually makes better sense etymologically. Molefi K.

Asante and his followers usually call their belief system 'Afrocentricity' rather than 'Afrocentrism', and refer to their associated academic discipline as 'Africology'. Erskine Peters (1991) has suggested a distinction between 'Afrocentric' to denote study of African-American life, and 'Africentric' for a focus on the continent itself and its historical heritage. Some such distinction might indeed be analytically useful, but Peters's terminology – quite apart from its pedantic air, and the value judgement he builds into it by viewing 'Africentrism' as the more creatively valid of the two spheres – has not been taken up by others.

2. Simon Jones's *Black Culture, White Youth* (1988) traces one strand of this in the British context.

3. One recent study, however (Merelman 1995), suggests that the teaching of black history in high schools remains primarily in the 'contributionist' mode – stressing the achievements of individual African Americans within US society – rather than being mostly Afrocentric in the strong sense. What both approaches have in common is a tendency to talk about black history in an artificial isolation, rather than exploring the complex interactions of different groups, whether in ancient Africa or in the modern USA. The texts themselves often have a curiously hybrid air. Asante's, as we shall see, eschews some of the wilder historical claims of his other writing, but retains and adds other very dubious arguments; while Crawford's mixes thoughts on curriculum reform drawing on John Dewey and multiculturalist theory with comparatively sober overviews of ancient Egyptian art and literature, but also with themes drawn uncritically from extremely unreliable Afrocentric 'authorities' such as George G.M. James and Yosef Ben-Jochannen.

4. Judgement on this 'scholasticism' also depends, of course, on arguments – rather complex ones – about the status of historical 'truth'. I do not try to make those arguments here, but simply note a belief that while historical writings are undoubtedly literary artifacts, and are always shaped and evaluated by many considerations other than factual or evidential accuracy, they can and must *also*, vitally, be judged according to their accuracy. In the specific context of African-American historical writing, I would wish to make a sharp distinction between works which deliberately adopt an 'epic', heroic and inspirational style of narration but none the less adhere to clear rules of evidence (good examples would be Vincent Harding's *There Is a River* [1981], or Nathan Huggins's *Black Odyssey* [1990]), and those which engage in wild and apparently deliberate mythmaking, whose statements bear no relation to the considered views of most specialists in their fields. There may be good reasons to be critical of the former – such reasons are well presented in Clarence Earl Walker's *Deromanticizing Black History* (1991) – but my target here is the second, much more fantastic kind of writing about history: a category into which almost all Afrocentricity falls. Nathan Huggins compares his and Harding's approaches, and offers a thoughtful defence of them, in his 'Integrating Afro-American History into American History' (1986: 163–5). Occasional attempts have been made – invariably by non-historians – to assert that *all* historical writing is 'inspirational' in intent, and that internal distinctions are thus irrelevant (see, for instance, Gilkes [1995: 30–32]). Only historiographical ignorance or philosophical naivety, I think, could sustain such a view.

5. There is a rather uncomfortable irony in my quoting with approval, here and later, the insistence of the young Pierre van den Berghe in 1970 on the irrelevance of race. The older van den Berghe, in more recent years, has drawn ever closer to sociobiological theories of history, with a concomitant belief that race is extremely relevant to nearly everything (1986, 1995). His later views, which I dislike, do not make his earlier ones any less compelling.

6. For Britain, see, amid a substantial literature, McDougall (1982); for Ireland the unmatched researches of Joep Leerssen (1986, 1988, 1996). It may be added that histories other than the European and the African are also replete with such fantasy: see, for instance, the racial theories propounded at various times by Arab (Al-Azmeh 1992), Chinese (Dikotter 1992), and South Asian (Robb 1995) writers, or the 'Aryanism' developed by both British Orientalists and Indian romantic culturalists (Trautmann 1997).

7. Other polemical assaults on US Afrocentrism include Lefkowitz (1992, 1996a), John

Miller (1994), some contributions to Collier and Horowitz (eds 1997), and (perhaps the most careful and measured brief critique) Blakey (1995). On Afrocentrism in the sciences, the critical literature is greater and probably better: see Gross and Levitt (1994); Kohn (1995); Montellano (1993) and Palter (1996a). The wider phenomenon of conservative counterattacks against the critique of Eurocentric historiography – what might be called the anti-anti-Eurocentric backlash – probably came earlier in France than in the Anglophone world (see, for instance, Bruckner [1986]; Finkielkraut [1988]).

8. There is also a quite distinct debate – albeit one which, in North America, has often been confused with the debate over Afrocentrism – around the politics of institutionalized multiculturalism; notably, what kinds of respect, recognition or formal rights should be granted to culturally distinct groups within plural societies? I cannot pursue that debate here – for major recent statements of position in it, see Gutmann (1994); Kymlicka (1995); Kymlicka (ed. 1995); Mendelsohn and Baxi (1994). I can only signal my scepticism as to whether humans can meaningfully be characterized as divided into discrete entities called 'cultures' and my sympathy for the 'universalist' and 'cosmopolitan' stances represented, for instance, by Jürgen Habermas and Kwame Appiah in the Gutmann collection, or Jeremy Waldron in the Kymlicka one.

9. See Duignan and Gann (1984); Isaacs (1963); Staniland (1991); Magubane (1987); Lynch (1978); Anthony (1994); Nixon (1994). Fredrickson (1995) traces both parallels and connections between black liberationist thought in the USA and that in South Africa; while Zack-Williams (1995) calls for an overdue dialogue between the concerns of African-diasporic cultural studies and those of development theory in Africa itself.

10. The generally middle-class character of Afrocentrism is emphasized by such Afro-American critics as Early (1995) and Marable (1995). No educational survey has yet managed to show that there is any positive relationship whatsoever between students' self-esteem and improving their academic, employment or economic performance. It is not even clear that African-American schoolchildren *do* overall express lower self-esteem than whites (see Mecca *et al.* 1989, a reference for which I am indebted to Kwame Appiah). The quintessentially contemporary US emphasis on positive self-image has few, if any, secure socioeconomic foundations. Molefi Asante, the most publicly prominent Afrocentric educator, denies in his reply to critic Diane Ravitch that enhancement of self-esteem is an objective of Afrocentric schooling (Asante 1991b); but this appears inconsistent with many of his other statements.

11. Analyses of that crisis are ever-proliferating. One from which I have learned especially is Hacker (1992). This is not, of course, to suggest that there is no connection between cultural transformations and economic progress, but only that an exclusive emphasis on the former is unlikely to aid the latter. Condit and Lucaites (1993) argue persuasively, as against the elitism of much of the thought analysed here, how much the discourse of equality in American history has owed to African-American inputs.

Part One

Ancestors and Influences

1

Race: What's in a Name?

The arguments over Afrocentrism, like the closely related ones which have recurred under different names for decades, are about history and culture, mentality and psychology, literature and linguistics, sex and economics; about Africa, Europe, America, the Atlantic and the Mediterranean. But above all, they are about race, and are conducted in the language of race. They invoke – sometimes overtly, sometimes in a kind of code – beliefs and theories about racial or ethnic identities. Theories of race and ethnicity are, of course, always claims about human group difference. The essential distinction is between those which see the differences that matter as being physical ones, and those which conceive of them culturally. Nowadays we usually describe the former as theories of race, the latter theories of ethnicity.

In the postwar world – especially in the West, and especially among liberals – there has been a powerful tendency towards the second language: to talk of human difference in terms of 'ethnic groups' rather than 'races'. The shift had both a directly political motivation – above all to refute the 'race science' of the Nazis – and a scientific one asserting, in essence, that race is not a biologically, genetically, anthropologically or sociologically meaningful concept. This latter proposition, denying that the language of race has any scientific validity, was given the official imprimatur of the United Nations in the postwar UNESCO Statement on Race. But the change to the language of ethnicity has not necessarily wholly severed the link with biology; for it is evident that lurking behind many usages – scientific, popular and bureaucratic – of the discourse of ethnicity are ideas about physical rather than – or as well as – cultural differences.[1]

Beliefs about physical differences have also, quite obviously, involved ideas that they correlate to characteristics other than the purely physical. If this were not the case, there would be little interest or controversy about distinctions between humans which are mostly rather minor and – in the case of the most observable ones – literally superficial. Why would anyone care that some of us are hairier, while some of them have shorter noses? In fact, claims about physical variations have constantly been linked to claims about differences in behaviour and capacities: above all, of course, in

19

intellectual capacity and/or psychological disposition. It is this association which has made it difficult for many of us to believe that ideas about physical variations among human groups could even in principle be neutral, objective, value-free. It is still less easy to accept that claims about psychological difference could be value-free: recent controversy over Charles Murray and Richard Herrnstein's book *The Bell Curve* (1994) has provided a striking new instance of how any such claims seem inevitably to carry strong and disturbing moral–political overtones.[2]

Statements such as 'science does not recognize the existence of race', however, induce their own kinds of scepticism, and these may be increasing in the 1990s.[3] The 'sciences' most directly concerned with these issues are generally thought of as clustering towards the 'soft' end of the intellectual spectrum; those least able to produce clear-cut and definitive results, with least consensus about methodology and the conditions of proof, most susceptible to subjective, emotive or ideological colouring – psychology, palaeoanthropology, archaeology, let alone history, cultural anthropology and sociology. And there has been a widespread, increasing recognition that science in general can never be simply and wholly value-free knowledge. A wide range of studies in the history and sociology of science, together with relativist theories such as those of Thomas Kuhn or the more extreme scepticism of Paul Feyerabend, have accustomed most observers to see how 'external' considerations – from the ambitions and emotions of individual researchers, through the protocols of professional institutions, to political ideologies – condition what scholars believe.

Three further kinds of influence have advanced the climate of scepticism. One is the critique mounted by social theorists, especially feminists, postcolonial polemicists and to some extent Marxists (a lesser extent, because classical Marxism both inherited the Enlightenment belief in scientific progress and rationality, and sometimes proclaimed scientific status for itself) directed at the gender, racial or 'Eurocentric', class and other biases frequently inscribed into what has counted as scientific procedure and proof. Second is an environmentalist critique, urging the negative consequences increasingly attendant on scientific and technical 'progress'. This is sometimes linked to what are often called New Age philosophies, which advocate the replacement of scientific thought by more spiritual, more humanistic (or, conversely, less 'speciesist'), more holistic world-views.[4] Third, a cluster of postmodernist, poststructuralist and textualist approaches, taking their methods and assumptions above all from literary theory and from particular currents of (mostly Franco–German) philosophy, subject all claims about 'scientific truth' to radical doubt. In their more fundamentalist forms, they assert instead that any such claims are merely rival narratives or discourses, none of which has any greater truth-value than any other, and none of which can be founded on anything outside itself.

All these controversies have had especially powerful resonance in the United States – with strong consequences for our main themes here. The USA is, it has often been said, not only an exceptionally 'multiracial' but an intensely race-conscious society. The categorization of and terminology for different racial groups have constantly been altered, as a moment's thought about the histories of people at different times labelled 'Indians', whether they are of Pueblo, Pawnee or Punjabi ancestry, will suggest. But the central object of the obsession has always been distinctions between black and white.[5] This has heavily influenced the way issues as apparently distant but emotionally charged as the racial make-up of ancient Egypt's population have been discussed.[6] Chicago University Egyptologist Frank Yurco rather plaintively moaned:

> When you talk about Egypt, it's just not right to talk about black or white. That's all just American terminology and it serves American purposes. I can understand and sympathize with the desires of Afro-Americans to affiliate themselves with Egypt. But to take the terminology here in the United States and graft it onto Africa is anthropologically inaccurate. (quoted in D'Souza 1991: 119)

An earlier generation of Afro-American scholars tended to share the same scepticism. Veteran popular historian and *Ebony* editor Lerone Bennett's view of ancient Egypt is typically guarded:

> If black people were a major element among the peoples who fathered Egyptian civilization, who were the Egyptians? The question bristles with thorns. The only thing that can be said with assurance is that they probably were not Caucasians. The evidence (which Bennett then goes on to summarize in an' even-handed way) suggests that they were a black-, brown- and yellow-skinned people who sprang from a mixture of Negro, Semitic and Caucasian stocks. (Bennett 1984: 7)

Such a presentation, with all its admitted uncertainties, probably represented a scholarly consensus, at the time, among those who had given the issue thought – and Bennett noted the variety of physical types and skin hues in which the Egyptians depicted *themselves*, while quite reasonably also pointing out that all of them 'would have been forced in the forties to sit on the back seats of the buses in Mississippi' (ibid.: 7). But in its mild caution, a view like Bennett's or Yurco's seems increasingly irrelevant to the present-day US storms over racial identity and African legacies: storms in which ancient Egypt and its peoples' possible skin colours have a surprisingly important role. To understand why, we need to go, if not quite so far as the Egypt of the Pharaohs, then certainly far back and far away from the modern United States.

Notes

1. For overviews, see Gould (1981); Stepan (1982); Barkan (1992); Kohn (1995).
2. See Jacoby and Glauberman (1995) for an extensive sample of responses – the great

majority of them hostile – to this book. It is a striking indication of the centrality of race to the American imagination, as against the lack of public debate about social class, that whereas the bulk of *The Bell Curve* actually deals with alleged differences of intelligence between classes rather than between races, the ensuing controversy focused almost entirely on racial questions. This included the surviving author, Charles Murray's, own media puffing for his work.

3. Kohn (1995) is a thoughtful overview of the current disputes.

4. For a scathing – and, in my view, overstated – assault on the 'myths of primitive harmony' often underlying such views, see Edgerton (1992). Keeley (1996), more tightly focused and better documented, offers compelling evidence for the pervasiveness of warfare and homicide among most 'primitive' peoples.

5. Or even – and perhaps increasingly – between African-Americans and 'everyone else', in so far as Afro-Americans remain sharply, perhaps uniquely, differentiated from the remainder of the population by almost every indicator from residential segregation to rates of intergroup marriage: see on this, amid a large and depressing literature, Massey and Denton (1993). For a strong argument that institutionalized educational multiculturalism is a necessary response to such circumstances – from a writer previously identified as rather unsympathetic to such stances – see Glazer (1997).

6. Many aspects of these American controversies could be captured only through a close attention to the sociology of knowledge and media studies: how claims about race, including the racial identities of ancient Egypt, have been played out in the US and other mass media. The present exercise in the history of ideas does not attempt to tackle that task except in passing. McAlister (1996) essays a small segment of it, in relation to the 1977–78 US museum 'tour' of exhibits from the Tutankhamun tomb.

2

Pan-Africanism and *Négritude*

The pioneering black political thinker Edward Wilmot Blyden, writing well over a century ago, neatly encapsulated the reasons why a language of Otherness, of absolute difference, has seemed powerfully attractive to those who felt themselves to be victims of racial vilification:

> It is a question of difference of endowment and difference of destiny. No amount of training or culture will make the Negro a European; on the other hand, no lack of training or deficiency of culture will make the European a Negro. The two races are not moving in the same groove with an immeasurable distance between them, but on parallel lines. They will never meet in the plane of their activities so as to coincide in capacity or performance. They are not *identical*, as some think, but *unequal*; they are *distinct* but *equal*. (quoted in Mudimbe [1988: 118]; original emphases.)

This polarization of alternatives resonates through more than a hundred years of argument over race, culture and human capacity in colonial and racially oppressive situations. It stated the cruel dilemma for victims of racist stereotyping: either accept a 'European' conception of human worth and achievement, and be judged inferior by it; or proclaim Otherness, a radically incommensurable ethos and destiny. Even if in practice individuals have mixed the approaches, and if increasingly self-conscious and sophisticated syncretic models have emerged, much intellectual as well as political debate still operates with these sharp polarities. Arguably, indeed, their antagonisms have become more extreme in recent decades. They are related to – though in principle distinct from – the more directly political clash of integrationist and separatist programmes, which inevitably had and has its most powerful relevance for culturally distinct groups within plural societies.

For sheer weight, intensity, persistence of negative prejudice, maybe no major human group has been so burdened by others' attitudes as have Africans – invidious though such comparisons always are. A mass of European literature over an extended historical period quite seriously posed the question whether Africans were human at all, and sometimes answered it negatively. Thus it was probably inevitable that some of the most dramatic affirmations of Otherness, as declarations of cultural independence, should come from intellectuals of African descent – and that they should come in the diaspora more on the continent itself. In the Americas, both access to education and publishing, and experience of cultural insecurity born from the destruction of or displacement from 'traditional' African modes of life and from long exposure to racist calumny, were greater than they were on the African continent.

One can trace diasporic responses asserting a specific African cultural ethos and destiny, a form of cultural nationalism, at least as far back as Blyden or, before him, Martin Delany and David Walker: Afro-American intellectuals of the pre-Civil War years. The most striking and influential cultural expressions of this stance came, however, from the Francophone Caribbean (and to a lesser extent the 'évolués' of French West Africa: the educated minority whom the colonial rulers judged to have attained to full-fledged Frenchness) with the _négritude_ literary movement of the 1930s and after. The pronouncements of its leading figures – Aimé Césaire, Léon Damas, Léopold Sédar Senghor – set the tone for much of the 'Third World' and ethnic minority cultural nationalism that has followed (see especially, from amid a vast literature, Mudimbe [1992]). _Négritude_ has, moreover, become one of the main influences on contemporary Afrocentric and similar theories: in part directly, in part through elective affinity, and even more through the mediation of what became labelled 'ethnophiloso-phy' and of the most ubiquitous presence in Third-Worldist cultural theory, Frantz Fanon. In subsequent commentary it has often also been linked – and sometimes misleadingly lumped together – with the political separatism of which Marcus Garvey's movement was the most famous expression; though intellectually one of the least coherent and, in terms of direct political impact, among the least successful. In fact, though, the founding figures of _négritude_ emphasized African cultural and psychological distinc-tiveness but did not, on the whole, have a separatist political programme or even, necessarily, any political programme at all.

One must thus beware of thinking of the _négritude_ movement and its descendants as only and always figures of nationalist, anticolonialist or even antiracist reaction. For a start, it is highly questionable how much of it can accurately be described as anticolonial. Its main precursor, Haitian 'noir-isme', was directed at least as much against an indigenous 'mulatto' elite as it was against neocolonial French or US influences in independent Haiti (see Dash [1981]; Nicholls [1979 chs 5–7]). Senghor and, even more, Césaire coupled their culturalist rejection of European hegemony with strong political loyalties to the French connection. _Négritude_ was, as Afro-American critic Charles Johnson rightly suggests, 'not philosophy. We have a doctrine, not analysis' (1988: 19). Indeed it may well be, as Valentin Mudimbe persuasively argues, that it was Jean-Paul Sartre, not the _négritude_ poets themselves, who turned a literary movement into a political philos-ophy, thus 'stultifying' it in the rhetoric of absolute Otherness: 'Senghor . . . had asked Sartre for a cloak to celebrate _négritude_; he was given a shroud'

(Mudimbe 1988: 85). And of course many other crucial oppositional thinkers of the African diaspora, like W.E.B. Du Bois, C.L.R. James and George Padmore, explicitly rejected cultural nationalism and adhered (most of the time) to more universalist and rationalist philosophies, derived in large part from Marxism.

The notion of Pan-Africanism, meanwhile, not only straddled these divisions but came over time to bear at least four fairly distinguishable meanings:

1. The aspiration for political co-operation, and awareness of a common experience of discrimination, among peoples of African descent wherever they may live (this was the earliest usage of the term).
2. The claim that people of African descent, wherever they live, have and should rediscover common sociocultural traditions derived from their shared origins. Some versions of this belief speak in terms of a distinctive 'African personality' involving shared philosophies, attitudes to life, or modes of expression and behaviour. In the Francophone world this latter variant came to be known as *négritude* or (in Haiti) *noirisme.* More recently in the Anglophone world, and especially the USA, similar beliefs have adopted the title Afrocentrism.
3. Belief in the need for the political unity, or at least much closer political, economic and cultural co-operation, between the states of the African continent (or, in some variants, its Sub-Saharan sector). This essentially political and geographical conception of the term is the most widespread *within* Africa, whereas outside it definitions (1) and (2) are perhaps more often meant: this has often caused misunderstanding.
4. In some situations, especially in South Africa, Pan-Africanism has become the political label of those who tend to stress the racial element in group conflict and identity as against emphasis on social class, political ideology, or universalist principles.

There is no one 'founder' of Pan-Africanism. W.E.B. Du Bois may be seen, perhaps, as the effective initiator of a political *movement* in the first sense above. The most important early exponent of the *idea* was probably Edward Wilmot Blyden, born in St Thomas in the West Indies in 1832. Blyden was one of the first to emphasize past African cultural achievements and the need for racial solidarity and pride. He also, however, adopted a somewhat mystical conception of African character, which he saw as essentially spiritual and ill-fitted for technical or scientific achievement. He was extremely hostile towards people of mixed ancestry, and in later life he became an apologist for European colonialism in Africa (Lynch 1967). Other important progenitors included Martin R. Delany (1812–85), a freeborn Afro-American from Virginia who asserted the cultural distinctiveness and African heritage of black Americans as well as campaigning for their political rights. He became an early advocate of 'back to Africa' ideas. Equally important, though this time more beyond the USA, was James Africanus Horton

(1835–1883), a London-trained Sierra Leonese surgeon who, for his critiques of racist theories and advocacy of West African independence, has been called the 'father of modern African political thought' (Fryer 1984: 277, quoting George Shepperson).

For the *négritude* concept itself, the most influential figure was Léopold Sédar Senghor, the poet and cultural theorist who later became President of Senegal. His beliefs and those of his circle were forged in France in the 1930s, under pressure of the prejudice which African and Caribbean students, visitors and *émigrés* encountered there. Senghor recalled – in a fairly typical experience, if a less bitter one than, say, that famously recalled by Frantz Fanon – that it was only on going to Paris that 'I became conscious of belonging to the basic category of Negro' (quoted in Vaillant 1990: 97). The idea that migrants, visitors or students from the different far-flung colonies of the French Empire had a shared identity was, then, in the beginning imposed mainly by the prejudices of others. Yet such categorizations did not overcome the divisions and mutual suspicions between Africans and West Indians in the Paris of the 1930s (ibid.: 99–102; see also Arnold 1981).

Nor did they by any means necessarily lead to a total rejection of 'Western civilization' and of universalist ideas; though this has often, in our own time, come to be seen as the most natural response. Senghor's pronouncements that African mentalities and approaches to knowledge were entirely distinct from those of Europeans gained a wide audience, and have had many followers – including, as we shall see, numerous contemporary American Afrocentric thinkers. He asserted: 'European reasoning is analytical, discursive by utilization; Negro-African reasoning is intuitive by participation' (Senghor 1964: 74). But this was not an absolute division: in his theory these were psychological tendencies, no more. They were complementary rather than antagonistic, and they were outweighed in significance by shared human traits. In Senghor's early writings the universalist category of humanism is persistently central, and it is invariably used as a *positive* term. Even subsequently, when he came to stress more and more insistently the basic contrast between European and African personalities, he continued to issue: 'Disclaimers and occasional reminders that all human qualities might be found, albeit in different mixes, among all peoples' (Vaillant 1990: 251). It was, again, left to Jean-Paul Sartre to provide the sweeping, essentialist claims which on the whole Senghor avoided.

Senghor's attitude was very far from the later 'Afrocentric' practice of ostentatiously – and fraudulently – disavowing any European intellectual influence: his debts to Marx, Durkheim and Weber, as well as to French literary models, were openly proclaimed, and there remained a kind of universalism in his ambitions: 'to make of *Négritude* a concept that might take its place among the great principles of his day, grand principles such as humanism and socialism' (Vaillant 1990: 251–2). He also remained selective in what he attacked about European legacies: he never, for instance, criticized Christianity as such. And he insisted that far from being intrinsically separatist, '*Négritude* is Africa's contribution to the coming universal civilization' (Senghor, quoted in Vaillant 1990: 266). The aspect of *négritude* which became most famous, Senghor's and Césaire's claim that African peoples had special qualities of intuition, spontaneity, creativity and spirituality as against the European strengths in logical and scientific thought, must be read in that context. Later uses and abuses of *négritude*, however, tended to retain the essentialist claim about specific racial mentalities while abandoning the universalist humanism in which Senghor embedded it.

Nor did the shocking experience of white hostility and cultural disdain by any means necessarily produce the populist response, seeking refuge in ideas of tradition and folk culture, which later appeared mandatory in some circles. Senghor and his colleagues in the movement formed around the Paris-based magazine *Présence Africaine* were artistic experimentalists, clearly parts of the cultural avant-garde of their day in France. That particular association has since appeared much weakened, even angrily repudiated, by many. Instead, the essentially negative reaction against alien domination has tended to become closely allied with populism, anti-intellectualism, and a rigidly functionalist notion of the 'committed' role of artistic, cultural and intellectual creation. These, of course, are familiar themes in the history of left-wing cultural theory; in recent years they have been turned ever more insistently to the service of Third-Worldist nationalism. Sometimes this takes ventriloquist forms, with theorists in advanced capitalist countries perceiving – and, indeed, prescribing – narrowly agitational roles for 'Third World' thinkers, writers and artists: roles which they apparently do not think it appropriate to demand of metropolitan intellectuals.[1] It also finds passionate expression in some 'minority' discourse and those seeking to legislate for it, as in the US Black Aesthetic movement of the 1960s. At their most extreme the demands echoed, consciously or otherwise, a Maoist kind of instrumentalism, as with black cultural nationalist Ron Karenga's 1968 call for black art to 'expose the enemy, praise the people, and support the revolution' ('Black Art', in Gates and McKay 1997: 1974). Karenga thus insisted, crudely, that 'any art that does not discuss and contribute to the revolution is invalid' (ibid.: 1973). As we shall discover, such anti-intellectual and culturally conservative notions have not only been a recurring presence in Afro-American life, but have gained a new lease of strength in our own times.

Note

1. An instance of a crude version of this stance is Gugelberger (1991); a more sophisticated variant is Jameson (1986).

3

African Origins and the Claim of Primacy

The study of human origins is inherently laden with ideology and emotion – more so than almost any other kind of intellectual inquiry. Certainly palaeoanthropology, the science of humanity's biological emergence and development, has been marked by a history of bitter and often highly personalized confrontations, as Roger Lewin's, or Erik Trinkaus and Pat Shipman's, fine popular histories of the subject show (Lewin 1987; Trinkaus and Shipman 1993). Most recently, the fierce antagonisms between Donald Johansen and Timothy White, leading rival research teams in Ethiopia, or between Milford Wolpoff and Chris Stringer, have hit the world's media headlines (e.g. Fitzgerald 1995). Indeed, a degree of emotional intensity unmatched in any other 'exact' science is imparted to the discipline by the very questions it asks. Where did we come from? How, and why, did our species turn into what it is?

That emotional resonance around the history of human physical emergence is equalled or exceeded in the case of the origins of civilization – or rather, of the bundle of attributes to some or all of which the title civilization is conventionally given: the births of agriculture, urbanization, literacy, large-scale political forms, ethical and religious beliefs, technologies, systems of abstract or speculative thought, and so on. In fact the emotional stakes are, if anything, higher for this latter question, because it interrelates more closely and evidently with contemporary political concerns. These include issues of race, nationalism and political geography – relating above all to the places of Europe on the one hand, Africa on the other, in the story. Archaeology has thus become even more intensely politicized than palaeoanthropology, on issues ranging from the relevance to the ancient past of modern theories of imperialism (Champion 1989), through the agonizings of South African archaeologists about their work's political implications (Martin Hall 1990), to the demands of Native American and other indigenous peoples for control over and reburial of their ancestors' skeletal remains (Layton 1994). Most generally of all, there is unending dispute in many different contexts between 'diffusionists' and 'isolationists': those who are keen to identify the patterns by which ideas, cultures or technologies spread from some places to others, and those who want to find independent – sometimes multiple – local roots for them. As we shall see, some proponents of each approach accuse the champions of the other of racism; and, perplexingly, both are sometimes right.

So far as human physical origins are concerned, it has long been widely accepted that the earliest directly traceable ancestors of *Homo sapiens* appeared in eastern Africa. The major controversies of recent years have been over *where* in East Africa the first identifiably direct proto-human was witnessed; such as those between Richard Leakey, whose discoveries were in Tanzania and Kenya, and Donald Johansen, who worked in Ethiopia.[1] The honour of being the cradle of humanity was, almost without doubt, Africa's. Many Africans, and writers and publicists elsewhere of African descent, have taken great pride in this. Some have erected substantial rhetorical structures on that basis, including a recent feminist subtheme claiming great significance for the fact that one major candidate for the title of earliest known human remains, Johansen's famous discovery 'Lucy', was female as well as African.

On the issue of the birthplace of the earliest hominids, then, first Johansen's 'Lucy', then Timothy White's 1994 discovery of considerably older hominid remains, also in Ethiopia, seemed to give the Africanists a decisive upper hand. However, there is still argument between those who think that modern humanity developed from several distinct hominid population groups, in several different regions, around the same time (e.g. Wolpoff 1989a, b; Wolpoff and Caspari 1997), and those who propose that not only did early hominids emerge in Africa, but modern humans also all share a much more recent common African ancestor.

Ideas about race are deeply involved in the background of this controversy, and became overt especially in the bitter exchanges over Carleton Coon's championing of the 'multiple origins' viewpoint, which he linked to claims that many thought overtly racist.[2] Both sides in the dispute call on genetic as well as fossil evidence. This has been most dramatically deployed on the Africanists' side, with the 1987 claim by Rebecca Cann, Mark Stoneking and Allan Wilson that all modern humans could be traced, on the basis of a worldwide DNA survey, to a single African woman who lived about 200,000 years ago (Cann *et al.* 1987). Inevitably, popular coverage of the scientific claim dubbed this putative universal ancestress 'Eve'. (It should be noted that 'Eve' is *not* the same lady as 'Lucy', who is roughly ten times as old.)

Eve, even more than Lucy, has evident utility for antiracists and universalists, as well as for those predisposed to claims of African priority. She is apparently powerful evidence for close human familyhood: we all have a relatively recent common ancestor. And she was African – though the fact that she was female reflects only the fact that mitochondrial DNA tests allow scientists to trace maternal, but not paternal, lineages far back in time; and of course they do not tell us her skin colour. There are strong arguments from fossil and other evidence, as well as genetic research, for believing that well after the first diffusion of hominids from Africa, a second dispersal of

clearly modern human beings – our more immediate and direct ancestors –
sallied forth out of Africa to populate the globe, replacing prior Neanderthal and other populations in Eurasia.[3] It is argued that this second group
were the descendants of 'Eve'. But the case was still not proven: critics have
claimed to find serious methodological flaws in Cann *et al.*'s work.[4] Alternative readings of the evidence might, it was suggested, propose non-African
or, indeed, multiple sites of origin. In 1997, however, dramatic and in many
eyes decisive new evidence appeared to support the Africanists' case.
Scientists at Munich University succeeded in extracting and analysing DNA
from Neanderthal bones, and found genetic variation so great that it
appeared impossible for Neanderthals and modern humans to have shared
a common ancestry. (See, amid the mass of global media coverage for these
findings, Mihill 1997.)

The ideas of multiple origins for modern humanity proposed first by
Franz Weidenreich and then updated by Carleton Coon – they even have
some echoes of pre-Darwinian 'polygenist' theories of human origins, which
said that different races were separate species – are given far greater
scientific rigour in Milford Wolpoff's work. Wolpoff and his co-thinkers, it
must be emphasized, do not attempt and would not desire to link arguments
about early human origins to contemporary racialized thought in the ways
Weidenreich and Coon did (though some other contemporary theorists,
like Richard Lynn and Philippe Rushton, certainly do proclaim such links).[5]
Erik Trinkaus and Pat Shipman suggest that the earlier storms had scared
scholars away from addressing these issues. Carleton Coon's critics had
exhibited 'outspoken moralizing and merciless judgemental quality . . .
stony undertones of political correctness' (1993: 322) in attacking his
alleged racism. They go on:

> The public attacks on Coon impressed an entire generation of anthropolo-
> gists with the notion that any discussion or even acknowledgement of racial
> differences would call similar censure down on their heads. . . . Race was not
> only not a fit subject to study: *it didn't even exist* . . . race went underground.
> By becoming unseeable, unknowable, and intangible, race became a threat-
> ening and all-powerful issue. (ibid.: 324)

There are, I think, better reasons than Trinkaus and Shipman suggest for
extreme scepticism about using the language of race. Their implication that
race was not a 'threatening and all-powerful issue' when its presence was
extremely overt, and that it became so only when it 'went underground', is
quite evidently false. But they are certainly right to suggest that its
banishment from the surface of scientific discourse has not necessarily
weakened its power. As we shall discover, it continues to raise its head in
almost every imaginable context: often with the ironic or tragic twist that it
is African and Afro-American intellectuals who have most vehemently
insisted on the reality and centrality of race to human history.

Moreover, hypotheses of a recent, common ancestor for all human groups do not necessarily buttress antiracist beliefs. Palaeoanthropologist William Howells and biochemist Vincent Sarich suggest that differentiation into the races identified today began only well after Eve, let alone Lucy. It came about 15,000 years ago, at the end of the last Ice Age. This is a claim that can be used – as it is, in highly polemical and controversial form, by Sarich – to argue that racial distinctions are extremely important. For such allegedly very large differences, both physical and cultural, among human groups as are shown throughout recorded history to have emerged so very quickly indicates that they resulted from intense pressures of natural selection. It is quite reasonable, then, to think that these also produced dramatic differences in the psychological nature of races: for instance, in intelligence or emotional make-up (Kohn 1995: 172–7).

The serviceability of such ideas, even if they are true, to racial theory, and especially claims of African inferiority, may, however, be doubtful. One reason for doubt is that it can be argued that Sarich makes a radically false inference: it is more plausible to think that rapid emergence of diversity reflects not just environmental selective pressures but intelligent adaptation to those pressures, indicating the shared high intelligence of *all* human groups. As we shall see later in relation to arguments over civilizational origins, both environmental determinism, and diffusionism as opposed to theories of multiple origins, can be deployed by all sides of modern historico-political debates.

Certainly it is hard to mount arguments based on human *physical* diversity which would mark off Africans from 'the rest' as a preliminary to asserting mental or behavioural differences. Africa is the most diverse of the continents in physical types with, for instance, both the tallest and the shortest people.[6] Nor is it easy to use environmental determinism to such ends, unless the simple fact of warm temperatures is to be the yardstick – which, as we shall see, it has often and crudely been, as for instance in some Afrocentrists' 'Sun People–Ice People' dichotomy or, in more rational fashion, by Cheikh Anta Diop and his followers. Beyond the basic fact that most of Africa is warmer, most of the time, than most of Eurasia, there are few environmental factors common to the whole continent – common to rainforest and desert, swamp and savannah, ecosystems rich in edible plants and animals and those extremely poor in them.

In any case, noting Africa's probable primacy in humanity's biological emergence provides no answer to the characteristic European sneers that 'humanity may have first developed in Africa, but has long ceased to continue developing there'. The struggle for the claim to have originated 'civilization' is even more important to present-day racial and other ideologies.

On one level, it might be said that there is no great argument here, certainly less than there is over the physical location of the earliest hominids – few scholars doubt that most, at least, of the major components of 'civilization' came together first in Mesopotamia, in the region of what is now Iraq. Any dispute on the lines of 'Which came first, Africa or Europe?'

might appear to be a red herring, for the evident answer is: neither. But things are not so straightforward as that. Certainly such major features of 'civilization' as literacy and urbanization appeared in Egypt very soon after they did in southwest Asia – and it remains possible that some did so a touch earlier.[7] It is also by no means sure that if such features did first occur in Mesopotamia, they necessarily spread from there to Egypt.[8] The developments may well have been parallel and independent of one another; just as some archaeologists believe that the crystallization of urban, literate cultures just a little later still in the Indus valley, and then in China, were autonomous rather than being products of diffusion. In other words, even if Egypt was not quite first, its culture may have been substantially original and indigenous – or as much so as any culture ever is.

For some, though, an argument that Egypt was first has a huge and specific emotional weight. This has been so especially for an old, albeit narrow, tradition of Afro-American thought. For more than two centuries, black scholars and publicists made the claim that civilization was African in origin a centrepiece of their efforts to vindicate the reputation and enhance the self-esteem of African-descended peoples. Identification of Pharaonic Egypt, or of regions further south like the 'Cushite' states of the upper Nile, or of 'Ethiopians' (a term often used, especially in nineteenth-century writings, as synonymous with 'Negro' or black African) as the originators of arts, sciences, technologies and political organization became a centrepiece of the fight back against white aspersion.

Denial that Egyptian civilization preceded that of Mesopotamia, it therefore came to be felt, must be the product of anti-African racism. Veteran Afrocentrist John Henrik Clarke alleges, for instance, that European scholars began to assert the priority of Western Asia, in an evidently dishonest and racist move, only after their claims about the 'whiteness' of the ancient Egyptians had been discredited (Clarke 1992: 9). The reasons for the centrality accorded to Egypt in that tradition are well summarized in Ivan Van Sertima's encapsulation of the Afrocentric view of ancient history. Egypt preceded everyone else, and Egyptian civilization in its turn derived in all essentials from further south, from the 'heartland' of the Upper Nile Valley and/or Ethiopia. Not only the historical claims, but the insistent, emotive language and the equally insistent racial categorizations are typical of the entire genre:

> Egypt was the node and center of a vast web linking the strands of Africa's main cultures and languages; the light that crystallized at the center of this early world had been energized by the cultural electricity streaming from the heartland of Africa; the creators of classical Egyptian civilization, therefore, were not the brown Mediterranean Caucasoids invented by Sergi,[9] nor the equally mythical Hamites, nor Asiatic nomads and invaders, but indigenous, black-skinned, woolly-haired Africans; Greece, mother of the best in European civilization, was once a child suckled at the breast of Egypt even as Egypt had been suckled at the breast of Ethiopia which itself evolved from

the complex interior womb of the African motherland. (Van Sertima 1989: 322)

None of these ideas is original to current American Afrocentrism, and few of them were even originated by Cheikh Anta Diop, the Senegalese historian often seen as the father figure of the movement. Afrocentric writer Tony Martin, unlike many of his colleagues, recognizes this in saying that 'Afrocentrism is a currently popular term for an idea that is as old as African American scholarly writing' (Martin 1993: 51). He could have said: considerably older. The next chapter surveys some of the ways in which black American authors from the middle years of the nineteenth century to the middle years of the twentieth used – and abused – ideas about the African past for a wide range of contemporary purposes, but above all to assert racial self-respect.

Notes

1. These disputes, marked as much by powerful clashing personalities as by scientific divergence, are discussed in Virginia Morell's vivid 1995 study of the Leakey family.

2. Trinkaus and Shipman (1993: 278–81, 312–24) surveys these battles, with more sympathy for Coon than I myself can muster.

3. Stringer and Gamble (1993); Lahr and Foley (1994); Stringer and McKie (1996); Nitecki and Nitecki (1994); Jones, Martin and Pilbeam (1992); Shreeve (1995).

4. See, for instance, Wolpoff (1989a, b). Trinkaus and Shipman (1993: 342–97), Shreeve (1995) and Kingdon (1993: 255–93) summarize the disputes. To this non-specialist, the arguments on the Africanist side of the debate presented in studies such as Stringer and McKie (1996) seem, for the moment, decisively convincing, and are further reinforced by the 1997 Munich findings.

5. Wolpoff and Caspari (1997) presents the multiregionalist theory at greatest length and in greatest detail, places it in the context of earlier debates on human evolution and race, and argues forcefully that neither Wolpoff's own version of it nor Weidenreich's earlier one offers any comfort to or holds any affinity with racist theories.

6. This diversity is, incidentally, a powerful piece of indirect evidence for the supposition that human evolution has been taking place for longer in Africa than anywhere else. Africa also appears to contain more genetic diversity than any other continent.

7. There is also an intriguing possibility – it can at present be put no higher than that – that sophisticated toolmaking, and a recorded number system, emerged in tropical Africa *much* earlier than anywhere else. Archaeologists Alison Brooks and John Yellen have uncovered at Katanda in former Zaïre bone harpoons and other implements which have been dated at c.90,000 years old, and are more advanced than any Eurasian finds of more than half that age. However, this remains an isolated find, the dating is controversial, and the significance for claims about African cultural primacy is regarded with great scepticism by many other scholars. Earlier in the same region, Belgian colonial geologist Jean de Heinzelin found what he believed to be evidence of a counting system, etched on bones, which he thought must have been communicated to ancient Egypt. This idea has been treated even more sceptically than have Brooks's and Yellen's finds. See Shreeve (1995: 235–63); Wolpoff and Caspari (1997: 326–9); and, for an excited, overstated Afrocentric view of the implications (based largely on Shreeve's earlier magazine articles), Finch (1994).

8. It might also be suggested that wherever in West Asia or North Africa the major features of 'civilization' originated, the Egyptian and Mesopotamian cultures interacted so

closely from – at the latest – 1500 BCE onwards that in important ways they formed a single civilizational complex. For a strong statement of this view, see Wilkinson (1993).

9. A reference to the long-forgotten and academically discredited Giuseppe Sergi, a late-Victorian ethnologist (see Sergi 1901).

4

Diasporic Images of Africa
before Afrocentrism

In numerous popular tracts, pamphlets, published sermons and occasionally substantial tomes from the mid nineteenth century to the early twentieth, African-American writers – a high proportion of them clergymen, the main 'organic intellectuals' of black communities – made reference to ancient Egypt, Nubia, Ethiopia and other African civilizations as part of their campaign for racial equality and respect. Such mainly little-known texts, glorifying ancient Africa, and especially Egypt, included the 1837 publication of Hosea Easton's *Treatise on the Intellectual Character and the Political Condition of the Colored People*; James Pennington's 1841 *Text Book of the Origin and History of the Colored People*; *Light and Truth* by Robert B. Lewis in 1844; the 1848 lecture by Henry Highland Garnet issued in print as *The Past and Present Condition, and the Destiny of the Colored Race*; William Wells Brown's 1863 *The Black Man: His Antecedents, His Genius, and His Achievements*; James 'Africanus' Horton's *West African Countries and Peoples* in 1868. From the 1890s the pace of such publication quickened, with such works as the prolific Joseph E. Hayne's 1887 *The Cushite*, his *The Black Man* of 1894 and his 1905 *The Ammonian or Hametic Origin of the Ancient Greeks, Cretans and all the Celtic Races*; W.H. Councill's 1898 *Lamp of Wisdom; Or, Race History Illuminated*; Charles T. Walker's 1900 *Appeal to Caesar*; Baltimore clergyman Harvey Johnson's 1903 *The Nations from a New Point of View*; Pauline Hopkins's 1905 *Primer of Facts Pertaining to the Greatness of the African Race*; John William Norris's 1916 *The Ethiopian's Place in History*; and James M. Webb's *The Black Man, the Father of Civilization, Proven by Biblical History*, also published in 1916.[1] Between the wars, late examples of the genre were Dr J.E. Blayechettai's pamphlet *The Hidden Mystery of Ethiopia* (1926); Drusilla Dunjee Houston's 1926 *Wonderful Ethiopians of the Ancient Cushite Empire*; Charles C. Seifert's booklets lauding black contributions to the visual arts across the millennia (1938) and the achievements of the fabulist Aesop, identified as a 'Negro' (1946), as well as a more substantial work, *An Introduction to African Civilizations*, co-authored by Willis N. Huggins and John G. Jackson in 1937. The charismatic Harlem clergyman Adam Clayton Powell and the hugely popular prosopographer (collective biographer) Joel Augustus Rogers, author of *World's Great Men of Color* (1947/1972), took up similar themes; as did Marcus Garvey, whose ideas we examine more closely in a subsequent chapter.

Some of these were works of profound eccentricity, like Augustus T. Bell's obscure, mystical tract *The Woolly Hair Man of the Ancient South*, issued during Theodore Roosevelt's Presidency in approximately 1903; or Edward A. Johnson's 1931 *Adam versus Ape-Man and Ethiopia*. Some, especially among the earlier examples of the genre, relied almost entirely on biblical arguments. Others, though, were works of impressive – if sometimes ill-digested – autodidact scholarship, seeking to enlist a wide range of historical, anthropological and theological sources in their campaign for racial equality and the revision of the white world's historical judgements.

The very first known Afro-American political texts already contained the themes which were to re-echo through all the subsequent decades: identification with ancient Egypt as a great black civilization, at least partly the creation of 'Ethiopians', 'Negroes', 'Cushites' or 'sons of Ham'; belief that civilization originated in Africa and was carried thence to Greece and the world; assertion that this past greatness was a source both of racial pride and of hope for future achievement. David Walker's *Appeal to the Coloured Citizens of the World* in 1829 suggested that:

> When we take a retrospective view of the arts and sciences (we see) the wise legislation – the Pyramids and other magnificent buildings – the turning of the channel of the river Nile, by the sons of Africa or of Ham, among whom learning originated, and was carried thence into Greece. (quoted in Forbes 1990: 214)

And Walker had insisted on the basic similarity between ancient Egyptians and African-Americans: they 'were Africans or coloured people, such as we are – some of them yellow and some dark – a mixture of Ethiopians and the natives of Egypt – about the same as you see the coloured people of the United States at the present day' (Gates and McKay 1997: 183). Hosea Easton's *Treatise on the Intellectual Character ... of the Colored People* was, like Walker's, primarily an antislavery tract, invoking the African past to refute assertions of black inferiority. Drawing mainly on the Bible and apparently on the German scholar Barthold Niebuhr, Easton points to Egypt, Ethiopia and Carthage as great ancient African civilizations. The Egyptians had taught the Greeks, who had beforehand been 'a race of savages', as had other Europeans before African-derived wisdom was passed on to them via Greece and Rome (Easton 1837: 9–11). Such mighty past African achievements, despite later decline, offered promise of future greatness and acceptance of racial equality. If others would deal justly towards Africa, then within a few generations 'her sons will again take the lead in the fields of virtuous enterprise' (ibid.: 20). Men like Easton and his contemporary James Pennington, a black New York clergyman and leading abolitionist who wrote in similar vein but devoted more space to Africa and to historical claims than did Easton, proposed rational arguments – albeit based on scanty historical knowledge – about the African past and its possible significance for the future.

Pennington's *Text Book of the Origins . . . of the Colored People* (1841) was, as its title implies, intended as an educational primer, 'offered to families, and to students and lecturers in history'(3). It adopted an almost exclusively biblical and creationist framework, seeking, on numerous theological grounds, to rebut ideas that Africans were the 'children of Cain' or subject to 'Noah's curse' (ibid. 7–9).[2] Rather, Negroes were the descendants of Cush, which meant that there was biblical support for the idea of their consanguinity with ancient Egyptians: they 'were cousins. They were brother's children' (21). Moreover, they came under the same government and soon became one people, 'equals in the arts and sciences for which Egypt is admitted on all hands to have been so renowned' (22). Thus 'the arts and sciences had their origin with our ancestors, and from them have flown forth to the world. They gave them to Greece, Greece to Rome, and Rome to others' (47). Pennington is careful, however, to distinguish between 'Ethiopian' (a racial label synonymous with 'Negro') and 'African' (a geographical one). Thus – contrary to the widespread later habit among Afro-American publicists of claiming the whole continent's history as their heritage – he insisted that the Carthaginians, for instance, 'cannot, in any proper sense, be considered Ethiopians, and therefore that we have no proper connection with them' (27). The ancient achievements of Egypt and Ethiopia alone, though, were enough to prove the intellectual equality of the races (45). If there had been degeneration among Africans from the glorious past, as Pennington seemed to admit, it was on account of polytheism and idolatry (32). Slavery could not be justified on grounds of the character of Africans (39), or as natural, any more than it had biblical sanction: the American 'prejudice against color' was entirely irrational as well as irreligious, tending to breed injustice, cruelty, hypocrisy and heathenism in the entire nation (74–96).

Another, more prominent Afro-American publicist of the era, again a clergyman and militant abolitionist, who drew on a mixture of biblical and historical arguments to proclaim past African glories, was Henry Highland Garnet.[3] His *The Past and Present Condition, and the Destiny of the Colored Race* (1848) declared African descent from Ham, while rejecting allegations that this ancestry placed black people under a curse legitimating slavery (1848: 7); lauded the achievements of the ancient Egyptians and other noteworthy Africans such as Hannibal and St Augustine; and anticipated a theme which was later often to be elaborated by pointing out that when ancient Africans were scaling the peaks of civilization, 'the ancestors of the now proud and boasting Anglo-Saxons were among the most degraded in the human family' (ibid.: 12). And the formidable Alexander Crummell, in his collection of sermons published as *The Future of Africa* (1862), insisted that no race had a monopoly of cultural achievement, which indeed was always a product of cross-fertilization and mutual learning.[4]

Far less rational or careful was Robert B. Lewis, also writing in the 1840s.

Lewis may perhaps be regarded as the true father of Afrocentrism's wilder theories, for he proposed, in Immanuel Geiss's (1974) summary,[5] that:

> Athens was founded by an Egyptian in 1556 BC and Macedonia by a descendant of 'Hercules, an African'; Greece, Europe and the whole of America were originally settled by descendants of the Egyptians; the Indians were related to the Israelites of Egypt; Syrians, Greeks, Phoenicians and Romans were all negroid.

Practically every major figure of Antiquity, from Euclid to Jesus Christ, was of African descent (ibid.: 102–3). A latter-day variant of this theme has been to claim African ancestry for a striking range of more modern figures – Beethoven, Browning and Marx being especial favourites – as well as to highlight the alleged Africanity of people with even the most distant or minor trace of black ancestry, like Pushkin or Dumas.[6] Parallel assertions about famous individuals of the ancient world have continued to recur, based usually on little more than surmise or wishful thinking – as with the 'blackness' of Socrates, Cleopatra, or Augustine of Hippo (Lefkowitz 1996a: 26–48).

A few white authors echoed similar themes. As early as 1852 a white abolitionist, the Reverend F. Freeman, in a book called *Africa's Redemption*, cast in the form of dramatic dialogue which was a standard abolitionist trope, had expressed the idea at length through his hero's words:

> It may greatly startle some who have heard of 'the fame of Egypt's wisdom . . .' that Egyptians were in fact black and curly-headed. . . .
> [T]hat very light which long since blazed before the world in Greece and Rome, and which now rises to its noonday splendor under the auspices of Christianity in Europe and America . . . was kindled on the dark shores of Africa. (quoted in Hickey and Wylie 1993: 240–41)

Freeman cited sources from the Greek historian Herodotus to the eighteenth-century French antiquarian Constantin Volney[7] to support his argument for both the blackness of ancient Egypt and the formative Egyptian influence on classical European civilization. Thus a white – and by no means particularly radical – clergyman had already, in 1852, expressed most of the major themes of 1990s Afrocentrism.

In the 1860s the pioneer Pan-Africanist James 'Africanus' Horton, in his *West African Countries and Peoples* (subtitled 'A Vindication of the African Race') also argued that ancient Africa had been the birthplace of civilization. His view was less singlemindedly Egyptocentric than those of most writers in this vein. He emphasized, in the usual way, the debt of Greece and Rome to African knowledge, but also that of early Christianity, since 'fathers and writers of the Primitive Church, were tawny African bishops of Apostolic renown' (Horton 1868: 67).

Probably the most important thinker in these nineteenth-century circles was Edward Wilmot Blyden. Inspired by a desire to see evidence of great black achievements, he visited Egypt in 1866. At the sight of the Pyramids, he wrote, awe overtook him:

> This, thought I, was the work of my African progenitors. . . . Feelings came over me far different from those I have ever felt when looking at the mighty works of European genius. I felt that I had a peculiar heritage in the Great Pyramid built . . . by the enterprising sons of Ham, from which I descended. . . . I seemed to feel the impulse from those stirring characters who sent civilization to Greece . . . could my voice have reached every African in the world, I would have earnestly addressed him . . . 'Retake your Fame'. (quoted in Lynch 1967: 55)

Blyden's semi-mystical and ethnic-absolutist ideas anticipated those which are now the common currency of Afrocentrism. He believed that 'every race . . . has a soul, and the soul of the race finds expression in its institutions, and to kill those institutions is to kill the soul. . . . No people can profit by or be helped under institutions which are not the outcome of their own character' (quoted in Davidson 1964: 35).[8] In other respects, though, his views were more generously inclusive than those of many later cultural nationalists: he expressed highly positive attitudes towards Jews (Gilroy 1993a: 210–11) and more particularly towards Islam, to which he looked as a major vehicle for regenerating Africa (Lynch 1967: 67–71, 73–7, 124).

It is noteworthy that some of these early proponents of the 'Black Athena' idea drew from it radically different lessons from those advanced by contemporary Afrocentrists: lessons about the necessity of cultural inter-change and syncretism. Leading black abolitionist Williams Wells Brown argued thus:

> As the Greeks, and Romans and Jews drew knowledge from the Egyptians three thousand years ago, and the Europeans received it from the Romans, so must the blacks in this land rise in the same way. As one learns from one another, so nation learns from nation. (Brown 1863: 36)

Brown thought that *all* Africans originated in the Nile valley, and so all shared in this interchange of progress. His major thrust, like that of many other nineteenth-century black writers, was to refute accusations of African incapacity. Most of the material by which he sought to do this took the form of a series of mini-biographies of blacks with notable achievements in his own time: Benjamin Banneker, Henry Highland Garnet, Alexander Crum-mell, slave revolt leader Nat Turner (a bold choice of exemplar for an Afro-American writing in the midst of the Civil War!), Toussaint L'Ouverture and other Haitian revolutionaries, the poet Phillis Wheatley, and so on. Yet Brown also, more briefly, made a case for ancient African accomplishments, to establish the point that 'The negro has not always been considered as the inferior race. The time was when he stood at the head of science and literature' (32). This was proved, of course, by ancient Egypt – which, citing the familiar authorities of Herodotus and Volney, he believed to be a Negro civilization. Such early African greatness was contrasted – in another trope which Garnet and Crummell had already employed, and which was to be repeated time and again thereafter – with the primitive savagery of the early Anglo-Saxons to which Roman authors bore witness (33–5).

The first major scholarly historical work by a black American was also the first serious study *of* the history of black Americans: George Washington Williams's 1882 *History of the Negro Race in America*. The main bulk of the book was devoted to the struggles and achievements of Africans in the New World, and on this theme it was a remarkable piece of research for its time: Williams noted proudly that he had consulted over twelve thousand sources, about a thousand of which were mentioned in his footnotes (Williams 1882: vi). A preliminary section, however, gave an outline of African history itself, and this was perhaps inevitably less securely grounded than the later chapters. Williams began in the fashion which had already become conventional, underlining the 'Unity of Mankind' and refuting the idea of a 'curse of Canaan' (ibid.: 6–11). His references to ancient history were sketchy, but included the similarly standard claim that Egyptians' origins came from the south, referring to Meroë as 'that ancient city, the very cradle of Egyptian civilization' (6). He also anticipated much later speculation, both European and Afro-American, in speaking of prehistoric 'Negroes' in India, Japan and elsewhere (17–19). Relying heavily on Herodotus, as so many Afrocentric authors have done up to the present (e.g. 13, 15), Williams asserted not that the ancient Egyptians were a 'Negro' population as such, but that they were very dark and included a substantial 'Negro' *element* (14, 445–6), and that many of their kings were Ethiopians; and he provided a list of these kings (454–9). He did, however, insist that the Cushites (or Nubians), the true originators of civilization, were identical to the Ethiopians, and were true Negroes (6–7), and he made the usual assertion of a chain of cultural influences running down the Nile and over to early Europe:

> Greece and Rome stood transfixed before the ancient glory of Ethiopia! Homeric mythology borrowed its very essence from Negro hieroglyphics; Egypt borrowed her light from the venerable Negroes up the Nile. (22)

Williams was less impressed by what he knew of West African cultures: no doubt partly because his sole sources on them seem to have been European travellers' and conquerors' accounts.[9] He mentioned some of the major West African states and empires – Benin, Ashanti, Yoruba, Dahomey (23–44) – but his view of the last in particular was far from favourable; he writes of bloodthirstiness, cruelty and human sacrifice. Like so many other nineteenth-century publicists – and not a few later ones – Williams felt that some explanation was needed not only for supposed African backwardness but for what he perceived as a degeneration of African culture from its past heights. His interpretation involved several elements. Part was religious: 'what was the cause of the Negro's fall from his high state of civilization? It was forgetfulness of God, idolatry!' (24: the point is not expanded, but repeated elsewhere, e.g. 109). He pointed, as one might expect, to the corruption and destruction wrought by European incursions (67); though he had nothing but praise for the efforts of Christian missions in Africa. He also, however, put forward an idiosyncratic theory of racial degeneration. As the noble original Africans spread from their Nile valley homes to less hospitable climates, they declined physically and mentally into what European contemporaries scorned – and Williams, surprisingly, concurred with them – as the lowly 'Negro type':

> The Negro type is the result of degradation. It is nothing more than the lowest strata of the African race. Pouring over the venerable mountain terraces, an abundant stream from an abundant and unknown source, into the malarial districts, the genuine African has gradually degenerated into the typical Negro. His blood infected with the poison of his low habitation, his body shrivelled by disease, his intellect veiled in pagan superstitions, the noblest yearnings of his soul strangled by the savage passions of a nature abandoned to sensuality – the poor Negro of Africa deserves more our pity than our contempt. (109)

The slave trade – which, he thought, singled out for transportation the weakest members of the lowliest West African tribes – merely compounded this negative process of natural selection: hence what he saw as the generally poor intellectual and moral character of Afro-Americans. Given all this, it might seem surprising that Williams felt as able as he did to point to impressive achievements among the more 'progressive' members of the race in America, and to offer such hope for their future. The reason lay in his burning faith in the civilizing, moralizing power of a Western – and, above all, a Christian – environment. Colonialism and slavery had at least brought true religion to Africans, and in the United States, after Emancipation, the road to racial equality and assimilation lay open. And the ex-slaves would in their turn, play the key role in bringing civilization to Africa, as they were already doing in Sierra Leone and Liberia, those 'light-houses on a dark and stormy sea of lost humanity' (110).

Such themes had, as historian Leo Spitzer notes, strong resonances among early 'Creole' (repatriated victims of the slave trade and their descendants) intellectuals in Sierra Leone and Liberia themselves. One anonymous writer in a Sierra Leonean newspaper urged: 'Let it not be forgotten that we are the direct descendants of men that have built those stupendous Pyramids which have in all ages exacted wonder and admiration, and have baffled the most skilful of modern architects' (Spitzer 1972: 121). In his *Africa and the Africans* (1881) Charles Marke proclaimed that ancient Africa was filled 'with churches, colleges, and repositories of learning . . . and . . . was the seat of a most powerful government which contended with

Rome for the sovereignty of the world' (in ibid.: 121). J. Augustus Cole, visiting Indiana from Sierra Leone, urged that ancient Egyptians were black Africans; while A.B.C. Merriman-Labor suggested that modern West Africans were descended from Ethiopians, who were themselves descended from Cush, the son of Ham (ibid.). The Cushites had founded such great cities as Nineveh and Babylon, and were chosen by God 'to be the primitive leaders of the van of civilization and to teach mankind the first principles of good government' (quoted in ibid.: 122). Merriman-Labor, with like-minded West African publicists such as Abayomi Cole and Africanus Horton, proposed a cyclical view of history. Africans had once been the leaders of world civilization, a role which had passed from them to various successors – most recently the British – but which, the wheel turning again, they might hope to regain. Like the Afrocentrists today, they tended towards a view of history defined in strictly racial terms, including strong preconceptions about who precisely should count as a true African. Thus Merriman-Labor excluded 'Copts, Berbers, Kaffirs and Hottentots', with their 'yellowish' or 'brownish' skins, from his providential schema (in ibid.: 127).

Meanwhile, the flow of Afro-American essays in racial vindication continued into the new century. William Hooper Councill's *Lamp of Wisdom* was, its publishers announced, intended as a 'standard textbook for the Negro schools throughout our beautiful Southland' (1898: 6). The author himself, President of the 'Agricultural and Mechanical College for Negroes' in Normal, Alabama, and one of the era's most accommodationist black public figures,[10] saw its educational purpose as inseparable from that of racial uplift:

> I hope that by the light of this little 'Lamp of Wisdom' the world may see more clearly the merits of the Negro, and accord him a man's chance in the race of life and that the Negro himself may take fresh courage and press forward to grander achievements. (ibid.: 5)

Discussion of Africa in the book, which is cast largely in question-and-answer form, is relatively brief. There is a basic list of the continent's natural features and resources (9–13), a bald assertion that Afro-Americans are descended from the 'ancient Ethiopians', the partners of Pharaonic Egypt (16), and the usual rebuttal of the idea that blacks are subject to a biblical curse (14–16). Far more space is given to American history, much of it strikingly inaccurate, and to listing black achievements in America, with special emphasis on business success stories and an extended puff for Councill's own school.

Much more radical, and giving much more attention to Africa and its past glories, is Harvey Johnson's *The Nations from a New Point of View* (1903). Johnson, pastor of the Union Baptist Church in Baltimore and holder of a Doctorate in Divinity, started as usual with biblical history, before turning to the iniquities of modern civilization via extended discussions of race theory. Asserting that all Africans, including both ancient Egyptians and the forebears of Afro-Americans, are 'Hamites' – an affirmation supported largely by biblical citations – Johnson proceeded: 'Greek and Roman art and literature – yes, and that of all Europe and America at the present day – is of African origin; yes, the original production of the Hamites' (ibid.: 89).

Carthage was a Negro, not a Phoenician, city, while Rome was settled and civilized by Carthage (104–14). Hebrew, Greek and Latin were all, in origin, Hamitic languages (117). Greece, too, was an African creation (228–37); though Johnson admits that he is speculating somewhat in claiming that 'the Hamites – that is, Egyptians and Phoenicians – first settled the country, and the white tribes came in and settled afterwards' (231). Johnson was evidently more widely read than the majority of Afro-American publicists in this vein: he seemed to be well acquainted, for instance, with the racial theories of Johann Friedrich Blumenbach, on which he launched repeated attacks. He was also a vivid, punchy, sometimes witty writer, who pointed out sardonically that Europeans had historically been slaves long before blacks were (123), and concluded with a rather wonderful satiric diatribe on the failings and follies of white society, from the medieval European habit of putting animals on criminal trial (278–9) to the corruptions of Wall Street. Given this history, he suggested, the question so often asked of Africans should be thrown back upon Europe – can they ever really be trusted to govern or civilize themselves?

More naive and repetitive in style – though also more historically detailed – was the contribution of another Baltimore clergyman, John William Norris. His 1916 tract *The Ethiopian's Place in History* ran through the standard litany of claims: a biblical explanation of humanity's division into races, uneasily coupled with an invocation of Darwin in support of the view that 'everything indicates that the origin of man was in Africa' (Norris 1916: 2); the assertion that 'fourteen Ethiopian Kings ruled on the Egyptian throne' (ibid.: 1); and an insistence that Egyptians were black, and that Greece learned its wisdom from them:

> Superficial criticism, guided by local and temporary prejudices, has attempted to deny the intimate relations of the Negro with the great historic races of Egypt and Ethiopia. But no one who has travelled in North-Eastern Africa or among the ruins on the banks of the Nile, will for a moment doubt that there was the connection, not of an accident or of adventitious circumstances, but of consanguinity between the races of inner Africa of the present day and the ancient Egyptians and Ethiopians. (5)

The Pyramids, to which Norris constantly returns as benchmarks of African achievement, were at least partly of Negro construction; which 'shows that the Negro had attained to a very high mark of civilization three thousand years before the birth of Christ'. Greece, the first civilized European nation, rose only a thousand years later, and under African tutelage (8–9). 'The white man never conceived civilization. He has tried to improve on it; or on

Hamitic conception. . . . The white man claims superiority in all civilizations, but there is no evidence of it' (10). Cecrops, a Negro descendant of the biblical Mizraim, founded Athens and brought culture to Greece (20–21). The wisdom and religion of the Jews, too, were of African origin (34–8). Originally, all humans had been of one colour – and Norris implied, without directly claiming, that this colour was black. Later migrations into varying climates produced the differentiation of races (which is, of course, almost certainly true) (23). Appealing to Afro-American youth to recapture past greatness, Norris proclaimed:

> Your foundation, boys, is the civilization that produced the Pyramids. But, says the young black man, that is too far back. Is it? Well there is where you will build. God left the Pyramids as a mark of your rock base. (33)

The British-based black autodidact Theophilus Scholes likewise, in urging that 'The corner-stone of the world's civilization was laid by the Negro', insisted that all social advance was the result of cultural contact, of borrowings and interactions. Scholes is perhaps the most interesting of all these authors. Born in Jamaica in 1856, he had trained as a doctor in Edinburgh and Brussels and worked as a missionary in the Congo, also spending time in Nigeria and apparently teaching at the African Training Institute in Colwyn Bay, Wales (P. Bryan 1991: 47–51; Fryer 1984: 438–9). His main interest in his voluminous writings was criticism of British colonial policies, and especially the prejudice which barred educated blacks from the employment or the social respect which was their due. His was primarily, then, an elite and class-specific desire for reform, like that of most early West Indian and West African critics of colonialism in his day. Like almost all the others he was calling for the liberalization of the Empire rather than its total abolition – indeed, he compared British policies favourably with the more extreme racial stratification of the US South (Scholes 1899: 378–9).

In *Glimpses of the Ages* Scholes presented a detailed, rational defence of the unity of the human race and the Africans' unique contribution to its development. The main difficulty with his argument – from the perspective of 1905, when he wrote it, and even more so from that of today – is that he insisted on linking this to a religiously-grounded polemic against Darwinism (Scholes 1905 I: 154–64). Apart from that idiosyncrasy, Scholes's main lines of argument were eminently reasonable. He pointed out, quite rightly, that all the different groups identified by his contemporaries as distinct 'races' had great internal variations of colour and physical features, and that the still-influential 'science' of craniology had failed to prove differences in brain size between racial groups (ibid.: 35, 49–52). He accepted – indeed, lauded – the current pre-eminence of Europeans on the world stage, but pointed out that within recorded history European 'savages' had been much more primitive than African ones, as Roman writings about the Britons, Gauls and Germans showed (174–90, 395). He proceeded from this to make the now-familiar arguments about the blackness of the ancient

Egyptians (191–209) and the great achievements of Egyptian civilization, including its role as tutor to Greece: 'the adoption by the Greeks of these sciences and arts has directly and indirectly made the Egyptians the educators of modern Europe' (235; see also 337).

Reversing familiar European polarities, as so many black vindicationist writers did, Scholes divided human civilizations into the 'spontaneous' and the 'imitative'. Egypt, with China and Ethiopia, fell into the first category; Europe into the second: 'Europe has produced no indigenous civilisation' (323), but had drawn everything from Africa.

Scholes was a strong believer in the ideology of progress, which for him was the natural order of things. In his own time, however, he feared that world civilization was regressing, in defiance of the natural order, because of the 'lack of truth' in public affairs, especially in relation to race (xv). He saw his task as to challenge and remedy this, casting a truthful light on the capacities of the various races. His centrepiece was ancient Egypt, but he also pointed to the 'progressive' nature of some African peoples in the present (249), and to the achievements of Afro-Americans (251–64) and of 'great leaders of the Negro race' (264–80). In the end, he averred, it was *moral* rather than material progress which really mattered, and here blacks were showing the way to the future. He intended, he said, to follow up his two stout volumes on racial history with a further four tracing the moral issues raised by race relations (vol. II: vii, ix, 488). Apparently he never completed these: certainly they never found a publisher.

Many other black writers around the same time made related arguments. In a massive work published in 1913, *The African Abroad*, William H. Ferris emphasized the blackness of ancient Ethiopia, and argued that civilization spread from there to Egypt and thence onward. Ferris, a graduate of both Yale and Harvard in philosophy and theology as well as a close associate and admirer of Du Bois, here produced an extraordinary mixed-genre compendium of history, philosophy, autobiography and contemporary political comment. 'All I am or ever hope to be is expressed in this volume,' he wrote (Ferris 1913: 131); and, not surprisingly, it strikes the latter-day reader as the product of a brilliant but unfocused intelligence. In so far as the book has a unifying theme, beyond a general assertion of black dignity, it comes from the influence of Hegel, Emerson and Carlyle, a philosophy of history centred on the notion of heroism.[11] Apparently the only point on which Ferris publicly disagreed with Du Bois, whom he revered, was over the latter's famous 1897 pamphlet 'The Conservation of Races'. Du Bois thought that great individuals became so because of the collective racial forces they represented. On the contrary, said Ferris, only outstanding individuals made races or nations great (D. Lewis 1993: 173).

In line with this general theory, Ferris devoted considerable space to the nature of historical greatness among both whites and, more particularly, blacks: in an extensive section entitled 'The Negro as Hero' he discussed his candidates for the list of 'the forty greatest Negroes in History' (Ferris 1913: 927–80). These included Thothmes I and Amenhotep III of Egypt, the sixteenth-century West African emperor Mohammed Askia ('the African Charlemagne'), the Islamic scholars Ahmed Baba and Abderrahman Sadi of Timbuktu, and various modern figures.

Ferris's general approach was vindicationist, but it was far from being unmodified boosterism. He bemoaned the lack of regard for intellectual attainments he discerned among Afro-Americans, and the fact that his race had, in his view, 'produced so many good talkers and so few good writers' (ibid.: 255). Indeed, racial stereotyping and essentialism, sometimes uncomfortably similar to then current dominant white views of 'Negro' characteristics, are by no means absent from his book (e.g. 244–6). His boldest hopes were reserved for those people of mixed descent whom he called 'NegroSaxons', who might combine the finer qualities of the two racial lineages (ch. XIV *passim*).

Ferris's views of Africa and its ancient past combined some standard themes of the tradition, such as that Greece 'derived the genius of her civilization' from Egypt (431), with a more singular version of racial history.[12] He endorsed Sergi's theory of a prehistoric 'Mediterranean race' but, unlike most, denied its whiteness: the inhabitants of Sub-Saharan Africa were an offshoot of it, so that they, the Arabs, Phoenicians, Homeric Greeks and Etruscans were all closely related. The usual bugbear question of whether the ancient Egyptians were 'Negroes' thus diminished in significance – he described Egyptians, Ethiopians (or Nubians) and Negroes as three distinct but closely related groups, and certainly none of them was white:

> [T]he Ethiopians . . . were neither Negroes nor Egyptians. But they were a mixed or colored race the same as the colored people of America. They represented a blending of the Hamites, a Caucasian race who settled in North Africa and Egypt, and Negroes; or they were a branch of the Mediterranean race from which the Negroes were an offshoot. (463)

Ferris's historical and anthropological influences were an interestingly mixed bunch. Apart from Sergi he drew on those favourite standbys of Afro-American Egyptology, then and since, Herodotus and Volney; he made much use of craniology (though he also acknowledged the influence of Franz Boas, the main contemporary critic of skull measurement as a means of racial classification [429–30]); and quoted extensively from then-standard authorities on ancient history like professors W.C. Taylor of Dublin and George Rawlinson of Oxford.

George W. Ellis, writing just a year later, while he also laid stress on Egypt as a probable centre from which cultural influences diffused, broke newer ground in lauding ancient Ghana and other West African kingdoms. His main purpose and focus, though, were not historical but to describe and praise the achievements of the Vai people of Liberia, where he had been stationed as a diplomat. His work thus took its place in the already substantial Afro-American tradition of defending Liberia's reputation against white disparagers, but also stood as a pioneering – albeit uncritical – piece of anthropological fieldwork by a black American (Ellis 1914).

Many of the texts already mentioned included discussion, usually brief, of ideas drawn from physical anthropology – whether, by way of selective citation, to support their arguments or – more often, given the generally racist tenor of the European anthropological tradition – to attack such theories. A few Afro-American writers plunged more deeply into this field, seeking to turn the claims of nineteenth-century physical anthropology – so much of which was devoted to establishing African inferiority – on their heads, or to prove the 'Negroid' character of ancient Egypt. As we shall see, this, too, is a tradition which has continued until the present day, above all through the influence of Cheikh Anta Diop. Such efforts included Joseph E. Hayne's flowery, amateurish *The Black Man; or, the Natural History of the Hamitic Race* (1894) and the more extensive effort by veteran campaigner Martin R. Delany; though the latter's *Principia of Ethnology* (1880), despite the scientific pretensions of its title and the wide knowledge it reflected, actually relied almost as much on the old biblical arguments as it did on a critical examination of the era's race science. Delany's main purpose appeared to be to reiterate his long-held view that New World blacks should emigrate *en masse* back to Africa.

In some such writings the 'cradle of civilization' was pushed further south down the Nile, and Ethiopia was identified as the real source of Egyptian achievements, just as Egypt was of Greece's. This emphasis on Ethiopia had a triple function. First, Ethiopians (vagueness was, as it had long been, endemic over whether the label referred to the Amharic state or to Africans more generally) were less contestably 'black' than Egyptians, especially at a time when the academic mainstream sought to proclaim the latter as Hamitic, or perhaps Aryan. Second, links could be drawn both with the scattered Biblical references to Ethiopia and with the country's deep-rooted Christian faith – both moves with evident appeal to intensely religious Afro-American publicists.[13] Third, the continued political independence of Abyssinia, its successful repulsion of attempted colonial conquest by Italy, presented an inspiring contemporary message. All these themes were later to motivate identification with Ethiopia among a wide range of heterodox and syncretic religious movements in the New World, most famously in Rastafarianism.[14]

J.E. Blayechettai, a clergyman who claimed to be an Ethiopian prince who had been kidnapped by the 'Dervishes', to have escaped and received an English education,[15] was apparently an extremely popular lecturer on the black Church circuit in the 1920s. His pamphlets *The Pen of an African* (c.1922) and *The Hidden Mystery of Ethiopia* (c.1926) repeated the by now familiar themes that the arts and sciences had originated among the Ethiopians, who: 'were the first people to throw the flashlight of knowledge upon the shores of Egypt. Egypt handed it to Babylon, Babylon handed it to Greece, Greece handed it to Rome, and Rome handed it down to the western world' (1922: 36). He linked this with the missionary endeavour:

like Pennington, Williams and other precursors, he believed that Africa had
lost its earlier pre-eminence through abandoning God, and could have it
restored by embracing Christianity – though if Blayechettai were indeed of
Ethiopian birth, he could hardly have been unaware that Ethiopia *was*
already Christian, and had been so for many centuries.

Edward A. Johnson's *Adam versus Ape-Man and Ethiopia* was a much more
substantial but still more eccentric work. Opening with an extended,
confusing – and, indeed, apparently confused – comparison between
creationist and evolutionary theories of human origins, he seemed to want
to have it both ways: both theories supported claims that Ethiopia was the
cradle of humanity, and of civilization. The Garden of Eden, he suggested,
had been located at the source of the Nile; though he also said it extended
from there as far as Mesopotamia, and blended this assertion with ideas
about lost continents (Johnson 1931: 25–34). Everything had radiated from
there, he proposed, in an account drawing on the extreme Egyptocentric
diffusionist Grafton Elliot Smith, on Herodotus and Volney, and on the
more reputable authority of W.E.B. Du Bois. Egyptian culture was the
creation of Ethiopia, as is proved by the racial features of the Sphinx (ibid.:
158–9). Egypt was in fact no more than 'a colony of the mighty Ethiopians'
(165), though Europeans have conspired to credit Ethiopian accomplishments to Egypt, entirely ignoring Ethiopia's antiquity and glory, its status as
the birthplace of all knowledge (272).

George Wells Parker, in 1918, not only anticipated later reverse-racist
antitheses between benevolent African 'Sun People' and malign European
'Ice People' in his *The Children of the Sun*, but argued that the ancient Greeks
were not only indebted to Africa but *were* African, at least in the Homeric
age.[16] As Parker put it, in language which echoed his era's African-American
colour-caste hierarchies of 'yellows', 'browns' and 'blacks', the 'great
Grecian epics were epics of an African people and Helen, the cause of the
Trojan war, must henceforth be conceived as a beautiful brown skin girl'
(quoted in Winters 1994: 177).[17]

A similar kind of racial romanticism found expression a few years later in
Drusilla Dunjee Houston's *Wonderful Ethiopians of the Ancient Cushite Empire*
(1926/1985). Houston (1876–1941), a schoolteacher and journalist who
spent most of her life in Oklahoma City, had apparently been inspired by
W.E.B. Du Bois's *The Negro*, but her own work displayed little of Du Bois's
care and caution. *Wonderful Ethiopians* was projected as the first of three
volumes, of which the latter two were seemingly completed, but never
published, and were subsequently lost.[18] It announced that the 'Ancient
Cushite Empire of Ethiopians' had spread its influence across the Middle
East, central Asia and India, as well as creating Egyptian civilization and
providing Greece and Rome with their pantheon of gods. It was 'either the
successor or the most famous branch of the Atlantic race' (ibid.: 5),
suggested Houston in a formulation which revealed the influence (direct or
indirect) of Leo Frobenius's far-fetched theories. The historic greatness of
the Cushites could still be seen today: observing modern Nubia, 'we can

plainly see in the inhabitants their superiority to the common Egyptian type' (32) – though it remained quite unclear how Houston, who had not, apparently, visited Africa, knew this. Much of the historical legacy, however, had been lost; and as Houston lamented (in language which revealed how far she, unlike many later Afrocentrists, identified herself with ideas of Western civilization), some of the destruction of Egyptian monuments was the work of 'Englishmen and Americans, to the everlasting shame of *our* claim to culture' (91; emphasis added).

Varying the usual identification with Ethiopians, Nubians or Egyptians, the Moorish Science Temple, founded by Noble Drew Ali in Newark, New Jersey, in 1913, proclaimed that African-Americans were descended from the ancient 'Moors', or Moroccans (Gardell 1996: 37–46; McCloud 1995: 10–18). Ali's movement – through which, it is estimated, at least 15,000 Americans had passed by 1950, as (often rather temporary) adherents, whose successors in the 1990s may still have numbered as many as 40,000 – was the first of numerous, usually highly heterodox 'Islamic' movements flourishing in black America during the first half of this century. It was the most Africa-centred of these, though Ali's belief in ancestral Afro-American affinity to Morocco could never command widespread credibility. His organization, and other early US 'Islamic' groups, were to be largely overshadowed by the Nation of Islam, founded in 1930 by the mysterious Wali Fard Muhammad.

If the tradition of Afro-American interest in and glorification of Egypt is long, it is also subject to its own kind of retrospective romanticization. Thus James G. Spady, seeking to trace a lineage of black American Egyptology – which, he suggests, Cheikh Anta Diop was much the poorer for not knowing – includes some extremely marginal figures. He cites two 'outstanding pioneer black Egyptologists of the nineteenth century', Norbert Rillieux and John H. Johnson (Spady 1989: 294). French-educated Rillieux was a noted engineer who no doubt deserves to be better remembered for his achievements in that sphere, but the only apparent evidence that he was even *interested* in ancient Egypt is the report of an acquaintance that he once found Rillieux looking at hieroglyphs in a Paris library! Johnson, a free Afro-American in antebellum Georgia, was a popular polemicist who lectured in Atlanta in the 1840s on 'The Ancient Black Egyptians, Originators of the Arts and Sciences' (Spady 1989: 295–6). Spady cites a number of other names, without offering evidence that any of them had a serious knowledge of ancient Africa – or could have had, in the segregated education system of their day. He also drags in at length, as a kind of proto-Diopian, the pioneer black historian Leo Hansberry (ibid.: 297–304).[19] In fact Hansberry, though he had an interest in the Ethiopian past, neither wrote on ancient Egypt nor shared any of the irrationalist impulses of the Afrocentrists and Egyptomanes. He was not only the first Afro-American, but one of the very first Americans, to have a close research interest in African history. Ego-boosting myths of black Pharaohs and bygone glories, however, played no part in this.[20]

Both black and white writers, American and African,[21] missionary and secular, took up different varieties of the theme that West Africans – or (as in the 'Hamitic hypothesis', which we shall discuss later) their ruling elites, or major elements of their cultures – originated outside the region itself, the Nile valley being the most popular starting point. Some had other suggestions: Olaudah Equiano believed the Igbo were a lost tribe of Israel, and James Africanus Horton seemed to agree (Zachernuk 1994: 435–6). But most concurred on Egypt's primacy with Henry Highland Garnet, who complained in 1848 that the new European scholarship of his day was 'by an almost common consent . . . determined to pilfer Africa of her glory' by denying that Egypt was 'Africa's dark browed queen' (quoted in ibid.: 433).

In the early twentieth century, however, more scholarly Afro-American views of African history did begin to emerge, notably in the writings of W.E.B. Du Bois and Carter G. Woodson. Woodson, the generally acknowledged founder of African-American history as a professional discipline, had a lifelong interest in Africa even though his major research projects never centred there. Like most black contemporaries who took note of the issue at all, he was concerned to underline the Africanness of Egypt and its importance for the early development of civilization. But his approach was radically distinct from that of later racial romantics in several respects. He emphasized ancient Egypt's character as a 'mixed' civilization, a 'crucible of cultures . . . a land of mixed breeds or persons comparable to Negroes passing in this country (the USA) as people of color' (Woodson 1922: 5; see also Woodson 1936). His polemical book *The Mis-Education of the Negro* (1933) has been claimed as a crucial precursor of Afrocentrism – even, by Gerald Early, as 'the central work of the Afrocentric movement by a black American writer' (1995: 37).[22] Yet although its fierce denunciations of the way in which misrepresentation of the black past in United States schools had produced subservience or even self-hatred among African-Americans are congenial to later Afrocentrists – indeed, the Farrakhan movement, among others, endorses and promotes reprints of *Mis-Education* – Woodson neither placed special emphasis on the ancient African past, nor advocated separatism or counter-mythographies of lost African glory. His central complaint was that the American educational system failed to give a true account of black history: but it was mainly a teaching of black *American* history for which he called, and to which he devoted his life, not that of ancient Egypt or Nubia.

Perhaps above all, Woodson always expressed himself with due scholarly caution. He had clear views on political and racial justice, which indeed motivated his whole life's work; but he distinguished these from what he frequently called, in the usual language of historiography at that time, a 'scientific' approach to history-writing. As his friend A.A. Taylor said after his death, he 'divorced scholarship from leadership *per se*, refusing to function either primarily or specifically as a race leader' (quoted in Meier and Rudwick 1986: 11).

There can be little doubt that almost throughout his exceptionally long career as writer, thinker and activist, W.E.B. Du Bois was the most powerful influence on the ideas of the more highly educated black Americans – though among the poorer and less sophisticated, others such as Marcus

Garvey or Malcolm X may, for briefer times, have had greater impact. For instance, among the eighty prominent Afro-Americans who formed Harold Isaacs's panel for evaluating black American views of Africa in the early 1960s, Du Bois was the most frequently mentioned name. Isaacs's interviewees were by no means all positive in their evaluation of Du Bois's personality or teachings, but none seemed ignorant about or indifferent towards him (Isaacs 1963: 195 ff.).

In the fullest of his attempts at autobiography, *Dusk of Dawn*, Du Bois's references to an early and painful discovery of being 'African' evidently – and conventionally for the time – mean the impress of an American racial awareness – they do not involve any particular connection to the continent itself. Asked, when he was already in his nineties, by Harold Isaacs whether in his teens he had had any knowledge of Africa, he responded negatively, saying that even if he had sought for books on Africa in the Great Barrington, Massachusetts library near his home, he would not then have found any (Isaacs 1963: 206–7). At school, he recalled only being incensed that no images of Africans came up other than the stereotypical 'savage' in textbook galleries of racial types; and even at Fisk University, Africa 'was something in the background. There was always a lack of interest, a neglect, a resentment at being classed as Africans when Negroes felt that they were Americans.' Like many others, Du Bois credited anthropologist Franz Boas with awakening the interest he did eventually develop in Africa, but that was only after about 1914 (ibid.: 207).

In his important 1915 book *The Negro*, Du Bois offered probably the least romance-bound, most factually grounded view of Africa yet published by a black American writer. In tune with the general thought of his age, he placed great stress on the physical characteristics of different human types. Yet he also insisted that there could be no clear scientific definition of race, and entered an early complaint against the whole idea of a distinct 'Hamitic' race being responsible for Africa's major cultural achievements (ibid.: 16–17). Quite unlike later theorists of Africa as an especially beneficent physical environment for human development – a favourite view of some Euro-racists who thought that natural abundance explained Africans' supposed lack of development, and later of romantic Afrocentrists who claim that it accounts for allegedly superior African moral qualities – Du Bois emphasized the harshness of life there. Disease, parasites and poor soils made sheer physical survival harder in Africa than in any other continent, he believed (18–19). This view, at best oversimple, was shared by contemporaries like the great Haitian ethnologist Jean Price-Mars (1928/1983: 58–9, 76–8) and, less understandably, repeated almost verbatim by modern Afrocentrists like Chancellor Williams (1971/1987: 49–53).[23]

Du Bois accepted then current views that humanity first developed in Asia, and had entered Africa in the distant past (20–23). On ancient Egypt, he emphasized indigenous African roots for its civilization while also recognizing that it 'drew largely from without', mainly from western Asia (30). On the race of the Egyptians, he stressed their mixed character – trying to quantify the different types there, seeing only a minority as fully 'Negroid', urging that none was white in the modern sense, and comparing Egyptian physical appearances with 'the striking and beautiful types arising from the mingling of Negro with Latin and Germanic types in America' (33).[24] Except for the last, obviously subjective and personally important identification, none of this would be unacceptable to Egyptologists in the 1990s.

Du Bois then sketched the history of the continent across three millennia, giving most attention to the states of West Africa. He anticipated much later writing in arguing that the apparent degeneration of West Africa's kingdoms from the achievements of the past must be due to the advent of the slave trade, not to any internal cause (67–8). Overall, his account avoided sensationalism and special pleading, being a solid reflection of the state of knowledge at that time, despite his reliance on such questionable colonialist sources as Sir Harry Johnston and Florence Shaw, Lady Lugard. His most obviously *parti pris* passage related to Liberia, his brief description of which (69–71) gave no hint of the territory's disorganized and tyrannical state.

In later writings – including the greatly revised and updated reworkings of *The Negro* which appeared in 1939 as *Black Folk Then and Now*, and in 1947 as *The World and Africa* – Du Bois tended towards a more polemical tone – though he also took adequate account of new research on African history, including that of ancient Egypt. Some, such as Kwame Appiah (1992), have seen him as shading into a romantic racialism. Provided we keep in mind the distinction, important to Appiah's case, between racialism (belief in the distinctive characters of different racial groups, a pervasive mistake but not one necessarily implying prejudice or hostility to any group on those grounds) and racism (belief in a *hierarchy* of such groups, which does necessarily lead to prejudice and hostility – of which Appiah does not accuse Du Bois) the judgement is not unfair.[25] Certainly he tended increasingly towards a romanticized enthusiasm for Africa itself, as his emotional response on first visiting the continent in 1924 indicated (excerpted in Van Deburg, ed. 1997: 47–50). Some commentators have viewed Du Bois's choosing to spend his last years living in newly independent Ghana as evidence of this; though clearly the Communist faith he adopted in old age also had much to do with the alienation from America which induced his emigration. And even as he became ever sharper and more categorical in his denunciations of white prejudice, more pessimistic – if not bitter – about the prospects for racial and social justice in America, Du Bois never ceased to be a scholar as well as a propagandist. His successive writings on African history may not have involved original research of the same order as his justly famous works on the Atlantic slave trade, Reconstruction and black Philadelphia, but they remain considerably more factually reliable than many later Afrocentric publications.

In his imaginative writing, Du Bois sometimes reached for symbols of civilizational, or even biological, priority of Africans over Europeans. Thus in his best-known poem, 'The Song of the Smoke', he proclaimed:

> The blacker the mantle, the mightier the man!
> For blackness was ancient ere whiteness began.
> (Du Bois 1985: 8; also in Gates and McKay 1997: 612)[26]

Du Bois's final view, however, was less an affirmation of romantic racialized thinking than a dream of 'Third World' solidarity, also evidently influenced by the Communist beliefs of his last years. Africa took its place primarily as a means to that end:

> The actual ties of heritage between the individuals of this group vary with the ancestors that they have in common and many others, Europeans and Semites, perhaps Mongolians, certainly American Indians. But the physical bond is least and the badge of colour relatively unimportant save as a badge; the real essence of this kinship is its social heritage of slavery; the discrimination and insult; and this heritage binds together not simply the children of Africa, but extends through yellow Asia and into the South Seas. It is this unity that draws me to Africa. (Du Bois 1940: 117)

More obviously romantic and propagandist, though still generally sober and serious in their approach, were the writers who continued to produce 'contributionist' histories – narratives emphasizing the African contribution to world civilization, and the black contribution to American development – up until and into the Civil Rights era. Most ambitious in scope was the work of Joel Augustus Rogers, whose nearly fifty years of assiduous information-grubbing culminated in the massive, self-published *World's Great Men of Color* in 1947. Born in Jamaica in about 1880, he moved to the USA in 1906 and, while scraping a living in a variety of manual occupations and later as a newspaper columnist, produced a steady stream of popularly orientated historical works. The majority of these were self-published and remained in obscurity, though his most accessible texts, the picture-book *Your History from the Beginning of Time to the Present* (1940) and the vivid *100 Amazing Facts About the Negro* (1957), reached a wide audience and went through numerous editions. Himself light-skinned – and apparently initially shocked to discover that in the States, unlike Jamaica, people of his hue were discriminated against just as sharply as those of more obviously unmixed African descent (Kellner 1984: 309) – he developed a particular interest in the theme of 'race mixing' in history (see, for example, Rogers 1927, 1940–44, 1952). One aspect of this preoccupation led to the least intellectually convincing part of his labours: his obsession with claiming African descent for many famous historical figures usually thought of as white. They included what he called the 'five Negro Presidents' of the USA (supposedly, Thomas Jefferson, Alexander Hamilton, Andrew Jackson, Abraham Lincoln and Warren Harding) as well as such oft-invoked names as Beethoven and Browning.

Such claims represented the more questionable side of Rogers's very uneven attitude to historical proof: what St Clair Drake describes as his 'solid scholarship combined with considerable speculation' and 'temperate, sophisticated approach to the use of sources, which unfortunately was sometimes not strictly adhered to' (1987: 98–9). Rogers's procedures were certainly, at times, indiscriminate and uncritical. His biographical sketches of prominent 'men of color', though mainly focused on people of African descent, also included a rather random-seeming handful of Asian and Arab figures. His very first subject in *World's Great Men* was the ancient physician Imhotep, who – though probably (like Noah or Gilgamesh) based on a historical individual – is known mostly as an Egyptian god. He laid claim not only to numerous major figures of American and European history, but to the Prophet Muhammad, who was, as he insisted, 'a very black man' (1940: 32). And he rarely offered any critical assessment of his subjects: the fact that they were in some way prominent, and had at least some trace of non-white ancestry, seemed to be enough. His guiding principle, he said, was that 'the recital of the deeds of the great or the worthy was instinctive in humanity' (Rogers 1947/1972 I: 6). The only really negative portrait is of Marcus Garvey, whose enthusiastic supporter Rogers had once been. Garvey's doctrine 'was, in short, racial fascism', his methods 'twisted, archaic, perverse', his followers 'rabid' (ibid. II: 420, 427, 418). With this exception, Rogers's pictures of his subjects (who even included some noted African slave-traders) served primarily as unalloyed boosters to race pride.

Rogers's works have continued to be republished, and praised by more recent Afrocentrists: though he would probably have had little sympathy with their separatism. He insisted that race was only 'a concept that was thrust upon me (I had never felt otherwise than as a member of the human race)' (1947/1972 I: 7). His decision to include 'great bad men' in his books did not mean that he approved of them simply because they were black: 'I dislike conquerors, tyrants, and dictators, whatever their color' (I: 23). Nor do even his wilder flights of historical fancy approach the disregard for logic and evidence of many present-day Afrocentrists. Indeed, to compare his books, for all their faults, with much of the material published by Afro-American cultural nationalists in the 1980s and 1990s – writers who have higher degrees, secure and well-paid jobs and guaranteed publishing outlets, in glaring contrast to Rogers's lifelong struggle to be heard – indicates that in such circles there has, if anything, often been intellectual degeneration rather than development.

The lack of interest in – and sense of embarrassment or disdain towards – Africa which Du Bois noted in his youth was clearly widespread among Afro-Americans, and persisted well into the era of decolonization. Martin Staniland's survey of the black US press in the 1950s and 1960s found little more coverage of African affairs there than in the white-owned media, and attitudes that were often not dramatically different, with conventional stereotypes abounding (Staniland 1991; see also Weisbord 1973). Some Afro-American leaders and intellectuals, going further than shared stereo-types, even identified themselves with the idea of an imperialist 'civilizing mission' in Africa and elsewhere, and associated this with their own hopes for progress among black Americans. The notion of 'racial uplift', in varying forms, was common ground to thinkers as diverse as Du Bois, Garvey and Booker T. Washington. There may even have been a direct association of ideas between the perceived need to educate and civilize poorer, 'backward' black Americans and the supposed European endeavour to do the same in Africa. The ideas of one who made such connections in the 1900s, the novelist and journalist Pauline E. Hopkins, have recently and interestingly been traced (Gaines 1993). Her own contribution to the vindicationist genre was a 1905 pamphlet, evidently intended as an educational aid with its question-and-answer format and deliberately simple language. The level of historical knowledge displayed was, however, low even by the usual standards of the genre. Hopkins repeated the old biblical argument that the 'three races' of mankind were derived from the three sons of Noah (1905: 6), and peculiarly argued that black skin colour was actually a concentrated red, as one could see in blackberries and other fruit! Therefore: 'The real color of the African is really purple and nothing else' (ibid.: 8). In the standard fashion, ancient Ethiopians were held to have 'excelled all other nations' in 'wisdom and Literature' (15), though the only evidence presented for this is, once again, the Pyramids. From the ancient world the text then leaps suddenly over the centuries to urge and celebrate the modern 'restoration' of black genius: contemporary Afro-Americans show 'that they are descended from the once powerful and learned Ethiopians' by producing men of talent in all fields of endeavour (17).

Perhaps the most important and intriguing exponent of this kind of thought, however, was Alexander Crummell. His mixture of militant Christianity, authoritarian elitism, progressivism, Puritanism and racial solidarity, as brilliantly analysed by his biographer Wilson Moses, finds many echoes among latter-day Afrocentrists and other cultural nationalists. As Moses comments, that ideology, bringing together seemingly contradictory ideas of cultural assimilationism and political or physical separatism, derives not from slave culture, let alone any identifiably African influence, but from black Victorian intellectuals adapting to their own ends the racial chauvinism and militant muscular Christianity so ubiquitous in the majority Euro-American culture of their day (Moses 1989: 9–10). In terms of political ideologies in the narrower sense, the closest affinities are with organicist conservatives like Burke, Guizot or Carlyle (ibid.: 287–90). One can see the influence of this structure of ideas on Marcus Garvey – numerous disciples of Crummell passed into the Garvey movement – and later on the Black Muslims and Louis Farrakhan, extending into the moral authoritarianism, racial and sexual chauvinism, and organicism of many in the modern Afrocentric movement.

Notes

1. The near-ubiquity of these emphases among African-American public figures in the late nineteenth century is suggested also by their reiteration among numerous delegates

at the 1895 Atlanta 'Congress on Africa'. Delegates E.W.S. Hammond, M.C.B. Mason, and John Smyth were among those declaring a pride in their ancient Egyptian heritage: Bowen (ed.) (1896). For the wider context of nineteenth- and early-twentieth-century African-American nationalist thought, see also Moses (1978); Redkey (1969); Stuckey (1987).

2. For a succinct summary of the possible origins of such ideas of a curse on Ham and his descendants, legitimating African slavery, see Blackburn (1997: 64–76). There is a substantial prior literature on this question, much of it given a politically charged resonance by dispute over how far, if at all, early Judaic texts may be 'blamed' for helping to initiate a discourse of racial hierarchy: see Evans (1980) Isaac (1985); E. Sanders (1969); Hannaford (1996: 90–95).

3. On the career of this remarkable figure, see Schor (1977).

4. Neither here nor in his later collection, *Africa and Europe* (Crummell 1891), however, did he press the case for historic or prehistoric African greatness. On the contrary, his belief in the 'civilizing mission' that Afro-Americans could accomplish in West Africa was premised on conventional ideas about African backwardness and lack of civilization – though he also insisted that West Africa's natives possessed some fine moral and industrious qualities (e.g. 1891: 87–8, 194–5), and naturally repudiated ideas that the supposed backwardness reflected some invariant racial essence or natural inferiority.

5. I have been unable to locate a copy of Lewis's book.

6. The latter pair did indeed have one African-descended grandparent each, but such claims in regard to Beethoven, Browning and Marx (despite the last-named's family nickname of 'the Moor') are highly speculative.

7. Volney, among the first modern Europeans to suggest that the Ancient Egyptians were 'Negroes' and that civilization originated in Africa, has naturally had ever-renewed appeal for Afrocentrists. The Black Classic Press has kept his 1794 *Ruins of Empires* in print throughout the 1990s.

8. Such ideas were virtual commonplaces in Blyden's time, voiced also by a huge range of European ideologues: it is their recapitulation in the late twentieth century that is peculiar.

9. Only after publication of this book did Williams gain first-hand experience of Africa: for his involvement with the affairs of the continent, which centred on the Congo, see J. Franklin (1985, 1988); Skinner (1983).

10. Councill was clearly a dedicated educationalist, but also a man whose ambition and opportunism led him into a subservience to white Southern interests which went much further even than that of his greater rival Booker T. Washington. Enthusiastically endorsing segregation, denying any aspiration to social equality and even campaigning for the white-supremacist Southern Democrats, as Washington's biographer says, he 'fulfilled the Alabama white man's conception of a Negro leader' who 'could condemn the Yankee radical and proclaim the Southern white man to be the Negro's best friend' (Harlan 1972: 169). Ironically, he lost much of his white support after suing a railway company which refused to let him travel first class.

11. The medium through which Hegel's, Carlyle's and Emerson's ideas were transmitted to Ferris was evidently his Yale mentor George Trumbull Ladd, to whom fulsome tribute is paid. A strong sense of intellectual elitism, rather specifically focused on his own old universities, resonates through Ferris's work. He even suggests that Booker T. Washington, against whose philosophy of race leadership he mounts repeated attacks, would have been a better and wiser man had he studied philosophy at Harvard or Yale (Ferris 1913: 107)!

12. Ferris claimed that he had originally been quite uninterested in the racial identity of ancient peoples, until a reading of Sergi, Volney, and other authorities (1913: 476). His point seemed to be that his involvement with the issue was scholarly, as opposed to the romantic racialism of previous Afro-American writers on this theme.

13. On the history of this appeal, and of the 'Ethiopianist' trope in African-American religio-political thought, see Drake (1970).

14. Sebastian Clarke (1980: 36–52) sketches the reasons for the Rastafarians' enthusiasm for Ethiopia and their connections to both biblical stories and claims about ancient

history, from the standpoint of a sympathizer, though not a believer. Clarke, under the name Amon Saba Saakana, has subsequently become the most energetic British publicist for Afrocentrism. Chevannes (1995) is a more detailed, scholarly and detached account of the origins of Rastafari.

15. Claims treated with no doubt justified scepticism by historians: see Hickey and Wylie (1993: 254–5).

16. I have not been able to see Parker's pamphlet, but his fanciful views on the issue can be confirmed from the briefer compass of his contribution to the *Journal of Negro History* (Parker 1917).

17. Intriguingly, exactly the same title, *Children of the Sun*, was used just a few years later by the London University anthropologist W.J. Perry. Perry, a disciple of the extravagant theories of ethnologist Grafton Elliot Smith on the Egyptian origins of all human civilization, sought in his book to trace common traits, and common Egyptian roots, for the whole range of cultural phenomena across the entire globe (Perry 1923). The current Afrocentrists' revival of the language of 'Sun People' may owe something, at least indirectly, to both Parker and Perry. John G. Jackson's *Introduction to African Civilizations*, a major pioneering work of Afrocentric history, draws heavily on Perry (Jackson 1970: 73, 75–6, 83).

18. Biographical information is from W. Paul Coates's Introduction to the 1985 reprint of *Wonderful Ethiopians*.

19. John Henrik Clarke and Runoko Rashidi, among others, have also sought to enlist Hansberry as a premature Afrocentrist: see, for example, Clarke (1992: 11); Rashidi (1994: 25–6).

20. Hansberry, though a revered teacher and energetic organizer who sponsored, in 1925, what was probably the first-ever black American scholarly conference on African history, published little in his lifetime. Parts of his notebooks on African history, from which he drew in widely influential lecture series, were published posthumously under the editorship of Joseph E. Harris: a volume on Ethiopian history (Hansberry 1974), and one on classical authors' views of Africa which complements the better-known researches of Frank Snowden on the same theme (Hansberry 1977).

21. As we have noted, however, the romantic historiography of past African glories was seemingly far less widely subscribed to among continental African writers than among African-Americans. Perhaps the most extensive earlier African production in this vein, leaving aside the work of Diop, was that of the Ghanaian academic J.C. deGraft-Johnson (1954). A handful of African imaginative writers have taken up such themes, notably the Ghanaian novelist Ayi Kwei Armah, whose later work includes unanimist and (see Armah 1995) even Egyptophile currents closely akin to those of US Afrocentrists.

22. Two disciples of Molefi Asante, the most prominent present-day Afrocentric thinker, have proposed strong affinities between their hero's approach and the earlier example of Woodson's *Mis-Education* (Mooijman 1995; Garland 1995). Asa Hilliard, too, proclaims Woodson to be the crucial forefather of Afrocentrism (Hilliard 1994a: 134–5). Similarly – if with less uncritical enthusiasm – the theologian Cheryl Townsend Gilkes (1995: 27–30) views Du Bois and Woodson as the founders of Afrocentrism, and Asante as the current exemplar. Asante himself has credited Woodson with establishing many of the principles on which Afrocentrism in education now operates (Asante 1991/1997: 289, 294).

23. Very crudely and oversimply, it can be said that Du Bois was nearer to the truth than the European ideologists who proclaimed Africa's initiative-sapping natural abundance (a view which uncannily echoes contemporary claims that state welfare systems destroy capacity for self-improvement – claims which, in the USA, often specifically target African-Americans). Much of Africa does indeed have comparatively high densities of disease-bearing insects and parasites, agriculturally poor soils, unreliable rainfalls, and other obstacles to the stable development of complex human societies. To recognize this is not to endorse the rhetorical structures either of Chancellor Williams and his ilk, or of latter-day ecological determinists. It is noteworthy, however, that Du Bois – like Woodson in his relatively brief discussions of African history, and unlike many later Afrocentrists – sought to explain cultural development in environmental rather than racial terms.

24. And Du Bois's most famous pronouncement of all, the musing on African-American 'double consciousness' in his *Souls of Black Folk*, explicitly counterposes the 'Egyptian' and the 'Negro' as two quite separate racial groups (Du Bois 1903/1961: 16).

25. Though see the extensive debate and critiques on this question in Bell *et al.* (eds) (1996), as well as Lott (1992/3).

26. Berghahn (1977) discusses images of Africa in Du Bois's imaginative writings, but greatly overstresses what she calls their 'rigid Eurocentricity' (116), largely because she fails to place them in the context of his non-fictional production. Conversely, Moses (1996), in stressing Du Bois's 'Afrocentrism', perhaps overstates the similarities between his thought and that of later US Afrocentrists, including an allegedly shared political authoritarianism.

5

The Birth of Afrocentrism

Meanwhile, with the growth of a substantial body of professional historians in black America, the appeal of the older romantic chroniclers seemed to decline. The wild theories of a Robert Lewis, or J.A. Rogers's pious efforts to celebrate the memory of any African with any known achievement in any sphere, became irrelevant or even embarrassing to a new cohort of far more skilled researchers in a new and more open political atmosphere. Any listing of the major Afro-American historians of the past few decades would include such names as Mary F. Berry, John W. Blassingame, John Hope Franklin, Vincent Harding, Darlene Clark Hine, Thomas C. Holt, Nathan Huggins, David Levering Lewis, Manning Marable, Wilson J. Moses, Benjamin Quarles, and Sterling Stuckey. Of these, only perhaps Stuckey and Harding could be identified at any time in their careers with cultural nationalist or separatist ideas – and neither of them has anything much in common with Afrocentricity. As Meier and Rudwick comment: 'Most of the publishing black scholars were never separatists' (1986: 229). The other side of the same coin is that the Afro-American publicists who did hold separatist or cultural nationalist views were not, with very few exceptions, productive scholars. They polemicized, but they did not research. They made speeches, and latterly granted media interviews, but they did not write.[1]

Much the same is true of Afro-American scholarship about Africa itself. It must be added, however, that relatively few African-American historians chose to specialize in the history of Africa; not that it was made easy for them to do so, to say the least, until quite recently. The first American historian to undertake fieldwork in Africa was black: George W. Brown, in the 1930s – but significantly, he did his research, on Liberian economic history, under the auspices of the London School of Economics rather than any American institution. A number of prominent African historians, together with a larger number of European Africanists, took American university posts from the 1960s onwards, including Kenneth Dike at Harvard and Boniface Obichere at UCLA, but they seem to have had little impact on Afro-American thinking. It may, though, be worth underlining that the writings of black American scholars specializing in African history rarely partook of the emphases, or the prejudices, of Afrocentric cultural nationalism:

if anything, considerably less so even than those of the major African-
American historians of the USA itself. It is perhaps indicative in this regard
that in very many cases, I have no idea at all of the racial identity of
American Africanists whose names and work I know, whereas equivalent
information has effectively been thrust to my attention for the vast majority
of scholars working on US subjects.

Separatism did raise its head in academic African studies, though not in
so widespread or successful a form as in scholarship about Afro-America. In
1969 some black members of the US African Studies Association split off to
form a blacks-only African Heritage Studies Association. As the new Association's title suggested, its members tended to be attracted to a rather pious
or celebratory, rather than a critical, approach to African studies. The story
of the battle is worth a brief retelling, for in a sense it marks the first
emergence from obscurity on to centre stage of Afrocentrism in North
America.

At the end of the 1960s, the African Studies Association, with over 1,500
members plus some three hundred affiliated institutions, was a veritable
academic empire presiding over one of the fastest-growing of all intellectual
fields. It was also a predominantly white organization, reflecting the then
still overwhelmingly white composition of American academia and even of
scholarly African Studies: as of 1968, its governing Board apparently had
only one black member, the distinguished Harvard political analyst Martin
Kilson. In this era of Black Power and Vietnam, of dramatic turmoil
throughout America's university campuses as in society at large, that
situation could not go unchallenged.

In 1968 a 'Black Caucus' was formed within the ASA, led by John Henrik
Clarke of Hunter College, New York – though allegedly many of its members
did not actually belong to the Association at all. The Caucus raised a series
of demands for sweeping change in the ASA's mode of government, ethos
and purposes. The campaign culminated in dramatic scenes at the Association's 1969 annual convention in Montreal, when black radicals disrupted
and effectively closed down the event. The atmosphere was clearly explosive,
verging at least on outbreaks of physical violence. One angry ASA member
wrote of 'being menaced . . . harassed, insulted and denied either freedom
of speech or a meaningful dialogue' (B.D. Bargar, *African Studies Newsletter* –
hereafter *ASN* – 2, nos. 6–7: 16–17). After forcing the closedown of the
official conference sessions, the Black Caucus presented a statement:

> African peoples attending the ASA Conference have demanded that the
> study of African life be undertaken from a Pan-Africanist perspective. This
> perspective defines that all black people are African peoples and negates the
> tribalization of African peoples. . . . African peoples will no longer permit
> our people to be raped culturally, economically, politically and intellectually
> merely to provide European scholars with intellectual status symbols of
> African artifacts hanging in their living rooms and irrelevant and injurious
> lectures for their classrooms. (*ASN* 2, 6–7: 1–2)

The black militants, headed by Clarke and by Professor Chike Onwuachi of Fisk University, also had more practical demands: for an immediate change in the 'ideological framework of the ASA which perpetuates colonialism and neo-colonialism'; that African studies be made more 'relevant'; for control over research funds; and for half the members of the ASA's Board to be black (ibid.: 2). Simultaneously, they announced the formation of an all-black African Heritage Studies Association 'at which all Black persons attending the conference were welcome' (ibid.: 1). Amplifying the list of demands, Clarke said the aims were: 'Reconstruction of African History and cultural studies along Afrocentric lines while effecting an intellectual union among black scholars the world over' (Clarke 1970: 10). The phraseology here is interesting – apparently one of the first times the term 'Afrocentric' – or, for that matter, 'cultural studies' – had been used in this way.

The Black Caucus and the AHSA – it remained unclear how far these were just two names for the same thing, though it was apparent that the same few individuals dominated both – were evidently, by no standards, large bodies. Comparing all the rival statements published in the *African Studies Newsletter* and elsewhere, one finds a maximum of ten names: Clarke, the subsequently notorious Leonard Jeffries, Onwuachi, Michael Searles and Nicholas Onyewu of Federal City College, Washington DC, Shelby Faye Lewis (Southern University, Baton Rouge), Nell Painter (San Jose College), Jan Douglass ('of New York City'), Inez Reid and Herschelle Challenor. Nor could they be called a distinguished group in academic terms. Apart from their leader, the prolific but unscholarly John Henrik Clarke, and Nell Painter, who had worked in Ghana and subsequently emerged as a major historian and author of important books (on American, not African, history), I can trace only *one* of them as having produced any substantial publication, then or subsequently – and even this was only as one of three co-editors of a book.[2] It was not at all clear who they spoke for, apart from themselves – as Henry L. Bretton ironically admitted, their claim to be 'the authorized spokesman for hundreds of millions of people' left him 'limp with admiration, as a political scientist' (*ASN* 2, 6–7: 19). Even Clarke himself seemed to concede that 'the main aims and objectives of the AHSA had not been made known to any appreciable number of the attending black intellectuals' at Montreal (Clarke 1970: 9). Indeed, one ASA official alleged that Clarke had played a rather slippery double game, pursuing private summitry on the one hand and demagogic appeals on the other (James L. Gibbs, *ASN* 2, 6–7: 13–14). But then these were heady times for self-appointed revolutionary vanguards. Alongside the ASA Black Caucus marched the Radical Caucus – also, by its own admission, all of ten cadres strong – which not only demanded that the Association officially adopt an anti-imperialist programme but affirmed: 'we no longer consider ourselves a caucus and have renamed our group the Pan-Africanist Radical Baraza' (Resnick 1970: 14–15[3]).

The radicals' calls for 'relevance' were themselves thoroughly double-edged, as Pierre van den Berghe acidly commented. A demand that expatriates' research be relevant to African governments' priorities 'unwittingly presents us with a sophisticated blueprint for intellectual neo-colonialism by showing Western scholars a way to survive in Africa by serving the needs of the new ruling class' (Van den Berghe 1970: 334). For Clarke and his co-thinkers, such concerns were probably rather beside the point: in a forum supposedly devoted to Africa, they were interested in *American*, not African, 'relevance'. As one of them, Nell Painter, proclaimed, their protests were launched 'not only because the ASA needs readjustment, but also because it is an integral part of racist America' (*ASN* 2, 6–7: 30).

At Montreal, some senior ASA members proposed a compromise formula conceding many of the black radicals' demands, including the demand for 50 per cent representation on the Board. A postal poll of the membership, however, indicated that a large majority opposed such a formula (*ASN* 2, 1: 2–3). Dozens of members, including several of the most prominent US Africanists and of the ASA's black members, endorsed an angry statement protesting 'that the ASA has been forced to accept racialist principles and to divide its membership into racial categories'. The statement alleged that most Black Caucus members did not even belong to the Association, condemning the disruption of meetings 'by physical force' and the black radicals' 'scorn for orderly democratic principles' (*ASN* 2, 6–7: 22). One ASA member, Ann Beck, must have spoken for many when she insisted: 'I personally cannot accept the thesis implicit in the statements of the Black Caucus that race determines a scholar's qualification to analyze and synthesize the African past' (ibid.: 17). Another, Arthur Keppel-Jones, proved that overheated rhetoric was certainly no monopoly of the radicals with his view: 'I recognize Nazi stormtroopers when I see them, and am no more willing to submit to bullying from black ones than from white' (ibid.: 27).

The idea that the African Heritage Studies Association – which another critic, Henry L. Bretton, called an '*ad hoc* coalition formed under unspecified conditions and circumstances by unidentified persons representing obscure causes' (ibid.: 19) – should be able to nominate half the ASA's Board members was clearly unacceptable to many, probably most, of those involved. On the other hand, it seemed unacceptable to the AHSA militants that anyone *except* them should choose the Board's black membership. If the latter were to be subject to open election, they allegedly said, 'the right Blacks would not be elected' (Cowan 1970: 344).

Negotiations between the ASA and AHSA, not surprisingly, soon broke down, and thereafter two distinct bodies operated – though the ASA remained far the larger and indeed, it would appear, retained more black members than did its Afrocentrist rival. ASA President L. Gray Cowan, insisting that this was a political rather than a racial issue (surely, in that atmosphere, a false antithesis if ever there was one), tried to write *finis* to the affair by asserting, rather unconvincingly: 'I welcome the presence of the AHSA and ... hope that the parallel interests of the two groups will bring them closer together in the coming years' (Cowan 1970: 345). The real last word, if there could be one, probably belonged rightfully to Martin Kilson. A year after the initial storms, he resigned from the Board expressing his 'disgust' at what he saw as white members' timid fumblings over the affair. Their behaviour was 'profoundly sycophantic in its guilt-ridden relationship to the silly political posturing and bizarre intellectual antics of black militants' (*ASN* 3, 7: 20).

Outside academia, meanwhile, a somewhat different story prevailed. There existed a flourishing 'underworld' of largely self-taught enthusiasts, working outside academic institutions and often in manual occupations, publishing in tiny black-owned imprints and not infrequently publishing themselves, their work often to be found only in the then few bookshops and even fewer libraries catering specifically to the African American community.[4]

Musicologist John Corbett's interviews with Alton Abraham, the Chicago mystic who was for decades a confidant and associate of the great bandleader Sun Ra, provide a window into one small segment of that world, including both its wonderful ambitiousness amid straitened circumstances and its severe intellectual limitations. In the early 1950s, Abraham recalled:

> [W]e were already doing ancient biblical research and research in astrology and researching the origin of mankind. . . . Found out that all people came from one source, civilization had its beginning in one particular area. Those that know know that that area is either the area around the Tigris and Euphrates rivers, or it's in certain parts of Africa in that area [*sic*] . . . I have a library of over fifteen thousand books dealing on those subjects . . . we wanted to do some things to prove to the world that black people could do something worthwhile, that they could create things . . . we studied composers like Beethoven, and we read the books of Schopenhauer, Nietzsche. . . . We had studied the prophecies of the pyramids, and the prophecies of Nostradamus. (Corbett 1994: 218–21)[5]

It was a world in which, successively, Garveyism and the Black Muslim movement had substantial influence. Here, impulses of racial uplift, religious and/or mystical leanings, political activism and autodidact scholarship intermingled in a rich stew of ideas. It was a tradition which stretched back to nineteenth-century pamphleteers like Augustus T. Bell and John William Norris. It included writers who have now, posthumously or in old age, achieved unwonted prominence in the climate of revived cultural nationalism from the early 1980s onwards, like George G.M. James, Joel Augustus Rogers and Yosef Ben-Jochannen. These men's writings bear all the marks of an autodidact subculture in which huge but indiscriminate erudition, antiquarianism, deep suspicion of all 'established' intellectual authorities, and a strong streak of mystical, occult and eschatological beliefs mingled. It is a milieu which has some striking similarities to the religio-political intellectual 'underworlds' of English plebeian radicalism delved into by historians like Christopher Hill and Edward Thompson – see, for instance, Hill's *The World Turned Upside Down* (Hill 1972) and Thompson's *Witness Against the Beast* (Thompson 1993) – or even those unearthed in Carlo Ginzburg's work on medieval European popular philosophy and witch cults (Ginzburg 1980, 1983, 1990).

Indeed, there are some direct parallels and connections between these different worlds of 'secret' knowledges, from early modern Europe, through John Milton's or William Blake's London, to contemporary Chicago or Harlem. Specifically, there is a fascination with and glorification of ancient Egypt – within which, as we shall see, a Masonic-ritualistic thread has continued to run. More broadly, there is a shared anti-rationalist and counter-Enlightenment world-view. Egypto-mystical writings like Godfrey Higgins's *Anacalypsis* of 1833, long forgotten in most circles, found a continuingly fascinated readership among African-American autodidacts, and were often reissued by Afrocentric publishers.[6]

In part at least, the coming of Afrocentricity to the academic milieu and to global media attention represents the 'coming in from the cold' of these previously marginal currents – an inclusionary move which owed far more to political than to scholarly changes. In the original heyday of cultural nationalism among Afro-Americans, from the mid-1960s to the mid-1970s, its impact on research and the study of history was rather small. In the 1990s the situation is very different in terms of public profile. Whether it is to be a new departure also in terms of substantial work, the establishment of a firmly grounded new paradigm, still remains to be seen; but on the evidence we shall survey in subsequent chapters, it seems unlikely.

Notes

1. For broader overviews of the development of African-American historical scholarship, see Hine (1986); Meier and Rudwick (1986); Novick (1988 ch. 14). It is notable that none of these, nor any academic survey of American or Afro-American historiography which I have read, discusses the 'alternative' tradition of largely amateur research which forms Afrocentrism's main intellectual lineage, and is my main focus here. The only major attempt to bring the two currents together, to my knowledge, is St Clair Drake's *Black Folk Here and There* (1987, 1990), which is considered elsewhere in these pages.

2. Jeffries and Reid apparently both hold doctorates in African studies from Columbia University – the former's on the politics of the Ivory Coast, the latter's on the Congo Democratic Republic – but neither appears to have published significant scholarly work. Painter's major work includes her 1977 and 1996 volumes: these and her statements on historical method (e.g. 1986) indicate a philosophy of history poles apart from the boosterism of the John Henrik Clarke school. Meier and Rudwick (1986: 214), based on interviews with Painter, discusses her ideological evolution as a historian.

3. I read Resnick's statement several times, struggling with my common-sense instinct that it must surely be a put-on. Unfortunately, it seems to have been written with a straight face.

4. And sometimes not even there: even the Schomburg Library, the world's premier research collection on African-American subjects, does not have fully comprehensive holdings of such materials.

5. Sun Ra's biographer traces the stages of the bandleader's own immersion in esoteric

Egyptology, which played so large a part in his music and thought: they included the works of Albert Churchward, Gerald Massey, Count Volney, Helena Blavatsky, Pyotr Ouspensky, George Wells Parker, Godfrey Higgins and George G.M. James (Szwed 1997: 61–73, 106–9).

6. See also C. Hill (1977: esp. 69–79, 299–301); K. Thomas (1971: esp. 318–32); and above all Yates (1964, 1972). Another direct – if subterranean – connection may be found in the Swedenborgian tradition. Emmanuel Swedenborg and his followers, like many later Afrocentrists, believed that Africans were inherently more spiritual in outlook than other groups, and looked to them for a revival of Christian values: on this, see Fredrickson (1995: 62–3).

6

The Masonic Connection

George G.M. James's book *Stolen Legacy* has achieved posthumous fame as a founding text of Afrocentrism, and especially of the argument that the ancient Greeks 'stole' all their knowledge from black Egyptians. James's book, however, is as much a mystic-ritualistic, and more specifically Masonic, work as it is an Afrocentric one. His major sources include Masonic, Theosophical and Rosicrucian works (these currents sometimes overlap: for instance, the Theosophists founded the first and only Masonic lodges to admit women) lauding the ancient Egyptians as originators of an esoteric wisdom and ritual which has passed directly to present-day cults and secret societies. Among these sources are C.H. Vail's *The Ancient Mysteries and Modern Masonry*, D. Davidson's *The Great Pyramid: Its Divine Message*, Annie Besant's *Esoteric Christianity*, H. Spencer Lewis's *Mystical Life of Jesus*, and the *Rosicrucian Digest*. James's central plea relates not – as with most Afro-American works in related vein – mainly to the need for racial uplift, but to his desire for 'the solution of the problem of universal unrest' (James 1954/1992: 151). Although this is hardly a specifically Masonic sentiment, it is precisely the idea and the wording held forth by the more messianic advocates of Freemasonry as the aim of their movement, especially in the writings from the first few decades of this century to which James makes frequent reference.

George James would thus appear, from internal evidence, to have been a Mason, and to have been strongly influenced by the more esoteric aspects of Masonic lore.[1] More generally, the sources on which Afrocentric writers have fastened have included many works by Masonic chroniclers. These works had their own reasons (drawing on the Hermeticist and Rosicrucian tradition, which we now know to have been the crucial formative influence on Masonry) to emphasize both the foundational status of ancient Egypt as source of all knowledge and the persisting – if hidden – power of that knowledge, including strong, direct connections from Egypt to northern Europe. Such ideas could readily be pressed into service by Afrocentrists for their own, very different purposes. Vail, Besant and the *Rosicrucian Digest* are also utilized by Ben-Jochannen, as are S. Clarke and R. Englebach's *Ancient Egyptian Masonry*, Levi H. Dowling's *The Aquarian Gospel of Jesus Christ*, an anonymous but evidently esoteric work entitled *The Lost Books of the Bible and the Forgotten Books of Eden*, and so on.[2]

Martin Bernal notes the importance of both Rosicrucianism and early Freemasonry in influencing the 'triumph of Egypt' in eighteenth-century European thought (Bernal 1987: 173–7, 180–81). Bernal misses or chooses not to stress, however, the mystical and mythographic elements in this – perhaps because he does not wish to draw attention to the more intellectually disreputable strains in beliefs which accord with his own. Nor does he note how a Masonic influence has continued, more or less underground, into twentieth-century Egyptology, including its Afrocentric versions.

As David Stevenson has shown (1988), the real origins of Freemasonry lay in seventeenth-century Scotland. Myths of Egyptian origin were, however, a part of the movement from the start, for it drew a great deal from earlier Neo-Platonist and Hermeticist occult ideas. The Hermetic movement, whose greatest thinker was Giordano Bruno, took inspiration from a body of mystic writings attributed to Hermes Trismegistus, a supposed Egyptian sage often identified with the god Thoth. In reality the works thought to be those of Hermes dated from the second and third centuries CE, but belief in their vast age, Egyptian origins and mystic power was widespread (Yates 1964). Not knowing that the sacred texts actually postdated Jesus, adepts were also impressed by the seemingly uncanny anticipations of Christian teachings they contained. Hermetic doctrine, with its near-fanatical high regard for supposed ancient Egyptian wisdom, was well known in Britain around 1600, and David Stevenson is able to show strong, direct connections between its enthusiasts and the probable founders of what we now know as Freemasonry (Stevenson 1988: 77–96). Thus references to Egypt, and a belief that Masonic symbolism and ritual had sources in the Egyptian Mysteries, were central to Freemasonry at the very outset. These ideas seem to have had a new lease of life in the early decades of the twentieth century. They were given renewed force, no doubt, by a wide range of contemporary intellectual currents: the late-Victorian revival of irrationalist and mystic ideas, the ubiquitous obsession with racial doctrines and myths of origin, and the flood of new information on Egypt itself, culminating in the 1922 discovery of Tutankhamun's tomb. A few contemporary Afrocentric writers appear still to buy the myth of Hermes/Thoth wholesale and without question, as does Wayne B. Chandler – whose credulity extends even to believing that Hermes lived for three hundred years, using secret regenerative processes which, Chandler hopes, we may soon rediscover (Chandler 1994: 218–19).

An especially interesting case is the use made by Afrocentrists of writings by Albert Churchward, an English medical man, ardent Freemason and amateur Egyptologist writing in the first few decades of this century. He is cited as an authority by such figures as Molefi Asante (1990: 96–104), John G. Jackson (1970, 1972) and Henry Olela (1984), and repeatedly by Yosef Ben-Jochannen.[3]

Albert Churchward's aim was to demonstrate that the 'secrets' of Freemasonry descended directly, in unbroken line, from the wisdom of ancient

Egypt. Egypt was the origin not only of civilization but of a true or natural religion, of which all later faiths are offshoots and merely partial expressions (this, too, is a notion which goes back to Giordano Bruno and the Hermeticists). The Egyptians 'had observed and studied the laws of nature, and founded a code of laws, as a result, that no other nation has ever improved upon since' (Churchward 1920: 114). From Egypt humanity spread out across the rest of Africa – but only those who remained in Egypt evolved on to the higher civilizational and spiritual levels. Elsewhere in Africa they stagnated: 'No higher development has ever taken place in this branch of the human' (ibid.: 87). The Egyptian masters sent out colonies all over the world: though Churchward seemed ambivalent over whether this included the Americas, saying in one place (ibid.: 117) that they probably had *not* gone there, but in others (160–61; 1921: 287–347) assuming that they had, since he cites 'evidence' including supposed ancient Mexican portrayals of 'Horus of the Double Horizon'.

Not only were all other civilizations and belief systems derivative of the Egyptian, but the Greeks and Jews debased the Mysteries. The Greeks and Romans 'only practiced a perverted and debased form of the old Egyptian Wisdom' (Churchward 1920: 177). As for the Jews: 'In no land or literature has the Mythical mode of representation been perverted and reduced to drivelling foolishness more fatally than in some of the Hebrew legends' (ibid.: 157). Some other cultures, by contrast, revealed surprising virtues: 'Ireland appears to have retained a truer form of the original than any other country, possibly because we know that direct communication was maintained from Egypt to Ireland to comparatively late periods' (195).

Apart from Churchward's racist belief – standard for his time – that in Africa apart from Egypt no human development could be observed, his structure of ideas was obviously congenial to African-Americans searching for historical sources of pride. Africa was the originating point of humanity, of all knowledge and civilization. Egypt taught the Greeks, Romans, Hebrews and everyone else all that they knew; indeed, they could only degenerate from the perfection of Pharaonic forms. All wisdom that was to be found anywhere in the world had been carried there by Egyptian emissaries. All that remained to be added by the Afrocentrists was an insistence that the Egyptians themselves were black.

But Churchward's real agenda could not be adopted by the Afrocentrists. He addressed himself explicitly, if not solely, to fellow Freemasons. The purpose of his extraordinary mythomania was to convince these 'Brothers' that their society descended from and was the repository of the wisdom of the ancient Egyptians. More – that their historic task was to recover that wisdom, unite, and combat the world menace of Socialism (which Churchward always capitalizes). His desire to elevate the status of Egypt and make it the birthplace of all human knowledge was entirely driven by these specifically Masonic and anti-socialist convictions, as his writings repeatedly emphasize. 'From the dawn of civilisation to the present moment two active and opposing forces have been engaged in deadly conflict' – that is,

Socialism and Freemasonry (Churchward 1920: 216). Primitive humanity had been socialist, and any attempt to 'return' to socialism would be an unnatural step backwards: 'TGAOTU (The Great Architect of the Universe: the semi-coded Masonic term for a transdenominational Supreme Being) will not allow such a retrograde movement: it is against His Periodic Laws ... any and every nation which attempts it will always be destroyed' (ibid.: 114). Elsewhere he proclaimed: 'His will is for the continuance of the British race – the highest type of the human development at present – and [that] the (1914–18) War was ordained for the destruction of Socialism, or so-called Democracy' (1921: 478).

Churchward was an extreme but not a unique case. Numerous Masonic, Theosophical, Spiritualist and other esoteric writers around that time were proposing such theories. Charles H. Vail's *Ancient Mysteries and Modern Masonry* (Vail 1909) was an American version of the same Egyptocentric argument, heavily drawn upon by Ben-Jochannen and James. C.W. Leadbeater, a former Anglican clergyman, then a Theosophist and '32nd Degree Mason', similarly traced modern Masonic 'mysteries' directly from the Pharaohs – and could substantiate his claims in a way unavailable to most others, for much of his knowledge came from mystic visions, from 'seeing beyond the visible plain' (Leadbeater 1926/1986).

There have, of course, been numerous other attempts, of varying degrees of crankiness, to trace ancient or medieval origins for Freemasonry. Among the most ingenious and popular recent efforts is John G. Robinson's *Born in Blood* (1989), which finds the birth of Masonry in the twelfth-century Knights Templar. None, though, has been as recurringly popular as the Egyptian myth. This may most probably have passed into Afrocentric writings through the network of Prince Hall Masonry, the blacks-only lodges established in parallel with and unrecognized by the main US Masonic orders. The latter were – and apparently in some places still are – exclusivist and white-supremacist in orientation; strong connections between Southern Masonry and the Ku Klux Klan have even been alleged. Be that as it may, middle-class blacks led by War of Independence veteran Prince Hall founded their own lodges – the first in Boston in 1775. What became the Prince Hall network, named after its founder, began in 1787, also in Boston, to be followed by a nationwide organization in 1797, eventually with over 200,000 members. It is reasonable to presume that myths of Egyptian origin for the 'craft' had an especially eager audience there, and that the Masonic circles formed an important conveyor for the stories about Egyptian wisdom which surface in Afrocentric writing.[4]

Masonic and other fraternal male orders seem to have been even more central to the life of black America than to white, especially for members of or aspirers to the small black middle class. In Philadelphia in the 1890s, Du Bois reported, there were nineteen black Masonic lodges, plus six 'chapters', five 'commanderies', three of the 'Scottish Rite' and a drill corps (Du Bois 1899: 224). Although it was not so well organized or wealthy as a rival fraternity, the Odd Fellows, Freemasonry was evidently an important part of the life of better-off black Philadelphians. Such secret societies, Du Bois rather obscurely claimed, 'naturally had great attraction for Negroes' (ibid.: 222). Nearly fifty years later St Clair Drake and Horace Cayton, in their classic Chicago study *Black Metropolis*, saw the Masonic lodges as being, with the Churches, the 'traditional bulwarks of organized middle-class life – the conservors of the traditions' (1945: 669). As early as 1890 'a dozen or so' Masonic lodges existed among black Chicagoans (ibid.: 49); though by the 1940s the authors felt that black Masonry 'has within the last twenty years lost most of its influence' (669).

Among major Afro-American political figures, we know that early Civil Rights advocate William Monroe Trotter was a very active member of the Prince Hall Grand Lodge in Boston; and that his more famous rival Booker T. Washington joined the Lodge specifically to combat Trotter's influence there – but had his invitation to deliver the Lodge's centennial speech withdrawn after bitter internal dissension among members (Harlan 1983: 103–4). The arch-manoeuvrer Washington, who also sought influence in the Odd Fellows, was clearly aware of the importance of Freemasonry as a power base among bourgeois African-Americans.

Such secret orders, Washington's biographer says, 'figured largely in black middle-class life', where they 'sustained black group life and racial solidarity' (Harlan 1983: 101). It seems a reasonable presumption that Du Bois and other Niagara Movement luminaries, as well as Trotter, were members at some time, though Du Bois's latest and fullest biographer (D. Lewis 1993) does not mention this. Garveyites, too, sought to take advantage of Masonic connections to spread the message of their movement: John Bruce, one of Garvey's most effective media proselytizers, had exhorted fellow Masons in 1919 that 'Masonry (was) the medium through which to give the right direction to the thought and policy which is to govern and control the race' (quoted in Stein 1986: 82). We can take it, I think, that George James – and, no doubt, other early Afro-American enthusiasts for the 'Egyptian origins of civilization' – took many of their ideas from those circles. The tradition is alive and well: Anthony Browder, representative of a younger generation of Afrocentrists, devotes himself to uncovering the 'Nile Valley Presence' in Europe and the Americas, largely through claims that Masons, including the USA's Founding Fathers, passed on ancient Egyptian wisdom through a mass of symbols and structures (Anthony Browder 1992: 189–217).

A wide variety of African-American nationalist organizations, especially those expounding new and esoteric religious doctrines, display a Masonic influence in their beliefs and rituals. This is evident in the Moorish Science Temple (Gardell 1996: 41–2), and in its more successful indirect successor, the Nation of Islam. The Black Muslim movement, however, was and is fiercely critical of Freemasonry, with Malcolm X (whose own father had apparently been a Mason as well as a Garveyite) denouncing them on several occasions during his time as a Nation of Islam spokesperson (B. Perry 1992: 195–6; X and Haley 1965: 252–4). In part, this hostility represented Black Muslim dislike of the generally middle-class and conservative character of Afro-American Freemasonry. More fundamentally, however, it expressed a rivalry over claims to possession of ancient wisdom, with Elijah Muhammad's creation myth of black people originating in Mecca (and before that the Moon – Essien-Udom 1962: 148–9) challenging the Masons' Egyptocentric version.[5]

Black Muslim doctrine was modified and softened slightly in Elijah Muhammad's last years, then thoroughly under his son and successor, Wallace (Warith Deen) Muhammad. Beliefs in the imminent end of the white world, in whites as devils, in lunar origins, and so on, were dropped, and the movement shifted towards the international mainstream of Sunni Islam (Gardell 1996: 99–118; Lee 1988: 73–101).[6] Despite this, the movement's book service continues to sell and recommend a decidedly odd range of works, including reprints of numerous esoteric Masonic and Egyptological books like those of Churchward and Gerald Massey.[7] Meanwhile Islamic–Masonic rivalry has persisted – as indicated, for instance, by widely distributed works like *Al-Islam, Christianity and Freemasonry* (1985) by the African-American Mustafa El-Amin, a follower of Warith Deen Muhammad: a book largely devoted to 'exposing' (in seemingly very knowledgeable fashion) the allegedly dangerous, conspiratorial, anti-religious nature of Freemasonry, with special reference to its perils for black Americans. El-Amin's work also partakes of some classic Afrocentric emphases, in arguing that Freemasonry, Christianity and Islam all carry legacies of ancient Egyptian wisdom. Only Islam, however, perpetuates the truth and greatness of this legacy: Christians and, still more, Masons pervert them (ibid.: 81–93). On the other hand, El-Amin denounces the earlier Black Muslim claims that whites are demonic, and those who 'taught racism, and called it Islam' (46).

Not all accepted the moderated, de-racialized new mode, however. Louis Farrakhan left Wallace Muhammad's movement in 1978, and his breakaway organization reinstated the old millennial and racially exclusivist beliefs (Gardell 1996: 119–86; Lee 1988: 103–23). Farrakhan himself featured more as a political than as a religious leader – rather in the mould of Malcolm X, even though Farrakhan had called for Malcolm's death after his break with the Nation of Islam, and has persistently – though unprovenly – been accused of some involvement in his assassination (an accusation he has vigorously denied). Louis Farrakhan continues to preach the Black Muslim belief that the Freemasons are a demonic white-supremacist conspiracy which, using secrets stolen from Islam, masterminds the exploitation of black peoples worldwide (Gardell 1996: 148–9). Although Farrakhan's movement cannot fully be identified with Afrocentrism as such – indeed, many Afrocentric writers have expressed vehement hostility to Islam – it shares many of the same general cultural nationalist features, while some specific elements often identified with Afrocentrism, notably anti-white and anti-Jewish prejudice, are found in particularly heightened form among Farrakhan's followers. This is a matter we shall explore further below.

Notes

1. Should it need saying, my discussion here of such esoterica and its influence on African-American intellectuals is not intended to imply that Freemasons in general subscribe to such beliefs. For the vast majority of adherents in all countries, Freemasonry is evidently a purely social and charitable activity.

2. As Mattias Gardell notes (1996: 38–42), Dowling's *Aquarian Gospel* was extensively plagiarized by Noble Drew Ali to provide the theological underpinnings for his 'Moorish Science Temple'.

3. For instance, throughout his 1972 'magnum opus': 46, 123–6, 172, 211, 250, 252, 324, 364, 419, 424; while all Churchward's books are listed in the 'Select Bibliography'; see also Ben-Jochannen 1971: 10, 29, 72, 581 and other references, and Ben-Jochannen in Addai-Sebo and Wong (1988: 99). Modern reprints of Churchward's major works are also produced and sold by various African American organizations.

4. For general histories of Afro-American Freemasonry, see Muraskin (1975); B. Williams (1980). Lefkowitz (1996a) notes the Masonic influences on Afrocentric views of ancient history, but she offers an oversimplified and in some respects erroneous view of the routes by which they fed into modern writings. Her genealogy runs from Jean Terrasson's *Sethos*, through Vail, to George James, omitting such crucial mediators as Churchward and Massey, and the whole nineteenth-century Afro-American tradition of Egyptomania, and failing to take account of standard authorities like Yates.

5. As an aside, I wish to float tentatively a notion on the possible source of the original Black Muslim myth about the creation of white people. The story propagated by Elijah Muhammad and his disciples – of whites being created by the genetic engineering of a 'mad scientist' on an isolated island – has some intriguing, and strikingly close, similarities to the plot of one of Sax Rohmer's hugely popular – though deeply racist – Fu Manchu novels, *The Island of Fu Manchu*, published in 1941. One Farrakhan follower, Paul Lawrence Guthrie, has recently attempted to provide historical substantiation for Muhammad's story (Guthrie 1992), but he does so by way of an astonishing *mélange* of citation from speculative Victorian works about ancient myth, and more modern esoteric texts. Discussion of contemporary historical or scientific sources is entirely absent. My thanks to Michael Francis for bringing Guthrie's book to my attention.

6. For sympathetic, somewhat uncritical but enlightening surveys of the development of Islam in the United States, mainly among African-Americans, see Barboza (1994); Gardell (1996); McCloud (1995), Gardell's being now the most detailed account.

7. See the mail-order lists published by the African Islamic Mission, Inc., of Brooklyn (for which I am indebted to Marek Kohn). Almost all Churchward's and Massey's books – other than the latter's poetry – are available in reprint from this organization, as are numerous other works of early-twentieth-century romantic Egyptology, but *not* the 'mainstream' Afrocentric texts of writers like Ben-Jochannen, Asante or Chancellor Williams.

7

Caribbean Currents

A strikingly high proportion of the glorifiers of the African past who achieved United States prominence – including Marcus Garvey, J.A. Rogers, George G.M. James, and latterly figures as diverse as Yosef Ben-Jochannen, Ivan Van Sertima and Louis Farrakhan – were of West Indian origin.[1] The Anglophone Caribbean also had its own independent tradition of Afrocentric mythography, which fed powerfully into Rastafarianism and other 'Ethiopianist' movements. The most influential formulator of such ideas in that context seems to have been a rather mysterious character named L.F.C. Mantle, who appeared on the Jamaican scene in 1935 claiming to have served with the British Army in Palestine, to have travelled in Ethiopia and Tibet, to have earned a Doctorate in Divinity, and to be both a rabbi and a faith healer in the 'Divine Science of Jesus the Christ' (Post 1978: 168). In fact, it turned out, he had done none of these things, his previous career having been as an ice-cream vendor and railway brakeman in Cuba. Discredited, he vanished from view again; but as Ken Post says: 'Nevertheless, despite the personal eclipse of Mantle, his "hidden secrets", reinforced by the contributions of others, produced a quite formidable body of doctrine' (ibid.: 169; see also S. Clarke 1980: 39).

Mantle, like many others, asserted a dual identification: of all black people as Ethiopians, and of Ethiopians, in their turn, with the Jews of the Bible. The ancient Ethiopians from whom New World blacks were descended had been the originators of civilization, which then travelled down the Nile to Egypt, and from there to Greece, Rome and hence to all European cultures:

> Ethiopians were the instructors of Music, founders of Arts, Science and Philosophy.... The Ethiopians were the architects that laid the plans and measured the spaces and laid the foundations of the Pyramids of Egypt ... and put the finishing touch on the face of the Sphinx.' (quoted in Post 1978: 170)

Europeans, including the whites who now falsely claimed the title of Jews, were descended from Adam, as they claimed – but Adam was created only

in 4004 BCE, while the Ethiopians had existed 3,400 years before that (ibid.:
171). Here Mantle was making really rather ingenious use of archaic
European Creationist beliefs about the age of the earth – which he had
presumably imbibed from some fundamentalist Christian sect – and linking
them to a claim for black cosmological priority. He was also, however, in
effect reviving the 'polygenist' ideas of some nineteenth-century European
racial theorists, who had asserted that whites descended from Adam but
blacks came from a different, inferior lineage. Some of these themes were
to be found echoed, forty and fifty years later, in the rhetoric of Yosef Ben-
Jochannen, suggesting that he had directly or indirectly been influenced by
Mantle's teachings.[2]

The most lastingly significant of these Caribbean-born publicists, though,
was Marcus Garvey. On the centenary of Garvey's birth in 1987, the
authorities in several London boroughs, many American cities and a
number of Caribbean islands organized official celebrations. In Jamaica,
Garvey's birthplace, he was proclaimed 'First National Hero'. His remains,
once obscurely interred in Bethnal Green, London, are now placed in a
Jamaican national memorial. The 1987 Sunsplash – the annual Kingston
reggae festival – took place on a stage over which frowned Garvey's massive,
idealized portrait. Beneath this icon, it is reported, every performer felt
obliged to compete in homage to the hero. This only capped an already
substantial history of invocations of Garvey's image in reggae lyrics: allusions
and hymns of praise which often credited him with prophetic or superhu-
man powers.[3] Throughout the African diaspora, a concept which itself owes
much to his legacy, Garvey's posthumous reputation seemed ubiquitous.
The flood of centenary publications ranged from semi-literate pamphlets to
scholarly tomes.

It is hardly surprising that some observers have found this retrospective
lionization virtually incomprehensible. After all, Garvey died in poverty,
leaving a legacy of seemingly comprehensive failure. His Universal Negro
Improvement Association, which had once claimed over six million members worldwide, was reduced to tiny and mutually antagonistic fragments.
His business ventures, run with almost staggering incompetence, had all
long since collapsed and had brought him a five-year US prison sentence
for fraud. The Jamaican colonial authorities, too, had imprisoned and
deported him, while the Liberian government had angrily repudiated his
project of settling black American colonists on its soil. He had been both
denounced and ridiculed by every other significant Afro-American politician
and intellectual of the age: as a demagogue, a charlatan, a lunatic, a petty
dictator, a black fascist.

None of these accusations is wholly off the mark, though equally none is
quite fair. Garvey was not mad, but he was bombastic, illogical and
sometimes virtually incoherent in his public statements. He was probably
innocent of deliberate, consistent dishonesty in his financial dealings, but
his ineptitude and blindness to subordinates' failings brought economic
disaster to thousands who trusted him. He was a scurrilous and unscrupulous

polemicist: not *merely* a demagogue, but a demagogue none the less by any definition of the term. He was no more a genuine fascist than he was a consistent follower of any social theory, but his political practice was wholly authoritarian and he proclaimed affinities with Mussolini and Hitler – even accusing them of stealing ideas from his movement.

Despite all this, and despite his record of failure, there was truth in the centenary claims that Garvey was one of the most influential figures of the twentieth century. Beyond the frequent confusion of his thought and the almost comic-opera disasters of his business career, Garvey's sheer energy and charisma shine through. Even his limitations could be made to work for him, for they mirrored those of his intended audience. They helped him win a mass following of the black US urban poor and a scattering of adherents across the Caribbean and the Atlantic, which inevitably eluded the more rationalistic, universalist appeals of better-educated, clearer-thinking leaders like Du Bois.

The major biographical studies on Garvey have been the work of admirers, and have tended to focus on the nature of Marcus Garvey's own personality, leadership and ideas, effectively reproducing the elitism and personalized nature of the movement itself (e.g. R. Lewis 1987; Martin 1976).[4] Few have attempted to look at the social character of Garveyism, the kinds of people who supported him and why. It seems, however, that despite the large number of poor and working-class blacks who joined the organiz-ation, Garveyism remained a movement of the middle class in terms of leadership and ideology. It was increasingly, as Garvey's projects ran into insuperable difficulties and fierce criticism from other black leaders, a movement of the small black bourgeoisie's more marginal or aspirant rather than securely prosperous members; but it never embraced a socially radical agenda, never allowed poorer working men and women into positions of leadership, and even the populist appeals which Garvey did make to the poor were highlighted only after his initial hopes of mobilizing the Afro-American elite had been rebuffed (Stein 1986: *passim*). In this at least, later Afrocentrists and cultural nationalists were indeed to prove true followers of Garveyism.

In his view of black and African history, Garvey drew on the various ideas earlier expressed by the wide range of romantic Afro-American, West Indian and African historical writers we have surveyed – there are clear echoes of people like Blyden, Crummell, Hayne and Scholes in his rhetoric – and distilled them into a mythologizing but hugely influential synthesis. A number of amateur historians and popularizers of inspirational beliefs about the black past were associated with the Garvey movement and published in the UNIA paper, the *Negro World*, including J.A. Rogers, John Edward Bruce, William H. Ferris and E. Ethelred Brown. And Garvey's own speeches and writings were peppered with historical references. African history, for Garvey, should be a source of inspiration and emotional uplift to blacks, coupled with a systematic derogation of European claims about the past. Whites, proclaimed Garvey:

made human sacrifices, ate the flesh of their own dead and the raw meat of
the wild beast for centuries even as they accuse us of doing; their cannibalism
was more prolonged than ours; when we were embracing the arts and
sciences on the banks of the Nile their ancestors were still drinking human
blood and eating out of the skulls of their conquered dead; when our
civilization had reached the noonday of progress they were still running
naked and sleeping in holes and caves with rats, bats and other insects and
animals. After we had already fathomed the mystery of the stars and reduced
the heavenly constellations to minute and regular calculus they were still
backwoodsmen, living in ignorance and blatant darkness.
     WHY BE DISCOURAGED?
     The world today is indebted to us for the benefits of civilization. They stole
our arts and sciences from Africa. Then why should we be ashamed of
ourselves? Their *modern improvements* are but *duplicates* of a grander civilization that we reflected thousands of years ago, without the advantage of what
is buried and still hidden, to be resurrected and reintroduced by the
intelligence of our generation. ('African Fundamentalism' [1925] in J.H.
Clarke 1974: 157; original emphasis.)

The history of the race, then, was the property of the race; – its most
valuable property, which had been stolen by whites and must be reclaimed:

     White historians and writers have tried to rob the black man of his proud
     past in history, and when anything new is discovered to support the race's
     claim and attest the truthfulness of our greatness in other ages, then it is
     skillfully rearranged and credited to some other unknown race or people.
     Negroes, teach your children that they are direct descendants of the greatest
     and proudest race who ever peopled the earth; and it is because of the fear
     of our return to power ... why [*sic*] we are hated and kept down by a jealous
     and prejudiced contemporary world. (Garvey 1925/1986: II: 82)

As this implies, Garvey – like many of the earlier advocates of past African
greatness – proposed a cyclical as well as a race-deterministic theory of
history, in which Africa had once led the world, had lost its primacy
(through white depredations and lies, Garvey insisted) but would now
regain it – by the efforts of Garvey and the UNIA themselves. It was clearly
the blacks of the New World who would lead the African renaissance, not
those of the African continent, for Garvey held conventionally disparaging
views about the state of 'civilization' among Africans, which contrasted
dramatically with his romanticization of the continent's past. His ideas for
UNIA colonization in Liberia were, like those of Crummell and others, very
much an Afro-American version of the 'white man's burden' ideology: the
advanced and intelligent Afro-American colonists would guide and civilize
the backward natives.
     Little in Garvey's view of history, then, was original: he merely put into
even more polemical – and vastly more popularly accessible – form the by

then conventional themes of several generations of Afro-American chroniclers. But whereas they had been mostly figures of the utmost obscurity, Garvey's message had a worldwide influence. The characteristic rhetoric of Afrocentric ideas about the past, even today, owes more to Garvey than to anyone else.

In recent years Garvey's admirers have claimed to find his influence absolutely everywhere in black politics and thought. Tony Sewell describes a peculiar assortment of leaders – from Du Bois, through C.L.R. James, George Padmore and Kwame Nkrumah, to Louis Farrakhan – as Garveyites (Sewell 1990: 53–76). Liz Mackey asserts equally indiscriminately:

> Whether black Americans marched on Washington with King, or prayed to Allah with Malcolm X, or armed themselves with the Black Panthers, or simply came to see that 'black is beautiful', they all embodied the legacy of Garveyism. (1987: 65)

The most bizarre appropriation, however, came from Marcus Garvey's own eldest son, a schoolmaster in Jamaica, who suggested in an essay published in 1974 that his father's black nationalism be updated into an 'African National Socialism'. 'It seems certain', Marcus Jr claimed, 'that the world will one day be faced with the Black cry for an African "Anschluss" and the resolute demand for African "Lebensraum"' (J.H. Clarke 1974: 387). This dreadful, uncomprehending mimicry of the century's greatest barbarism is as untrue to Garvey's real legacy as is Rupert Lewis's Marxized Marcus, and far more disreputable. Indeed every attempt to reconstruct a coherent theoretical Garveyism founders as surely as did the aged vessels of his Black Star Line, wrecked on the sheer inconsistency of the man. Almost everything about his career and thought is irrelevant or actively damaging to modern antiracism and anticolonialism – except his very simple core message. That message was of self-respect, self-confidence, self-assertion for the Americas' poorest citizens; faith that the future could be theirs if they made it so. For that one basic claim and its impact, his influence can hardly be overstated. This, in addition to his emphasis on Africa as spiritual home and source of values, has been the basis for his influence on subsequent Afrocentric ideas. The unfortunate thing is that much of his irrationality, his authoritarianism and his mass of prejudices have also been passed on.

The most ubiquitously cited intellectual inspiration for African-American militants, from the 1960s onwards, has been a very different kind of Caribbean thinker from the racial romantic Garvey; the Martiniquan psychologist and political theorist Frantz Fanon (1925–61). More recently, ideas drawn selectively from his writings have become a major direct or indirect influence on Afrocentric and cultural nationalist thought; though as we shall soon see, his thinking was in reality poles apart from theirs.

At the time of the 1960s US ghetto uprisings, *Liberator* magazine editor Dan Watts claimed that 'every brother on a rooftop (with a gun, that is) can

quote Fanon' (quoted in Van Deburg 1992: 61). Among the founders of the
Black Panthers, *The Wretched of the Earth* was given almost literally holy status.
Bobby Seale said he had read it six times even before forming the party
(Seale 1970: 41), and thereafter he and Huey Newton would pore over it
obsessively, especially for its criticisms of cultural nationalists (ibid.: 51).
Eldridge Cleaver called it the Bible of the black revolutionary movement
(Cleaver 1971: 43, 44–6). For Stokely Carmichael, Fanon was 'one of my
patron saints' (Carmichael 1968: 150). The celebrated prison writer and
militant George Jackson repeatedly cited Fanon, usually in conjunction with
Marx, Lenin and Mao, among his personal gurus (Jackson 1971, 1972:
passim).

Even David Hilliard – seemingly less interested in theory than any other
top Panther leader, and under whom the party became deeply mired in
drug abuse, financial corruption and sexual exploitation – claimed a deep
study of Fanon. His account is important for the apparent painful honesty
with which it tracks a poorly educated street militant's encounter with
'revolutionary' theory. Initially, Hilliard the school dropout, not surprisingly, found *Wretched of the Earth* incomprehensible:

> I'm lost. I have the dictionary in one hand, the book in the other, and I can't
> get past the first page, can't get past the first paragraph, barely the first
> sentence. I might as well be reading in a foreign language. Practically every
> word is unknown to me. (Hilliard and Cole 1993: 120)

Later, though, under Seale's tuition: 'I listen, tracking the subtleties of
Fanon's thoughts, not uncomprehending now. It's complicated, this stuff, I
think – not simply what Fanon is saying, but being a revolutionary.
Revolution is a science' (ibid.: 152). And later still, in prison, Hilliard
poignantly reconnects the semi-religious initial impact of Fanonist ideas
with the way the Panthers, in their turn, had become icons:

> One of the inmates sends me a dog-eared page from a copy of *Wretched of the
> Earth* that Huey had left behind. . . . The words are no longer foreign to me.
> Earlier this fall I have actually visited Algeria . . . met some of the revolution-
> ary leaders who knew Fanon. My stomach clenches with its familiar ache.
> We've come a long way since Huey was first here; we've become a part of
> history. (ibid.: 267)

Maulana Karenga, the most prominent among the 1960s cultural nationalists against whom American Fanonists like the Panthers raged, had, by the
1980s, given Fanon a prominent place in his pantheon (Addai-Sebo and
Wong 1988: 177–8). Less militant – or at least more strategically minded –
black leaders like Roy Innis and James Forman also lauded the Martiniquan's message. By the end of 1970 *Wretched of the Earth* had allegedly sold
an astonishing 750,000 copies in the USA (Van Deburg 1992: 60–61). Black
intellectuals as diverse as Henry Louis Gates and Cedric Robinson still

thought Fanon's legacy well worth fighting fiercely over in the 1990s (Gates 1991; Robinson 1993). Molefi Asante, the leading Afrocentric thinker, insists on the centrality of Fanon's ideas to his intellectual formation (Asante 1993a: 138). The current of Fanonism is more diffuse, certainly less activist, and more academic than it was in the 1960s, but it still flows in a remarkable range of different Afro-American milieux.

However, Fanon's ideas were radically different from those advocated, and sometimes foisted on to him, by successive generations of African-American cultural nationalists. Often, indeed, the 'Fanonism' they have proposed has been little more than a dogmatic caricature of Fanon's own ideas. Seeing the position of Afro-Americans as a colonial one, and emphasizing the supposed transformative power of spontaneous revolutionary violence, this caricature has also perceived the colonial situation itself purely in terms of violence: a distortion actually much more pronounced in Fanon's philosophical mentor Jean-Paul Sartre than in his own work. Fanon's discussion of decolonization is far more subtle than that, proposing a quite complex explanation which has been ignored equally by his admirers among 1960s revolutionaries and among 1980s–90s cultural theorists.[5]

Fanon's importance lies primarily in two very different books: *Black Skin, White Masks*, a study of the psychological effects of racism and colonialism, written in his twenties; and *The Wretched of the Earth*, a more directly political analysis of decolonization and its aftermaths. Two further books, *Toward the African Revolution* and *A Dying Colonialism*, are collections of articles, mostly about Algeria.

Broadly, we can speak of two different 'Fanonisms' having operated since the man's premature death. The first to emerge took its cue primarily from his last book, *The Wretched of the Earth*; the second, more recent, (mis)reading has relied mainly on the earlier *Black Skin, White Masks*. The second Fanonism, which has been taken up by literary theorists like Homi Bhabha, is beyond the scope of our present discussion, as is the 1990s creation of a 'Fanon industry' (see, amid a rapidly proliferating literature, L. Gordon *et al.* [eds] 1996; Read [ed.] 1996). The first (in his own life the last) Fanon, though, is seen above all as a critic of bourgeois anticolonial nationalism, and as a theorist of revolutionary liberationism. This he certainly was. In 'The Pitfalls of National Consciousness', which occupies the later pages of *Wretched of the Earth*, he attacked African nationalism as the ideology, or tool, of the native middle class, a class essentially parasitic in nature and unable to do more than act as go-between from the metropolitan bourgeoisie to the African masses. In its search for political power this small group posed falsely as an agent of radical transformation. It was obviously tempting, and became rather popular, for Afro-American militants not only to identify their position with the colonial situation described by Fanon (here North American 'Fanonism' connected with theories of internal colonialism, as we shall soon discover) but also to see the African-American middle class and the Civil Rights leadership reflected in the mirror of Fanon's African bourgeoisie.

For all this, aspects of Fanon's ideas could readily be appropriated by cultural as opposed to revolutionary nationalism, and even by the Afrocentrists whose world-views, one may be sure, he would have scorned. He cannot be thought of as a thoroughgoing democratic theorist. He seems to have been profoundly ambivalent about single-party systems: lamenting the abuses of power which were already solidifying in his lifetime, he none the less never wrote of one-partyism as objectionable in principle. Being 'on the side of the people' – especially the peasantry – is for him a supreme value; but democracy as such does not appear to be. Notions of national culture are dealt with in ways ranging from apparently uncritical invocation to deep scepticism of their possible appropriation by reactionary national leaders: though possibly this reflects not so much indeterminacy on Fanon's part as a shift, interrupted by premature death, towards more critical views. He frequently blurs notions of racial identity and oppression with the idea of colonialism; but here, too, it may be that this near-identification, which was the source of much of his appeal both to 1960s Afro-American militants and to recent cultural critics, was being increasingly jettisoned in his last writings. Certainly he was less and less prone to see identities between African, French and American 'racial' situations.

In any case, Fanon had never believed that racism in itself conferred identity: even if, in the most polemical passages of *Wretched of the Earth*, he wrote as if he thought colonialism did so. His criticisms of *négritude* were early and sharp. In 1955 he was already scorning the tendency of West Indian intellectuals, reacting against their earlier desired assimilation to European norms, to identify themselves with imagined African characteristics:

> He discovered himself to be the transported son of slaves; he felt the vibration of Africa in the very depth of his body and aspired only to one thing: to plunge into the great 'black hole'. It thus seems that the West Indian, after the great white error, is now living in the great black mirage. (Fanon 1964/1970: 37)

Fanon had little apparent interest in the classic *négritude*–Afrocentrist themes of rediscovery of historic African glories. He had, of course, encountered the early writings of Cheikh Anta Diop in *Présence Africaine* circles; but he referred to them only by way of a rather lukewarm expression of 'interest' and only in the context – notably oblique to Diop's main concerns – of comparing literary production in African languages favourably to that in Caribbean dialects (Fanon 1952/1970: 21). Notions of a common 'racial' culture, and the general 'racialization of thought' (Fanon 1961/1967: 171), which he discerned among African and diasporic intellectuals – as among their Arab counterparts – were in his view likely 'to lead them up a blind alley' (ibid.: 172). Awareness of difference would, and should, grow instead; realization that 'The Negroes of Chicago only resemble the Nigerians or the Tanganyikans in so far as they were all defined in relation to the whites' (ibid.: 173–4). But – and it is a crucially limiting 'but' – his alternative to the racialization of thought he increasingly disliked was to propose a notion of *national* culture – apparently internally homogeneous – which is eventually no less restricting: 'every culture is first and foremost national', he insisted (ibid.: 174). He spoke at one point of the need for a 'National consciousness, which is not nationalism' as the only route to *inter*nationalism. To try to 'skip the national period' on the route to wider solidarities, pretending that national identity was outmoded, was not only a 'mistake' but the prating of 'pharisees' (ibid.: 198–9). As with so many others who have produced similar formulations before and since, Fanon failed utterly either to specify how 'national consciousness' differed from nationalism, or what the routes might be from that consciousness to cosmopolitanism. Nor was he wholly immune from romantic cultural nationalist tendencies to idealize certain expressions and political mobilizations of 'tradition'. Perhaps most famously, his essay on women's participation in the Algerian revolution ('Algeria Unveiled', in Fanon 1959/1965), for all its complexity and all its genuine commitment to a notion of women's liberation, is finally trapped in what was to prove a hopelessly romanticized and overoptimistic assessment of the female role in a revolutionary and then an independent Algeria; and particularly of the significance of the 'return to the veil' within this. Women's emancipation is finally but comprehensively subjugated to the imperatives of anticolonialism. Michel Foucault was later to fall into exactly the same trap in relation to the Iranian revolution, and to reimposed veiling there (see Eribon 1992: 281–91, esp. 286).

It must be emphasized, though, how strongly Fanon's basic beliefs were universalist. He explicitly rejected identitarian claims, both political and epistemological: 'I sincerely believe that a subjective experience can be understood by others; and it would give me no pleasure to announce that the black problem is my problem and mine alone' (1952/1970: 61). He clearly had no sympathy with the relentlessly racialized identity politics which has been the trademark of Afrocentrism.

As a kind of pendant to Fanon's influence, one should note the later, lesser – but similar and often intertwined – impact of another radical black scholar, who shared many of Fanon's ideas and, like him, died tragically young: Walter Rodney. Rodney, born in Guyana and teaching during his short career in Jamaica and Tanzania as well as his native country, produced important writings on precolonial West African history, and on the Guyanese working classes. These scholarly works, however, were not the main source of Rodney's international influence. That came from a far more polemical, wide-ranging book he published in 1972, *How Europe Underdeveloped Africa*. The book's argument is well summarized by its title. It applied to Africa ideas first presented a little earlier by Latin American scholars in relation to their own continent. Some countries were poor, simply and directly, because others were rich: the former had been systematically 'underdeveloped' by the actions of the latter. Rodney alleged that African poverty, lack of industrialization, and so forth were the result of centuries of exploitation by Europe, especially through the Atlantic slave trade and then colonial rule itself. Africa's potentialities for indigenous economic growth had been blocked, turned back, stifled.

Or rather, it was European *capitalism* which had thus robbed and mutilated Africa, for Rodney's framework was a strongly Marxist one. Africa's miserable fate was the consequence of an unfolding world capitalist system first of trade, then of production, in which Europe and later North America occupied advantageous and exploitative 'core' positions, Africa a disempowered 'peripheral' one. Here, though, a crucial ambiguity in Rodney's message, and even more in the way it was received, became evident. Was his critique essentially directed against a world system in which capitalists exploited peasants and workers – the former disproportionately but certainly not exclusively white, the latter mainly but not all black, since there were major African partners in and beneficiaries of both the slave trade and colonialism, as well as, of course, deprived and dispossessed Europeans? Or was he attacking a system by which white European people cheated and exploited black African people? His historical method suggested the first; many of his more rhetorical passages, and his title, pointed more towards the second. The tension is unresolved in Rodney's book, though on the whole one might say that the socialist element predominates over the black nationalist one, especially when his other writings and political activities are taken into account. The more important point in the present context, however, is that the book seems to have been received and its message popularized far more in the second sense. With one side of his argument, the Marxist one, marginalized or ignored and the other, the nationalist one, amplified and simplified, Walter Rodney's ideas could readily be pressed into service for the Afrocentric cause.[6]

One aspect of Rodney's ideas which very conspicuously and unfortunately was *not* taken up in the United States was his attempt – tentative and, perhaps, again internally inconsistent but politically of great importance – to redefine then current slogans of 'Black Power' so that they were not exclusive to those of African descent. With his native Caribbean mostly in mind, he recognized that in several West Indian societies people of Indian descent were often poorer, and definitely less well represented in the political arena, than those of mainly African ancestry. Rodney therefore tried, in writing and in the left-wing opposition party he founded in Guyana, to produce a political unity of the underprivileged from both main population groups, urging the idea of 'blackness' as a label for shared experience of dispossession rather than for ancestry or ethnic exclusivity.[7] Such an attempt, fragile enough in the Caribbean, could not readily be transposed to other circumstances – as the short, troubled life of the notion of 'black' as common political identity for all non-white groups in Britain suggests – though Steve Biko's version of Black Consciousness philosophy in South Africa shared many of its features. In the United States, however, it looks to the outsider as though even the attempt was never seriously made. As varieties of cultural nationalism became ever more ascendant in Afro-

America through the 1980s and 1990s, 'blackness' as an exclusivist and essentialized signifier for those of African descent alone could only be reinforced. One of the casualties was the emphasis on economic deprivation and shared interests in wealth redistribution, which Rodney had championed.

Haiti was the second European colony after the United States to attain independence. It was the first state of predominantly non-European population to do so; and for many decades the only black-ruled postcolonial polity. For an even longer period, it served massive and multifarious symbolic functions: above all in the huge archive of North American and European writings displaying Haiti as evidence that people of African descent could – or (more usually, in this writing) could not – govern themselves and attain 'civilized' status. From about the same time, an almost equally large body of writing by both Haitian and non-Haitian black intellectuals represented it as incubator or exemplar of the future of the African-descended peoples. Indeed, almost every variety of Third-Worldist nationalist thought found early – often its earliest – expression in or in relation to Haiti. Central tropes of what were to be called *négritude* and Afrocentricity, in particular, found their first formulations among Haitian intellectuals from the 1920s onwards.

Under the impact of invasion and occupation by US Marines after 1915, numerous Haitian intellectuals undertook a revaluation of national identity: – and, rather as German writers had done in their era of Napoleonic French dominance, they began a reaching out to the peasant masses, their cultural beliefs and practices. This newfound nationalist enthusiasm for the peasantry was also stimulated by the emergence of widespread peasant revolts against the occupiers in 1918–20. The first pioneer in the consequent positive revaluation of rural Haiti and its African heritage was ethnologist Justin Dorsainvil, who drew on then current European psychological and evolutionary theories to present a picture of the Haitian people as still essentially African in character (Nicholls 1979: 152–4). The crucially formative work, however, was Jean Price-Mars's *Ainsi Parla l'Oncle* in 1928. Price-Mars's career was in many ways strikingly similar to that of his contemporary W.E.B. Du Bois: that of a polymathic scholar-activist massively learned in the European social sciences of his day, yet persisting throughout a long life (Price-Mars died in 1969 at ninety-two; Du Bois in 1963 at ninety-five) in affirming the dignity and significance of Africa's heritage. Price-Mars's book (translated as Price-Mars 1983) and associated writings affirmed both the basic cultural unity of black Africa and the strength of its persisting cultural influence in Haiti. There was in his celebration of peasant life certainly a strain of the 'conservative populism' which Nicholls finds characteristic of his thought, and which he links, perhaps somewhat unfairly, not only to early-nineteenth-century German Romanticism but to *volkisch* Nazi ideologues (Nicholls 1979: 157).[8] Undoubtedly, too, Price-Mars held a romantic view of rural Haiti as well as of Africa, and was peculiarly muted about its dreadful material poverty. Very probably some of the same charges of adhering to a damaging racial mystique, transposed all too readily from contemporary European theories, can be levelled at him as at Du Bois.

Yet just as we find little sanction in the life and work of Du Bois for later irrationalist appropriations of the Pan-African idea, so in Price-Mars we already encounter a powerful critique of the counter-racisms of 'writing back'. He was fundamentally a rationalist, a believer in cultural syncretism rather than in myths of purity, one who looked to an innovative future rather than a consolingly noble past. Even in lauding African civilizational achievements, he wrote of Haiti as 'the new social form which is slowly emerging from the confusion of mores, beliefs, and customs' (1983: 217).

The influence of Price-Mars and other rediscoverers of peasant tradition was soon felt in literary circles. The 1920s saw a dramatic stylistic and thematic shift, adumbrated by the 'Indigenist' movement. This involved an increasingly pervasive invocation of African and voodoo-related themes. Initially, as in the work of Jacques Roumain and Carl Brouard, the romantic celebration of African 'primitivity' was in the service of beliefs about Haitian culture as a unique Afro-Latin synthesis. Its political thrust was above all opposition to the American occupiers, and it maintained the previous generation's emphatic rejection of biologistic racism – even though an authoritarian streak, widespread Nietzscheanism, and occasionally (as in Roumain and Max Hudicourt) an enthusiasm for Mussolini, may be discerned in some of these writers (see Nicholls 1979: 158–64; Dash 1981: 65–97).

Thus, while there were some disturbing political undercurrents in the literature of the 1920s, its general tenor was fairly straightforwardly nationalist, and anti-racist. Only in the 1930s did a full-fledged culturalist irrationalism and even counter-racism emerge, with the successor 'Griot' movement. This was eventually to have some alarming political offshoots, most evident in the career of a minor 'noiriste' poet, influential ethnological propounder of peasant cultural 'authenticity', and later one of the Western world's most brutal and erratic dictators. The different phases of François Duvalier's progress had far more than just biographical connections. In his earlier literary, ethnographic and historical work can be discerned the elaboration of a set of myths designed to legitimate the reign of terror he was later to install in Haiti.

Four elements predominated in the mix of ideas put forward by Duvalier and his collaborators (most important of whom was Lorimer Denis) in the 1930s and 1940s.[9] They all have disconcerting similarities to central themes in the contemporary US Afrocentrist-postcolonialist-nativist *mélange*. First there was an aggressive anti-rationalism, and a eulogization of peasant belief, tradition and legend. This served to delegitimize reasoned criticism of his dictatorship, especially that mounted by socialists, Marxists and, of course, foreigners. It also underpinned Duvalier's deft manipulation of superstitious popular fears, through his cultivation of powerful local *houngans* (voodoo priests), his use of psychic as well as physical terror by the paramilitary *Tontons Macoutes*, and his attribution of supernatural powers to himself.

Second was the exposition of an almost entirely fabricated view of the national past. This accorded absolute historical primacy to the intra-elite division between 'blacks' and 'mulattoes', wholly misrepresented this by presenting black powerholders, past and present, as representatives of the masses, assimilated class to colour, and bestowed spurious populist credentials on 'black' autocracy.

Third was an essentialist and organicist notion of racial character, into which ideas of culture, community and nationality were also rolled. This not only facilitated use of a nationalistic and, on occasion, Pan-Africanist or Third-Worldist discourse by the dictator, and further delegitimized all criticism as 'anti-national', but served more or less effectively to disguise the Duvalier regime's own abject dependence on US aid and approval.

Fourth was explicit and fierce rejection of liberal and democratic ideas, argued both to be undesirable in themselves and, under Haitian and other 'Third World' circumstances, to be the creatures of imperialist foreign enemies and their local apologists.

Thus we can see that some prefigurative and – directly or indirectly – globally influential discourses of cultural authenticity – of what was to be called first *négritude*, later Afrocentricity – had their origins in a very direct thrust for political power. Power, moreover, which was to be wielded by the successful self-proclaimed apostle of cultural decolonization – François Duvalier – in the most repressive, corrupt and vicious manner. These Haitian origins of the nativist and irrationalist ideology which has in recent years attained so powerfully renewed a global vigour have more than just Antillean significance. And it became evident in Haiti, as it was later to do elsewhere, how apt the discourses of cultural nationalism and racial assertion were for the legitimation of dictatorship. It is disturbing to find, in the 1980s and 1990s, a whole new wave of writing about race and identity which poses as *solutions* things which in Haiti, the first black postcolonial polity, have long since proved to be major parts of the *problem.*

Notes

1. For a general sketch of Caribbean intellectual influences on African-Americans in the USA, see V. Franklin (1992b).

2. The influence certainly need not have been direct, since similar beliefs have been widespread among the more esoteric kinds of African-American religio-political groupings, including the Nation of Islam.

3. Gutzmore (1988) notes just some of these; see also S. Clarke (1980); Sewell (1990); Waters (1985). Chevannes (1995: 99–109) deals more systematically with the myths associated with Garvey among Jamaican Rastafarians, and probes the probable origins of some of these.

4. Among the few trenchantly critical accounts of Garvey's career is Clarence E. Walker (1991: xxiii–v, 34–55), depicting him as a 'charlatan' whose appeals to racial unity were 'self-serving, empty slogans' containing 'proto-fascist elements', and whose ideology and following reflected Caribbean rather than Afro-American preoccupations (ibid.: xxv, 54).

5. What seems to me the most thorough and compelling latter-day interpretation of Fanon's thought is Sekyi-Otu (1996).

6. The book is recommended and advertised by the Farrakhan movement, and is praised (though misinterpreted) by leading Afrocentric scholars like Molefi Asante. For an earlier racial-essentialist appropriation of Rodney's message, see Uya (1982).

7. For the origin of these ideas in Rodney's thought, see R. Lewis (1994).

8. The most obviously direct point of comparison – though Nicholls does not actually make the connection – would be with the almost simultaneously published celebration of peasant life and culture by Nazi theorist Walther Darre: *Das Bauerntum als Lebensquell der Nordischen Rasse* (1929). On Price-Mars's thought and circumstances, see also Shannon (1996).

9. See, as sources for the following argument, Nicholls (1979: 167–72; 194–200; ch. 8 *passim*; 1985: chs 1–3, 12); Dash (1981: ch. 4); Trouillot (1990: chs 4–7); Ferguson (1987: ch. 2); Taylor 1989; plus two sensationalist accounts which none the less contain useful material: Abbott (1988: chs 3–5); Diederich and Burt (1969).

8

Afro-America as Nation, and as Internal Colony

I have suggested, I think uncontroversially, that Afrocentrism – at least outside Africa itself – is by definition a species of cultural nationalism. This means, rather obviously, that its adherents must conceive of themselves as belonging to, analysing and advocating the interests not just of an ethnic group, a community, or even a race, but a nation, in some way distinct from the majority (Euro-)American nationality. How could this nation best be described? The most recurringly popular answer among Afro-American nationalists has been: as an oppressed, colonized national minority within the United States. Indeed, it seems to me that although present-day Afrocentrists, unlike many previous brands of cultural nationalists in the USA, have not normally used the term 'internal colony' to describe their position, that idea – or one very like it – is a logical or even necessary foundation for their beliefs.

The notion of African-Americans as a distinct nationality has a long but uneven history.[1] Black political leaders and writers had intermittently referred to themselves as part of a separate national group from the earliest recorded statements of their political views up to the present. Yet such terminology was frequently vague in the extreme, with words like 'race', 'nation' and even 'tribe', or later 'culture' and 'ethnic group', being used loosely and often interchangeably – as, indeed, they have been in many other contexts. As August Meier suggests, many Afro-American publicists described themselves as a separate group or (less often) nationality to emphasize the way they were excluded and belittled by other Americans, but insisted that this separation was thrust upon them rather than desired: they themselves sought full acceptance as unhyphenated Americans. This ambivalence was neatly captured in the declaration by the assimilationist, conservative black journal the *Cleveland Gazette*, in 1886: 'Like other nation-alities constituting the American family, we have struggled for constitutional government and constitutional liberty' (Meier 1966: 53).

Invocations of the idea of Afro-American nationality, as this implies, did not necessarily involve advocacy of a political programme of national*ism*, let alone separatism. Their uses were often, perhaps, mainly tactical: asserting a collective identity as a means to stake claims to greater respect, resources

or power within American society, or to rally a constituency as a power base
for such ambitions – not to separate from it entirely. The conception of
nationality involved was thus nearly always a cultural one, rather than
partaking of the aim associated with nearly all political nationalisms since
the French Revolution: that of political independence as a 'nation-state'.
This is as true of Afrocentrism as of its precursors: very few of its
spokespeople appear to have any serious desire either for mass emigration
to Africa or for full political and geographical separation within the
Americas.

The concept of internal colonialism, by contrast, is a fairly recent one,
but it has had a very wide variety of applications right across the globe. It
has been taken up since the 1960s, especially but not only by left-wing and
Marxist thinkers, to denote processes such as English domination over
Wales, Scotland and Ireland (Hechter 1975), South African apartheid
policies (Wolpe 1988), class and ethnic stratification in Latin America
(Stavenhagen 1965, 1973, 1975), Israeli oppression of the Palestinians (Ram
1993; Shafir 1989; Zureik 1979), and the position of oppressed 'national
minorities' in numerous states. From one point of view, pretty much *all*
history can be seen as a history of internal colonialism: as indicated, for
instance, by Robert Bartlett's demonstration of how much the development
of medieval Europe was a story of conquest and colonization by a Latinate–
Frankish core over its neighbours (Bartlett 1993). Using the concept in the
present, however, has had more specific and politically charged connotations. It has implied taking sides in complex arguments over whether, how
far and in what ways the position of minorities within advanced capitalist
countries could be described as equivalent to that of colonized peoples in
the European overseas empires – a dispute that is felt to have strong political
implications. It was intertwined, often in confused ways, with the question
of whether the political struggles of people of African, Caribbean or Asian
descent in the USA, Britain or elsewhere in the Atlantic world should focus
primarily on their countries of residence or on those of their or their
ancestors' origin.

The most basic claim of any argument asserting that a situation is one of
internal colonialism is that there is an exploitative relationship between the
dominant community or communities within a state and minority or
peripheral communities. Thus the primary thrust is in most versions an
economic one, though often supplemented by stress on political disadvan-
tage or powerlessness. Frequently this stress on exploitative relations is
associated with the dominant group's economic activities being seen as
diversified, and associated with industrialization, advanced technology, and
high skill and wage levels. Evidently this picture connects with the colonial
analogy only if the differentiation is to some considerable degree a *spatial*
one: that there are exploiting and exploited *regions* within the state. If this
dimension does not exist, the exploitation is hard to separate analytically
from one of social class. On the other hand, a *merely* regional differentiation
would not seem to meet the case for seeing a situation as colonial. There

would also have to be at least a significant cultural differentiation between exploiters and exploited. Perhaps more, it might be necessary for significant numbers of those concerned to conceive of it as a national distinction.

Some advocates of the internal-colonial model would reject the stringency of these conditions, arguing that *either* geographical *or* cultural differentiation between exploiters and exploited is enough to define the situation as colonial. This is most evidently the case in applications of the model to African-Americans, who do not have a geographically distinct 'homeland'. But there are difficulties even in cases, sometimes described as internal-colonial ones, where both conditions apply – for instance, as Anthony Birch points out, neither Scotland within the UK nor Quebec in Canada has been marked by particularly specialized or non-industrialized economies, nor have their natives been underrepresented in positions of political power (Birch 1989: 67–8).

The concept of internal colonialism as a way to describe the situation of African-Americans really took off in the 1960s. It was closely associated with the political shift from Civil Rights integrationist campaigns to a rhetoric of Black Power, a revived separatism, and an increasingly revolutionary temper in some Afro-American circles. Yet the internal colony thesis also had a long prehistory, starting in the international Communist movement, in the Comintern's and Communist Party of the USA's 1930s 'black belt' thesis.

This has aptly been described as 'the most obscure and puzzling chapter in the history of American Communism' (Draper 1960: 315). Issues of race, on a global scale, had from the Third International's foundation been placed by Moscow under the rubric of 'the national and colonial question', or – in what was initially a near-synonym – 'the peoples of the East'. Otto Huiswood, one of the handful of early US black Communists, told the Comintern's Fourth Congress as early as 1922 that factors of racial and colonial oppression must be taken into account in relation to Afro-America. An international 'Negro congress' including Afro-Americans, it was suggested, should be called. Despite this, American Communists initially treated the issue of US blacks as essentially, if not solely, one of class. And since American Communism in the early and mid 1920s had virtually no black members, being overwhelmingly comprised of diverse European migrants' 'foreign language sections' (Buhle 1987: 121–43), the question was of largely symbolic importance.

The Comintern's Sixth Congress in 1928 radically transformed the official Communist line on Afro-Americans, as on a great deal else. In the context of Stalin's ascendancy in the Soviet Union's internal power struggles, and of the general turn to 'Third Period' ultra-leftism, the Congress adopted a new and militantly sectarian stance on questions of colonial liberation. The US situation was subsumed within this, with Afro-Americans in the 'black belt' states of the American South defined as an oppressed, colonized nation for whom self-determination should be demanded. For blacks in the industrial North, by contrast, only calls for racial and class equality were stipulated.

This bifurcation, and the reasoning behind it, were never clearly spelled out at the Congress. Evidently, though, they derived mostly from a schematic universalization of the Soviet Union's own nationalities policy – the officially proclaimed one, not the far more oppressive and centralizing reality. Neither black nor white US Communists themselves had called for this stance; indeed, most of them had argued strongly against defining the Afro-American situation as a 'national' one. In so far as there was a base of support for the idea among African-Americans, it seems to have come from the small nexus of black students who studied at the Soviet University of Toilers of the East during the 1920s.[2]

Thus US Communists were saddled with an evidently unworkable dual strategy: for the North, a piously proclaimed integrationism involving bitter hostility to all black nationalist or separatist groupings; for the South, advocacy of black self-determination including the right to secession (which would, naturally, be desirable under capitalism but not necessarily under a Soviet USA).[3] The former involved, in particular, bitter attacks on Garvey-ism, major if largely unsuccessful attempts to recruit in Harlem, and ostentatious purges of alleged racists in the CPUSA's own ranks. The latter, southern strategy included an outpouring of arguments for self-determination in Communist publications (including even maps showing the boundaries of the proposed 'black republic') and efforts to organize black sharecroppers and other poor farmers in the South. These had some shortlived success; but there is no evidence that slogans of national liberation contributed to it (Klehr 1984; Draper 1960: ch. 15). Both facets of the policy undoubtedly involved – as later Afro-American critics like Harold Cruse bitterly alleged – heavy doses of paternalism and manipulation.

The call for 'black belt' self-determination was largely abandoned – silently, without discussion – after the 1935 Seventh Comintern Congress. This new shift was again the result of Moscow's changing strategic needs rather than of any indigenous US – let alone African-American – initiative. The CPUSA dissolved the main 'front' organization which had been pressing for self-determination, the League of Struggle for Negro Rights. Officially, the doctrine had not been repudiated; and in 1946, with the demise of CPUSA leader Earl Browder's strategy of appealing to American 'exceptionalism' and patriotism, it was revived in what Draper calls 'a slightly watered-down version – as a programmatic demand and not as an immediate slogan of action' (Draper 1960: 355). According to one Party veteran, it aroused some enthusiasm among younger black members in the late 1940s (George Charney, quoted in Robinson 1983: 346).

Only in 1958, well after Stalin's death, was the 'black belt' thesis formally buried by the CPUSA. The great migration of Afro-Americans to northern cities and the rising tide of the Civil Rights movement apparently made such nationalist appeals – always dubiously compatible with orthodox Marxism – irrelevant. But within a very few years a new generation of black intellectuals was to revive the notion of an oppressed Afro-American *nation*. One of the first – and among the most historically informed – writers to employ it was Harold Cruse. As he argued in 1967:

> Africans and West Indians were never allowed to forget that they were colonial subjects. But the fact that the American Negro was also a subject, of a special kind of North American domestic colonialism, was never fully accepted either by the Negro himself nor by Africans or West Indians. Back in the 1920s, during the Haywood–Huiswood–Briggs controversy within the Communist Party, the West Indians did not want to classify American Negroes as colonials. It was not until 1962 that even the new Afro-American National-ists began to see the domestic colonialist nature of the Negro's position in the United States. (Cruse 1967/1984: 433)

The main point of the whole argument for Cruse, then, was not to explore the internal-colonial model in itself, but rhetorically to invoke it as further evidence of the irreducibly national-cultural nature of all 'left' politics in the USA. This is by no means an unreasonable view, since at least from some perspectives the whole history not only of Afro-American politics but of American socialism can best be analysed through the shifting loyalties and alignments of immigrant, ethnic or national groupings (see, for a more recent and less polemical analysis on these lines than Cruse's, Buhle 1987). One may, however, doubt Cruse's ethnicist (some would say anti-Semitic) insistence that the driving forces behind the disputes over Afro-American identity were largely Jewish and secondarily West Indian 'racial' chauvin-isms. His choice of 1962 as originating point of the revived awareness was, one suspects, dictated by the fact that his own first published discussion of the internal-colonial thesis (later collected in Cruse 1968) appeared then.

The rediscovered concept of internal colonialism received its most fully articulated Afro-American formulations in Stokely Carmichael and Charles V. Hamilton's book *Black Power* (1967/9), in Robert Allen's *Black Awakening in Capitalist America* (1969), and in Robert Blauner's *Racial Oppression in America* (1972). Carmichael and Hamilton suggested its immediate ancestry by quoting black sociologist Kenneth Clark and radical journalist I.F. Stone, who had evoked the colonial idea, as rhetorical trope and as analogy respectively, in 1965 and 1966 (Carmichael and Hamilton 1967/9: 19).

Neither Clark nor Stone had in fact developed the parallel further. Carmichael and Hamilton, in their effort to do so, initially identified colonialism as 'another name' for institutionalized racism (ibid.: 22). They immediately admitted that 'the analogy is not perfect', because of the lack of geographical separation of the races and the fact that Afro-America exported only labour, not goods, to the dominant sector. However, they suggested – pointing to South Africa and to what was then called Rhodesia – that the USA was not unique in the former, and that the latter was a 'technicality' (ibid.). They then pursued the argument for black Americans' colonial status through political, economic and social aspects.

Politically, they argued, US 'pluralism' was a myth in relation to racial questions, where all black assertions faced a white power bloc as monolithic as that formed by colonial rulers (22–6). What black political leadership there was amounted to no more than what they considered, evoking West African parallels, to be a precise analogy to colonial 'indirect rule' systems (26–32). On the economic front, they relied on a conception of 'normal' colonialism as necessarily motivated by the extraction of profit for the metropolis(32–3); and saw Afro-America as exploited in exactly the same way (33–9). Their focus here was overwhelmingly on northern, urban ghetto conditions rather than on rural or southern African Americans. Socially, they emphasized denial of equal status and racial defamation, which they believed had 'taught the subject to hate himself and to deny his own humanity' (47).

Yet at no point did Carmichael and Hamilton call Afro-Americans a national group, advocate violent revolution (despite saying, more as warning than in hope, that liberation would be sought 'by whatever means necessary' [187]), or imply belief in secession. Instead, their rather modest call was for 'new political forms which will be the link between broadened participation (now occurring) and legitimate government' (184).

Blauner's agenda was in a sense wider, for he wished to argue the validity not only of an Afro-American perception of their situation as colonial, but of the then new notion of a 'Third World' coalition among colonially oppressed groups in the USA. Even if invocations of such a coalition were largely dictated by immediate political motives, he suggested, the parallel was valid because:

> [T]he experience of people of color in this country does include a number of circumstances that are universal to the colonial situation, and these are the very circumstances that differentiate third world realities from those of the European immigrants. The first ... is that of a forced entry into the larger society or metropolitan domain. The second is subjection to various forms of unfree labour that greatly restrict the physical and social mobility of the group and its participation in the political arena. The third is a cultural policy of the colonizer that constrains, transforms, or destroys original values, orientations, and ways of life. (Blauner 1972: 53)

Thereafter Blauner narrowed his focus somewhat to concentrate on Afro-America. There, he – in common with most other radical analysts of the time, almost whatever their theoretical orientation – identified lack of black political representation, the undermining of cultural traditions, and social discrimination as the key problems. A further factor – separate labour status – was added only as an afterthought (ibid.: 84). He did, though, return to the theme of *geographical* separation as an element in internal colonialism (85–91; 95–102). In identifying the internal colony as a physical space, Blauner's focus – like Carmichael and Hamilton's and unlike that of the 1930s Communist theorists – was on the urban black ghettoes rather than the rural South. He saw the 1960s ghetto revolts, in this context, as movements for decolonization: but once again the conclusions drawn are not fully separatist or secessionist. Rather, Blauner called for the 'colonized' to be given the choice between local self-government (seemingly identified as little more than black-run inner-city authorities) and fuller participation in US national life (104).

Meanwhile, if these were unusually extended analyses, the less systematic, more purely agitational rhetoric of internal colonialism seemed, for a time, nearly ubiquitous. Eldridge Cleaver, for instance, used the notion in rather sketchy and haphazard ways, as part of a rhetorical case associating the struggles of US blacks with those of Third World peoples and a generalized notion of 'the oppressed' (e.g. 1970: 69–70; 108; 118–20; 1971: 44–6; and most extensively 1971: 80–94), though he initially employed the term itself only by way of a quotation from Nkrumah (1970: 108), and did not draw fully separatist political conclusions from its use. Only, it seems, after his association with the Black Panther party did he adopt the colonial analogy in a substantial way. And even then this was less a coherent presentation of a case than a moment in a polemic asserting the primacy of desire among Afro-Americans for land of their own (1971: 85), proclaiming the need for Afro-America to 'assume its sovereignty, to demand that that sovereignty be recognized by other nations of the world' (ibid.: 89), to articulate Black Panther calls for a plebiscite on black self-determination (91–2), and – rather inconsistently – to urge that guerrilla war was the only means for black liberation (92–4).

Poet and playwright LeRoi Jones, similarly, invoked the idea that 'Black is a Country' as part of a sweeping rhetorical claim for Afro-American struggles as 'only a microcosm of the struggle of the new countries all over the world' (Baraka/Jones 1966: 85). And most influentially of all, Malcolm X urged in 1965:

> We are living in an era of revolution, and the revolt of the American Negro is part of the rebellion against the oppression and colonialism which has characterised this era. . . . It is incorrect to classify the revolt of the Negro as simply a racial conflict of black against white, or as a purely American problem. Rather, we are today seeing a global rebellion of the oppressed against the oppressor, the exploited against the exploiter. (quoted in Marable 1984: 95)

And in his subsequently famous 1964 speech 'The Ballot or the Bullet', Malcolm X proclaimed:

> America is just as much a colonial power as England ever was. . . . What do you call second-class citizenship? Why, that's colonization. Second-class citizenship is nothing but twentieth-century slavery. . . . Just as it took nationalism to remove colonialism from Asia and Africa, it'll take black nationalism today to remove colonialism from the minds of twenty-two million Afro-Americans here in this country. (Gates and McKay 1997: 94)

Thus for Cleaver, Jones, Malcolm X and others, the colonial analogy was above all an argument in service of an African-American nationalist claim. This had not been the case in the 1930s, when Communists advancing the 'black belt' thesis were simultaneously bitterly hostile to Afro-American cultural nationalist groupings; nor was it the purpose of Carmichael, Blauner and others who sought to give the concept some analytical content. In the hands of black nationalist groups from the mid 1960s onwards, it was far less an analytical tool than a part of the emotional atmosphere of the day: one compounded of swirling currents of violence – in Vietnam, from white racists, from police and other state authorities, in ghetto uprisings, and among some black political organizations themselves – and of often undirected enthusiasm for African and other Third World independence movements. Its manifestations included the widespread invocations of Fanon's writings and those of various African independence leaders; though how widely these texts were actually *read* is, of course, quite another question. There was a popular adoption of names, dress, language codes (above all fragmentary Swahili) derived – or purportedly so – from African originals: the most systematized being Maulana Ron Karenga's 'Kawaida' doctrine. There was – far the most lastingly valuable legacy of the era – a sharply novel and politicized sensibility in the arts, especially poetry and jazz.[4] Moving behind the trends came a clutch of cultural nationalist 'Black Aesthetic' critical and cultural theories (traced, in polemical vein, in H. Baker 1984: esp. 71–87).

Amid this highly charged political and cultural environment, to complain at the lack of coherent social theory underpinning the era's use of internal-colonial imagery is almost beside the point. Many of the proponents of an African-American cultural nationalism were unashamedly irrationalist, drawing on the legacies of Garveyism and of the Nation of Islam in style if not in ideological substance. Some attracted charges of nihilism and even 'black fascism' from critics like Addison Gayle and later Manning Marable (Marable 1984: 120–21). Some interpreted 'Black Power' as meaning above all 'black capitalism'. Others, moving away from the more mystical or quasi-religious forms of cultural nationalism like that of Elijah Muhammad's Black Muslims (Essien-Udom 1964; Lincoln 1961), had their possible ideological evolution cut brutally short. This happened with the most charismatically influential figure of all, Malcolm X, leaving enduring controversy about his final political views and their significance – a controversy revived in the early 1990s when Malcolm's image, boosted by Spike Lee's high-profile film biography, attained renewed salience (see B. Perry 1992). And some black nationalist groups moved into violent insurrectionary action – albeit under a degree of state pressure or manipulation which is also lastingly controversial. The scale of such action was never very great; though between 1969 and 1975 twenty-six police officers were killed in gunfights with black militants (Gurr 1989: 212), and a somewhat larger number of armed radicals were killed *by* the police, sometimes in very murky circumstances. As Ted Robert Gurr comments:

It is evident that armed violence by handfuls of black militants was the last deadly derivative of a movement that won most of its victories through peaceful protest in the early 1960s. Black militancy had largely subsided by the early 1970s. . . . In the 1980s FBI reports and journalistic sources provide no evidence of any further organized violence by black militants. (ibid.: 213)[5]

If the logical conclusion of beliefs that Afro-America was an oppressed nation or internal colony was armed revolution – as many militants proclaimed, especially in the late 1960s – then that conclusion was not pursued by any numerous group to any significant degree.[6] Where there was large-scale violent action, as in the various inner-city disturbances or such incidents as the Attica prison uprising of 1971, almost all the deaths were by the guns of state forces. Affairs like the Attica revolt, which ended in the deaths of twenty-nine prison inmates and ten guards whom they had taken hostage (investigation proved that the dead guards were almost all killed by the bullets of their 'rescuers', not by the prisoners), involved much Third-Worldist and liberationist rhetoric. The Attica prisoners included among their demands a call for 'speedy and safe transportation out of confinement, to a non-imperialistic country' (Wicker 1978: 396), but this does not seem to have been accompanied by any articulation of the black radical prisoners' *own* situation as a colonial one, rather than as part of some generalized category of the oppressed. In California especially, some prison militants identified themselves with 'Third World' revolution, and saw themselves as a potential insurrectionary vanguard; but they were a small, isolated group increasingly cut off from US political realities, as the fates of George Jackson and then of the 'Symbionese Liberation Army' miserably demonstrated (see the disenchanted retrospective analysis in Cummins 1994).

Another apparently logical deduction from the belief that Afro-Americans were an internal colony of the USA was the idea of geographical separation and self-determination – of carving out an independent 'black republic' within the USA. American Communists' advocacy of this idea in the 1930s had met an unhappy fate, but some groups revived it in the 1960s. Best known by far was the Nation of Islam, whose demands for independent territory to be granted by way of reparations for past black suffering varied wildly with time and circumstances – from wanting two US states to be ceded to them, through to an insistence that twenty-five would not be too many (Van Deburg 1992: 140–44). It is doubtful, though, whether this kind of evidently impractical demand played a major role in the movement's popular appeal. A much smaller group, the Republic of New Africa, had clearer-cut proposals, which they put before the public in 1968. The states of Alabama, Georgia, Louisiana, Mississippi and South Carolina would form the new black republic, funded by $400 billion 'start-up' money from the US government. If these modest demands were not met, the territory would be seized by force, liberated by the 'New African Security Force' and its urban guerrilla sympathizers. The new sovereign republic would devote itself to reviving authentic African values, which apparently included compulsory military service, a tightly controlled press, hostility to trade unions and encouragement of polygamy (Van Deburg 1992: 144–9). The Republic of New Africa, too, has retained or revived a certain influence into the 1990s: the bestselling memoirs of former Los Angeles ghetto gangster 'Monster' Kody Scott attribute his conversion from violent crime to their ideas, and those of Afrocentrism more generally (Shakur 1993). The organization has played an active part in the campaign for the US government to pay reparations, compensating African-Americans for centuries of slavery and exploitation (see Van Deburg [ed.] 1997: 333–41).

As 1960s black militancy fragmented or wound down, still other black radicals persisted in – or made their way towards – various kinds of socialist politics: most often a variety of Marxist—black nationalist syntheses. It was in these circles that the internal-colonial model remained persistingly alive. Thus LeRoi Jones, renamed Amiri Baraka and in transit from cultural nationalism to Marxism–Leninism, asserted of his home town:

> There is a clearer feeling in Newark, than in any other city I have ever been in, of Colonialism. Newark is *a colony*. A bankrupt ugly colony, in the classic term, where white people make their money to take away with them. ('Newark – Before Black Men Conquered' [1969], in Baraka 1979: 178; original emphasis)

And a few years later, having come to (at least temporary) ideological rest with an aggressively crude Maoism, he returned to the theme, now by way of proclaiming that blacks in the US 'Old South' were a nation as defined by Stalin:

> It is this Afro-American nation, which still exists in the Black Belt South, that was and is oppressed by U.S. imperialism, in the same fashion imperialism oppresses other nations in the Third World (Asia, Africa and Latin America). But since the Afro-American nation actually exists on the land base of the United States, the approach to its liberation is somewhat more complex than many of the colonial questions whose solution is to be made by revolution, though make no mistake, the only solution to the Afro-American national question is by violent armed revolution, socialist revolution! ('Black Liberation/Socialist Revolution' [1976], in ibid.: 211; also in Baraka 1984b)

But the apparent clarity of this Maoist version of the internal colonialism thesis is deceptive; for Baraka argued elsewhere that although the Afro-American bourgeoisie had made gains since the 1950s:

> what is being created with this largely false 'clout' the black bourgeoisie and petite bourgeoisie have achieved as a result of the black mass struggle, is a kind of neocolonialism, although the black nation in the United States is *not*

a colony but an oppressed nation, fighting for the right of self-determination. ('"Clout": What Is It?' [1977], in Baraka 1984b: 74; original emphasis)

Unlike Third World national liberation struggles – which, according to Maoist orthodoxy, might include the participation of the national bourgeoisie – the Afro-American struggle would apparently necessarily be led by the working class, and result in socialism. This followed from the fact of the USA's advanced capitalist status; but it is quite unclear what is meant by – or what the significance may be of – persistently describing black Americans as a nation subject to imperialist (sometimes called colonial) domination, but *not* actually a colony. If it is not a colony, and if its hoped-for revolution will necessarily be a socialist one, what is the point of insisting on its absolute right to self-determination or secession (as Baraka does in 'Marxism and the Black Community' in 1984b) – even if the latter were physically possible? This begins to read like Malcolm X recast in pseudo-Marxist language; or, alternatively, the disputes of the Second International repeated as farce. In fact Baraka's eventual position, expressed in a dreadfully dogmatic and obfuscatory Maoist jargon light years away from the vivid style of his literary and cultural writings, seemed to be that Afro-Americans in the 'black belt' *were* a nation with the right to secession, while those elsewhere were not (e.g. 'Black Liberation Today', in Baraka 1984b, esp. 102–5). In other words, he had reverted to precisely the stance adopted by the Comintern during the 'Third Period'. This view, though, was neither clearly nor consistently formulated.

In somewhat similar vein, and a little earlier, George Jackson's prison writings, adopting a mixture of separatist and Maoist–Leninist beliefs much influenced by the Black Panthers' ideas, regularly referred to the position of US blacks as a colonial one, though again without fully developing the idea, and simultaneously putting forward a highly schematic two-class model of American society, proclaiming that its political system was fascist (Jackson 1972; see also Cummins 1994). Other, less personally prominent analysts also continued with or reverted to the internal-colonial thesis during the 1970s and 1980s. They included veteran 1960s radicals like James Forman (1981) and James Boggs (1970); and the theoreticians of several minuscule Trotskyist and Maoist formations.[7] As Cornel West says, the thesis:

> with its ahistorical racial determination of a nation, its flaccid statistical determination of national boundaries, and its illusory distinct black national economy ... functions as a poor excuse for the absence of a sophisticated Marxist theory of the specificity of Afro-American oppression. (West 1988: 20)

But as West also remarks, for all their inadequacies, such notions remained hegemonic among African-American socialists. The image retained force even among analysts who rejected its literal validity *tout court* rather than, like Baraka, ambivalently and inconsistently. Thus Manning

Marable adopted a specifically colonial trope for the title and polemical thrust of his *How Capitalism Underdeveloped Black America* – alluding to Rodney's *How Europe Underdeveloped Africa* – urging that Black America was deliberately 'underdeveloped' by US capitalism:

> Blacks are an integral and necessary part of an imperialistic and powerful capitalist society, yet they exist in terms of actual socioeconomic and political power as a kind of Third World nation. As a result, Black America shares some similarities with other national minorities or oppressed nationalities within European countries. (Marable 1983: 10)

Yet he insisted that 'the race/class dialectic in the United States cannot be adequately or accurately described as neocolonial' (ibid.: 135), and did not in fact ordinarily speak of African-Americans as a *nation*.

More recently the concept of internal colonialism has sometimes come to be used in virtually scattergun fashion, applied to any and every situation of racial minorities. Thus African-American feminist writer Andree Nicola McLaughlin, in a global sketch of black women's positions across the Anglophone world, coins the term 'people of colony' – on the analogy of people of colour – to embrace black Americans, British and South Africans, New Zealand Maori, and various Pacific islanders (McLaughlin 1990: 152). This involves her not only in embracing the aggressively anti-liberal and anti-pluralist perspective of extreme Maori cultural nationalists (ibid.: 159–62), the minority black British current which rejects even a hyphenated 'British' identity (163–7) and the internal colonialism thesis for Afro-America (167–74), but also in endorsing the 'primacy of the land' thesis of South Africa's PAC – without apparently even being aware that this is a minority view rejected by the far more widely supported ANC (156–9). And bell hooks can lament at length – and rather oddly, given the evidence we have just surveyed – that analysis of Afro-America has failed to use the language of colonialism or think of US blacks as being in a colonial situation.

hooks asserts:

> there hasn't been a major discourse of decolonization in the US ... words like 'colonization' and 'decolonization' aren't allowed to play a role. ...
> [The] reproduction of the drama of victimization is totally tied to the lack of a whole critical theory and practice around colonization and decolonization. (in Gilroy 1993b: 217)

hooks is not entirely wrong when she goes on to argue that reincorporating the concept of colonialism into Afro-American social thought might force a renewed internationalism as opposed to the present fixation on the USA's, and American blacks', uniqueness, and might facilitate greater attention to issues of class, economics and gender (ibid.: 222–3). But in her apparent lack of interest in the fate of past uses of the idea – by no means always internationalist, or involving attention to concrete economic problems, let alone to gender – she fails even to ask why such earlier intellectual movements fragmented, failed and lost their popular appeal. The reason, surely, is first and foremost that the notion of Afro-America as colony is simply not a coherent one.

Thus we see that the earlier uses of the idea of internal colonialism deployed it as an economic and/or sociological category; but it has increasingly been changed into a primarily cultural phenomenon. Yet whereas in some other cases – such as that of Ireland – this shift from economics to culture has been accompanied by an increasing sophistication of analysis, with theories of cultural imperialism being substantially more varied and subtle than analyses of economic colonialism, for 'internal colonialism' in Afro-America the reverse has been the case. Some of the analyses cast in predominantly socioeconomic terms have had considerable scholarly weight. The cultural interpretations have on the whole been shallowly polemical, irrationalist, and quite devoid of any serious proposals for social change.

There seems no reason, in any case, to suppose that any particular political strategy follows necessarily from adoption of the model. Conversely, no particular set of policy proposals necessarily requires adoption of the internal-colonial analysis rather than some other – except perhaps the call for revolution, which in some circumstances (like those of Afro-Americans) appears hard to sustain except through use of the colonial model. While revolutionary sentiments could in principle be mobilized among Afro-Americans, or Hispanic Americans, on some other basis – such as social class membership – a *specifically* racial- or ethnic-based insurrectionary politics would seem to require the colonial model as a necessary – though of course woefully insufficient – condition. Short of this, it is evidently possible to support strategies involving strong recognition of community rights on many other bases than that of defining the community as a nation or an internal colony. Indeed, it is hard to see what help such a definition gives to the advancement of such rights.

Notes

1. For general histories of such ideas and their contexts, see (amid a large literature) Geiss (1974); Hall (1978); Moses (1978); Pinkney (1976); Stuckey (1987).

2. C. Robinson (1983: 306–7) places the roots of the concept among these, especially Harry Haywood; see also McClellan (1993).

3. On these ideas and disputes see Cruse (1967/1984: Part II *passim*); C. Robinson (1983: 291–311); Haywood 1978.

4. On the relations between 'black power' politics and free jazz, see Baraka/Jones (1967); Kofsky (1970); Wilmer (1980).

5. The view that violent protest achieved almost nothing for African-Americans, or was actually counterproductive compared to the record of peaceful agitation, is strongly endorsed in perhaps the most careful historical overview of a century's black liberationist politics: Fredrickson (1995).

6. It would have been an illogical conclusion in any case, since contrary to much

contemporary and subsequent rhetoric, the great majority of former European colonies' decolonizations were achieved without significant military conflict.

7. See summaries and references by Cornel West and Lucius Outlaw in M. Davis *et al.* (1987: 83–4, 116–17, 260); and West (1988: 19–20, 26).

9

African Cultures and the New World

Debate over African survivals or cultural retentions in the Americas has been intense and complex for several decades now. Initially this was a highly polarized dispute, conducted between those – like Melville Herskovits (1941/1958) – who made very strong claims for a near-ubiquity of recognizably African cultural traits among Afro-Americans, and those – like black sociologist Franklin Frazier – who asserted that such retentions were negligible. Neither extreme position appears tenable in the light of more recent research. John Thornton (1992: Part II) gives an even-handed overview of the current state of scholarship on the issue, stressing particularly that the search for this or that African 'trait' or 'survival' is misleading, since cultures exist in some sense as totalities, and are always in a state of change. He also emphasizes, as do Robert Farris Thompson (1983) and a growing number of others including now – most influentially – Paul Gilroy (1993a), how what emerged was a specifically black _Atlantic_ cultural complex, rather than one which was African, European and/or American. In relation to religious practices, for instance:

> The result was the emergence of a new Afro-Atlantic religion that was often identified as Christian, especially in the New World, but was a type of Christianity that could satisfy both African and European understandings of religion. (Thornton 1992: 235)

On the whole, we can say that historians and anthropologists have tended towards greater caution about the extent of continuing New World Africanisms, whereas literary and cultural critics have made stronger claims about them; though almost all serious scholars are more ready to recognize such 'survivals' than would have been the case two generations ago.[1] It is also fairly generally accepted that clearly identifiable African elements are far less significant in black North American cultures than in those of Brazil, or of several Caribbean territories. Whereas specific Africanisms can be traced in considerable detail in the popular culture, say, of Jamaica (see, for example, Alleyne [1988]; Glazier [ed.] [1993]) or among the Maroons of

101

Suriname (see Richard Price's remarkable *First Time* [1983]), and perhaps most of all in Haiti, scholars have been far less able to do so in the USA.

There are a number of reasons for this. Blacks formed a lower proportion of the population in even the most intensely slave-labour-dependent parts of the United States than they did in many Caribbean islands, in the Guianas or in the plantation regions of Brazil. Most US plantations were small – indeed, the word itself is often a misnomer for the family-run farms and workshops in which the majority of slaves laboured – as against the sometimes vast, industrial-scale slave enterprises of Santo Domingo, Bahia or Jamaica. At any given time, the proportion of African-born people in the enslaved population of the US South seems to have been considerably lower than in many regions further south and east – for the simple reason that life expectancy was normally greater in the former, so that labour forces were not so constantly, massively replenished by new imports. Additionally, large-scale importations of slaves ceased earlier in North America than they did in Brazil or Cuba, for instance. And it may well be that in the USA, the slaves living and working in any particular area, and thus in contact with one another, were more likely to be from a variety of linguistic and cultural backgrounds than elsewhere. It is notable that much of the strongest evidence of distinct Africanisms in North America comes from the coast and islands of Georgia and South Carolina, where these conditions were least evident: where, for instance, large-scale slave imports continued later, black–white ratios were higher and owners more often absentee than elsewhere in the USA. Here, to a greater extent than anywhere else in continental North America, scholars have found clear African continuities in language (e.g. L. Turner 1973), in social organization (Creel 1988), and in arts and crafts (R. Thompson 1969, 1983; Vlach 1978).

All these factors made the persistence of specific African cultural patterns less possible, and acculturation into new, syncretic but heavily European-influenced patterns more rapid and fuller in the USA than further south. It is also sometimes suggested that US slaveholders, or perhaps Anglophone ones generally, were less tolerant of their vassals sustaining African linguistic, religious, recreational and other cultural forms than were their equivalents in Spanish, French and Portuguese colonies: a distinction in its turn sometimes linked to religious differences – that is, the Catholic–Protestant division. Put more positively, the activities of Protestant Christian evangelists, notably Baptists, often anti-slavery in temperament, produced greater 'Euro-peanization' – or, more accurately a more novel, original syncretic culture – than there was in places where an extremely *laissez-faire*, if not merely indifferent, Catholic hierarchy held sway.

Inevitably, the debate on African retentions has been a highly politicized one, for reasons Thornton summarizes: 'Denying the survival of African culture among Afro-Americans has constituted a denial of the Afro-American past and a possible Pan-Africanist present; affirming it accepts the past and the present' (1992: 210). Or – as Melville Herskovits argued at an early stage in the controversy – the old view that Afro-Americans had no historical past, no African inheritance, worth considering might be thought 'one of the principal supports of race prejudice in this country' (1941/1958: 1). But a further dimension of politicization has also come into the picture. Since it is often difficult, if not impossible, especially in the United States, to identify Afro-American cultural traits as deriving from *particular* African peoples, it has become politically important for some intellectuals to emphasize that distinctions between those peoples were essentially insignificant, so that descent from a generalized 'Africa' becomes more meaningful. This concern evidently coincides with that of people within Africa itself who want to emphasize elements of cultural unity or shared tradition, for their own quite different political motive of strengthening support for continental political unification. Two quite different kinds of Pan-Africanism thus enter into a marriage of convenience. Hence, in part, the appeal of ideas like those of Cheikh Anta Diop for Afro-American cultural nationalists, which will be traced below.

Diop's work, however, was essentially unknown in the Americas before the 1970s. In its absence, one major early influence in English on the notion of a unified African culture, or belief system, was a highly romanticized book by the German Africanist Janheinz Jahn (1961). Drawing on Karl Jaspers's philosophy of history, Malinowski's anthropology, and Placide Tempels's misguided construct of 'Bantu philosophy', Jahn posits a common African culture based on a few key concepts – or, rather, key*words* – whose explication, he believes, accounts for anything and everything.

On the other hand, Jahn's judgements on New World black cultures were equally sweeping and ill-informed – but this time in directions quite antithetical to Afrocentric desires:

Millions of Afro-Americans in South America, the Antilles and the United States grow up in a European-American environment and without any knowledge of African culture. Except for the colour of their skins they are Americans like any others. Yet the others think this colour a blemish and let those in question feel it. Thus the Afro-American is constantly reminded of his origin, which has otherwise often lost all meaning for him.' (Jahn 1961: 21)

Only white racism, then, gives any kind of significance to African origins. This is a view with few, if any, supporters today – though one might suggest that what Jahn misdescribes as a reality would be held by some commentators – like Arthur Schlesinger (1992) – to be a desirable aspiration.

Several critics have suggested that it is misleading to think in terms of a simple opposition between the survival or disappearance of 'Africanisms'. As Leslie H. Owens says:

[T]he predominance of an African majority in most areas (of the New World plantation systems) continued the pattern of African blood ties and alertness to history that distinguished their immediate past. . . . The reach became more difficult with time, but such blood ties should be labelled more than simply lingering 'Africanisms'. They unlock an institutionally structured way of ordering the world and provide a practical link to a past that could not be erased. (Owens 1986: 27)

Henry Louis Gates, making a similar point, tends towards the more 'Afrocentric' pole of the argument, though without associating himself with the more sweeping claims made by those who identify themselves as Afrocentrists – his views are too heavily shaped by regard for rationality, logic and respect for the evidence for that. And he betrays his deep ambivalence about the evidentiary status of some of his own arguments by entitling his own chapter on the subject, in his major work *The Signifying Monkey* (Gates 1988), 'A Myth of Origins'. Furthermore, he is far from asserting some kind of pure or all-determining African descent for characteristic black American folkways. As he says: 'Afro-American culture is an African culture with a difference as signified by the catalysts of English, Dutch, French, Portuguese, or Spanish languages and cultures' (ibid.: 4). Nor is he in the business of seeking to claim that any kind of cultural homogeneity or unity existed within the African continent, or even those parts of it which mainly supplied the slave trade. Rather, he wants to suggest that a syncretic Pan-African culture, such as could not have existed on the continent itself, was created through the mixing which the Atlantic slave trade itself produced, which 'did serve to create a dynamic of exchange and revision among numerous previously isolated Black African cultures . . . a truly Pan-African culture fashioned as a colorful weave of linguistic, institutional, metaphysical and formal threads' (ibid.: 4). His particular concern is to trace a genealogy for the figure of the 'trickster' in Afro-American culture, which he sees as recurring in folktales from Brazil or Haiti to the USA, and in numerous contemporary Afro-American writings including those of Zora Neale Hurston, Ralph Ellison and Ishmael Reed. He finds the origins of this figure in the Yoruba god Esu-Elegbara, with a direct analogue in Legba among the Fon:

> these variations on Esu-Elegbara speak eloquently of an unbroken arc or metaphysical presupposition and a pattern of figuration shared through time and space among certain black cultures in West Africa, South America, the Caribbean, and the United States. (6; see also ibid.: 3–43 *passim*, as well as Okpewho 1994)[2]

It may be noted that ancient Egypt and Ethiopia play no part whatsoever in Gates's schema.

Historian V.P. Franklin argued, as against both assimilationist and revolutionary interpretations of black American political trajectories, that a consistent thread of cultural resistance centred on the idea of self-determination had always been manifest, and had always also been the theme with greatest popular appeal among African-Americans. So far, the argument would have evident appeal to cultural nationalists and Afrocentrists, but in Franklin's view this was a specifically *American* form of resistance to oppression. And he certainly did not believe that cultural values directly transposed from Africa were at the core of it. They could not be, since the African peoples involved in the Atlantic slave trade 'were diverse in experiences, language, cultural practices, and many other aspects' (Franklin 1992a: 4). Rather, the 'Afro-American cultural vision was forged in the crucible of slavery', and (here he agrees with Cornel West, James Cone and other analyst-advocates) owed more to Christianity than to any other source (Franklin 1992a: 204–5). Wilson Jeremiah Moses takes a similar stance, noting the arguments over African retentions in African-American religion, and seeing belief in these as an important politically mobilizing myth, but arguing none the less that the main roots of American black nationalism and its persistent messianic elements lie much more in North American Christian – especially New England Puritan – eschatology (Moses 1993: esp. chs 1–4). It is perhaps unsurprising, in the light of the evidence, that Afrocentric writers have generally shown little interest in African-American popular culture and folklore: even apart from the cultural elitism which so often seems to mingle uneasily with their intellectual populism, all too little of it supports their claims about unbroken and all-powerful African continuities in the New World.[3]

Africa has been a persistent, but decidedly a minor, theme in Afro-American literature. A certain rather crude statistical indication of the relative sparseness of reference to the continent in African-American poetry is that of 381 poetry and verse selections included in the monumental *Norton Anthology of African American Literature* (Gates and McKay 1997), just thirty-three include some kind of explicit reference to Africa, and of these only nine could be said to make the continent a central theme.[4] Perhaps the most famous early example is Countee Cullen's 1925 'Heritage', which sets up, then calls sharply into question, romantic images of an ancestral homeland, leaving a message not of simple affirmation but of ambivalence, doubt, distance, estrangement (Gates and McKay 1997: 1311–14). Langston Hughes's 'The Negro Speaks of Rivers' linked together ancestral 'memories' of the Euphrates, the Congo, the Nile and the Mississippi (ibid.: 1254). The passionate affirmation of historic African glories came perhaps most single-mindedly from Barbadian former missionary and anticolonial campaigner Peter Blackman:

> I smelted iron in Nubia when your generations still ploughed with
>   hardwood
> I cast in bronze in Benin when London was marshland
> I built Timbuctoo and made it a refuge for learning
> When in the choirs of Oxford unlettered monks shivered unwashed.
>   ('My Song is for All Men': Breman 1973: 113)

The experimental modernist Melvin B. Tolson, in his extraordinarily dense 'Libretto for the Republic of Liberia', laden with scholarly allusions and dozens of footnotes, similarly urged that 'Alfred the Great (had) no University of Sankore' (Gates and McKay 1337) and, amid a plethora of references to different aspects of the African past, underlined his debts to such proto-Afrocentric works as Du Bois's *The World and Africa* and the writing of J.A. Rogers. Tolson was awarded the 'Order of the Star of Africa' by the Liberian Republic for this poetic tribute, though it may be doubted how many of the West African state's dignitaries actually read and got to grips with a work which is at least as hermetic as anything by Olson, Pound or Zukofsky.

Such explicit and detailed invocations of the African past were, however, exceptional. It was with the Black Power movement of the 1960s and its literary analogue, the Black Arts movement, that something describable as a literary Afrocentrism really became evident. Examples of African and, more, of wider cultural nationalist invocations in the Afro-American poetry of the era – and to some extent subsequently – could be multiplied, but few of the major figures of black literature other than Baraka made this an important focus of their work. Afro-Caribbean writers have been somewhat more prone to feature African themes as major components in their work than have African-American ones. Here too, though, it remained a minority theme. An especially important instance, drawing far more on real knowledge of African cultures than most, is the epic poem *The Arrivants* (1973) by Barbadian Edward Brathwaite, who had taught in Ghana for seven years. Brathwaite is also the author of major scholarly works on Caribbean society, including its African-descended components. In the USA, the poet Langston Hughes was very much in the minority with his well-informed fascination for Africa, expressed both in extensive tours of the continent and in detailed knowledge of emerging African literatures (Rampersad 1988: 234–40, 292–3, 347–9, 353–6, 400–66).

In the novel, the African image was considerably less frequent still. Alice Walker has been one of the few front-rank writers to have featured African themes and settings; and although *The Color Purple* (1983) included a familiar romanticization of Africa, this was sharply undercut in the more recent *Possessing the Spirit of Joy* (1992), a harrowing story of African clitoridectomy and its consequences. Although other major African-American novelists have evoked images of Africa, they have usually done so – as in Toni Morrison's *Song of Solomon* (1977) or Paule Marshall's *Praisesong for the Widow* (1983) – through the prism of American folklore rather than with direct reference to Africa itself – or, as with Charles Johnson's *Middle Passage* (1990), the evocation has been sardonically de-romanticizing and intertextual.[5] Questions of nationalism, Africanism and identity politics have been, it seems, a far more significant presence in Afro-American literary theory and criticism than in imaginative literature itself.

Phillip Brian Harper's analysis of the 1960s Black Arts movement, the main creative precursor to current Afrocentric trends, lays stress on its rhetorics of violence and anti-white feeling (Harper 1993). He suggests, however, that these were not only largely a matter of literary posturing, but (despite the loud protestations to the contrary) directed mainly towards a white readership. The discourse was then to be 'overheard' by Afro-Americans, who were to be impressed by the fierceness with which the common foe was being addressed.[6] But the notion that the main target of hostility was a white oppressor-figure was also deceptive, since the poetry's constantly reiterated focus is on *intra*-racial divisions, with repeated attacks on those blacks who supposedly aspired to white values, sold out the revolutionary cause, and so on. By contrast, calls for black pride, unity and purposefulness were empty, constantly predicated on the apparent assumption that to make such a call is in itself a revolutionary political act: no sense emerges of what such feelings, once aroused, are to be mobilized *for*. The violent rhetoric of Black Arts poetry is designed to 'quell ... ambivalence' about identity and purpose, not in fact to call to any purposive action. It not only stresses intra-racial divisions but 'itself actually serves to produce such division' (ibid.: 254).

Related complaints have come from Afro-American critics Nathaniel Mackey (1992, 1993) and, at greatest length, Charles Johnson (1988), who also assail the extreme cultural conservatism they discern in cultural nationalist and Afrocentric rhetoric. Mackey contrasts an *artistic* practice of 'othering', which is 'to do with innovation, invention, and change' – 'other' as verb – with a *social* practice, making 'others' nouns, which is 'to do with power, exclusion and privilege' (1992: 51). The former, characteristic of African-American creativity, whether in literature or in the jazz avant-garde, has been marginalized by the 'neotraditionalism that has taken hold of late' (ibid.: 68) in Afro-American cultural circles. Black writers are once again, or still, being 'read racially, primarily at the content level, the noun level; as responding to racism, representing "the black experience"' rather than as innovators, original creators, members of 'a counter-tradition of marronage, divergence, flight, fugitive tilt' (68). He instances as models of innovatory artistic 'othering' figures like Wilson Harris (on whom he has elsewhere written perceptively: 1993 esp. chs 10–12), Aimé Césaire, Edward Kamau Brathwaite, and musicians Thelonious Monk, Sun Ra, and Henry Threadgill (Mackey's own fiction has, in an exceptional way, mingled the tropes of the literary and of the jazz experimentalists). The populism and neo-traditionalism of Afrocentric and related currents have no more room for such experimental creators than the white cultural mainstream does: in truth, they probably have less.

At the opposite pole to Harper's, Johnson's and Mackey's informed scepticism lie those currents of literary theory and criticism which celebrate organicist, traditionalist and supposedly African values. This sometimes takes expression in vehement proclamations that interest in theory or innovation is in itself Eurocentric (e.g. Joyce 1987a, b, 1991, 1994). Paul Gilroy was surely correct to allege that in such polemics there is not only an 'anti-political configuration' on all sides, but: 'There was no escape from the hermeneutic claims of ethnicity and nationality, only an argument over the precise ethnic recipe involved in being able to walk that walk and talk that talk' (Gilroy 1992: 197).

Arguably, the whole discourse about American Africanisms started in popular culture, and finds its most potent expressions there. Some of the most vigorous and complex debates over African cultural retentions in the New World have related to music, especially the blues and jazz.[7] The medium through which Afrocentrism has had the widest public resonance – apart, perhaps, from the bitter media disputes over its role in schools – is rap music. Some high-profile rap groups have aligned themselves closely with various Afrocentric currents – in very varied ways, ranging from the aggressive reverse racism of Ice Cube to Arrested Development's idyllic visions of African pastoralism. A smaller but still significant number endorsed at various times the Farrakhan movement or the less powerful rival 'Five Per Cent Nation of Islam' (Decker 1994; Gardell 1996: 293–301). Among the bigger names in rap and hip-hop culture adopting such stances have been Public Enemy, Ice Cube, Sister Souljah, Queen Latifah, Brand Nubian and Prince Akeem. Earlier, when jazz was a more popular and youth-orientated music than it is today in black America, jazz evocations of Africa may have played a somewhat similar role (see Weinstein 1992). Editors of the journal *Public Culture* suggest that 'Afrocentricity could not have existed without (Alex Haley's) *Roots*. After *Roots*, we can say that the academic version of Afrocentrism is preaching to the already converted' (Appadurai *et al.* 1994: xi). Although their short essay then proceeds to a series of highly essentialist statements in the format of 'The Black public sphere is . . .', their stress on the importance of a mass-selling piece of popular literature and its televisual adaptation, both partaking of a perhaps uneasy, but symptomatic, hybridity between history and fiction, has some force.

A continuity can be seen, for instance, in the images alluding to ancient Egypt featuring on the cover art of black American performers' album releases throughout the 1960s and 1970s. Paul Gilroy suggests that these 'proved to be an important means for communicating pan-African ideas in an inferential, populist manner'. Intriguingly, too, such images often presented ancient Egypt 'in a way that emphasized its continuity with contemporary technological and scientific achievements' (Gilroy 1993b: 241).

Gilroy's recent writing, meanwhile, has included a move towards ever sharper criticism of Afrocentric theories – not least for their unacknowledged but intense North American parochialism. Gilroy also sees in the transition from Exodus-based to Pharaonic narratives of identification and ancestry a historic watershed, symbolizing a major moral regression in some Afro-American circles:

> Blacks today appear to identify far more readily with the glamorous pharaohs than with the abject plight of those they held in bondage. This change betrays a profound transformation in the moral basis of black Atlantic

political culture. Michael Jackson's repeated question 'Do you remember the time?' (of the Nile Valley civilizations) has, for example, recently supplanted Burning Spear's dread enquiry into whether the days of slavery were being remembered at all. (Gilroy 1993a: 207)

Appropriation of the 'Exodus' narrative, with its liberatory identification with slaves escaping oppression, has now been replaced by a fixation on the supposed glories of Pharaonic Egypt – an identification, in effect, with the oppressors. Much the same, one might add, could be said of Afrocentrism's desire to redirect the focus of black American historical attention from the struggles of Africans in the New World (a story in large part of resistance and defiance, however much some radical scholars may have exaggerated and romanticized the resisting elements in slave culture) to attend instead to visions of precolonial African state-building (a history preoccupied with rulers and conquerors). There is a danger in Gilroy's alternative proposal, though, of forgetting a third participant in the 'Exodus' story, the victims of the victims, the Canaanites who were dispossessed by the fleeing Israelites: an omission with evident contemporary Middle Eastern political resonances.[8]

'It's a Black Thing: you wouldn't understand', says a T-shirt slogan one still occasionally sees on both sides of the Atlantic. That is not a view Gilroy has much time for. There is, he insists, a wide spectrum of cultural and intellectual expression which is very specifically black; but it is so not by virtue of roots and inherited codes, still less of some mystic transhistorical racial essence. The 'ethnic absolutism' and 'cultural insiderism' that sanction such claims are a constant target of his critique, especially in their latest manifestations like the resurgent rhetorics of black macho masculinity, with its associated familial, misogynist and homophobic tropes, and the US Afrocentric movement.[9]

Equally problematic are notions of unbroken 'cultures of resistance' extending from African roots across all diasporic black societies (see, for Caribbean-British evocations of such ideas, B. Bryan et al. 1985; H. Campbell 1985). In relation to similar claims made on behalf of the Rastafarian movement, Alrick Cambridge rightly points out that their:

> assumption is that the Ras Tafarian culture of resistance is a universal essence built into the nature of the collective racial group (the subject of racial domination), and expressed through the group's black identity. Further, each black personality of the collective racial group is then assumed to be a bearer of the universal black identity, an essence transmitted across historical times, geographical boundaries and generations. (Cambridge and Feuchtwang 1992: 64–5)

To see modern Afro-Caribbean, African-American or black British musical forms, culturo-religious assertions such as Rastafarianism, or features of self-presentation such as dress or hairstyle, as manifestations of a continuing, unbroken culture of resistance is not only mistaken but mystificatory. Rather, most of these should be understood as particular cultural movements, the product of very specific circumstances in the recent past, which – in expressing opposition to dominant European-derived conceptions of human capacities (especially Caribbean colonial and later British or American racist ones) – manifest oppositional or counter-assertive modes of self-identification, albeit of a largely symbolic kind.

The romanticism Gilroy and Cambridge criticize, it might hardly need stressing, has by no means always been reciprocated on the African continent itself. There exists a whole subgenre of travel literature by black Americans telling of their experiences – sometimes deeply painful and disillusioning – of estrangement and incomprehension when exposed first-hand to modern Africa; of finding themselves seen by locals – and, indeed, coming as never quite before to see themselves – as first and foremost Americans.[10] *Roots* itself was quite differently received in West Africa than in America:

> On leaving the Gambia, I was asked by a Mandinka immigration official if I intended to return and make a film like *Roots*. The Gambian government had acquired a copy of *Roots* for its mobile cinema. It had not been well received. 'We don't want to see any more dressed-up Americans pretending to be Mandinkas. It was a ridiculous pantomime,' the official told me. (Haydon 1985: 12)

The enthusiasm for *Roots* – and for roots – which helped to launch Afrocentrism might well then seem, like much that followed, to be no more than 'Afro-kitsch' when viewed from the African continent itself. Certainly that is the harsh judgement of Mali-born film historian Manthia Diawara, now teaching in New York. As Diawara sneers: 'it is nothing but a kitsch of blackness. It is nothing but an imitation of a discourse of liberation. Afrocentric academics fix blackness by reducing it to Egypt and *kente* cloths' (Diawara 1992: 289).

Naturally, though, if one rejects any notion of evidence, of seeking conscientiously for chains of historical causation, and opts instead for mystical notions of transhistorical essence, no such testimony or argument counts. One can continue to say virtually *anything* about New World Africanisms. Thus O.R. Dathorne could assert, in the *Présence Africaine* tribute volume for Cheikh Anta Diop: 'Rastafarianism is the current proof of the manner in which the invisible linkage to the African ancestor operates. Always present, yet invisible, it serves as a means of confirming social identity' (Dathorne 1989: 131).

Gloria I. Joseph's muddled tribute to the pioneer Afro-American feminist Sojourner Truth represents a particularly unreflective version of this current. She asserts that Truth's career and views can be understood only from 'within the framework of African cosmology and epistemology' (1990: 38) – a claim which would doubtless have bemused Truth herself. This framework is described in the familiar – inflated and mystical – ways: in terms of holism, communitarianism, spirituality, and the rest. Furthermore, it is suggested that the 'underlying goals' of the African world-view are 'perennial happiness and peace' (ibid.: 43, 46); an assertion which empties it of any determinate meaning or social, political or moral distinctiveness. It is a pseudo-religious, not an intellectual, claim. Equally ersatz-mystical, not to mention dispiriting in its elitism, is the hymning of Anita Hill (in an otherwise rich, stimulating collection of essays on the Hill–Clarence Thomas controversy) by Nellie Y. McKay:

> [W]hen Anita Hill stepped from her plane back onto her home soil and greeted her well-wishers, the African queens from whose loins she sprung must have beamed on each other in great approval ... in the splendour of her own radiance, she was an unconquered African-American queen. (in Morrison [ed.] 1992: 287)

As Itabari Njeri (1993: 39) caustically notes, none of those who weave imaginings about their African ancestry ever claims descent from the village thief. They are always 'sprung from the loins' (the archaic language is itself revealing) of kings and queens.

Notes

1. For a sense of the sheer range of views on all this, see, amid a vast literature, Berry and Blassingame (1982); Blassingame (1979); Creel (1988); Fox-Genovese (1988); Genovese (1981); V. Harding (1981); Holloway (1990); L. Levine (1977); Mintz and Price (1992); Mullin (1992); Raboteau (1978); Small (1987) Sobell (1987); Stuckey (1987); R. Thompson (1969, 1983); Vlach (1978). Perhaps the best and most judicious recent brief overviews are Thornton (1992) and Kolchin (1993), esp. chs 2 and 5. For the broader intellectual history of ideas about Africa, I have found the most stimulating recent research to be that of V.Y. Mudimbe (1988, 1991, 1994).

2. Once again, this would be a much stronger case in relation to Haiti, to some other parts of the Caribbean, and to Brazil than to the USA. In the former, clear evidences of African-derived religious systems have been traced by many scholars (Legba is, for instance, one of many Yoruba and Fon gods to be found in the Haitian *voudou* pantheon), whilst for the former they are far more tenuous.

3. One of the very few exceptions, Tolagbe Ogunleye, tries to get around the problem by claiming that those (especially whites) who have studied Afro-American folklore have, in conspiratorial fashion, played up its 'obscene' elements, which 'are not representative of the African American worldview nor our national culture', and ignored the morally elevating African ones (1997: 440).

4. This total includes the song lyrics and other vernacular pieces included in the *Anthology*, but not the verse sections intertwined into Jean Toomer's novel *Cane*, reprinted in full there. Naturally there are borderline cases, notably invocations of Africa or Ethiopia as metaphor for the African-American condition, like Frances W. Harper's 'Ethiopia' (Gates and McKay 1997: 412). These I have counted as 'African' poems: thus my rough totals overstate, if anything, the presence of African themes in the tradition.

5. Jane Campbell (1986) has interesting reflections on the mythic uses of history in Afro-American fiction; Berghahn (1977) is an earlier survey of images of Africa in this literature up to the 1960s.

6. Similarly – and equally plausibly – O.R. Dathorne (1994: 111–12) has argued that the militant rhetoric of a Malcolm X or a Louis Farrakhan is really addressed mainly to whites rather than to its ostensible black audience.

7. See, for example, Calt (1994); Charters (1981); Finn (1986); Floyd (1995); Lipsitz (1994); P. Oliver (1970); Small (1987); Toop (1984).

8. See Edward Said's 'Canaanite Reading' of Michael Walzer in Said and Hitchens (1988).

9. Like the work of Kwame Appiah, that of Paul Gilroy has drawn fierce attack from Afrocentrists, many of whom seem to regard criticism by fellow black writers as especially blameworthy, akin to racial treachery. Two British-based Afrocentrists have assailed Gilroy's *Black Atlantic* as the work of an 'Africophobist ... a pathetic effort by a feeble-minded, irremediably traumatised and deculturalised numskull to pillorise [sic] the great heritage of the African humanity' (Ekwe-Ekwe and Nzegwu 1994: 19–20). They express elaborate doubt over whether Gilroy, given his views, can really be of African descent (ibid.: 19), and hint heavily that his work is part of a Jewish conspiracy (22).

10. Richard Wright's *Black Power* (1954) is a pioneering instance; Eddy Harris's *Native Stranger* (1992) a major recent example.

Part Two
Visions of History

Hamites, Semites and Statue-Stealers

A great deal of the African-American and 'black Atlantic' polemic we have described was motivated by reaction not only against general vilification of Africans, but more specifically against what became known as the 'Hamitic hypothesis', which gained widespread assent among European writers in the later nineteenth century and the first decades of the twentieth. Light-skinned peoples of ancient Egyptian, Indo-European or even 'Aryan' origin, it was believed, had spread across Africa, where they generally formed a small elite ruling over mentally and physically inferior subject races. All significant cultural achievements could be attributed to their influence. But as they interbred with their subjects, the racial type deteriorated and the civilizations they had founded declined. Hence the degeneration widely believed to have overtaken certain West African regions; as in Benin and Yorubaland, where the artistic achievements of the past could not be denied, but seemed hard to square with supposed present 'savagery' unless racial degeneration was posited (Coombes 1994; Fagg *et al.* 1982; Ben-Amos 1980). Ancient Egypt itself was sometimes also seen as having succumbed to this process of degeneration.

The view that all African achievement was the product of outside 'Hamitic' influence was widely propagated by the noted explorer, colonial official and author Sir Harry Johnston, and reformulated in more scholarly terms and with pronounced Egyptocentric bias by the romantic anthropologist Grafton Elliot Smith;[1] but its most influential exponent was the British ethnographer Charles G. Seligman. His *Races of Africa*, which continued to be reprinted and treated in many circles as authoritative as late as 1966, stated bluntly: 'The civilizations of Africa are the civilizations of the Hamites' (Seligman 1930: 61). Elliot Smith thought that 'the smallest infusion of Negro blood immediately manifests itself in a dulling of initiative and the "drag" on the further development of the arts of civilization' (quoted in Trigger 1994: 331).

The Hamitic hypothesis was very widely accepted, even unquestioned, for a long time: see, for instance, the surveys of its influence in Shaw (1978), and many contributions to Robertshaw (1990). Seligman himself – or 'Sligs', as he was apparently known to his many friends – commanded massive respect and prestige among colonial-era British and other anthropologists, as the star-studded contributors' list to his *Festschrift* underlined (Evans-Pritchard *et al.* 1934). Virtually every major figure in the field paid obeisance to his influence: from Bronislaw Malinowski to Melville Herskovits, Louis Leakey to Marcel Mauss, Audrey Richards to George Pitt-Rivers. 'Sligs' was, as Saul Dubow remarks, 'a key intellectual broker in the world of inter-war British anthropology' (1995: 85–6).

In the world of French-speaking African studies, similar views were just as widely held; thus the pioneer archaeologist Maurice Delafosse, among many others, went in search of ancient Egyptian and other 'white' cultural influences in the Ivory Coast, and of course found them in abundance. Such ideas were still powerful in France in the 1950s, with the synthesizing works of D.P. de Pedrals – which were to have a major impact on Cheikh Anta Diop and, through him, on modern Afrocentrism. For some reason, fantasies of Jewish origin for various African civilizations seem to have been especially popular among French colonial historians (Holl 1990: 300). German writers, too, made their contribution, which was in theoretical terms perhaps the most influential of all, beginning with Friedrich Ratzel in the 1880s and culminating in the massive, highly idiosyncratic efforts of Leo Frobenius (e.g. 1913, 1933). Frobenius, whose theories about outside influences on African cultures included the notion that some of these (like the artworks of the Yoruba) came from Plato's 'Atlantis' and were thus essentially Greek, while many others were the gift of the Hamites (see his late, synthesizing *magnum opus*, 1933 *passim*), and whose 'fieldwork' methods included outright theft of art treasures from Ife in Nigeria, was also a major influence on Diop and has, astonishingly, continued to inspire and be praised by American Afrocentrists.[2]

In a younger generation, even Basil Davidson, among the most passionately pro-African and antiracist of all European writers on Africa, put forward a version of the Hamitic hypothesis in his early book *Old Africa Rediscovered* (Davidson 1959: 29–31) – at least to the point of believing that there was an identifiable racial group in Africa called Hamites; though he took pains to repudiate the racist assumptions usually developed from that belief. And a substantial number of African and other black writers, as we shall see, adopted versions of the Hamitic idea – at least after it had been decoupled from the originally associated belief in a biblical 'curse of Noah' legitimating slavery. Subsequently, the idea of successive waves of Hamitic invaders and culture-carriers has been entirely abandoned by serious scholars.[3] Perhaps its last gasp was in John R. Baker's massive, anachronistic and frankly racist 1974 book *Race*, where the elderly anthropologist Baker still cast around desperately for scraps of outdated 'evidence' showing that supposed African cultural achievements actually came from almost anyone other than 'Negroes' (Baker 1974: esp. 401–17). Only among radical Afrocentrists has a revised version of the myth gained new life today; though some of them also still devote considerable energy to assailing the older Eurocentric version, despite its moribund state (e.g. Reynolds-Marniche 1994).

The Hamitic hypothesis was an especially clear-cut instance of diffusionist beliefs among archaeologists and ancient historians. These were the conventional wisdom of the late nineteenth and early twentieth centuries. As we have noted, they could be appropriated for racist and colonialist ends, and in relation to Africa they usually were; but in other contexts they could be pressed into service by radicals. For the great Marxist archaeologist V. Gordon Childe, diffusionism was morally appealing as a counter to extreme nationalist claims, especially those of interwar German historians, about the purity and indigeneity of particular cultures (cf. Trigger 1989: 254–5). In the postwar world, however, the 'New Archaeology' largely dispensed with diffusionism, stressing instead the overwhelming influence of particular environments on historical development, including the recognition that similar environmental pressures could produce similar cultural or technological adaptations in widely separate places, without contact between them (Trigger 1989 is an admirable summary of the shifting paradigms). Afrocentrism's extreme diffusionism makes it something of an oddity or anachronism in current historiography; as several critics of Martin Bernal, for instance, have pointed out, his reliance on a strong diffusionist model imparts a strangely nineteenth-century air to his work (Baines 1991a; J. Hall 1990).

There were two especially important sites of contestation around claims that any civilization in Africa must have come from outside: the highly developed state systems of West Africa, with their widely admired artworks; and the monumental stone structures of southern Africa, especially Great Zimbabwe. Many Europeans simply refused to believe that the cultural achievements they encountered in both regions could possibly be the work of black Africans.

Early European 'discoverers' of Great Zimbabwe proposed a bewildering variety of external origins for the builders of these massive, eerily impressive structures. The two favourite theories, proposed together or separately, were that they had been Phoenician, and that the monuments were connected with biblical tales of King Solomon's goldmines and the Queen of Sheba. The story had much earlier origins, appearing in Portuguese travellers' tales (based apparently on Swahili reports, not direct observation of the sites) in the sixteenth century (Garlake 1973: 51–5). It continued to haunt British imaginations: it and associated Hamitic themes recur throughout Henry Rider Haggard's numerous and formulaic African novels, in which almost any admirable or intelligent black person – and especially each of Haggard's various African *femmes fatales* – is routinely insisted to be light-skinned and/or of 'non-negroid' features.

The first excavations and chronicling of Great Zimbabwe were carried out by J. Theodore Bent in 1891. As Garlake comments:

> He approached the problem of Great Zimbabwe firmly believing, like almost everyone else, that its origins must lie with a civilized and ancient people, who must therefore necessarily have come from outside Africa. (1973: 66)

But the objects he uncovered – wrecking large parts of the site in the process, and thus making the job of later archaeologists extremely difficult – suggested to him parallels from as far apart as Assyria, Cyprus, Egypt, Malta and Arabia. This mishmash of tenuous comparisons should, as later writers have pointed out, have suggested to Bent that there was something wrong with the whole approach, and that perhaps the unthinkable should be thought: that the culture responsible for the buildings was indigenous. Naturally, the notion did not strike him. Nor did such ideas trouble Richard Nicklin Hall, whose custodianship, writing and amateurish excavations in the 1900s further damaged the site and mythologized its history (ibid.: 71–5).

Inevitably, the later colonial regime and the white-minority state of 1965–80 sustained and promulgated belief that white, possibly Semitic, certainly non-African incomers must have created the great stone structures and their associated artworks. This became an important element in white settler ideology, while African nationalist opposition to it was capped by their choosing to name their own state-in-waiting after the ruins (see Garlake 1982; Frederikse 1983: 9–15). The latter's belief that Great Zimbabwe's creators must be indigenous, their own direct ancestors, was of course also highly ideological rather than scholarly. But the overwhelming weight of archaeological evidence, as more careful and less racist researchers than Bent or Hall began working on it, supported their claim. Even in the first years of this century – contrary to careless assumptions that scholarship in Edwardian Britain was monolithically aligned with the racist Hamitic hypothesis – the leading lights of archaeology and ethnography 'emphasized the complete lack of any alien influence at Great Zimbabwe'. They included Sir Arthur Evans, Sir Hercules Read, Sir John Myres and David Hogarth (Garlake 1973: 79). The genuine scholars who worked on the ruins had no doubt that the builders were indigenous. David Randall MacIver, following his visit in 1905, suggested a medieval date and the clear affinities of the structures' building techniques to known Shona practices. More decisively, in 1929 Gertrude Caton Thompson, leading a pioneeringly all-female scientific team, demonstrated the indigeneity of the builders (Caton Thompson 1931). As Martin Hall (1995) has recently emphasized, however, even these champions of the view that Great Zimbabwe was a distinctively African achievement were not free of conventional negative stereotypes about African mentalities, with Caton Thompson claiming that the buildings indicated 'pre-logical' and even 'childish' traits. Conversely, a few African nationalists appropriated the idea of alien builders for their own purposes: in 1915 Matthew Zwimba argued that the structures showed that Europeans had once occupied the area but had been driven out by the locals. The experience, he implied, could and should be repeated (Ranger 1970: 22).

The edifices, it transpired, were far more recent than had been assumed: they were built in the thirteenth and fourteenth centuries (most probably mainly in the 1320s), almost two millennia after any putative Phoenician incursion. The people who built and inhabited them were without serious doubt indigenous, directly connected to the slightly later kingdom of Mwene Mutapa, or Munhumutapa, for which we have substantial documentary evidence (Connah 1987: 183–213; Garlake 1973: 174–8; Beach 1980; Mudenge 1988). The site was both a major religious centre and the heart of an extensive system of trade: clear evidence of trade links to India and China has been uncovered. But it was not unique, except in its size and complexity; dozens of other significant stone structures existed in the region, if none so dramatic as this. Regional political and trading shifts led to its abandonment, probably in the sixteenth or fifteenth century. The civilizational succession to which Great Zimbabwe belonged, however, was disrupted, and its traditions were largely lost, only in the 1830s.[4]

But if local nationalist political thought concurred with expert opinion on the indigenous origins of the culture Great Zimbabwe symbolizes, Pan-African nationalist assertion elsewhere pressed a quite different case. For Cheikh Anta Diop, in line with his general theories (see below, pp. 163–92), its inspiration simply had to be Egyptian. He pointed vaguely to the famous carved soapstone birds of Zimbabwe, claiming that they were Egyptian falcons, and to the image of the crocodile also found in both Egyptian and Zimbabwean sculpture, and suggested that the area 'may well be an extension of the land of the Macrobian Ethiopians mentioned by Herodotus'. He even linked the suffix 'we' in Zimbabwe and similar names to Egyptian plural 'w' endings (Diop 1974a: 157, 172–3, 183). Meanwhile, fanciful theories premised on the belief that the Great Zimbabwe complex must be of at least mainly non-African origin have not disappeared, despite the near-universal professional consensus on its indigeneity. The South African architect and amateur archaeologist Wilfrid Mallows could still be found arguing, in 1984, that its purpose had been as a prison and holding centre for the Arab slave trade, designed by non-African traders, with the local role in its construction being only that of manual labour and, later, clumsy imitation of Arab or Indian masters (Mallows 1984).

The West African case was even more complex, as historian Philip Zachernuk has recently indicated. Late-nineteenth- and early-twentieth-century Nigerian writers, thinking about their past, exhibited a range of interacting influences which cannot be reduced to the simple polarities of nationalist versus colonialist or assimilationist viewpoints. Some adopted the Hamitic hypothesis to their own ends. And some, like various Afro-American writers of the nineteenth and early twentieth centuries, even accepted the view that their recent ancestors had 'degenerated' from the higher civilizational point reached by their Egyptian or other migratory forebears (Zachernuk 1994: 431–7; see also Atanda 1980: esp. 70–73).

While some uses of the myth of external origins were anticolonialist, and proclaimed a common origin for all Nigerian, or all West African, peoples and cultures as a rhetorical strategy for political unity, others were highly particularist. One of the most popular suggestions was that the Yoruba of Western Nigeria originated from Egypt – or, at least, that major features of their religion and culture did so. This was argued by the priest and pamphleteer J. Olumide Lucas in the 1940s, and he held that it explained the unusually progressive and intelligent character he attributed to his people. Lucas's work on this idiosyncratic but evidently popular theme gained him a Doctorate of Divinity from Durham University in 1942 (Zachernuk 1994: 447).[5] No such tradition, it may be noted, seems earlier to have featured among the Yoruba themselves – though some of them, at least after the advent of Islam in Yorubaland, fancied Meccan origin; and their earliest and most important published historian, Samuel Johnson, speculated that they might have migrated from Nubia, via the Arabian peninsula, to their present homes (Johnson 1921: 3–7).[6] Johnson made no suggestion that Yoruba language or religion derived from either Upper Egypt or, indeed, Arabia. Heroically, the Afro-American amateur historian Don Luke later sought to show that Yoruba religion, in its turn, must have shaped that of the Vikings (Luke 1985: 233–5).

Increasingly in the late colonial years, and evidently reflecting the growth of regional-ethnic antagonisms in Nigeria, amateur local historians 'often adopted the Hamitic Hypothesis tradition in the search for historical primacy and cultural superiority over other Nigerian groups' (Zachernuk 1994: 451). S.O. Biobaku claimed in 1955 that the Yoruba came from Meroë, the ancient kingdom of the Sudan. Emmanuel Ughulu claimed Jewish origin for the small Esan tribe. Frederick Numa believed the Urhobo were of Egyptian descent; and so on (ibid.: 450–52). Race in the broader sense – black versus white – seemed to have little place in these polemics. Egyptian connections 'could be employed without having to worry whether the Egyptians were black or white; it was the claim to a distinguished past which mattered' (452). But as the colonial order's cultural preconceptions declined in salience during the post-independence years, appropriations of the Hamitic syndrome dwindled away too.

White supremacist versions of the Hamitic myth maintained their influence longest, as one might expect, in South Africa. Using and misusing evidence first from physical anthropology and then from linguistics, some South African scholars retained faith in the Hamites right through the apartheid era, and no doubt beyond (Dubow 1995: 20–119: esp. 74–95). Unfortunately, the world has probably not heard the last of this discredited idea, whether from white Africans or black Americans.

Notes

1. Smith's career exemplifies the interrelationship between arguments over humanity's biological origins, and those over the origin of civilization: he was both a major participant in controversy about the Neanderthals and the Piltdown Man scandal, and an influential proponent of theories on the Egyptian roots of all world cultures.

2. On Frobenius's personality, career, views and influence, see Jahn (1974); Marchand (1997) – neither of which sufficiently notes the sheer eccentricity of many of his ideas.

3. For overviews of current thinking on these issues, see Connah (1987); R. Oliver (1991); Phillipson (1993); Shaw et al. (1993).

4. It had been assumed that abandonment resulted from the *mfecane*, the major population shifts and disruptions of that era; though if more recent arguments that the *mfecane*'s destructiveness has been exaggerated are correct, this view may require revision. Mudenge (1988) suggests that a combination of internal dynastic rivalries and Portuguese incursions caused the decline of the Munhumutapa kingdom.

5. Cheikh Anta Diop several times drew on and expressed agreement with Lucas's theories, which so well corresponded with his own. See Diop (1974a: 184–6, 1987: 216–17). On the Yoruba historiographical context, see Falola (ed.) (1991).

6. Atanda (1980) notes that Muhammad Bello, Sultan of Sokoto, had recorded similar beliefs in the early nineteenth century. Indeed, this appears to reflect a more general set of West African ideas about Meccan origins, which may have been invented – or, less probably, merely revived or elaborated – with the rapid nineteenth-century spread of Islam in the region.

The Lure of Egypt

Ancient Egypt's fascination for modern humanity has remained persistent, ever-recurring.[1] Obsession with Egyptian mysteries, including notably successive, imaginative theories on the 'meaning' of the Pyramids, has been a staple of occult and latterly of New Age thought. This bizarre tradition was founded in 1859 by John Taylor, but reached its canonical, subsequently ever-renewed expression in Charles Piazzi Smyth's vast mid-Victorian labours to demonstrate that the Pyramids were the product of direct divine guidance, storehouses of multifaceted mathematical, scientific and spiritual (he believed, specifically Christian) knowledge.[2] Piazzi Smyth also proposed that the internal passages of the Great Pyramid represented, in symbolic form, the entire progress of human civilization (France 1991: 185): an idea which harked back to the Renaissance 'art of memory', and was expressed in the architectural symbolism central to Masonic rites – as we have seen, these rites have formed an important link between the mystic Egyptianism of earlier centuries and the Afrocentrism of today.

Occultist and other far-fetched theories about ancient Egyptian mysteries, secrets of the Pyramids, and so on, seem to have a never-ending capacity to renew themselves: bestselling recent examples include Robert Bauval and Adrian Gilbert's *The Orion Mystery* (1994) and Graham Hancock's *Fingerprints of the Gods* (1995). Ancient Egypt is, apparently, a favourite location for the past lives of believers in reincarnation (Lowenthal 1985: 18). In the genre fiction of horror, fantasy and the occult, from Thomas Moore (*The Epicurean*) and Edgar Allan Poe ('Some Words with a Mummy') through Bram Stoker (*The Jewel of Seven Stars*), Théophile Gautier ('The Foot of the Mummy', 'One of Cleopatra's Nights'), Arthur Conan Doyle ('Lot No. 249'), Shane Leslie ('As in a Glass Dimly'), and H.P. Lovecraft ('Imprisoned with the Pharaohs') to Anne Rice in the present, Egypt has been among the most favoured of all themes. Novelists outside those genres, too, have turned their hands to the world of the Pharaohs and seen it as a repository of lost wisdom, if rarely with very distinguished results – from the Abbé Terrasson's 1731 *Sethos*, which in a sense started the whole thing,[3] to Norman Mailer's incredibly turgid *Ancient Evenings* (1983) or adventure writer Wilbur Smith's recent romances based around the search for ancient

Egyptian secrets, *River God* (1993) and *The Seventh Scroll* (1995). Henry Rider Haggard varied his South African tales with several featuring ancient Egyptian settings, like *The World's Desire, Moon of Israel, Morning Star, The Ancient Allan,* and *Cleopatra*; while the better-known (and better) *She* and *Ayesha* have strong Egyptian occult themes. Less numerous but hardly less central to the modern Western imagination have been operatic evocations, from Mozart's Masonic *Magic Flute* to Verdi's *Aïda* and Philip Glass's *Akhnaten.* In the cinema, major peaks have included *The Mummy* (1932), Cecil B. deMille's *Cleopatra* (1934), Howard Hawks's extravagant epic *Land of the Pharaohs* (1955), and Steven Spielberg's *Raiders of the Lost Ark* (1981). In art and design, Egyptian influences and pastiches have recurred time and again (as traced in Curl 1994).

Christopher Hill notes how '[t]he idea that there was a secret traditional wisdom, Egyptian or Hermetic' (1972: 93) runs as an often subterranean but always important stream through English thought, often linked to politico-religious radicalism among those who 'wanted to democratize these mysteries; to abolish mumbo-jumbo men, whether priests, lawyers, or scholars' (ibid.: 93; see also 196–200). E.P. Thompson emphasizes:

> In London in the 1780s – and, indeed, in Western Europe very generally – there was something like an explosion of anti-rationalism, taking the forms of illuminism, masonic rituals, animal magnetism, millenarian speculation, astrology (and even a small revival in alchemy), and of mystic and Swedenborgian circles. (Thompson 1993: xiv–xv)

Much the same could be said of the 1980s and 1990s, and in many ways Afrocentrism has been a part of that new explosion. In the earlier manifestation, however, *anti*-Egyptianism was an important thread among radicals and believers in the democratization of mystic knowledge – a current which Martin Bernal, among others, completely ignores. Pharaonic Egypt was identified, by William Blake and Henry Fuseli (following earlier radicals like William Warburton, Thomas Blackwell, and above all the republican John Toland), as well as by Constantin Volney in France, as the scene of knowledge's appropriation by a priestly elite. The priests used their monopolistic hold on the mysteries to enthral and delude the masses; and such practices had passed via Moses into the Judaeo-Christian world (Mee 1992: 126–9, 157–9, 195–7). Far more recently, Afro-American novelist Ishmael Reed's wonderfully subversive *Mumbo Jumbo* (1972) revives similar themes.

But radicals continued to look for positive messages from ancient Egypt too. For instance, Joel Barlow's revolutionary epic poem *The Conspiracy of Kings* (1792), drew on Volney to propose a new universal 'religion' of humanity based on Osirian myths (Mulford 1987); while the 'religion' of reason' with which the French revolutionaries temporarily dethroned Catholicism included numerous Egyptian elements among its better-known Greek and Roman borrowings (Notre Dame cathedral became, for a time, the Temple of Isis[4]). This suggests once more that enthusiasms for ancient

Greece and for Egypt were by no means such historically antagonistic traits as Martin Bernal and other Afrocentrists seem to assume.

Blackwell and Warburton also, it may be noted, accepted the tradition recently rediscovered and made much of by Afrocentrists: that Pythagoras, Socrates and Plato had received their wisdom from Egypt – in other words, they fully believed in what Bernal calls the 'Ancient Model' (Mee 1992: 128–9), even though Bernal places Blackwell and Warburton among the 'Romantic Philhellenes' supposedly responsible for belittling Egypt (1987: 196–7, 208, 210). Enthusiasm for ancient Egypt was, however, widespread among central Enlightenment figures too. The young Edward Gibbon's first projected book (which he later burned) was on the Pharaoh Sesostris (Porter 1988: 45). He later abandoned the belief that it might be possible to link Egyptian, Greek and Jewish histories together – a renunciation which he ascribed to maturer judgement, but which Bernal seems to see as a kind of regression typical of the age (Bernal 1987: 185) or even, obscurely, as a surrender to racism (Bernal 1991: 203, 273).

The particular appeal of ancient Egypt to Afro-Americans hungry for evidence of black historical achievement is catered to by the Association for the Study of Classical African Civilizations (ASCAC). This body, which claimed over 800 members in 1987, sponsors conferences and Nile valley study tours. ASCAC's founders and leaders were among the most extreme Afrocentrists on the US intellectual scene: Karenga, Ben-Jochannen, Jacob Carruthers, John Henrik Clarke, Asa Hilliard and Leonard Jeffries – the last serving as the body's Secretary. Its 1987 meeting, held at Aswan in Upper Egypt, was said by the organizers to attract 700 participants, most of whom also signed up for a fifteen-day trip around Pharaonic sites, guided by Ben-Jochannen and others. The conference title clearly indicated its intentions of racial feel-goodism rather than scholarship: it was 'Back to the Blackland', reported *West Africa* magazine (Anon. 1987). More recently a younger US Afrocentrist, Anthony Browder, who runs the 'Institute of Karmic Guidance, Inc.' in Washington DC, has conducted annual Egyptian study tours. In 1991, to popularize these, he published *My First Trip to Africa*, 'co-authored' with and narrated in the words of his seven-year-old daughter Atlantis (Browder 1991).

Meanwhile, what do serious scholars say on these controversial questions of early African and Egyptian history?

What is perhaps most remarkable is how long images of a historyless – or, at least, undeveloping – Africa persisted and, conversely, how the more popularly orientated historians of the continent felt that they had to hammer home time after time the point that theirs was a real subject. Such insistences, moreover, were heavily overdetermined by the language of race: by a notion that in establishing that there was indeed an African history, one was making a significant point in defence of the human dignity of African and African-descended peoples. To speak of the African past at all – it appeared still to be felt long after the message should have become otiose – was to intervene in antiracist struggles. Thus Basil Davidson's 1984 television series 'Africa', a fine work of historical popularization, felt it necessary to emphasize the point time and again: an overinsistence which could in some eyes smack of apologetics. 'Africa once had its own cities, its own civilizations,' urged Davidson (who had already been driving home this message in his books for over thirty years) in Episode Two.

It seemed at least as necessary to underline the connections between ancient Egypt and the rest of Africa, to insist on the 'continuous community of peoples extending right across the Sahara' (Davidson in Episode One). Or, more dramatically, to ask: 'What had they (the Pharaohs) to do with Africa? How could this grand hierarchy of gods and spirits have anything in common with the superstitious mumblings of the black peoples of inner Africa?' The camera then cuts to the Cairo Museum and to the 'negroid' features of the young King Tutankhamun – and then to Cheikh Anta Diop. Here, though, Davidson (often seen as the white historian most sympathetic to 'Afrocentric' viewpoints) feels that it is important to establish a critical distance from the Senegalese writer's ideas on the blackness of ancient Egypt. He describes Diop as 'one of the most outspoken' African historians on such matters. Diop, centre screen, points to the cover of his own book *Parenté génétique de l'égyptien pharaonique*: a painting showing Egyptians as 'pure' blacks. But, says Basil Davidson, this is the *only* Egyptian image he knows which makes that point so unequivocally.[5] Ancient Egyptians mostly depicted themselves as 'reddish-pink', though some were evidently black, or Nubian. The programme – which, one suspects, had featured Diop and his views mainly as a pious political gesture – thus simultaneously affirmed continuities between Egypt and Sub-Saharan Africa on cultural levels, and cast doubt on them in terms of 'racial' identity.

Such nervousness, such overinsistence on African historicity, even marked – indeed, pervaded – a more apparently scholarly project: the *UNESCO General History of Africa*, whose multiple volumes began appearing in 1981. The very first sentence of the first volume's 'General Introduction' stated simply: 'Africa has a history' (Ki-Zerbo 1981: 1). Is it even imaginable that a book about any other part of the world could feel compelled to begin with such a statement, so plaintive or truculent in its nakedness?

In the preface to that first UNESCO volume, the organization's Director-General, Amadou-Mahtar M'Bow, felt more exercised about the fault-lines *within* the continent. He insisted on Africa as a single entity, and on past imperialist falsifications designed to obscure this:

emphasis was laid on everything likely to lend credence to the idea that a split had existed, from time immemorial, between a 'white Africa' and a 'black Africa'. . . . Hermetic frontiers were drawn between the civilizations of Ancient Egypt and Nubia and those of the peoples south of the Sahara. (Ki-Zerbo 1981: xvii)

Ancient Egypt and its legacies are at the heart of these anxieties, as they are at the core of the Afrocentric view of the world. We shall be seeing in various contexts what ideological uses have been made of the Pharaonic state; but it is necessary to offer a brief and inevitably quite inadequate summary of the real condition of historical knowledge about Egypt and its external relations.

The society's dominant features were its reliance on the annual Nile floods, its powerful divine kingship, and its highly unified, apparently homogeneous character. Ancient Egypt was evidently the most sophisticated, as well as the largest, political state to have been created in the world up to that time, and remained probably the largest *unitary* state throughout its 3,000-year existence. An extremely elaborate structure of government, including a huge state sector of employment and a kind of welfare system, came into existence, and was underpinned by an equally elaborate ideology of state power (Kemp 1989; Jansen 1978; Kitchen 1982 offer varying views on Egyptian state ideology). How we judge this may well depend on our attitudes to state power in general. It was, however, essentially – if not solely – a *legitimating* ideology, inseparable from religious beliefs about the Pharaoh: there is no sign in Egyptian writings of elements of a critical or analytical view of politics, such as was to be pioneered by Plato and Aristotle – unless we believe that the latter drew heavily on unknown Egyptian sources; a view held by many Afrocentrists but one for which there is no clear evidence. There is no sign, either, that anyone even envisaged alternatives to the king's power. As Michael Mann says:

> All politics, all power, even all morality apparently resided with him. The crucial term *Macat* (or Ma'at), denoting all the qualities of effective government, was the nearest the Egyptians came to a general conception of 'the good'. (1986: 110)

It was a highly stratified society, albeit one which apparently had few and weak 'vertical' divisions: there is almost no evidence of segmentation by clan, tribe or region among the population. Slavery in the full sense seems not to have been widespread, though there may have been more of it in the New Kingdom than earlier, and certainly, as in almost all pre-modern societies, war captives were enslaved. However, the large numbers of people constrained to labour on the vast state building projects – temples, tombs, pyramids, fortresses, and so on – must have existed in a slave- or serf-like position, although there is no evidence that this status was necessarily permanent or inherited, and they were paid 'wages' in food and other commodities (Egypt did not have a monetary system).

The real powers of the Pharaoh must none the less have been less extensive than official ideology proclaimed – the nature of the sources poses great interpretive problems here, because the documents and inscriptions are almost all statements of how successive rulers *wanted* their might and achievements to be seen. Certainly there were long periods when regional power figures, the nomarchs, thwarted, evaded or challenged the authority of the Pharaoh.

In briefest summary, one might categorize the major Egyptian achievements which influenced the rest of the world as follows:

Pharaonic Egypt gave to the world the idea of the individual human soul,
conceived of as surviving beyond death, and as being judged according to
the good and ill deeds of the individual. Thus the idea that there exists a
system of cosmic justice, of rewards and punishments, can be thought of as ?
an Egyptian invention: it opened the way to universalist moral principles far
more clearly than, say, ancient Jewish or Greek religious beliefs can be said
to have done. It may well be, too, that monotheism was an Egyptian
invention – albeit one repudiated by Egyptian society itself – briefly
instituted by the 18th Dynasty Pharaoh Akhnaten. What kind of influence,
if any, Akhnaten's experiment had on the later evolution of Judaic monotheism remains highly controversial.

Often muddled and extravagant claims have been made by Afrocentric
historians about the alleged Egyptian origins of various religious doctrines.
Yosef Ben-Jochannen claims in one place that the Judaeo-Christian Ten
Commandments are taken from the *Osirian Drama* (Addai-Sebo and Wong
1988: 115), and in another that they come from the 'Negative Confessions'
found in the tomb of Ramses VI (ibid.: 130). Maulana Karenga says they
derive from the 125th chapter of the *Book of Coming Forth by Day* (ibid.: 23).
In fact, chapter or spell 125 is the same as what was once oddly – or
oxymoronically – called the Negative Confessions, better titled 'The Declaration of Innocence' (Faulkner 1985: 29–34), and it could also loosely be
called part of an 'Osirian drama'. Whatever it is entitled, the connection
with the later Mosaic Commandments is tenuous: the Declaration lists
numerous sins which the speaking soul has not committed in life, and a very
few of these sins overlap with those forbidden to Moses. That is the whole
extent of the resemblance. More generally, the inflated claims made by
Ben-Jochannen and other Afrocentrists for the preternatural wisdom and
spiritual greatness of the *Book of Coming Forth by Day* seem extremely far-
fetched. The 'book' contains much that is incomprehensible to the modern
reader, and much that is absurd (though whether there is more of either
than there is in the sacred texts of modern world religions is a moot point).
There is a 'Spell for preventing a man from going upside down and from
eating faeces' (Faulkner 1985: 185–8) as well as another against eating
faeces and drinking urine (ibid.: 65); one for 'eating bread, drinking beer,
purifying the hinder-parts, and being alive in Heliopolis' (80); several for
repelling snakes, and one for repelling a beetle (58, 60), and so on, and
on.[6] Yet more implausibly, the *Book of Coming Forth by Day* has been claimed
as the inspiration or basis for Aristotle's treatise *On the Soul*, though in fact
there is no resemblance beyond the basic subject matter: both works deal
with the idea of the soul, but one is an abstract philosophical treatise, the
other a set of spells for the afterlife (see Lefkowitz 1996a: 8, 138–9).

In terms of philosophical thought, our assessment of Egyptian achievement must again be heavily shaped by whether we accept or reject
speculative claims that much Greek philosophy was – in the words of

African-American publicist George James – 'stolen Egyptian philosophy'. In the absence of definite evidence for such beliefs – some of which are unprovable, some plausible, some evidently erroneous (for instance, James claims (1954/92: 125–30) that Aristotle plundered the great library of Alexandria to steal the ideas wrongly identified as his, whereas in fact the library was founded only after his death) – we can judge only by the surviving Egyptian texts themselves. These offer elements of an extremely complex and subtle system of religious belief, some of which might properly be called philosophical, especially if the stories they tell are to be interpreted as symbolic or allegorical.[7] A strong case can indeed be made – as it is by Jan Assmann – for seeing this system of belief as evolving, under the New Kingdom, into a full-fledged and dynamic theology, more complex than early Judaic monotheism (the very simplicity of the latter being a means by which the ancient Hebrews marked themselves out as different from the Egyptians) and pioneering the concept of the historicity of human existence (Assmann 1995: 209, 1996).

Even this view, however, does not make Egyptian religious thought 'philosophical'. Kwame Appiah's judgement is that it cannot be seen as more than a systematized but uncritical folk philosophy, a set of beliefs lacking in any procedures for interrogating their own status (1992: 162). In that light, it is *not* philosophy in the modern sense, and has little of value to tell us today. This seems accurate, though we should also bear in mind Barry Kemp's argument that Egyptian religion:

> grew up in a world where, in the absence of serious rivals, no one felt the need to develop a more cogent and complete form of communication. Persuasion was never necessary. . . . Although some Greek visitors attempted to record their impressions of aspects of Egyptian religion, Egyptian priests failed to develop in time a sufficient interest in explaining their beliefs in cogent form to outsiders, a process which would, in itself, have led to significant internal modifications. Egyptian thought cannot, therefore, be recreated as a living intellectual system. (Kemp 1989: 2)

If this is so, and if it contrasts – as it so evidently does – with all the ways in which early Greek philosophy *has* remained a living system to subsequent ages, it does not necessarily bespeak an inherent superiority of Greek over Egyptian thought, simply different historical circumstances. Or so Kemp believes: I am not so sure. Because Greek thinkers, unlike Egyptian ones, *did* seek to communicate their beliefs to outsiders, to persuade, to offer reasons for particular beliefs, there seem to me to be good grounds for holding Greek thought to be, if not necessarily intrinsically superior, then certainly superior in usefulness for *us*. Here lies a large part of the explanation for the Afrocentrists' persistent failure to follow up their proclamations of the importance of Egyptian philosophy with any specific arguments about *which* Egyptian beliefs should be important to us, and why. Moreover, one crucial element in early Greek thought appears to be entirely missing from that of Egypt: a philosophy of nature such as Greeks from Heraclitus onwards developed, which enabled the eventual emergence of scientific inquiry.

Did the Egyptians themselves practise 'science' in any clear or conventional understanding of the word? This is an area where some very sweeping – indeed, wild – claims have been made by successive generations of speculators from Renaissance Neo-platonists to modern Afrocentrists. But if we leave aside for the moment that vast range of mystical beliefs about an arcane 'lost wisdom of the Pharaohs', secrets of the Pyramids, and so on, then we must surely answer: No, the ancient Egyptians had no science in the modern sense, or anything vaguely resembling it. Certainly they had considerable technological skills, for which their monumental architecture presents the most impressive evidence. But this was a highly conservative – though not static – civilization. Technological innovation seems to have been remarkably slow-paced. The failure, for many centuries, to make significant use of iron, despite knowledge of the relevant techniques, is a striking instance. As Basil Davidson comments:

> it had required at least a thousand years for the highly evolved and in many ways matchless civilization of Egypt to pass from regarding iron as a curious rarity to accepting iron technology as a necessary part of daily life. (1974: 47)

In this respect, later Sub-Saharan African cultures showed much greater innovation and adaptability.[8] In Robert Palter's view, drawing on a wide range of authorities in the history of science, Egyptian astronomy was crude and uninformed by any mathematical theory, clearly inferior to that of the Babylonians, let alone the Greeks. Much the same can be said of the Egyptians' mathematics, while their medical practices mixed valuable practical techniques with mystical pseudo-remedies, radically different from Greek approaches (Palter 1996a).

Clearly the Egyptians possessed elaborate arithmetical and geometrical knowledge, which enabled – among other things – their startling architectural achievements, their ability to calculate time and create calendars, and the complex administration of the Pharaonic state itself.[9] But it seems to have been an *empirical* rather than a theoretical knowledge, as Barry Kemp comments:

> it reflects the basic Egyptian mentality that each problem is dealt with as a specific and individual case rather than as an application of general mathematical principles. Practised scribes must have developed a degree of mathematical intuition, but the idea of pursuing this as an end in itself – to create the subject of mathematics – did not occur to them. (Kemp 1989: 116–17; Palter [1996a: 227–41] broadly supports this view)

The breakthrough to the development of mathematical theories has always been attributed to the Greeks, and there is little – if any – hard evidence to call the attribution into question. The notion that these 'Greek' discoveries were in fact taken over from the Egyptians – a crucial claim for much Afrocentric thought – remains entirely speculative.

Finally, Egypt produced, as we have noted, an extremely powerful and long-lasting form of state. Various attempts have been made to suggest that this had a very wide-ranging influence: the colonial anthropologist Charles Seligman (1934) argued that divine kingship could be found throughout Africa, and must have been diffused from Egypt. This belief was supported also by the Egyptologist Wallis Budge, and in part by ancient historian Henri Frankfort. As late as the 1960s some standard textbooks were still reproducing it, albeit stripped of the overtly racist element in Seligman's theories (B. Ray 1991: 184–96). The idea has been repeated, with quite different ideological intentions, by the Afrocentric writers Cheikh Anta Diop, John G. Jackson and Molefi Asante. Looking north from the Nile, Patricia Springborg (1992) sees strong – albeit concealed – Egyptian influences on ancient Greek thinking about kingship and rule. All these claims, however, are somewhat tenuous: the actual evidence of ideas about kingship paralleling Egypt's either in Sub-Saharan Africa or in the Aegean is extremely thin, and they all ignore the environmental influences on forms of state, although there is good reason to think that the ecology and geography of the Nile valley was the crucial influence on the nature of Egyptian kingship.

What of the influence and relations of Egypt south down the Nile valley and west across the Sahara, rather than north over the Mediterranean and east to Palestine or Mesopotamia? A massive body of European writing, in the last century and the earlier part of this, proposed an extreme diffusionist model: almost everything worth noting elsewhere in Africa (or, in some versions, everywhere in the world) had spread there from the Nile. Much more recently, Afrocentric historians have reproduced exactly the same view; the only real difference being that for the earlier diffusionists the carriers of civilization were 'white' Egyptians, while for their modern counterparts they were 'black' Egyptians, Nubians or Ethiopians.

So – were the Egyptians 'black'? We have noted, and will continue to trace, the intense ideological charge which dispute over ancient Egypt's racial make-up has carried. In September 1991 *Newsweek*'s front cover emblazoned the question 'Was Cleopatra Black?'.[10] To serious modern Egyptology, by contrast, the question is simply not a meaningful or significant one. The major contemporary overviews of Pharaonic Egyptian history (e.g. Baines and Malek 1980; Trigger, Kemp, O'Connor and Lloyd 1983; Kemp 1989; Grimal 1992; Spencer 1993) all raise the question of Egyptian race or phenotype only in passing, if at all. The most important recent work on ancient Egyptian biological anthropology, similarly, includes only a brief and dismissive reference to the issue, in just one of its numerous papers (Armelagos and Mills 1993: 2). Contributors are far more interested in what the archaeological evidence can tell us about themes like ancient Egyptian health, medicine, diet, flora and fauna (Davies and Walker 1993). Quite rightly, they seem to think the race question an irrelevance, or an intrusion of inappropriate modern ideology into the study of ancient history. Where modern Egyptologists have more fully addressed the question of the ancient Egyptians' racial character, they have more often than not done so while protesting at the artificiality of the whole issue, and arguing that the question 'were they black or white?' is downright foolish.[11] As two biological anthropologists comment, obsession with such dubious questions has been 'in part responsible for diverting energy and interest away from biocultural studies within the modern ecological framework' (Armelagos and Mills 1993: 2). The idea of calculating the presence of distinct racial 'types' in the ancient Egyptian population harks back to the absurd and discredited researches of Samuel George Morton in the 1840s: he thought he could do it by measuring skulls (Gould 1981). Morton's theories were a major formative influence on the development of American 'scientific' racism and the eugenics movement – and these in their turn were extraordinarily influential on Nazi race policies, as the young German historian Stefan Kuhl has recently shown (Kuhl 1994).[12] Given this sinister lineage, it is as peculiar as it is disturbing to find arguments about the race of the Egyptians being put forward today as supposed contributions to antiracist politics.

There may be good reason to believe that the population became more ethnically heterogeneous over time: so much so that one recent work on Egypt after the Pharaohs, under its Persian, Greek and Roman rulers, is entitled (a touch modishly, if not fancifully) *Life in a Multi-Cultural Society* (J. Johnson 1992). For most of the Pharaonic period, however, it is the quite unusual *lack* of internal cultural differentiation which is most striking. Michael Mann puts the point more strongly:

> The degree of common cultural participation in a single (and, naturally, highly unequal) society was unique. This was as close an approximation to a unitary social system ... as we find throughout recorded history. (Mann 1986: 113–14)

Some modern writers have tried to assess the proportion of clearly 'negroid' types in the Egyptian population – Eugen Strouhal reckoned it at 1 to 5 per cent (1971: 1), and argues that it increased under the New Kingdom as a result of Egyptian southward expansion. His claims, though, are vitiated by highly dubious environmental-determinist beliefs; he thinks that 'Negroes' failed to survive long in Egypt because they were ill-adapted to its arid climate (ibid.: 9)! Certainly various 'alien' population elements entered Egypt at different times. For instance, large numbers of foreign mercenaries were employed, apparently largely of Nubian and Libyan origin.[13] Many of them no doubt settled, intermarried and became Egyptian – there are records of numerous 'Sherden' (Libyan mercenaries) renting agricultural land under the 20th Dynasty (Kemp 1989: 311); while there is clear evidence of Nubian slaves, but equally of Pharaohs of Nubian origin, under Egypt's New Kingdom (Shinnie 1996: 82–3). There is evidence also of substantial Greek and other immigration in the post-Pharaonic period.

No serious contemporary scholar, however, appears to doubt that the great bulk of the predynastic and Pharaonic population was of indigenous African origin (see, for example, Hoffman 1991; Rice 1991).

The African-American physical anthropologist S.O.Y. Keita has argued, no doubt correctly, that the real issue is not the Egyptians' race (an inherently undecidable question, based as it is on a historically varying ideological concept) but 'population affinity' – to whom were the Egyptians most closely related (Keita 1993: 297)? If we insist on pursuing physical rather than cultural traits, we should investigate the biological affinities between different ancient peoples rather than their shade of pigmentation; and on this the classical texts tell us nothing (ibid.: 312).[14] His provisional conclusion is:

> the Egyptians of the earlier periods, especially in the south, were physically a part of what can be called the Saharo-tropical variant range and retained this major affinity even while diversifying. The base population of 'Egypt' included the descendants of earlier populations, and some Levantines and Saharan immigrants. (ibid.: 305–6; see also Keita 1990, 1992)

He also points out that most European Egyptology, over a long period, accepted that the Egyptians were a mixed but largely African population. Only a minority view insisted on their being 'white'; even adherents to the Hamitic myth saw the Egyptian 'Hamites' as fairly dark-skinned (ibid.: 302–7). In other words – as the evidence of self-depiction would lead us to expect – this was a people predominantly of indigenous African origin, whose skin hues may have exhibited just, or almost, as wide a range as do those of peoples across the contemporary 'Saharo-tropical' region, from Algerian Berbers to southern Sudanese.

Perhaps the most interesting recent contribution to the debate has come from a physical anthropology research team headed by C. Loring Brace. They pursue the time-honoured approach of trying to assess population affinities through analysis of skull types; but with a new sophistication and with quite different intentions from the old craniologists or their Afrocentric epigones. A Morton in the 1840s, or a Diop more recently, analysed a few rather crude general features of skull type, and sought from these to determine the race of the deceased. Brace and his collaborators have looked systematically at a range of two dozen micro-features (Brace *et al.* 1993: 4–5), and insist that the whole language of race is an obfuscation.[15] The claims made or implied by Bernal, Diop and others, therefore, 'are hopelessly simplistic, misleading, and basically wrong' (ibid.: 22). We can get answers to the question 'who were the Egyptians?' only if we discard that language. The ancient Egyptians were neither 'black' nor 'white'; they were Egyptians, a population of largely indigenous origins and a high degree of continuity across time – including, it seems probable, continuity up to the present. What we can meaningfully ask – and to some degree answer – is who they were related to. The answers Brace & Co. believe they can give with some confidence, based on their craniological analyses, are striking. The ancient Egyptian population had very few affinities with that of Sub-Saharan Africa: ties to other parts of North Africa, to the European Neolithic and, more distantly, to India are more evident (ibid.: 9–12, 18–20). A continuum of gradually changing types can be discerned stretching down the Nile valley, including changes which may imply long-term adaptation to different climates (20–21). Shomarka Keita, though evidently more sympathetic to Afrocentric ideas than are Brace and his co-workers, is in broad agreement. His cranial analyses indicate diversity, with a range of skull types intermediate between those found in Europe and those in Sub-Saharan Africa, with remains from the Upper Nile showing more frequent 'African' features than those further north, and with evidence of increased intermingling over time (Keita 1990, 1992).

It thus seems reasonable to assume, from the physical as well as other evidence, that in Pharaonic times, as today, the further south one went up the Nile, the darker the inhabitants' skins tended to be; but there is certainly no good reason to think that at any point along the great valley some clear dividing line could be found between lighter-skinned or 'mixed' Egyptians and 'all-black' Nubians. Nor is there any reason to believe that the graduations of phenotype that were encountered were granted any kind of ideological significance.[16]

The mass of evidence from Egyptian self-portraiture, and Egyptians' depictions of others, remains extremely hard to interpret – as the exchange between Diop and Davidson cited above may suggest. White supremacists have been able to argue, with very little evidence, that where darker-skinned or 'negroid' people are depicted in Egyptian art, these are invariably slaves, captives or uncivilized foreigners bearing tribute. Even very recently one archaeologist, Emily Vermeule, in the course of attacking Martin Bernal's views, seems to assume that warfare between Pharaonic Egypt and Nubia must have reflected racial antagonisms (Vermeule 1992: 92: compare the mythography of Chancellor Williams, discussed below). Afrocentrists have responded, on almost equally shaky evidential grounds, by underlining the 'negroid' facial features in statues of this or that Pharaoh or high priest. A particularly popular – and particularly far-fetched – claim is that the Giza Sphinx's nose was deliberately destroyed (by Napoleon, in one version) to hide the evidence of its 'negroid' character.[17]

Afrocentrists have also suggested that the reddish-brown colours most common in Egyptian self-portraiture represent a conventionalized rather than a realistic image. This may well be so: certainly Egyptian art was highly stylized. Men are usually depicted as darker-skinned than women, which most probably reflects a conventionalized colour-coding (Yurco 1989). Cheikh Anta Diop (1991: 68), in a far-fetched argument, links this to the present-day use of skin-lightening creams by some West African women. Afro-American art historian James Brunson has tried to reinforce claims about the blackness of the Egyptians by suggesting, in another very strained argument backed up by highly selective reproductions of Egyptian portraiture, that where people are depicted in red or yellow colours this is symbolic, but when they are black, this is naturalistic (Brunson 1989)! Egyptian portraiture of Nubians evidently also had a conventional or stereotypical element (Torok 1991), though there is no doubt that despite the broad range of skin hues with which both Egyptians and Nubians are depicted, the latter are on average darker.[18]

But if there *was* some ideological reason for ancient Egyptians habitually to depict themselves as lighter-hued than they were, as the Afrocentric argument seems to imply, then it would suggest that there was an aversion towards darker skin in Egypt: a notion for which there is again no evidence, and one which runs quite counter to the Afrocentrists' other claims (on this see Vercoutter [1976]; Snowden [1976, 1996]). Cheikh Anta Diop sought to short-circuit the whole argument by saying: 'as the Egyptians were black, their painted iconography . . . could represent only black people' (Mokhtar 1981: 74). Challenged by Jean Vercoutter as to why they had not used a carbon black pigment, which they well knew, to depict themselves, but employed a red colour instead, Diop responded, with baffling illogicality 'that this red colour was indicative of the black Egyptian race' (ibid.: 75).

Literary sources also provide only rather limited and ambiguous evidence on Egyptian phenotypes. Egyptian written texts themselves make almost no reference to physical appearance. Later Greek and Roman ones have many scattered allusions to the skin colour and other features of varied African peoples, including Egyptians. Frank M. Snowden has argued repeatedly (1970, 1983, 1989, 1996) that these distinguish fairly clearly between different physical types, using the term 'Ethiopian' for those whom later eras would call 'Negroes' or 'black Africans' and definitely *not* describing Egyptians as equivalent to these people in looks. It is therefore seriously misleading for Martin Bernal and other Afrocentrists to use the labels 'Egyptian', 'black' and 'African' interchangeably, or to state or seek to imply that ancient Egyptian phenotypes were like those of, say, contemporary Ghanaians.

Genetic research is beginning to provide new evidence, suggesting, for instance, that an earlier rigid, caste-like separation perpetuated by close intermarriage, including brother–sister matrimony, broke down in the post-Pharaonic period, perhaps because Christianity imposed a taboo on such marriages. Claims once advanced by Egyptologists like Flinders Petrie that the biological segregation of rulers from ruled by in-group marriage reflected a racial distinction between aristocrats and peasants, however, now appear implausible (Brothwell and Chiarelli 1973). Attempts to assess the ethnic make-up of the population through DNA analysis are almost as unlikely to give definitive answers as were older methods like skull measurement and blood-group classification. They almost certainly will not answer the question which obsesses Afrocentrists – or at least, not in any satisfyingly clear-cut way, for there is no single gene governing skin colour.[19] Loring Brace and his collaborators point out that skeletal analysis continues to have one major advantage over genetic research, in that one can test prehistorical or other specimens without remaining unmodified cell tissue (Brace *et al.* 1993: 4). DNA analysis may, however, give some more hard information than we now have of how much continuity there has been between ancient Egypt's population and the inhabitants of the modern Republic. Much Afrocentric speculation, of course, depends on undocumented assertions that the relatively light-skinned people of the lower Nile today descend from Arab conquerors rather than earlier residents.[20] We may reasonably guess that continuing research will validate none of the simple, ideologically charged images of ancient Egypt which dominated first European, then Afrocentric, writing: patterns of interrelation, population movement and mingling will appear ever more complex as our knowledge grows.

Notes

1. For overviews, see Fagan (1977); France (1991); Vercoutter (1992); Wilson (1964) – the last work gives especial attention to American mystical and occultist ideas about Egypt. Saad el Din and Cromer (1991), though focused mainly on the attractions of modern Egypt for imaginative writers, constantly notes the crucial role of ideas about the ancient past in this appeal.

2. See Leonard Cottrell's caustic dissection of Smyth's reveries (1955: ch.11): 'The Great Pyramidiot'. Piazzi Smyth's ideas have remained attractive, however, to some contemporary Afrocentrists. He is quoted with enthusiasm, for instance, by John G. Jackson (1970: 100–01) amid that author's general passion for occultist ideas about ancient Egypt; while in the younger generation of Afrocentric writing, Anthony Browder draws, apparently indirectly, on many of his characteristic themes. Related ideas on the monuments' hidden wisdom have been propounded by the Nation of Islam: Gardell (1996: 153–4).

3. Lefkowitz (1996a, b) has claimed *Sethos* as the sole fountainhead of all subsequent Afrocentric fantasy about an 'Ancient Egyptian Mystery System'. In fact, as we have seen, such ideas have a much more diffuse ancestry.

4. It has been suggested that this was oddly appropriate, since allegedly the cathedral was built on the site of what had originally, in the Roman era, been a temple dedicated to Isis (Browder 1992: 190).

5. Hence its constantly recycled appeal to Afrocentrists – for example, its use as frontispiece to Van Sertima (ed.) (1994).

6. Assmann (1992) – among numerous works by the same author – offers a far more scholarly and nuanced view of the possible relations between Egyptian and Jewish religious doctrines.

7. Major recent contributions to debate on the nature of Egyptian religion and myth include Assmann (1989, 1992); Baines (1991b). Perhaps the strongest advocate of the view that ancient Egypt did possess a full-fledged philosophical system, which fed strongly and directly into later Sub-Saharan thought, is the African historian Théophile Obenga, a disciple of Cheikh Anta Diop (whose work is discussed below, pp.179–81). Obenga, unlike most of the Afro-American publicists who have made similar claims, at least attempts to give an account of the *content* of this philosophical system (1973, 1989, 1992, 1995 *passim*). A major recent African-American effort in the same direction is Carruthers (1995).

8. The fullest survey of ancient African ironworking is now Shaw *et al.* (1993), which includes eight chapters tracing its history in different parts of the continent. See also the excellent brief summary in Isichei (1997: 69–77).

9. George Joseph (1991), while he is self-consciously revisionist and anti-Eurocentric in approach, gives what seems to the non-expert a balanced picture of ancient Egyptian as well as other African and Asian mathematical knowledges. Far more extreme claims about

Egyptian mathematical wisdom have become the common currency of some US Afrocentric circles: see, for example, Lumpkin (1983a, 1994); Moore (1992b).

10. The answer would probably be no, even if one thought it meaningful to call the Pharaonic Egyptians black, since Cleopatra's ancestry was mostly – if not entirely – Greek. See Lefkowitz (1996a: 34–52) for the historical evidence, and S. Haley (1993) for an identitarian reflection on the emotional-symbolic issues raised by the question in one black classicist's mind.

11. See Yurco (1989); Kelly (1991); Snowden (1989, 1983; and, from an otherwise sharply opposed point of view, Keita (1990, 1992, 1993). Drake (1987) includes one of the most detailed available discussions of Egyptian attitudes to skin colour and their historiography, seeking deliberately to balance the views of 'vindicationist' black writers against more conventional scholarship. The more moderate and scholarly Afrocentrists tend to concur with Keita, his protégé Keith Crawford (1994), and Ivan Van Sertima (1994b: 75), who denounces the posing of the issue in black/white terms as a 'trap', if not downright racist.

12. For the early and formative influence of such ideas on South African 'scientific' racism, see also Bank (1996).

13. Grimal (1992: 253, 268–9); Kemp (1989: 176, 227, 292); Save-Soderbergh (1991: 189–90). Cheikh Anta Diop, strangely, thinks of these ancient Libyans as 'white' (1974a: 215).

14. To cut a complex story short, the 'typological' approach to studying anthropology, prehistory and ancient history – based on the assumption that humans can be divided into fairly clear-cut racial groups – lost favour from about 1945 onwards. It was replaced by a 'populational' approach, suggesting that sharp 'racial' divisions cannot be discerned among human groups, only 'clines' or gradients of variation, like the lines on a weather map. This new approach was pioneered by Sherwood Washburn and Frank Livingstone (see Livingstone 1962 for the classic expression). Afrocentrism and the 'race science' of a Roger Pearson or Richard Lynn represent twin reactions against it.

15. The measurements used by the old – and usually overtly racist – physical anthropologists were the 'cephalic index' (ratio of breadth to length of skull; for skulls of the deceased, the term is 'cranial index') and 'facial angle' – how much the face slopes forward from top to bottom. The standard belief was that the more steeply the face sloped, the more primitive and stupid its owner. Contemporary physical anthropologists focus instead on a large number of very small variations in skull shape, deliberately excluding those which are subject to strong environmental selective pressures, and almost unanimously reject the language of race.

16. Trigger (1978); Trigger et al. (1983: 352, 361); Yurco (1989); Drake (1987); Kelly (1991); Snowden (1983, 1996); Bard (1996). Afrocentrists are not, however, the only contemporary scholars who continue to employ anachronistic and misleading terminology: see, for instance, Jasper Griffin's attempt to distinguish between Egyptians and 'Nubians, who really were black' (1996: 69).

17. See, for instance, Alexander von Wuthenau's lament, which seems to think of the statue as a living person: 'What a sad story this is. To destroy the nose of a Black woman for some idiotic reason, the worst of which would be a vicious racist complex' (1987: 57). Browder (1992: 222–6) rehearses this idea at some length, accompanied by a series of pictures of various dates and provenances 'proving' that 'Napoleon must bare [sic] some responsibility for the damage done to Her-em-akhet. Others may try to defend him and place the blame on the shoulders of someone else, but in the final analysis, the nose knows.' The Sphinx has been almost as popular a focus for esoteric theorizing as have the Pyramids – with a recent Afrocentric version involving claims that its age must be vastly greater than is usually thought, and its builders a long-lost, pre-Pharaonic black African civilization (see, for example, Finch [1994: 47–51], an argument largely reliant on stories in the magazine Condé Nast Traveller!).

18. On Egyptian depictions both of themselves and of others, and the little that can reasonably be inferred from them about ethnic character or differentiation, see also Bard (1996); Drake (1987); Snowden (1996). It may be noted here that much discussion of

such questions has been bedevilled by stereotypical ideas drawn from Victorian physical anthropology about the physical characteristics of 'the typical Negro' – ideas which bear little relation to the actual diversity of African physical types. Once again, extreme Afrocentrists are often as guilty of such stereotyping as the defunct European writers they so repetitively attack, and much more so than contemporary 'mainstream' scholarship.

19. I am grateful to my brother, Roland Howe, a biochemist working on the technological aspects of 'genetic fingerprinting', for advice on the state of the art in this field. Hedges and Sykes (1993) discusses the technical difficulties in extracting and analysing DNA from ancient skeletal remains.

20. The latest major synthetic work on African populations is firmly of the opinion that 'It was not that Arabs physically displaced Egyptians. Instead, the Egyptians were transformed by relatively small numbers of immigrants bringing in new ideas, which, when disseminated, created a wider ethnic identity' (Newman 1995: 79).

Nubia and 'Inner Africa': the Ideological Uses of African State-Building

Apart from the racial make-up of the Egyptian population itself, both academic and political interest has centred on relations between Egypt and the states and peoples to its immediate south – usually labelled 'Nubian' – like Napata, Meroë and Axum, which at different times ruled much of what is now southern Egypt, the Sudanese Republic and Ethiopia.[1] There are major shortcomings, yet again, with the current state of our knowledge on these questions. Archaeological research in the Sudan, Ethiopia and neighbouring regions has been vastly less extensive than that in Egypt, and has been hamstrung by political problems – both Sudan and Ethiopia have been embroiled in recurrent civil war, famine and border disputes, and Sudan is now ruled by a repressive and xenophobic Islamist regime. As Bruce Trigger points out, so-called fundamentalist Islam discourages interest in the ancient past, because by definition it belongs to the *jahilia*, the age of ignorance before the Prophet (Trigger 1994: 345). Upper (southern) Nubia, in particular, has been only very patchily researched, while archaeological work was focused in the north by the massive effort to document sites facing obliteration from the Aswan Dam project (Edwards 1989). What William Adams said in 1977, concerning the huge contrast between our knowledge of ancient Egypt and the vast gaps in understanding of Nubia, would be less wholly true today, but not *much* less:

> Egypt, at the lower end of the Nile, has the longest recorded history in the world. Inner Africa, at the headwaters of the same river, has almost the shortest. Nubia, the land between, alternates for 5,000 years between history and dark ages. (Adams 1977: 1)

Moreover, the historical and archaeological research which has been done has been largely by scholars whose training and previous work had been as Egyptologists. As David O'Connor (1990) points out, this may have predisposed them to look for Egyptian influences rather than assess Nubian cultures in their own right or in relation to Sub-Saharan Africa. Indeed, one of the first pioneers, Karl Richard Lepsius, was a racist committed to the dogma that nothing he discovered in the upper Nile could be of 'Negro' origin; while later scholars, like James Henry Breasted and George Reisner, similarly insisted on Egyptians as part of the 'Great White Race' whose culture owed nothing to Africa. The nature of the Egyptian sources, so much more abundant than the Nubian, also imposes problems – it tends to reflect Pharaonic assertions about their power and superiority over the peoples to their south, creating images of Nubian and other African states as poor relations to Egypt's might, which modern European preconceptions have only reinforced. Even scholars who saw themselves as friendly to the Sudanese shared such assumptions (Trigger 1994: 335), while the methods of early physical anthropology were 'crude enough to have allowed confirmation of any historical theory that they wished to champion' (ibid.: 331). Much Upper Nubian archaeology has been site-specific rather than directed towards long-term perspectives on social and economic change, and has focused on monumental structures rather than remains which would give insight into ordinary people's lives (Edwards 1989: 1–2). Partly because of all this, we still know very little about the patterns of early settlement in Upper Nubia (Newman 1995: 72). Nor do we know the geographical extent, or much about the political structures, of the successive Nubian states, nor whether they had a continuous existence or whether there were breaks or periods when rival dynasties contended for power (Edwards 1996: 1).

The racial identity of the Nubians themselves has been predictably contentious. There is little doubt that they were on the whole darker than most Egyptians. Egyptian art invariably depicts them as being so: though, as we have noted, this offers only ambiguous evidence, and there is a severe paucity of known coloured Nubian artistic self-depictions, which would have provided a fascinating point of comparison. The most prominent and prolific historian of Nubia, William Y. Adams, insists that Nubian 'blackness' is a highly variable, socially constructed category:

> I have seldom referred to the Nubians as 'black', not out of any racial sensitivity but because they have only intermittently been black. By that I do not mean that their skin colour or facial features have changed significantly in the historic period; I believe in fact that they have remained pretty much the same since the earliest times. But race is largely in the eye of the beholder. . . . There have certainly been periods when they have been subject to prejudice and oppression as a result of their dark skin colour, and when to call them 'black' would be sociologically meaningful in today's terms. There have also been times when they were subject to the same attitudes and treatment not because of their skin colour but because they were unlettered barbarians, or because they were Christians surrounded by Moslems. (Adams 1977: 8)

There have even, Adams adds, been historical periods when Nubians allied with their northern neighbours to exploit still darker-skinned peoples further south: in such circumstances, he suggests, twentieth-century social categorization might make them temporarily 'white'. His view that the actual physical appearance of the area's inhabitants has remained little changed across thousands of years, however, is generally supported. Peter Shinnie suggests that both skeletal and ancient pictorial evidence 'show ancient Nubians as an African people fundamentally the same as modern ones' (1996: 13). The coming of Arab overrule 'has had a powerful linguistic, religious and cultural impact but has . . . not had a great influence on the appearance of the people' (ibid.: 14).

Thus Adams's and Shinnie's view of populational continuity in Nubia has won ever wider acceptance, accompanied by abandonment of Egyptocentric diffusionism and by emphasis on the continuity, indigeneity and environmental determinants of Nubian culture – all this being very much in line with the general trends of thought in world archaeology (Trigger 1994: 338–42).[2]

Afrocentrists, however, have often proposed the idea that the Nubian kingdoms *preceded* the Pharaonic Egyptian state, and provided its teacher and inspiration.[3] No archaeologist has supported this view. Bruce Williams has, it is true, argued that a Pharaonic-type kingship may well have emerged in Nubia earlier than in Egypt, and influenced the latter. But even he does *not* proclaim a Nubian 'origin' for the Egyptian state: rather, he speaks cautiously of Nubian 'participation' in its evolution, and of Nubia having 'helped fashion pharaonic civilization' (Williams 1980: 21, 1987: 15). Even in this, his is very much the minority view. As Peter Shinnie comments, the evidence for it is slight, and it has not won widespread agreement: the Qustul burials on which Williams builds his case 'may well indicate powerful chiefs, and use of royal symbols, but these may be "imported" from Egypt' (Shinnie 1996: 51; see also Adams 1985). Afrocentrists like John Henrik Clarke rather predictably scorned Williams for so tentatively suggesting something that they had long since 'known', without evidence (Clarke 1986: 45).[4] Again they are reproducing the beliefs of early-nineteenth-century chroniclers, drawing on notions from classical authors like Diodorus of Sicily (Trigger 1994: 325). But it was almost certainly not the case that urbanization, state-building or kingship emerged first in Nubia. Evidence of very early human settlement, such as stone implements, is more abundant in Nubia than in the northern Nile valley; this, however, may indicate not earlier habitation but, rather, that further downstream, potential sites of primordial tool use have been washed away or buried deep in silt from the Nile's millennia of annual floods (Phillipson 1993: 96–7; H.S. Smith 1991; Trigger 1976: 32–48; Krzyzaniak 1991). Around 2300 BCE (this and all other dates relating to ancient Nubia are subject to much uncertainty and dispute among scholars), however, when Egypt was already a major, literate polity with a powerful monarchy and monumental stone buildings, the contemporary Nubian culture (what historians still, for lack of hard information, label the 'C-Group' culture) lived only in relatively small agricultural settlements – even though the monumental burials at Qustul suggest to some scholars that much of lower Nubia was united under a single political authority. Luxury goods were few, and seem to have been mostly of Egyptian origin: over a third of Nubian 'C-Group' graves include objects of probable Egyptian provenance (Shinnie 1996: 63–4; see also W. Adams [1977, 1984]; Trigger [1976: 49–62]; Sherif [1981]; Spencer [1993]). Intensive agriculture apparently developed a little earlier in the lower Nile valley than it did further south – in about 4100 as against 3800 BCE. (Wetterstrom 1993; Newman 1995: 42–5). It probably did not spread either from Egypt to Nubia or *vice versa*, but was brought to both by migrants from the Sahara, driven into the Nile valley by desertification.

The earliest major urban remains identified in the Sudan, those of the Kerma culture, are little – if any – earlier than 2000 BCE, over 1,000 years later than Egypt's (Trigger 1976: 82–102); see also Bonnet [1992]; Hassan [1993]; O'Connor [1993a, b]; Shinnie [1996]); while Meroë's great structures date from 1,500 years later still. The major Kerma culture, with its monumental architecture, arose only after the end of Egyptian occupation from c.1800 onwards: we still know very little of its political, cultural or social arrangements, and can say only that the city of Kerma was *probably* the centre of an independent Nubian state (Shinnie 1996: 67–72). Thereafter, broadly, Nubia flourished when Egypt was weak (W. Adams 1977: 141). Only when Egyptian 'imperialism' in the south collapsed, in Adams's view, did the resulting power vacuum allow the 'meteoric' rise of the Napata kingdom (ibid.: 247, 292). Human populations and some early tool-making and agricultural techniques, therefore, may have travelled down the Nile from Upper Egypt and/or Nubia (see also Strouhal 1971); but urbanization, literacy, large-scale state structures, and so on, almost certainly went mostly the other way. One major indication of this is that all earlier written inscriptions in the Nubian kingdoms are in Egyptian hieroglyphs. Only in the later years of the last great Kushite state, Meroë, did an indigenous – and still only partly deciphered, and untranslated – Meroitic script and language gradually replace Egyptian.

On the other hand, the kingdoms of Kerma, Napata, Meroë and Axum were by no means mere inferior imitators of Egyptian civilization, as European ideologists constantly assumed. Their cultures were a synthesis, involving many Egyptian elements but also many not found further north. Technologically, for instance, Meroë was in some respects more advanced than Egypt, including perhaps in the scale and sophistication of its ironworking: though the huge Meroitic iron industry which some archaeologists believe to have existed, on account of the slag heaps which still dot the desert by the city, probably attained that scale only one or two hundred years either side of Christ's lifetime (Phillipson 1982: 167). The Nubian Kerma culture was literate by about 1700 BCE (Trigger *et al.* 1983: 173–4). Most strikingly of all, although the Pharaohs occupied much of Nubia during the Middle Kingdom (c.2000–1800 BCE) and again under the 18th Dynasty (c.1500), the Kushite kingdom was able to conquer Egypt itself in about 750 BCE (W. Adams 1977: 260–67; Shinnie 1996: 96–103) thereafter Nubian Pharaohs ruled Egypt for about a century as the 25th Dynasty, which certainly suggests that the relative politico–military weight of the two was less loaded in Egypt's favour than historians had tended to assume.

There has been a clear – albeit slow – shift in scholarly perceptions of Nubia's importance. To some degree this has now gone beyond the sphere of specialist scholarship into the world of the museum and the art gallery. Warsaw's National Museum, from 1972, was apparently the first in the Western world to give separate space and attention to Nubian artifacts rather than merely annex them to those of Egypt. The British Museum has more recently followed suit – since 1991 – though still within a format depicting Nubia as essentially an appendage to Egypt. The first major international exhibition of Nubian art, in 1978, sought to provide a new perspective distinguishing what was indigenous from what was Egyptian-inspired; while the massive display of African art from across the continent, shown at London's Royal Academy in 1995–96 and New York's Guggenheim in 1996–97, gave Nubian pieces a prominence and a separate discussion which would not have been likely even a decade back (Phillips 1995; Torok 1995). This has been followed, in 1997–98, by exhibition in Paris and other European cities of a substantial selection of materials from Sudan's own museums (Wildung 1997).

Such revisions – which, one might confidently predict, will go further in the near future – are unlikely, however, to lead to widespread acceptance of the view which romantic Afrocentrists would prefer: that Nubian civilizational achievements both preceded and outstripped those of Egypt. Few experts have pressed the case for Egypt's links with and debts to Nubia and the remainder of Africa so far as the captions at New York's American Museum of Natural History, whose African exhibits now (1998) carry texts seemingly owing more to Afrocentric lobbying than to scholarly consensus. These claim that ancient Egypt's 'ideas as to cosmology, mythology and medicine also came from the southern part of the continent', and refer to 'an ancient and vital interchange of ideas as well as of objects throughout the continent'.[5]

William Y. Adams's massive effort to reconstruct Nubian historical experience, which quite deliberately adopts a stance of identification with the Nubians, sees them as developing a creative civilization, but none the less primarily as the exploited victims of Egyptian imperialism, an 'external proletariat' for the 'overshadowing colossus to the north' (Adams 1977: 668–9). Bruce Trigger's work (1976) adopts a similar perspective. Indeed, both Adams and Trigger adopt explicitly colonial images to describe Egypt's relation to Nubia. Trigger suggested:

> The Egyptians had no respect for the technology, religion, or customs of the Nubians. Like European colonists in Africa more recently, they dismissed the local technology and failed to appreciate religious practices or patterns of kinship and reciprocity that were based on principles that were radically different from their own. The Nubians were portrayed by the Egyptians as scantily clad barbarians living in thatched huts. (1976: 110)

He sees the nature of Egyptian occupation in Nubia, under the Middle Kingdom and the 18th Dynasty, as directly colonial: the 'native' rulers who were prepared to collaborate with the Pharaohs were assimilated into Egyptian culture, while the peasantry laboured as serfs for Egyptians and Egyptianized Nubians (ibid.: 130). Adams reaches for similar images, saying that the oft-repeated Egyptian label for their southern neighbours, 'miserable Kush', 'expresses succinctly the disdain which civilized peoples have often felt towards their barbarian neighbours. Something of the same attitude is conveyed in the nineteenth century term "Darkest Africa"' (1977: 163). Elsewhere he explicitly compares Egypt's role in Nubia with modern neo-colonialism (ibid.: 669–71), and calls it the first colonial empire known to history (Adams 1984).[6] Even the 'major cultural renaissance' of Meroë represented an offshoot of a much wider classical civilization. In this it was like Egypt itself in its later years, under the Ptolemies, 'provincial expressions of a world civilization' (ibid.: 295).

All this may be more than a little one-sided – indeed, Bruce Trigger has not adopted so sharp a view of Nubian inferiority to Egypt in his later writings. David O'Connor urges, by contrast, that 'even ancient Nubian chiefdoms – let alone states – were much larger and more powerful than has been allowed for, and [that] our perspectives on the historical relationships between Egypt and Nubia need to be accordingly adjusted' (1991: 145; the point is reiterated and developed in O'Connor 1993a, b); though he admits that this remains a speculative and contestable view (1991: 159). Egyptian influence was, as one might expect, stronger in Lower than in Upper Nubia (Edwards 1989: 139–40; see also Leclant 1981; Hakem 1981). It seems to have diminished with time; Meroë's material culture, form of literacy and politico-religious practices appear less heavily shaped by Egypt than those of Kerma. In the post-Pharaonic era, when – Adams and Trigger had suggested – Lower Nubia was virtually deserted, it has recently been argued that archaeological evidence from Qasr Ibrim shows the continuation of a vigorous culture and political authority, clearly southern in inspiration: a striking instance of what one scholar rather oddly calls 'Africa in Egypt' (Horton 1991).

Perhaps the most concerted attempt to 'redress the balance', to see Meroitic civilization as an independent and truly African entity rather than a mere offshoot of Egypt's, has been the work of Cambridge scholar David Edwards. Bemoaning, as others have done, the 'Egyptocentric bias' in most studies of Nubia, he urges instead 'investigation of the indigenous background to the (Meroitic) state, viewed from the perspective of sub-Saharan Africa' (1996: 3). He devotes a degree of attention unusual among archaeologists to theories of the state, drawing especially on the work of Michael Mann, and suggests viewing Meroë in relation to the later state systems of the Sudanic (or Sahelian) belt, like Darfur, Kanem, Bornu, Songhai, Mali and Ghana.[7] Comparing features of these, he proposes a 'Meroitic–Sudanic model' of the state (ibid.: 21–2), with social power resting on control of water supplies (23–6) and of manufactures (27–8), but above all of long-distance trade (28–47). The key to royal power lay in dominance of the 'prestige-goods economy' (39), so that 'it may be proposed that monopoly long-distance trade and the systems of elite alliances, forged through the medium of locally unobtainable prestige-goods, provided a key integrative force in the creation of a large-scale political unit such as the Meroitic kingdom' (47). As the tentative phraseology may suggest, Edwards concedes that his is in large part a speculative model, offering far more questions than answers, given the severe paucity of evidence on Meroë's social, economic and political structures. Nor does he deny a major premiss of older views about Meroë: that it was a 'peripheral state' in relation to the Egyptian Empire (29). It would seem probable, though, that his perspective of reinserting Nubia in its African context will be the wave of the future.

The successive states of the Sudanese region and the upper Nile, then, were not just Egypt's poor relations, its epigones or offshoots. But nor, most probably, were they the precursors and tutors of Egypt, as some Afrocentrists assert. For Nubia, as for Libya, economic and cultural interaction with Egypt was two-way, but with Egypt the more powerful partner through most of the Pharaonic era. As for Ethiopia, literacy and urbanization seem to have been implanted there, heavily influenced by South Arabian invaders, only in the last millennium BCE: two thousand years or more after Egypt's flowering (Phillipson 1993: 169–72). The first great state in the Horn of Africa, Axum, flourished only at the time of the Roman Empire, from the first century CE onwards (Munro-Hay 1991). Our knowledge of what is now Somalia in Pharaonic times – perhaps the biblical 'Land of Punt' – is extremely scanty, and largely derived from Egyptian sources (Kitchen 1993). Still, the whole project of judging Nubia's or Ethiopia's history by comparison with Egypt's may be a distorting one. They were major, creative civilizations in their own right, whose development deserves to be assessed on its own terms. It should hardly need adding that speculation about their inhabitants' skin colour, skull shapes, or DNA make-ups contributes nothing whatsoever to the task. Yet the extreme Afrocentrists' romantic thirst for certain racial categorizations, of the classically Victorian kind, persists. Thus Peggy Brooks-Bertram can lament that the fragmentary skeletal remains which may – just possibly – be those of the Kushite Pharaoh Taharka have not been analysed for 'racial designation'. This, she believes, 'is a very critical area of needed research because of the possibility of answering the question of the race of Kushites. Perhaps for example, with new technology, we can even reconstruct the face of Taharka and study the bone fragments for racial clues' (1994: 185–6). Existing technology, as we have seen, will permit no such chimerical quest; and few people other than romantic racialists are likely to regret that fact.

In the end here, for Nubia as for Egypt, amid great gaps in our knowledge, we are inevitably in territory where value judgements intermingle intensely with historical inquiry. It is largely a matter of which language we find more appealing, and why. Do we prefer phraseology like Martin Bernal's references to 'pharaohs one can usefully call black' (1987: 242), or that of Loring Brace and his collaborators, with their insistence that:

> The 'race' concept did not exist in Egypt.... Since it has neither biological nor social justification, we should strive to see that it is eliminated from both public and private usage. Its absence will be missed by no one, and we shall all be better off without it. R.I.P. (1993: 26)

For whom is Bernal's terminology 'useful'? And who are Brace and company's 'we'?

As one moves further south or west from the upper Nile valley, speculation and uncertainty become ever greater – but the claims of first the Eurocentric, later the Afrocentric, diffusionists, become ever more grandiose. It is simply ahistorical to argue or assume that the character of Sub-Saharan African kingdoms was, or could have been, similar in all essentials to that of ancient Egypt. To do so is to ignore not only the sheer variety of African state systems, but also the massive influence of environment on political forms. The nature of the Egyptian state was in significant part dictated by its location: the long, thin cylinder of the Nile valley where a high population density could be sustained in the areas reached by the river's floodwaters, but beyond whose limits lay almost uninhabitable desert. Few, if any, other African states, at any stage in history, had such clearly fixed natural boundaries as did Egypt. Arguably, those physical limitations were a major factor inducing strong, elaborate state structures. Without them, people would escape the demands of the state by migration, and awareness of this kept the machinery of control at a relatively low level. The Pharaonic state rested on maintaining the irrigation system derived from the waters of the Nile, and on extracting and redistributing the surplus produce and labour freed from agriculture. It benefited from superb internal communications along the Nile itself, and from the fact that neither essential metals nor substantial wood supplies existed within the country. Access to these, therefore, depended on foreign trade or war, and could thus be effective royal monopolies. No subsequent Sub-Saharan state had such a basis. In many cases, African state power rested on control over long-distance trade, which was important but not fundamental in the Egyptian case. None depended on large-scale public works, and apparently none was mainly reliant on taxation of agricultural producers.

Furthermore, very many of the larger Sub-Saharan states relied on substantial standing armies – the most famous examples being the Zulu and other military states of southern Africa in the eighteenth and nineteenth centuries. Ancient Egypt appears to have had only a minimal standing army, at least under the Old and Middle Kingdoms. Slavery, too – as opposed to enforced but waged labour on state building projects – seems to have been relatively unimportant to Egyptian life, whereas it was crucial to the social structure of many later Sub-Saharan states. It is simply not true that most or even many African state systems conceived of their monarchs as divine (as opposed to sacred), as did the Egyptians. On the contrary, a very wide variety of elective, limited or quasi-constitutional monarchies existed across the continent: most typically, systems where the king's power was checked by an assembly of chiefs or elders. Federal systems of city-states, as among the Yoruba, are also not rare. None of these has anything much in common with Egyptian kingship. In case after case, research on precolonial African states has shown that they embodied mixtures and competing forms of authority, with rival legitimating ideologies. Power was never either unitary or uncontested (see, for a sample of such accounts, Feierman 1974; Joseph Miller 1980; Vansina 1978). Moreover, Africa is well known to have had many highly decentralized polities, without formally constituted or inherited political authority: these are often, though questionably, called 'stateless' societies. They are quite literally at the opposite extreme from ancient Egypt in the spectrum of world history's political forms.

Scholars remain largely in the dark about the extent and nature of influences from ancient Egypt to the rest of Africa, and vice versa. The image proposed by William Adams (1977) – of Nubia as the 'corridor' of culture contact between Egypt and Sub-Saharan Africa – has not been followed up by much substantial knowledge about what actually passed along the corridor. Indeed, another specialist, J.A. Alexander, has argued that the upper Nile was not a corridor but a cul-de-sac, with very little evidence of cultural transmission either way (1988). John Iliffe, similarly, thinks that 'Egypt was remarkably unsuccessful in transmitting its culture to the rest of the continent' (1995: 26).[8] Graham Connah's careful overview takes this side too. He can find 'very little influence' from either Nubia or Egypt on the rest of Africa: 'Surely corridors usually lead to a few rooms, but the Nubian corridor, in which so much happened, does not seem to have led anywhere' (1987: 65). In 1967 Peter L. Shinnie pointed out that not a single object of certain Meroitic origin had been found west of the Nile and south of the Sahara (Shinnie 1967: 167); and this is apparently still true today.

In one sphere where there *is* substantial evidence of trading or other contacts – in the large number of cultivated plants found both in Egypt and in Sub-Saharan regions – the evidence suggests that transmission was almost entirely from south to north. Only much later, with the medieval growth of trans-Saharan trade routes, did agricultural goods move from North Africa to the south (Blench 1991). In general, it would appear that trans-Saharan trade was on a very small scale between the birth of the Pharaonic state and the introduction of the camel in the early centuries of the Christian era (Connah 1987: 97–9). Much earlier, though, prior to desertification, when north-central Africa was still fertile – and, indeed, large parts of it were covered with great lakes – the story may have been very different. Only scanty archaeological evidence so far fills out John Sutton's pathbreaking suggestion, made over twenty years ago, of an 'aquatic' civilization flourishing from as far back as 9000 BCE until 2000 BCE in the midst of what is now the Sahara, before it dried up (Sutton 1974). The likelihood seems to be that the first pastoral and agricultural inhabitants of the Nile valley migrated into it from the Sahara around 5000–4500 BCE (Hoffman 1991; Wetterstrom 1993). Some of the answers to our questions about Egypt's relations with Sub-Saharan cultures may lie here, with the almost wholly unexcavated relics of those who hunted, fished and grazed their animals where now there is only sand and rock. In many ways, then, the issue remains open, as Peter Garlake comments:

> Philology has so skewed our understanding of that (Egyptian) civilisation that, until the archaeology of settlements is fully addressed, Egypt's place in African history and the influences that permeated to and from the far interior will remain in the realm of polemic. (1995a: 31)

More fundamentally still, there is little – if any – basis, across most of Africa, for the idea – fundamental to Afrocentric mythography – that the continent's historically known societies originated in massive, long-distance population movements out of the Nile valley. In the *very* distant, prehistoric past, it seems probable that human settlement across Africa – as, eventually, across the whole of the rest of the globe – resulted from two successive migrations out of an original 'cradle' in East Africa: of australopithecines three million years ago, and of early humans perhaps 200,000 years back. Right at the other end of human history, the present locations of major ethnic groups in southern Africa are the end-product of very modern (eighteenth-century) and often violent population shifts consequent on white colonial incursions and Zulu expansion. These became the basis for a racial mythology of their own, with apartheid apologists using them to assert either that South Africa's black peoples are just as much 'immigrants' as whites are, or that the original homes of the main ethnic groups were, by remarkable coincidence, the small and impoverished enclaves assigned to them under the Bantustan system. But the belief proposed in Cheikh Anta Diop's theories and heavily stressed in those of Afrocentric ideologues like Chancellor Williams, Yosef Ben-Jochannen and Molefi Asante is nothing to do with either the prehistoric or the most recent migrations. It is that vast population movements took place in historical times. All African societies, they assert, owe their fundamental unity to their founders' having spread at some ill-defined point – at the birth of Pharaonic Egypt, at its collapse, and/ or in the era of Arab conquest – from some equally ill-defined northeastern region of origin: Egypt itself, 'Nubia', or 'Ethiopia'.

This belief is quite without evidential support. It is true that many African peoples, like those elsewhere in the world, harbour myths of origin tracing their ancestry to places other than those they now inhabit. But across much of eastern, central and western Africa, the overwhelming weight of modern archaeological, linguistic and other evidence suggests in many cases that for thousands of years the ancestors of modern peoples inhabited roughly the regions still held by their modern descendants. A complex pattern of migration there has certainly been, but where we have clear evidence for

it, much of it has been migration *within* regions of Africa, not right across
the continent.[9] Modern archaeologists have little doubt that agriculture
and early technologies had several different points of origin in Africa
rather than diffusing from one single starting place (Andah 1993; Muzzolini
1993). Where there are strong reasons to think that most modern inhabitants descend from long-distance migrants, the probable patterns do not
fit the Diopian schema at all: as in the rainforests of equatorial Africa,
whose main present inhabitants spread there by a very gradual process
between 5,000 and 2,000 years ago (Vansina 1990: 49–57), or with Bantu
speakers.

The original cradle of the Bantu language group, spoken virtually right
across the southern half of the continent, most probably lies in what is now
southeastern Nigeria and Cameroon (Vansina 1990: 49; Phillipson 1993:
198–205; Newman 1995: 140–49); certainly not in the Nile valley. According
to an alternative means of language classification referring to greater time
depth, the two main groupings, the Niger–Congo and Nilo–Saharan, spread
respectively from the Niger valley and the southern Sahara (Blench 1993:
136). The spread of a language group does not necessarily mean the
physical migration of entire peoples, displacing previous inhabitants –
though almost undoubtedly, migrants speaking variants of the Eastern
Bantu linguistic subfamily moved east and south (not west, as claims about
Egyptian or Nubian origins would suggest), usurping the territories of
Pygmies, Khoi and San. Even the myths of origin (themselves, one may
suppose, frequently of recent origin) are often fairly localized ones, with
peoples as diverse as the Masai, the Kikuyu, the Asante and the Igbo
identifying their legendary birthplaces as within a few hundred miles at
most of their present dwellings. As an Igbo elder insisted to historian
Elizabeth Isichei in 1972: 'We did not come from anywhere and anyone
who tells you we came from anywhere is a liar. Write it down' (Isichei 1976:
3).[10]

Similarly, the notion that the eighth-century Arab conquests produced
massive destruction and disruption – an idea also crucial to the theories of
Chancellor Williams, Molefi Asante and other American Afrocentrists – is
simply not supported by the evidence. In parts of the Maghreb, it is true,
historians have sometimes argued that pre-Islamic social structure and
agrarian life were profoundly disordered by the Arab conquests: not so
much the initial coming of Arab overrule, which probably involved only
minimal population movements, as by the eleventh-century spread of
nomadic peoples, and especially the Banu Hilal westward from Egypt. But
as Albert Hourani sums up the current state of knowledge:

> Modern research has shown . . . that the process was not so simple as this. . . .
> It may have been the weakening of authority and the decline of trade, and
> therefore of demand, which made it possible for the pastoralists to expand.
> No doubt their expansion caused destruction and disorder, but it does not
> appear that the Banu Hilal were hostile to settled life as such; they were on

good terms with other dynasties. If there was a shift in the rural balance at this time, it may have resulted from other causes, and it seems to have been neither universal nor perpetual. . . . The expansion of pastoralism, in so far as it existed, was possibly therefore an effect rather than the main cause of the breakdown in the rural symbiosis. (Hourani 1991: 104)

Moreover, the expansion of the Banu Hilal and other Arab tribes, like the initial Arab conquests, does not seem to have involved sufficiently large numbers to transform the make-up of the Maghreb's population. The spread of the Arabic language and Arab culture was mostly the result of Berbers and other indigenous Maghrebian peoples assimilating to the culture of the conquerors, rather than a wholesale replacement of one set of inhabitants by another. The whole idea of massive Arab migrations into and across North Africa may well even have been largely the invention of early Islamic historians, especially Ibn Khaldun (see also Hasan 1967; Newman 1995: 77–83). The apparent medieval decline of North Africa almost certainly owed far more to the ravages of the Black Death than to Arab conquest and forced population movements (Dols 1977; Iliffe 1995: 47–9). And finally, there is no evidence at all that the disruptions which did ensue had a major impact further south, beyond the Sahara. The whole structure of explanation proposed by those historical mythographers who believe in a cataclysmic flight of African peoples from Egypt or Nubia across the whole continent, fleeing an Arab holocaust, rests on nothing.

A further major theme in Afrocentric historical fantasy should also be noted: the tendency to deny, against all the evidence, that chattel slavery existed in precolonial Africa – or to insist that, if it did, it was a marginal, small-scale and benign phenomenon. One might set against this romanticization Orlando Patterson's estimates of the scale of precolonial African slavery, in the fullest comparative global study of slavery ever attempted. Patterson suggests that in the major early states of West Africa – Islamic Ghana, Mali, Segou and Songhay – slaves constituted over 30 per cent of the population. In the states of the central Sudan and the Hausa city-states, it was between 30 and 50 per cent. In the Fulani kingdoms established after the *jihad* of the eighteenth century, between 30 and 66 per cent of the people were enslaved; while in the states of what are now Senegal, Gambia, Sierra Leone and Ghana, figures ranged from 30 to 75 per cent. Among the precolonial Yoruba, from a third to a half of the population existed in servile status, while in many of the states of Central Africa – among the Kongo, Luvale and Lozi, for instance – the figure was over 50 per cent (Patterson 1982: 354–6).

Internal African slavery and slave-trading were undoubtedly on a very significant scale, and long predated the advent of European slave-raiding; though it remains quite possible – indeed, likely – that their growth was greatly stimulated by the effects of European demand, so that African slavery in its later, most extensive and many of its harshest forms can reasonably be 'blamed' in part on Europe. One estimate (P. Manning 1990: 171) has it that the number of people enslaved within Africa, across the sweep of modern history, equalled the number exported by the Atlantic and Red Sea trades. Important aspects of intra-African economic interchange, like trans-Saharan trade routes, included or were even pioneered by the trade in human beings (Savage 1992). Nor is it true that slavery within Africa was largely 'domestic' and therefore, by implication, relatively benign: large-scale plantation slave-labour systems were introduced in several parts of the continent, albeit probably most often under at least indirect European or Arab influence (see, for example, Cooper 1977; Sheriff 1987; Lovejoy 1983: 31–2, 164–7, 190–209, 223–7).

The nature and extent of precolonial formal education in Africa has also been the site of extravagant assertions by Afrocentrists. Journalist Lynell George describes a history class in an Afrocentric private school in Los Angeles:

> Brother Reginald begins with a beautiful vision of the past. Not full of slave ships, sharecropping, and whips and chains, but of grand Egyptian kingdoms and universities (like the Grand Lodge of Luxor at Kemit or the University of Sankore at Timbuktu) filled with vast libraries and peopled by unheralded thinkers. (George 1992: 95)

In reality we know almost nothing of the educational system at Luxor: not a 'university' but some kind of seminary for Egyptian priests. The 'university' of Timbuktu, or Sankore (the latter was actually the name of a mosque), is, however, near the heart of romantic Afrocentrism. Chancellor Williams (1971/1987) presents a quite fanciful account of this 'university', together with the claim that there must have been a lost, but once comprehensive, 'West African elementary and secondary school system without which there could not have been a University of Sankore with such high standards for admission' (ibid.: 206). Ahmad Babo (as Williams calls him, though 'Ahmed Baba' would be more accurate) – few of whose works have survived, and who may well in any case have been a Berber rather than a 'black' West African – is suggested to have been the sixteenth-century world's greatest scholar (207–8).[11] Quite apart from its fantasy element, Williams's account is caught in an awful dilemma: he cannot deny that education at Timbuktu was Arabic and Islamic, but he wants somehow to combine glorification of this centre for African scholarship with his overarching schema of belief that the Arabs and Muslims systematically destroyed African civilization throughout the continent.

Cheikh Anta Diop, as usual, is more rational in his claims. He points out that the state of learning in medieval Timbuktu may have been equivalent to that in Paris at the same time, but he certainly does not pretend that it was clearly superior. He notes how its overwhelmingly Koranic emphasis might hamper the development of secular and scientific inquiry. And he emphasizes that in both cases, in Africa and in Europe, the Arabs were intermediary for the introduction – or reintroduction – of classical scholarship in the Middle Ages (Diop 1987: 176–95; 1991: 325–6).

It seems pretty certain that Timbuktu was not a 'university' in anything like a modern sense, but rather – like al-Azhar in Cairo, or indeed like medieval Oxford and Paris – a centre where various individual religious teachers passed on sacred knowledge to private pupils.[12] Little has survived of the writings produced by its scholars – though the remnants include two of the most important early written sources for the region's history, the sixteenth-century *Tarikh el Fattach* and *Tarikh el Sudan* – but quite clearly their learning was overwhelmingly in Islamic tradition and jurisprudence. Afrocentric writers who ignore this, and seek by omission to evoke in their readers' minds images of something equivalent to a twentieth-century university, are engaging in more or less deliberate, even deceptive, anachronism.

The obsession with Timbuktu, like so much else in contemporary Afrocentrism, reproduces nineteenth-century and earlier European fantasies. The idea that the city was a vast, fabulously wealthy conurbation in the heart of the desert haunted European imaginations and inspired a series of ill-fated expeditions in search of it, across many decades. When Europeans did eventually reach Timbuktu in the 1820s, they found the reality (of a rather decayed, largely mud-built, modest-sized town) thoroughly anticlimactic – though the earlier beliefs have an afterlife in continued proverbial uses of the town's name as figure for the distant and mysterious.[13] Timbuktu's significance may also have been exaggerated even among more sober historians, because our surviving written sources for the history of its region come overwhelmingly from the *ulama* of the city itself (Gomez 1990).[14] The Islamic scholars of Timbuktu were undoubtedly a learned religious community, but their influence apparently did not extend beyond West Africa. There is no clear evidence that they were treated as equals, or even referred to, by the Islamic jurists of longer-established centres like al-Azhar. Even within the region, for political reasons, under the Songhai Empire the scholars of Gao, although less erudite than those of Timbuktu, had greater influence (ibid.: 22). Timbuktu's eminence was relatively short-lived, dissipating when many of its scholars were forced to flee after Sunni Ali Ber's conquest in the early 1470s (ibid.: 8).

But Timbuktu was also a major trading centre, including the slave trade. Even during the nineteenth century, it has been estimated that 1,000–2,000 slaves were exported every year northward from the city across the Sahara (Lovejoy 1983: 150). One of the city's most renowned scholars and centrepiece of Chancellor Williams's mythography, Ahmed Baba (1556–1627), wrote a book fiercely condemning the enslavement of fellow Muslims, but accepting its legality and normality in relation to infidels: 'the reason for slavery is non-belief. . . . Whoever is captured in a condition of non-belief, it is legal to own him, whosoever he may be' (quoted in Lovejoy 1983: 30).

Timbuktu was, it is clear, the most important but far from the only West

African centre of Muslim scholarship. There was evidently considerable learning and literacy, mostly of Islamic inspiration, in precolonial West Africa. To that extent, standard European stereotypes of an illiterate Africa must indeed be qualified quite substantially. Large parts of Sub-Saharan Africa, especially in the savannah belt and the eastern coastal regions, had written languages quite independent of European influence: literacy was mainly in Arabic, but later in such African languages as Hausa and Swahili as well. Alex Haley's depiction, in *Roots*, of his hero Kunta Kinte coming from an educated, book-owning household before his enslavement may be romantic, but it is by no means ridiculous (Haley 1976). But equally evidently, much of this learning was, in the post-medieval world, a kind of museum piece. In the 1820s Sultan Bello of Sokoto, on meeting Hugh Clapperton – apparently the first European he had seen – and learning that he was a Christian, asked him whether he was a Nestorian or a Socinian (Perham 1960: 33)! Clapperton gave the Sultan a copy of Euclid in Arabic, for which he was extremely grateful, saying that his family had previously had a copy obtained in Mecca, but it had been lost in a house fire (Davidson 1964: 68). What the medieval spread of Islamic scholarship in Africa really indicates, on a world-historical perspective, is how extensive the reach of Islamic learning was compared with the far more modest attainments at the time of Western thought. As Marshall Hodgson says: 'Occidental culture was confined to its own little peninsulas. Thomas Aquinas was read from Spain to Hungary and from Sicily to Norway. Ibn al-Arabi was read from Spain to Sumatra and from the Swahili coast to Kazan on the Volga' (1993: 132). But that recognition of the intellectual power and influence of medieval Islamic culture is no part of Afrocentrism's intentions at all.

The use of sources in Afrocentric historical writing has been as questionable as the narrative such writing constructs. By far the most important classical source for the Afrocentric view of Egypt and its relations to Greece has been Herodotus, whose account of information he gleaned during travels in Egypt has long supplanted an earlier reliance on the scanty biblical references to Africans. Herodotus's own allusions to skin colour or other racial features are in fact equally scanty, which might well be thought evidence of just how irrelevant such matters were in the Mediterranean world of his time – a view, suggesting that Antiquity was effectively free from colour prejudice, which has been extensively argued by Afro-American historian Frank Snowden (1970, 1976, 1983). Those few references in Herodotus – really only two, and both oblique – have been repeated, mantra-like, time after time by modern-day polemicists obsessed with the Egyptians' phenotypes.

This illustrates one facet of the uses of Herodotus: an uncritical enthusiasm for him as a source of supposed hard facts, which ties in with the whole enterprise of historical retrieval as racial retrieval. This has been the often lonely, self-taught, obsessional activity – until recently, almost entirely outside the academy – of people like Yosef Ben-Jochannen or John Henrik Clarke. But coexisting with this is another aspect of Herodotus's appeal, less clearly acknowledged but evidently often operating in the very same writers as the first. Herodotus is the great father of *muthologos*, the mingling of myth and history, of an anti-rationalist discourse: antithesis to the slightly later Thucydides, the founder of a rationalist historical tradition. He is also the great ur-exponent of history as *istorin*, finding out for yourself, mixing discovery with subjective experience, affect – maybe even, in the slogan of Molefi Asante: 'soul as method'.[15]

It is arguable, however, that Herodotus's ideas about non-Greek cultures should not be seen mainly as a result of investigation, accurate or otherwise, and assessed for their truth or falsity. Rather – as François Hartog has sought to show through an extensive discussion of Herodotus's depiction of the Scythians – the ideas expressed may be mostly *symbolic* ones. The Scythians function in Herodotus's writing – so Hartog argues, and despite the Greek historian's repeated insistence that he bases his account on personal observation – as symbolic barbarians, not-Greeks, inverting Greek values, embodying the opposite of everything Greek; especially in their nomadism, contrasted with the Greeks' rootedness.[16] Elsewhere, Hartog has suggested that Egypt also served primarily definitional, stereotypical functions for Greek thought (Hartog 1986).

The abuse of sources such as Herodotus is not, however, the most serious fault of Afrocentrism as history. The unanimist, diffusionist model of African history proposed by Diop and by modern American Afrocentrists, ironically enough, results in a disparagement of African cultural creativity just as thoroughgoing as that imposed by the Hamitic myth and other long-discarded European misconceptions. If, as they tend to believe, cultures, institutions and ideas across the whole continent are merely copies of originals developed in ancient Egypt, then Africans have created nothing new for four thousand years or more: quite evidently a ridiculous as well as a demeaning view. It also involves a kind of state-worship, celebrating the power of rulers, conquest and military might as evidences of glorious African achievement and blind to the oppressions which precolonial African rulers, like state powerholders everywhere, visited on their subjects. Successive generations of Africa's historians have identified themselves with the rulers: precolonial chroniclers who were, more often than not, court officials; imperial apologists lauding the 'civilizing mission' of the colonial state; historians of the early post-independence years cheering on the new rulers' efforts at 'nation-building' and 'development'. Contemporary Afrocentric ideologues merely repeat the pattern, the only real difference being that they, more than their predecessors, seek their heroes in the past rather than the present, in mythicized warrior kings and queens of bygone ages: a Shaka, an Nzinga, a Mutota. Our knowledge of ancient African civilization remains extremely incomplete. As Graham Connah aptly puts it, we have 'a series of islands of information projecting from a sea of uncertainty and ignorance' (1987: 214). But that is no reason to fill the gaps between the islands with fantasy.

Notes

1. Uses of the term 'Nubia' have been rather vague and shifting, referring sometimes to the whole of what is now the Sudanese Republic, southern Egypt and even parts of Ethiopia, sometimes to the much smaller area where the Nubian language is spoken today.

2. The texts accompanying Nubian exhibits at the British Museum, recently updated, are intriguing here in their very reticence. 'The ancient Nubians', visitors are told 'shared a broadly common ethnic background with the Egyptians, but their physical characteristics showed variations of skin colour, physiognymy, and skeletal proportions.' Another caption, however, points outs how clearly Egyptian portraiture distinguished Nubians from themselves.

3. For example, Diop (1991: 103–8): an argument resting on a single artifact from a Nubian grave; an artifact which, it seems evident, Diop misinterprets as well as overinterprets; see also J. Jackson (1970: chs 2–3), Anthony Browder (1992: ch.1); Brunson (1991); or, in far wilder and less coherent fashion, Ben-Jochannen (1972: *passim*).

4. Drake (1987): 163–4, 312–13), again, seeks to mediate between these viewpoints.

5. This is at best speculative, and in its reference to material objects quite unsupported by archaeological evidence. Other texts exhibited at the museum are yet more questionable. They claim that there was no 'real' slavery in precolonial Africa: it was 'in fact, serfdom, a more humane institution and primarily a way of dealing sensibly (!) with war captives and criminals. . . . Even after Arab and European slave traders introduced real slavery (!), many African rulers at first treated their slaves with respect.' Elsewhere it is suggested, peculiarly, that 'there is probably a greater knowledge of the Yoruba religion, for instance, in Harlem than in Nigeria'.

6. Such language is also reflected in the British Museum, which boldly heads one section of its exhibits 'Egyptian Imperialism in Africa'. It is not clear why such labels are thought more appropriate for this relationship than for other conquests of one polity by another in the ancient world, unless for the questionable reason that it is still thought of as a domination by 'whites' over 'blacks'.

7. On these states, see also McIntosh and McIntosh (1984, 1993); O'Fahey and Spaulding (1974); Levtzion (1973, 1985); Abdullahi Smith (1976); Hunwick (1985).

8. The problem with such a formulation is only its intentionality: the apparent presumption that Egypt tried – or *should* have tried – to spread its influence south and west. As John Baines comments, Egyptian culture was 'highly interconnected and inward-looking in its organization and style . . . many Egyptian cultural traits did not travel well' (1996: 33–4). In relation to its size and power, Egypt seems for most of its history to have been unusually lacking in expansionist ambitions (ibid.: 43–4).

9. See Connah (1987); Oliver (1991); Phillipson (1993); Isichei (1997); and contributions to Robertshaw (1990); Shaw *et al.* (1993) for summaries of the evidence.

10. Vansina (1995), surveying recent evidence from historical linguistics, stresses that there was no single massive Bantu 'migration', 'expansion' or 'explosion', but a very long, slow, uneven set of processes involving successive dispersals of individual languages. Isichei (1997: 46–55) is a clear summary of the state of historical knowledge on these and related issues.

11. For a detailed – though in large part necessarily speculative – study of Baba, see Zouber (1977). The romantic and grossly exaggerated view of Timbuktu's intellectual significance is reflected in exhibit captions at the American Museum of Natural History, where it is wrongly asserted that it 'became a center of learning so famed that scholars came from all over the Islamic world to discourse together and to consult its priceless library'.

12. See Saad (1983); Gomez (1990). Hiskett (1984) and Levtzion (1973) give the wider context; and for a superb evocation of this educational model in a situation where it continued into the present, in Iran, see Mottahedeh (1985).

13. Gardner (1968) gives a vivid account of the legends and the eventual European

penetrations to the city. Gardner's epigraph, taken from Thackeray, neatly evokes the mysterious appeal of Timbuktu to both European adventurers and later Afrocentric romantics:

In Africa (a quarter of the world)
Men's skins are black, their hair is crisp and curled;
And somewhere there, unknown to public view,
A mighty city lies, called Timbuctoo.

14. Though see Hunwick (1996) for contrary arguments, offering reasons to believe that Timbuktu's religious scholars were more autonomous from the Songhai state, or more powerful *vis-à-vis* it, than Gomez suggests.

15. For balanced overviews of Herodotus's merits and faults in the framework of both classical and modern historiography, see Momigliano (1990); Lateiner (1989). After Herodotus, the other ancient author most often cited by Afrocentrists is Diodorus of Sicily, who wrote almost 400 years later. Diodorus, who apparently visited Egypt in 60–56 BCE, makes wide claims about Egyptian influences on Greek learning, derived from tales told to him by Egyptian priests. There are good reasons for scepticism about most of his assertions, as Mary Lefkowitz (1996a: 57–61, 71–80), Lawrence Tritle (1996), and other classical scholars explain.

16. Hartog (1988). Edith Hall's (1989) study of images of the 'barbarian' in Greek drama offers a rather similar message in less Parisian-theoretic ways; while Liverani (1990) gives a wider understanding of the ideological uses of ancient historical texts.

13

African Unity and African Philosophy

Many of the philosophical underpinnings of contemporary Afrocentric beliefs can be traced, ironically enough, to a handful of colonial-era European writings on African views of the world. The first and most influential of these was *La Philosophie bantoue* (translated as Tempels 1959), which appeared in 1945. The author, Father Placide Tempels, was a Franciscan missionary living in the then Belgian Congo, now the Democratic Republic of Congo. He believed that the peoples of the Bantu language group (which includes most of west, central and southern Africa) shared a common philosophy centred on a concept of vital force. Everything in the universe possesses this force, including inanimate objects, but it is most powerful and important in human beings: still active in the departed ancestors as well as the living. Humanity, 'Muntu', is thus at the centre of the universe, the measure of all things, at the head of a hierarchy of beings but intimately connected with all by the flow of energy between individuals, between the living and the dead, the human, the animal, vegetable and inorganic. Preservation of this cosmic order is the yardstick for ethics: evil is that which disrupts it or diminishes the flow of vital forces, good that which preserves and enhances. All people had some knowledge of these forces and a responsibility to act so as to preserve them; but greater knowledge and more active powers of intervention in the circulation of energy were the exclusive domain of magicians, those whom Europeans misnamed witchdoctors.

This basic system of beliefs, according to Tempels, was shared by all the many peoples of the huge and diverse Bantu language family – though his own research had embraced only one of these, the Baluba. Moreover, it was shared and understood by all individuals within each of these societies; even those whose Western education or lifestyles might be expected to have made them abandon it. All 'Bantu' behaviour was to be explained in terms of the system, including what appeared to outsiders to be illogical or unreasonable behaviour – for the system itself, though internally coherent, was (in the word the French anthropologist Lucien Lévy-Bruhl had popularized to describe African beliefs) 'prelogical'.

Tempels's motivation was – as one might expect – specifically Christian and, many would add, also specifically colonialist. He believed that by understanding the 'Bantu' world-view his fellow whites in Africa, especially missionaries (for the book was clearly aimed at them rather than Africans, who must presumably – by Tempels's own arguments – already 'know' its contents), would be able to build on the elements it had in common with Christianity, purge it of its illogical and 'magical' residues, and so lead the natives towards a more civilized, morally perfect life. Despite this, his ideas had a strong appeal to many African intellectuals. Tempels was, after all, insisting that Africans possessed a coherent philosophical system rather than just a mass of superstitions. For this, his African fans were prepared to forgive or overlook much, including his rather low opinion of the content of that system. Those African thinkers attracted to Tempels also ignored, or misunderstood, his opinion that while the Bantu had a philosophy in the sense of an organized system of beliefs, it was not a 'true' philosophy comparable to the Western tradition, in that they were not critical, self-aware beliefs.

There were further attractions. Bantu thought, as Tempels described it, was outside the 'logocentrism' (or emphasis on the speaking, knowing, rational individual) which first Heidegger and the existentialists, later Derrida and the deconstructionists, saw as the defining feature – indeed, since they were hostile to it, the original sin – of Western philosophy. Thus for people swayed by existentialist ideas, who naturally included many Francophone African students, the Bantu as described by Tempels were natural soul mates. For those influenced by *négritude*, too, the emphasis on intuition and affect rather than logic which Tempels attributed to Bantu thought was attractive, because it chimed with their own convictions. And the suggestion that the same structure of thought was shared by all members of all African societies, across a very large part of the continent, was pleasingly parallel to the Rousseauian claims about a unified general will opposed to colonialism, in which nationalist politicians traded.

After *Bantu Philosophy*, the second European-authored work to have an important impact in such circles was *Dieu d'eau, entretiens avec Ogotemmeli* (translated as Griaule 1965) in 1948, by the French anthropologist Marcel Griaule. The book was based on Griaule's interviews with a blind elder of the Dogon people in the then still French-ruled Mali. The old man explained to Griaule an elaborate Dogon cosmogony, philosophical system, and set of religious beliefs. Like the system Tempels discerned among the Baluba, the Dogon world-view centred on a single all-pervading principle: [1] 'Nommo', which meant simultaneously the Word, creative power, water, and the divine twins whose creation had set the world in motion. Also like Tempels's Bantu system, these Dogon beliefs were handed down supposedly unchanged from the distant past, and were held unanimously by all Dogon – or so Griaule implied. Critics responded that this was an impossibly idealized and undynamic picture of 'tradition', one which might well represent not so much the shared ideas of the Dogon as the personal interpretations of the individuals Ogotemmeli and/or Griaule. As Kenyan philosopher D.A. Masolo put it, it was a 'mixture of dogonized Griaule and griaulized Dogon' (Masolo 1994: 69). More recent anthropological field-work suggests that Dogon in general do not share – indeed, disclaim – much of the knowledge and beliefs attributed to them by Graiule/Ogotemmeli (Van Beek 1991). It was even suggested that Ogotemmeli might have been deliberately hoodwinking Griaule, especially in relation to the strikingly advanced knowledge of astronomy attributed to Dogon tradition (see below, pp. 269–70).[2]

Griaule's findings were appealing to many African intellectuals, especially those influenced by Senghorian *négritude* or by existentialism, for the same reasons as were Tempels's, and with the important addition that significant parallels could be discerned between Dogon beliefs as presented by Griaule and ancient Egyptian religion. Soon African philosophers began to apply and develop their ideas, the first important figure to do so being the Rwandan Alexis Kagame in the early 1950s. Perhaps inevitably, Kagame and those who thought like him were more concerned to emphasize the rationality of African belief systems than was Tempels: Kagame was particu-larly insistent on tracing similarities between Bantu philosophy and that of ancient Greece (see Masolo 1994: 84–102). Shortly thereafter, John S. Mbiti elaborated a view of traditional African religious thought, stressing its coherence and sophistication, its congruence in important respects with Christian belief, its association with a distinctive, non-linear conception of time, and once again the alleged great similarities of belief systems across a large part of the continent (Mbiti 1969).

In this way what was dubbed ethnophilosophy was born, and Tempels, Griaule, Kagame and Mbiti have remained its most influential exponents, though they have many followers.[3] As we shall see, the main ideas also migrated across the Atlantic and had a major impact among Afro-American thinkers. But it soon came under sharp attack from African philosophers themselves.

The central focus for assault was the uncritical attitude ethnophilosophy maintained towards the ideas it examined. At its worst and lowest, ethnophi-losophy amounted to little – if anything – more than collecting the proverbs and folktales of a people and presenting them as if they were a philosophical system. Such collection may (so the critics conceded) have antiquarian or curiosity value, but to see its limitations as a form of knowledge, one has only to imagine trying to conduct any serious discussion in such a form:

> Dr A: Are you going to vote for the Government, or do you think we need a change?
> Professor B: Well, look before you leap, as my mother always said.
> A: Aye, but nothing ventured, nothing gained.
> B: Still, a bird in the hand is worth two in the bush.
> A: Maybe, but a change is as good as a feast.
> [*Interjection from a non-philosophical bystander.* How about the idea of a coalition?]

B: Mmm . . . they say many hands make light work.
A: But too many cooks spoil the broth.
B: If you can't stand the heat, get out of the kitchen.
A: Out of the frying pan, into the fire.
B: There'll be a cuckoo in the nest, mark my words.
A: Or a dog in the manger.
B: It's no use crying over spilt milk.
A: That's just sour grapes.

At this point, in the cultural model apparently preferred by some advocates of ethnophilosophy and Afrocentrism, Professor B concedes the argument because she recalls that Dr A is older than her, or because he is male, or because he has mentioned grapes, whose proverbial sexual connotations make them an unfit subject for mixed company.

Ethnophilosophy is based on beliefs that in every 'culture' there is a system of metaphysics, largely unchanging over time, generally if not unanimously shared among the members of the community in question, and unique to that community. This is a highly questionable assumption, as critics like Paulin Hountondji, Marcien Towa and Kwasi Wiredu have pointed out: it is indeed, they have said, an unfounded and even absurd one. Adding to the absurdity is the widespread claim that a single such metaphysical system exists across the whole African continent; and that (as some ethnophilosophers soon began to add) it derives in all its essentials from ancient Egypt, which itself drew it all from some unspecified parts of the continent further south, and in its turn provided all the major intellectual resources for Greek – and thus for European – thought.

Hountondji, a Marxist philosopher from Benin who had studied under Louis Althusser in Paris, labelled this basic error of ethnophilosophy 'unanimism'. Hountondji, and many others, pointed out that the belief systems of African peoples were vastly more varied than the ethnophilosophers asserted, and often incompatible with one another. To assume, furthermore, that all members of a particular society – rich and poor, male and female, rural and urban, and so on – share the same beliefs is to subscribe to a myth about a singular 'African mind' of the very kind shared by colonialist discourse and conservative forms of nationalism alike. Hountondji is thus sharply critical of the whole ethnophilosophical project. In his view, quite apart from its analytical flaws, it is a form of sentimental exoticism which panders to European prejudices about inferior African rationality (Hountondji 1983).

Moreover – and this was a point the Ghanaian philosopher Kwasi Wiredu made with particular force – there is no great value in merely *describing* traditional beliefs, whether or not they are labelled 'philosophy' and even if (unlike many of the ethnophilosophers) one describes them accurately. To do so is neither a serious contribution to philosophical knowledge nor of relevance to the practical tasks facing modern Africa. Any philosophy worth the name, in Wiredu's opinion, must involve properly critical and logical methods; and these methods are not culture-specific but universal (Wiredu 1979, 1980, 1992). Using such tools, one must analyse *critically* and, where appropriate, *develop* such insights as may be contained in 'traditional' African beliefs. Doing this is not abandonment of one's own cultural traditions but creative use of them, part of a task of development in which all the world's peoples are involved. *Not* to do it, Wiredu insists, is to acquiesce in the inherent authoritarianism of 'traditional' oral cultures where the ideas of the long-dead, interpreted by the elderly and the powerful, exercise tyranny over the minds of the living. The Cameroonian Marcien Towa, making a similar point in a more openly politicized, Marxian manner, charges that ethnophilosophy and *négritude*, with their hostility to innovation, science and technology, entail servitude to an unholy alliance of colonial or neo-colonial exploiters and local African powerholders (see Masolo 1994: 164–78; Bjornson 1991: 202–5).

The critique of ethnophilosophy has more recently been pressed further by the Kenyan D.A. Masolo (1994), the Zaïrois Valentin Mudimbe (1988, 1991, 1994), and the Ghanaian Kwame Anthony Appiah (1992). Masolo attempts an overview rather than a polemical intervention; but there is no doubt where his sympathies lie. His judgements on the post-Tempels ethnophilosophical currents are scathing; he correctly shows how vastly superior in rigour and pertinence have been the 'Eurocentric' analytical approaches, whether primarily influenced by Anglophone linguistic or pragmatist traditions or by Marxist and other more evidently politicized approaches. And he is simply scornful of American Afrocentrism. Mudimbe, engaged in even wider-ranging analyses of conceptions of Africa, drawing on theological (especially in Mudimbe 1991) and ethnographic as well as philosophical literatures, and adopting a framework heavily influenced by Michel Foucault, is less evidently *parti pris*; but he, too, concludes with harsh judgements on the ethnophilosophical tradition as 'a type of convenience history' (1988: 192) and 'primitivist strategies' (ibid.: 195).

After Hountondji, Towa and Wiredu, the most powerful attack on ethnophilosophy and associated assumptions has been made by the philosopher Kwame Anthony Appiah. His polymathic and polemical book *In My Father's House* (Appiah 1992) has become probably the most widely read work in the field. He echoes and extends the criticisms made by Wiredu and others. As Appiah points out, the mere description of a belief system without any critical assessment can have no more than curiosity value:

> [I]t might, I suppose, lead to intellectual tolerance, but it might just as easily lead to chauvinism or total incomprehension: 'So they believe all that; so what? They're wrong, aren't they?' (ibid.: 151)

But, he says, the ethnophilosophers never go beyond this descriptive stage. They stop just where serious thought must start.

Such assault on the views of Tempels, Kagame and their followers in Africa implies in the North American context – as we shall see in detail later on – equally sharp rejection of the founding assumptions of the Afrocentrists, who have launched predictable counterattacks. Victor O. Okafor, for instance, charges that Appiah's *In My Father's House* 'plays into the hands of those who need a legitimation of the Eurocentric view of Africa' (Okafor 1993: 210). It is striking, however, that such critiques appear not to engage with the *content* of arguments like those of Mudimbe, Wiredu, Hountondji or Appiah at all. They merely repeat the supposed need, on usually unstated political or psychological grounds, to retain belief in a distinctive, continent-wide and unanimously held African – and African-diasporic – world-view. Nor do they note the fact – potentially embarrassing to them – that their hero Cheikh Anta Diop agreed at least in part with the critics of ethnophilosophy, urging that the systems of thought described by such writers as Tempels and Kagame 'cannot be considered to be a philosophy in the classical sense' (Diop 1991: 323). Beyond that, what underpins this insistence seems to be a notion that a belief or an idea found in Africa, however trivial, incoherent or false, is of significance merely because it is African. Such a notion is dismissed, with varying degrees of impatient scorn, by thinkers like Wiredu, Hountondji, Mudimbe, Appiah, Towa and Masolo. For many people in North America, by contrast, haunted by a pressure of racism and its legacies far more direct than that experienced by the intellectuals of independent Africa, it remains emotionally compelling.

It is dangerous for someone largely without formal philosophical training, and without knowledge of many of the languages whose special features are important to these debates, to venture overall judgement on them. However, such a non-specialist can attempt to evaluate the formal features of the contending arguments: the standards of logic, coherence, lucidity, amount of evidence deployed, and so on. In these respects it seems to me that there is simply no contest. The critics of ethnophilosophy – Hountondji, Appiah, Wiredu, Towa, Masolo, and the rest – seem to me to adhere to generally higher standards of argument than their opponents. Their views are expressed in more lucid form (with the partial exception of the Althusserian jargon disfiguring Hountondji's early work!), they proceed more often by reasoned argument as opposed to mere assertion or description, their work is more coherent. To some, no doubt, that view simply shows that I have an irredeemably Eurocentric conception of coherence.

Notes

1. Kwame Appiah's satire hits the point exactly:

Soon to be published:*THING: Western Culture and the African World*, a work which exposes the philosophy of ING, written so clearly on the face of the English language. For ING, in the Euro-American view, is the inner dynamic essence of the world. In the very structure of the terms do*ing* and mak*ing* and mean*ing*, the English (and thus, by extension, all westerners) express their deep commitment to this conception . . . Here we see the fundamental explanation for the extraordinary neophilia of western culture, its sense that reality is change.' (1992/3: 13–14)

2. Clifford (1988: 55–91) gives some biographical detail on Griaule, with a postmodernist interpretation of his work which seeks to dissolve questions about the accuracy of its findings by viewing it as 'a complex, negotiated, historically contingent truth specific to certain relations of textual production' (60).

3. Serequeberham (1991) reproduces some of the key texts. Masolo (1994) is an excellent overview and critique, as are the briefer surveys in Bodunrin (1984) and Gyekye (1987). Some recent phases in the debates, including convergence between their preoccupations and those of postcolonial cultural theory, can be traced in the various contributions to Eze (ed.) (1997).

14

Cheikh Anta Diop

By far the most important single figure in the development of what is now called Afrocentric thought is the Senegalese historian Cheikh Anta Diop. Indeed, one might say that every significant idea or claim put forward by Afrocentrists today was earlier expressed by him (though as we have seen, many of them also have a much older, more diffuse ancestry). The only real exceptions to this are the wilder, more mystical and more racially exclusivist assertions made by extreme Afrocentrists. These Diop did not anticipate; for although his work involves many unsustainable claims, his was primarily a career of rational intellectual inquiry. Not only did his writings precede those of the currently high-profile US Afrocentrists, they are in almost every respect superior.

Very few academics can ever have had popular record albums named in their honour. It is an index of Cheikh Anta Diop's reputation, especially posthumously, that the leading Senegalese group Super Diamono titled one of their best-known LPs with his name. Diop was born in Senegal in 1923 and died there, relatively young, of a heart attack in 1986. His background was that of an aristocratic Wolof family: later acquaintances often remarked on his patrician manner and bearing, and elements of social and ethnic disdain seem to creep into the way certain Senegalese ethnic groups or 'castes' are described in his writings.[1]

His early education was Islamic, but he achieved a scholarship to the Sorbonne in Paris, initially to study mathematics. There, his interests seem to have diversified remarkably, involving both a specialism in nuclear physics and a growing enthusiasm for Egyptology. His historical writing was to face widespread opposition – not only for the idiosyncratic and adventurous nature of the theses he advanced, but for the fact that these came from someone not conventionally trained in the relevant disciplines. He believed there were more sinister reasons for hostility – in taking up Egyptology, he was approaching hidden secrets: 'I noticed that whenever a Black showed the slightest interest in things Egyptian, Whites would actually begin to tremble' (Moore interview 1989: 372). He remained in France from 1946 to 1960, receiving his MA and doctorate from Paris, though the latter was awarded only after considerable controversy and initial rejection. He also taught at Paris high schools, and participated in the activities of the *Présence Africaine* group. From 1961 until his death he headed the radiocarbon laboratory at IFAN (the Fundamental [originally the French] Institute of Black Africa) at Dakar University. In 1981, belatedly, his historical work was given institutional recognition when he was appointed Professor of Egyptology and Prehistory at Dakar. This did not prevent his champions, like obituarist Babacar Sall in *West Africa*, from alleging that the University neglected and failed to support him through the years. Sall described Diop as 'an intellectual liberator fighting against the falsification of history, against academic charlatanism. All his life he did this work in a terrible solitude' (Sall 1986: 1162). Ironically, the University itself was renamed in Diop's honour after his death.

Alongside his academic career, Diop pursued an intense but decreasingly successful political involvement. He was a founder of the Rassemblement Démocratique Africaine in Paris, and its student organization's Secretary-General from 1950–1953. Returning to Dakar, he established the Bloc des Masses Sénégalaises in opposition to Senghor's government, but this foundered as many members accepted offers to join the ruling party. Diop held firm against such blandishments, but soon thereafter a one-party state was effectively proclaimed, and his efforts to found new opposition parties – first the Front National du Sénégal, then the Rassemblement National Démocratique – met with official bars. Still, in Senegal's relatively mild version of authoritarianism, Diop and his supporters remained able to voice open dissent throughout the 1960s and 1970s. Gradually, from the mid 1970s onwards, Senegal moved back towards a multi-party system, but with few benefits for Diop's RND, which won just one seat in the 1983 elections.

The major intellectual influences Diop acknowledged were interestingly diverse. In his early Paris days, Aimé Césaire was evidently the greatest formative presence, both personally and through his writings (Moore interview 1989: 403–5). More broadly, Diop stressed the ancient Greek Stoic materialists – Democritus, Epicurus, Lucretius – together with Marx and Engels, Lenin, Stalin and Plekhanov, Hegel, Goethe, Alfred de Vigny, the historian of Antiquity Fustel de Coulanges, and Albert Einstein (Diop quoted in Gray 1989: 122). The views on ancient history in Diop (1987) are heavily – indeed, excessively – reliant on the now thoroughly outdated work of de Coulanges. The presence of the Greeks is intriguing in a list of inspirations drawn up by someone so strongly associated with the claims of Egypt's priority over Greece. Interesting in a different way is the emphasis on a Marxism of a strongly orthodox Soviet cast, including Stalin himself. Doubtless this reflects the Parisian leftist intellectual milieu of Diop's youth. He was to continue a close if sometimes somewhat timelagged engagement with French and Marxist thought despite his Afrocentrism: his last major book, for instance, includes substantial critical discussion of Jean-Paul Sartre and of French Marxist anthropology (Diop 1991: 185–207, 223–4).

Diop's ideas were evidently formed early in his career, and changed little thereafter. In lectures and articles in 1950 and 1952, he was already proposing his main themes: the character of ancient Egypt as a black African civilization, the continuity of its cultural influences across the continent and across the centuries, the culturo-historical unity of Africa. His first book, *Nations nègres et culture* (partially translated in Diop [1974a]), appeared in 1955. In 1960 he published *L'unité culturelle de l'Afrique noire* (originally translated as *The Cultural Unity of Negro Africa* in 1963; republished in English as Diop [1989]). In the same year were issued *L'Afrique noire précoloniale* (translated as Diop [1987]) and a more directly political tract, *Les Fondements culturels, techniques et industriels d'un état fédéral d'Afrique noire* (Diop 1960; an updated version is translated as Diop [1984]). The first three books were all based on successive versions of his doctoral thesis, which may partially account for the considerable degree of repetition within them. The fourth reflected another lifelong concern, which his historical writings were designed to support – his political Pan-Africanism and opposition to the colonial and postcolonial 'Balkanization' of the continent. *Antériorité des civilisations nègres* (1967; partially translated in Diop [1974a]) substantially repeated earlier arguments by way of a response to critics – especially the Dakar professor Raymond Mauny, who had been one of the first to attack Diop's theses at length. In *Parenté génétique de l'égyptien pharaonique et des langues négro-africaines* (1977) he sought to marshal considerably more linguistic evidence than hitherto in support of his claims for Egyptian influence across black Africa. A sequel to this, supplementing its arguments with extra evidence from linguistics, appeared posthumously as *Nouvelles recherches sur l'égyptien ancien et les langues négro-africaines modernes* in 1988. His final major work was the most ambitious. *Civilisation ou barbarie: Anthropologie sans complaisance*, published in 1981 (translated as Diop [1991])[2] placed his long-held views on Africa in the context of a general theory of human development. Diop also composed many articles and addresses – perhaps most influentially, papers for the two major conferences of Pan-African intellectuals held by *Présence Africaine* in 1956 and 1959, and his chapter in the *UNESCO General History of Africa* (Mokhtar 1981) – but on the whole these do little but repeat themes from his books in briefer or more polemical form (many of these, mostly on issues of contemporary African politics, are collected posthumously as Diop [1990]).[3]

Given this lifelong dedication to a single package of ideas, Diop's theses may be summarized quite briefly. Both the biological origin of humanity, and the emergence of civilization, took place in Africa. Egypt was the cradle of the latter, was specifically a black or Negro civilization, and was the fullest flowering of a cultural system unifying the whole African continent. That cultural system not only originated most important aspects of human social and intellectual development, but was distinct from Eurasian societies in its matriarchal, spiritual, peaceable and humanistic character. Ancient Greece – and hence all European civilization – took almost everything of value usually claimed to be theirs from this antecedent African-Egyptian culture. Africa, Diop urged, must recover the glories of its ancient past, rejecting the colonial and racist mystifications which had obscured those glories, and progress to the future by drawing on the lessons of the old Nile valley philosophies. The political corollary of this is the need for a single, federal African state which, taking confidence from the unique greatness of past African achievements, will stand equal with Europe and the rest of the world.

It would be wrong, however, to imply that Diop's thought was entirely static. The three books deriving from his doctoral research included many very polemical assertions, some of which, he was later to suggest, had always been intended as hypotheses, provocations to others to conduct new research, rather than firmly held beliefs. Later work, especially *Civilization or Barbarism*, his 1981 *magnum opus*, was often rather less dogmatic in tone (though the tendency was not all one way, as the thoughts on comparative historical sociology in *Civilization or Barbarism* are often more sweeping and questionable, though based on wider reading, than those in the earlier *Precolonial Black Africa*). It also indicated a closer engagement with more recent theories, especially French Marxist anthropology, with its revival of the notion of an 'Asiatic Mode of Production'. Diop took over the theory of an Asiatic Mode with modifications (predictably, he preferred to call it the *African* Mode of Production); though he was still open to the charge of often relying on out-of-date sources. If his primary purpose was always to establish the historico-cultural unity of Africa, the ubiquitous influence of ancient Egypt and the 'blackness' of the latter, a secondary but recurrent theme in his work followed an essentially Marxian problematic: to explain what he saw as the millennia-long stable equilibrium of African societies, the lack of social revolutions in their history (see esp. Diop 1987, 1991 Part II).

Echoes of the *Annales* school of French historians could also be found in Diop's later writings, but largely without direct citation. Clearly what he was attempting had at least elective affinities with the work of *Annales* godfather Fernand Braudel and others: like them, he was interested in a history which did not narrate events, but described very long-term changes in demographies, economies and cultures. He was essaying a vision of the 'longue durée', to use Braudel's famous rallying-cry, in Africa. But this also meant that classic faults of the *Annales* approach were replicated – indeed, compounded – in Diop's writings. There was little attention to chronology or even development over time: comparison between different precolonial African societies all too often seemed to juxtapose motionless entities rather than trace dynamic interaction. As two younger Senegalese researchers, Mohamed Mbodj and Mamadou Diouf, have alleged, his comparative method was 'organized in terms of stratification, and therefore of immutability' (1986: quoted in Gray 1989: 26).

Some of this was inherent in the nature of the sources – establishing chronologies for precolonial African history is always notoriously difficult, since neither oral tradition, nor archaeology, nor linguistic evidence can provide a precise framework of dates. But it was exacerbated by what Jean Duvignard reasonably complained was Diop's tendency to 'lyrical generalisation and poetic assimilation' (quoted in Gray 1989: 24); and it was equally evident in cases where a fairly clear chronological account and a picture of development over time *were* available. Thus Diop's discussions of ancient Egyptian culture seemed to treat the near-3,000-year history of the successive Pharaonic states as a single, static entity.

This was something which his later view that Pharaonic Egypt was the original version of the 'Asiatic Mode of Production' only intensified (see, among several such discussions, Diop [1967: 124–89]). What Marxist theoreticians routinely abbreviated as the 'AMP' was itself a notably non-developmental, homogenizing concept; and it was remarkably close to the standard European prejudice against which Diop was protesting – that Egypt and later African societies were stagnant civilizations, whereas ancient Greece and modern Europe were dynamic ones. Perhaps worse, his treatment of comparative world revolutions in *Civilization or Barbarism* (1991: chs 9–11), and his attempt to formulate 'laws of ethnic relations' (ibid.: ch. 7), jumped over centuries and continents with blithe abandon. It sometimes seemed as if, to Diop, all history was contemporary, the question of the Pharaohs as immediate as that of neo-colonialism in Senegal: that his conception of time was non-linear (see Jewsiewicki 1989: 4–5; 1992: 106–7), almost in the manner frequently associated with African cosmographies by the more obscurantist ethnophilosophers (e.g. D. Pennington 1985) or the most scornful European chroniclers.

We should perhaps remember, in mitigation, that Diop's early work had been conducted not only before the major impact of Braudel's great book on the Mediterranean world, which established the validity of a history not based on events, but before publication of Jan Vansina's groundbreaking work on African oral history, or Joseph Greenberg's historical linguistics; before the Leakeys made an African origin for humanity almost indubitable; before the 1960s revival of a serious Marxist historiography – indeed, before many people took the idea of an African history seriously at all. Even in his later life, Diop operated in a Francophone milieu where African historical research remained seriously underdeveloped by comparison with the English-speaking world (see, for example, Klein 1986).

Yet much of Diop's work was evidently and badly flawed by its reliance on out-of-date sources, a tendency which deepened as he grew older. As Augustin Holl remarks, right up to his death Diop 'behaved as if nothing new had occurred in African archaeology in general, and especially in West African archaeology, history, linguistics, and social anthropology' (Holl 1995: 207). His enthusiasm for the work of Leo Frobenius is a striking case in point. Frobenius – whose damaging early influence on European Africanism we have already noted – was a highly idiosyncratic German writer active in the 1890s, whose ideas may have appealed to Diop because of his belief in Egyptian influences on West African civilization, or simply because he was less nakedly racist than most Africanists of his time; but he had not been taken seriously by specialists for decades even at the time of Diop's first publications. The character of Frobenius's efforts (memorably

satirized in Yambo Ouloguem's novel *Le Devoir de violence*) is well summed
up in the savage assessment of J.D. Fage:

> encumbered by mystic theories relating to Atlantis, to an Etruscan influence
> on African culture, and so on . . . a self-taught eccentric whose work is flawed
> not only by his outlandish interpretations but also by his rapid, crude and
> often destructive methods of fieldwork. (Fage 1981: 37–8)

In his contribution to the *UNESCO General History of Africa*, Diop relied
mainly on authorities dating anywhere from the 1830s to the 1930s,
referring to not a single work on African or Egyptian history that had
appeared less than twenty years before his essay's publication (Diop 1981:
passim). Nor does he appear anywhere to have discussed any historico-
philosophical theory that developed, even in France, during the 1960s or
1970s: for instance, I have found only one passing, uninformative reference
in all Diop's writings to that highly influential and controversial younger
figure in the field, Michel Foucault (Diop 1985: 19).

In *The Cultural Unity of Black Africa*, Diop builds his argument mostly
around disagreements with the theses of J.J. Bachofen, Lewis Henry Morgan
and Friedrich Engels rather than any more contemporary anthropological
theory. The peculiarity of this procedure will be apparent: here, as too often
elsewhere in his work, Diop was pursuing a debate with the Victorians
(Bachofen wrote in the 1860s, Morgan in the 1870s, Engels in the 1880s),
and failing to take modern research into account. This was poor enough
when Diop did his original work in the 1950s, worse when he repeated his
ideas virtually unchanged in the 1970s and 1980s, absurd when his Anglophone fans still cite his theories as the last word for the 1990s.

In his last book, *Civilization or Barbarism*, he makes much of Grimaldi Man
fossils and their alleged African origins – reflecting ideas which had been
discredited long before the book was written, for it is generally accepted
nowadays that the Grimaldi fossils do *not* represent either a distinct human
subspecies or evidence of migration from Africa – and even flogs the dead
horse of the Piltdown Man forgery (1991: 13–16, 25–9, 39–52). He affirms
similarities between prehistoric European cave paintings and those of
southern Africa (ibid.: 11–15) – failing to note that as even Joseph Ki-Zerbo,
a Diop fan, admits (Ki-Zerbo 1981b: 660), the Sub-Saharan rock paintings
are newer than those in the Sahara, and both are considerably less old than
the European Palaeolithic specimens. There is good reason to think that
the rock art of southern Africa reflects a very old artistic tradition, going
back as far as 28,000 years (Phillipson 1993: 74–8), but most of the extant
remains are relatively recent, so comparison of its images with the European
ones cannot provide evidence of influence in either direction; and there is
no other kind of evidence for such influence or diffusion (Ki-Zerbo 1981b:
660, 675; and see also Whitney Davis 1990; Garlake 1995b).

Perhaps the most striking and surprising anachronism of all, the most
remarkable instance of Diop's failure to keep abreast of new developments,

was that the post-1960s explosion in Africanist history-writing, including the substantial body of work by African historians themselves, barely features in his work. The Bibliography to *Civilization or Barbarism* includes several references to commentaries on his own earlier books by his American disciples – some of them effusions of very dubious value – but hardly a single piece of modern African historical research. Earlier, mentioning the decline in the power of Yoruba kingship, he remarked: 'It would be helpful to know whether this shrinkage of royal power preceded or resulted from the British occupation' (1974a: 224); whereas if he had paid any attention at all to African historiography he would have known of a mass of literature illuminating this point, from Samuel Johnson's pioneering chronicle (1921) onwards.

Writing in the context of Senegalese intellectual history, and especially the new climates of thought preceding independence, Michael Crowder sees Diop's significance as above all political. His work 'gives an extreme idealization of African history' (Crowder 1967: 55), and 'contain[s] marked elements of counter-racism' (ibid.: 57). The impact of these negative tendencies, however, was in Crowder's view, shortlived:

> What is important is that a Senegalese, of undoubted scholastic attainment, had reinterpreted the history not only of his country but of the continent as a whole, so that it could be put on equal terms with that of Europe. (ibid.: 55)

Certainly Diop's purpose was primarily polemical and political. He repeated throughout his career the claim that adopting his view of ancient Africa and Egypt offered a way forward politically, culturally and psychologically for twentieth-century Africans. As early as 1956 he told the First International Congress of Negro Writers and Artists: 'the ancient Egyptian and Pharaonic civilization was a Negro civilization ... all Africans can draw the same moral advantage from it that Westerners draw from Graeco-Latin civilization' (Diop 1956: 349–51). This notion of 'moral advantage', vague as it may sound, was a constant with him, and became one of the ideas which has resonated most strongly among later Afrocentrists. And in his last major book he reiterated the same thought: 'A look towards the Egypt of antiquity is the best way to conceive and build our cultural future' (1991: 3). He even suggested elsewhere that a programme of educational reform could be drawn from his historical views: 'The new African humanities must build themselves on the foundations of the antique pharaonic culture. Ancient Egyptian and Meroitic should replace Latin and Greek in (teaching) programmes. Egyptian law should take the place of Roman law' – and Egyptian philosophy should be taught with that of Greece to show their affinities (1977: xxv; see also 1991: 215–16). Diouf and Mbodj indeed allege that for Diop: 'history is nothing but a means to serve the realization of a political plan' (1992: 120).

Diop did not feel, however, that this political purpose was at odds with scholarship. Indeed, he insisted many times that his work was of value only 'provided it does not depart from a strictly *scientific* terrain' (Moore interview 1989: 375; original emphasis). His 1967 book *Antériorité des civilisations nègres* carried an epigraph from Brecht: 'La vérité est concrète' – truth is concrete. What distinguished his views from the Senghorian version of négritude, he argued, was precisely his attention to the world of ascertainable facts rather than racial mystique:

> my work in history, sociology and linguistics kept to the path of objective verifiable reality. By throwing light on the falsifications to which the historical past of the black man has been subjected, these historical, sociological and linguistic studies serve to reinforce the cultural personality of Africans. (Moore interview: 406)

Diop was also critical, on similar grounds, of ethnophilosophy. The study of African thought would, he believed, become scientific only when ethnophilosophical cosmogonies:

> occupy their chronological place like a mummy in its sarcophagus. . . . It is essential, therefore, to break away from the atemporal structural study of African cosmogonies, because by isolating oneself from the historical framework, one becomes exhausted in a false battle. (1991: 4)

If Diop saw the differences between himself and the Senghorian mainstream of *négritude* thought as the distinction between mysticism and science (see 1991: 217–18), Senghor was inclined to see them as mostly generational (quoted in Gray 1989: 41). But fundamentally, apart from directly political disputes, these were different conceptions of the role of race in history. Senghor's final message, as we have seen, was humanist and universalist; Diop's – albeit with modifications and inconsistencies – was exclusivist and essentialist. Senghor, symptomatically, did not see the ancient Egyptians as 'black', but as a mixed population (see Gray 1989: 44–5), and associated this perception with his general positive view of hybridity or *métissage*.

Was Diop himself a racist? One must answer: no – though one must qualify this answer by saying that his thinking was always intensely, if not entirely consistently, *racial* in its assumptions. He argued several times that denial of the reality of race was merely a latter-day Eurocentric evasion:

> The Europeans, all the Occidentals, say there is no race. But they know very well what a white man is . . . every time these relationships are not favorable to the Western cultures, an effort is made to undermine the cultural consciousness of Africans by telling them 'we don't even know what a race is' (Finch interview 1989: 366–7; see also Diop 1991: 16–17)

Race as genotype, he always believed, although it was important from a scientific point of view, was uninfluential historically; in the story of societies and their relations, phenotype was all.

All of humanity's historical and social relations, from the beginnings of time right up to the nineteenth century, were ethnic relations, founded on phenotype . . . humanity has been governed essentially in its development by these ethnic confrontations. (Finch interview: 368)

In an earlier interview, however, he had qualified this sweeping view, suggesting that racism in anything like the modern sense was *not* ubiquitous in Antiquity, though it could be discerned in the Assyrians and the Romans. He often used the discredited term 'Aryan' in his earlier writings, though he dropped it in *Civilization or Barbarism*, and even earlier he insisted that his employment of it 'has nothing to do with either racial purity or any other racist-intended notions' (Moore interview 1989: 376–7).

Yet Diop certainly did not seem to believe that this past history of racial conflict was either desirable, or inevitably fated to continue in future. Indeed, a rather vague kind of idealism governed his view of potential futures (see Moore interview 1989: 378–9). Racial coexistence would be possible 'in a truly Socialist state, or a state that has adopted a high moral philosophy' (Diop 1991: 124). He was convinced that acceptance of his theories would lead to the unification first of Africa as a whole, then of all humanity:

The rediscovery of the true past of the African peoples should not be a divisive factor but should contribute to uniting them, each and all, binding them together from the north to the south of the continent so as to enable them to carry out together a new historical mission for the greater good of mankind. (1981: 51)

And he appeared – usually – to want to insist, too, that when he spoke of race, he really meant *culture*. 'When we talk about personality, meaning the personality of collective groups, we can only mean a *cultural personality*' (Moore interview 408; original emphasis). If this appears to slide towards the besetting sin in racialized thought – of confounding race with culture – his treatment of the latter concept also seemed radically inconsistent. In interview in 1976, he said: 'I consider culture as a rampart which protects a people, a collectivity. Culture must above all play a protective role; it must ensure the *cohesion* of a group' (Moore interview 375; original emphasis). Elsewhere, however, he appeared to take a less essentialist view, and to look forward to a future of greater cultural intermingling. In replying to his critic Raymond Mauny, he even apologized for 'returning to notions of race, cultural heritage, linguistic relationship, historical connections between peoples, and so on. I attach no more importance to these questions than they actually deserve' (1974a: 236).

Diop was certainly not among those who saw all Africa's ills coming from
outside – though of course this was his main emphasis – or entirely
romanticized precolonial African cultures. For instance, he recognized lack
of literacy, and practices of passing on knowledge only through initiation
from the elders, as major weaknesses. This was:

> [N]ot the best way to transmit or generalize examination of scientific
> knowledge. Nor does this system allow for the critical examination of
> scientific theories. This has been extremely harmful to the technological and
> social development of traditional black societies. The monopoly of knowl-
> edge by a restricted group of religious men has been detrimental. (Moore
> interview 382)

Diop's initial arguments for strong connections between ancient Egypt
and Sub-Saharan Africa were something of a grab-bag of disparate elements,
most of them sketchily described – though in later writings he was
considerably to expand the list, especially in relation to supposed linguistic
affinities. He mentions totemism, without putting forward any specific
common features at all on this front (1974a: 134–5; though see also 1967:
71–96); circumcision, for which the only specific instance he gives of beliefs
paralleling the Egyptian comes from Dogon cosmology (1974a: 135–8);
divine kingship, on which he relies entirely on Charles Seligman's far-
fetched theories (ibid: 138–9; see also 1991: 181); cosmogony, for which
Father Tempels and, again, Marcel Griaule on the Dogon are the sole and
unquestioned authorities (139–41; see also 1967: 108–14), and which
suggest to Diop an 'identity of mental structure . . . of genius, culture, and
race' between Egyptians and 'Negroes' (ibid.: 140–41); a supposedly shared
matriarchal system, although Diop fails to offer any evidence whatsoever
that ancient Egypt *was* matriarchal (142–5); and kinship patterns, in relation
to which he appears to wander off the point altogether to mention tenuous
similarities between names of gods and to assert, both irrelevantly and
groundlessly: 'When Mohammed was born, Arabia was a Negro colony'
(151). Finally he turns to language, proclaiming that it 'is easy to prove the
profound unity of Egyptian and Negro languages' (153). In fact Diop was to
spend much of the rest of his life in a vain attempt to do just that.

The assertion which Diop throws in of seventh-century Arabia as a 'Negro
colony' (presumably intended to imply that the Prophet himself was a black
African, though it is intriguing that Diop, with his own Islamic upbringing,
never returned to any more detailed elaboration of this claim[4]) is not
untypical of his tendency to weaken his own credibility by inserting
implausible suggestions quite unconnected to his main theories. He speculated also about ancient contacts between Africa and the Americas, his
'evidence' being the vague similarities among *two* Eskimo words, one North
American Indian one, two Wolof ones, the name of a Mexican city, and
(quite bizarrely) an old German song title (1974a: 183)! This piece of wild
speculation, with Diop's subsequent assertion that the Inuit are black, later

helped to form the basis for quite elaborate theorizing (or mythologizing) by Ivan Van Sertima and his collaborators (Van Sertima 1977, 1985), as we shall see. In similar offhand style, Diop proclaimed 'no doubt on the southern and Negro origin of the megaliths in Brittany' (1974a: 194). He captioned an assemblage of illustrations in one book with a series of emphatic assertions about the 'negroid' nature of various Egyptian representations. The Pharaoh Dejezer was a 'typical negro'. Cheops was seen as 'resembling the contemporary Cameroonian type'. The Sphinx showed a 'typical negro profile ... it is neither Hellene nor Semite: it is Bantu'. In Egyptian work scenes, 'the suppleness of body and allure of movements' indicated their essential Africanicity (1967: Plates xvii, xviii, xix, xxxiv). Most tenuously of all, pictures of hairstyles (ibid.: Plates xxxv–xl) and of supposedly 'totemistic' images (Plates xliv–xlviii), or of the Malian Gao mosque, with its imagined resemblance to an Egyptian step pyramid (Plate lxxxiii), were held to prove intimate connections. In a later article (Diop 1973) he claimed, mainly on the basis of linguistic affinities, to be able to identify the precise original home of the Senegalese peoples in the Nile valley.

None of this is to say that there is *no* plausibility in arguing for connections between ancient Egypt and particular traits in specific, later, Sub-Saharan African cultures. However, a more careful scholar than Diop, Benjamin Ray, points out that while there are some superficially quite striking resemblances between Egyptian ideas – for instance, about kingship – and those of the Baganda kingdom in what is now Uganda, even there:

> If kingship ... had once been part of a unified kingship complex to which ancient Egypt belonged, surely Buganda and Bunyoro would have retained some elements identical to those of ancient Egypt. But none are to be found. (Ray 1991: 196)

Ray counsels great caution in presuming that similarities are evidence of direct influence. Not a single Egyptian artifact has ever been found in Sub-Saharan East Africa (ibid.: 196). The ideas about kingship which do seem to be similar are not uniquely African: parallels can be found all over the world (ibid.: 197–8). Remnants of ancient Egyptian kingship 'simply cannot be recognised' in East Africa (198).

It is possible, too, that the ritual and monumental burials, mostly dating from c.500 to 1000 CE, to be found broadcast from Mali, across the savannah, to present-day Gambia and Senegal or Igbo Ukwu in Nigeria, may be connected in some as yet unknown way to one another, and may even owe *something* to at least indirect influence by Egyptian practices of monumental burial (Shaw 1970; Phillipson 1993: 177–80). It is possible, but as yet still entirely speculative. One might suggest, however, that if there is a case to be made of the kind Diop urges, it must be validated by a significant number of detailed studies like Ray's or Shaw's. Diop's own sweeping, impressionistic and emotive presentation, so often based not only on tenuous evidence but on unwarranted generalization from the Francophone West African and especially Senegalese experience, has failed to convince those not already strongly predisposed to be convinced.

It is notable that in their lists of supposed proofs for ancient Egypt's 'Negro origin' (and, the other side of the same coin, later Egyptian influences across the continent) neither Diop nor those who followed his hypothesis later mentioned the dog that conspicuously did not bark, to invoke the timeworn Sherlock Holmes cliché: material culture. If cultural contact and direct influence across the Sahara and down the whole length of the Nile valley had been considerable, one would naturally expect to find material objects of Egyptian origin broadcast across archaeological sites in the Sub-Saharan regions. Yet these hardly exist: the fact that archaeologists have found only a tiny handful of them, all very small and of unknown history, is a powerful piece of negative evidence concerning Egyptian influence further south or, indeed, vice versa.

Another of Diop's most constantly reiterated ideas was of an absolute contrast between African civilizations and those of the rest of the world (as he usually expressed it; though presumably he meant the *Old* World – and he had very little specific to say about South, Southeast or East Asia). The respects in which Africa was culturally unified, and sharply opposed to everywhere else, could be 'discerned in the organization of the family and of the State, in the concept of royalty, and in the philosophic and moral systems' (1959: 66). His greatest emphasis was on the first, family structure, to which he devoted major parts of two of his more important books, *The Cultural Unity of Black Africa* and *Civilization or Barbarism?*, as well as numerous articles and shorter passages elsewhere. The contrast was simple – Africa was matriarchal; everywhere else was patriarchal. It derived from environmental considerations (as we have seen, Diop was an extreme environmental determinist) and produced a huge range of contrasts in social organization, behaviour, character, beliefs and art: all of them, of course, contrasts in which the African way was superior.

This led him to numerous rather wild claims: such as that the Greeks routinely killed three-quarters of the children born to them by deliberate exposure (1959: 67); that Eurasia existed in a state of 'endemic war' as against Africa's peaceableness (ibid.: 70); that Eurasians were uniformly pessimistic, while African world-views were always based on optimism – so that only the former could have invented the idea of tragedy (1989: 152–65); and many more. Some of these are, of course, simple inversions of classic Euro-racist themes. European colonial writers had said that Africa was permanently embroiled in tribal wars, while Europe had achieved social peace, so Diop reversed the statement.

This argument, counterposing the Euro–Asian 'Northern cradle' and the African 'Southern cradle' of sharply contrasting civilizations, was most systematically developed in *The Cultural Unity of Black Africa* (1989), though he repeated it in several works up to and including *Civilization or Barbarism.* 'Of necessity,' Diop thought, 'the earliest men were ethnically homogeneous and negroid' (1981: 27). The sedentary and matriarchal roots of African society led to its being peaceful, organicist, solidaristic and collectivist. Cultures springing from the later 'Northern cradle' are individualist, competitive, preoccupied with blood and misery. They are devoted to 'An ideal of war, violence, crime and conquests, inherited from nomadic life, with as a consequence, a feeling of guilt and of original sin' (ibid.: 177). African cultures are also distinguished by the emancipation of women, by peace, justice and goodness, and by an ideal of human worth which, Diop bizarrely asserted, 'makes moral or material misery unknown (in Africa) to the present day' (ibid.: 177).

The Mediterranean formed a border zone, dominated by first matriarchal, then patriarchal, modes. West Asia, meanwhile, was a 'zone of confluence' between the systems (1981: 84–101): from there, patriarchy made inroads into Africa only with the coming of Islam (ibid.: 60–61).[5] The idea – latterly popular among feminists – that human societies in general had followed a chronological succession from matriarchy to patriarchy, however, was naturally one that Diop rejected with indignation; he therefore polemicized at length against anthropological theories which asserted this, like those of Lewis Henry Morgan, J.J. Bachofen and Friedrich Engels (1989: 5–46).

Also peculiar is the way in which Diop gives separate consideration to ancient Egypt, Ethiopia and Libya in turn, while he lumps all Sub-Saharan Africa together in an undifferentiated mass (1989: 47–64) – a procedure which threatens to repeat the very distinction that Diop is so often praised for challenging: one between literate 'high' civilizations and fundamentally less interesting 'lower' African cultures.

After his extensive but strikingly ahistorical discussion of family structures, occupying far the greater bulk of the book, Diop turned to a rather arbitrary-seeming list of 'other aspects of northern and meridional cultures' (1989: 130). He began with the idea of the state. In Africa this was founded, from the days of the Pharaohs, on 'xenophilia' (ibid.: 134) and the 'spirit of justice and piety' (149). War and conquest were entirely alien to it until they were introduced from outside (150). The origins of the state idea in the North, by contrast, were not only xenophobic and aggressive but 'very soon developed into a totalitarianism' (135). This difference could also be seen in the domain of religion: the gods of Africa were kindly; those of Eurasian cultures like Greece, Assyria and pagan Germany were aggressive, greedy and amoral (141–50). Philosophical systems – on which Diop approvingly cited the mystifying ideas of the colonial-era Belgian priest Maurice Tempels (138) – and imaginative literature (151–65) reflected the same essential division (the posthumously republished 1962/1989 makes the same arguments in rather more concise form).

Diop was evidently – even plaintively – aware of the limitations of what he could do as a solitary, multidisciplinary researcher, even hinting that charges of dilettantism might reasonably be levelled at his efforts. He spoke several times of his wish that a large interdisciplinary research team, which he might direct, should take over the baton from him (Finch interview [1989]: 361; Moore interview [1989]: 376; Van Sertima and Williams interviews [1986]: 291–5; Spady 1986: 92). Working without such a team, his sheer breadth of interests, the ambitiousness of what he was attempting, no doubt help to account not only for the scepticism with which he was viewed by many specialists, and for his failure to keep up with contemporary research in his various areas of concern, but for the heterogeneous, almost fragmentary nature of his last major work.

Civilization or Barbarism, though it is Diop's most substantial and in many ways most interesting book, juxtaposes bewilderingly diverse kinds of argument without any very evident logical order of exposition. It starts with an overview of human origins, based on alarmingly outdated evidence and reiterating a somewhat redundant case for Africa as cradle of *Homo sapiens*; then proceeds, via reflections on the Atlantis myth and the birth of Egyptian civilization, to sweeping claims on the whole history of tribal organization, race, social class, states and revolutions, including extensive but ill-integrated discussion of Marxist ideas about the 'Asiatic Mode of Production'. A brief interlude on the nature of cultural identity and intercultural relations – again quite startlingly ahistorical – is followed by two long chapters, radically unconnected with what has gone before, on ancient Egyptian 'science' (mainly mathematics, where he once more seems overwhelmingly reliant on works dating from the 1920s and 1930s; Robert Palter [1996a: esp. 235–6, 240–41] has no trouble in showing how ill-evidenced are Diop's claims in this sphere) and 'philosophy' (including a strangely assorted collection of religious doctrines which embrace such 'philosophical concepts' as 'girl', 'female noble', 'to remember', 'the desert' and the number five [1991: 360–61] and their supposed influence on Greece [see also, as an earlier and sketchier version of this argument, Diop 1967: 216–30]).[6] As an *omnium gatherum* of Diop's different preoccupations, *Civilization or Barbarism* is a kind of summation to his career. As a coherent argument, or as a book with any appearance of having been composed *as* a book rather than a collection of disparate fragments, it is a bewildering anticlimax, a failure.

Diop's concerns may have been diverse, but they were not universal. His interest in religion was apparently slight. He rarely emphasizes it in his major writings, beyond passing comments that, for instance, Akhnaten would be recognized as the 'first prophet' of monotheistic belief were it not for racism (Finch interview 1989: 364–5). His own Islamic upbringing plays little, if any, overt role in his work (Diop 1987: 162–75 is indeed quite critical of Islam's influence in Africa); nor, unlike many more mystically inclined Afrocentrists, does he make any significant claims about the truth-value of the Egyptian beliefs he studied. Equally unlike them, Diop's writings show no particular hostility to Christian or Judaic faiths – and he seems entirely free of one major disturbing tendency in latter-day Afrocentricity, anti-Semitism. For that matter, Diop was not even particularly anti-Zionist: in interview, he expressed nothing stronger than disappointment with

Israeli foreign policy, especially in relation to Israel's links with South Africa, and predicted that eventually Israeli and Arab cultures would merge because of their great intrinsic similarities (Moore interview 1989: 394–6).

Among the earliest and most powerful objections to Diop's work was that proposed by Raymond Mauny, who was for many years Professor of African history at Dakar, Senegal, and among the most important pioneers of archaeological research in Francophone Africa (de Barros 1990: 162–7 traces his career and influence). Mauny's review essay was thought sufficiently important to be still reprinted in a *Problems in African History* textbook as recently as 1993 (Collins 1993), and Diop replied at length in his *Antériorité des civilisations nègres* (in Diop 1974a; for the French original, which also takes on Jean Suret-Canale and Maurice Devisse, see Diop 1967: 231–79). Without doubt, Mauny's case had some notable flaws. If Diop relied excessively on an uncritical reading of sources whose reliability was already very suspect in the light of the state of knowledge when he began researching, such as Frobenius or D.P. de Pedrals, Mauny's critique depended on some equally tainted authorities. His source for controverting Diop on the racial make-up of the ancient Egyptians was Carleton S. Coon's work, almost the last would-be authoritative exposition of classic European racial 'science' (see esp. Coon 1962). In relying on it, Mauny placed himself on the worst possible ground in both scholarly and political terms.

Coon's underlying argument – that several (probably five) quite separate hominid groups had existed for at least several hundred thousand years and had thereafter converged, but only very imperfectly and unevenly so, towards a 'civilized' condition – may help to indicate why views which were the polar opposite of this, extreme diffusionism and environmental determinism, were so attractive to anti-Eurocentrists like Diop. However, Diop's diffusionism – quite apart from the apparent shakiness of the evidence he can adduce for particular instances of cultural diffusion – is one of his Achilles heels. He merely assumes, without argument, that any idea or practice found in different places must have started in one of them and then spread or been carried to the others. The Greeks, he insisted, can have had no 'autonomous thinking' enabling them to 'create civilization': otherwise they would have done so before their contact with Egypt (Finch interview 1989: 363). This overlooks the powerful arguments and evidence, from a host of spheres of human activity, that similar cultural forms, beliefs and practices can arise quite separately in distinct and distant societies. Moreover, there is an irony in Diop and his followers adopting naive diffusionism as an antiracist creed. The original extreme diffusionists were themselves racists or cultural supremacists, believing that all human achievements had begun with one group – Greeks, or 'Aryans', or whoever – and been carried (usually by physical expansion and conquest, as in the Hamitic hypothesis for Africa) elsewhere. Diop has taken over the structure of argument, shifted the original location to one more congenial to him, and reproduced all the faults of the earlier European versions.

Much of the argument for diffusionism and Egyptian origins in the work of Diop and his disciples rests on a highly selective, rather idiosyncratic comparative ethnography of African societies. Quite apart from the inadequacies of the account thus given, which appear to be numerous, there is a basic methodological flaw in this procedure, as Jan Vansina explains:

> The social and cultural differences among related peoples are a product of their past history. It would therefore seem proper first to document such differences precisely at a given moment in time and later to explain the differences as divergence from the original situation to the situations today. . . . The variants would then be seen as a set of transformations from the single ancestral situation to the multiple contemporary ones. Each variant would be a step in a *logical* pathway of development. . . . Yet such an exercise is not a *historical* reconstruction. Historical and logical developments need not be identical. For example, it could easily be argued that marriage with bridewealth is a logical transformation of the practice of exchanging one woman for another. But it cannot be demonstrated by this deduction alone that the latter practice is in fact anywhere older than the former. . . . There does not seem to be a way to avoid anachronism if one relies only on a comparison of contemporary cultural or social features. Straightforward comparative ethnography cannot be used as a source of history. (Vansina 1990: 9–10; original emphasis)

It should hardly need to be added that the difficulties are compounded, not resolved, if one's initial step is to document *similarities* rather than differences, as Diop does; and if, moreover, this documentation seems extremely *un*systematic and proceeds from an a priori assumption that diverse peoples are necessarily related.

It is beyond my competence to assess in detail the linguistic evidence for the cultural unity of ancient Egypt and later black Africa, which Diop advances in successive books. However, the non-specialist can reasonably seek to evaluate the general principles and methodology by which Diop's ventures into historical linguistics proceed. These, too, appear extremely unsystematic, in ways that greatly weaken his overall case, and despite their ever-increasing elaboration – the 1977 *Parenté génétique* included a Wolof–Ancient Egyptian lexicon of over 200 pages.[7]

The basic flaw is that in order to trace the history of languages, to identify shared roots, patterns of evolution and divergence, it is entirely inadequate simply to list similar-sounding or possibly related terms in different languages. Almost however long the lists are, they can provide little more than an a priori case for investigating the possibility of common origins. Not all similarities imply links; while such listing of similarities cannot tell us much at all about the history of the language users: when, how, by what routes did one language influence the other, or (perhaps more likely[8]) how and when did both diverge from a shared ancestor?

The fundamental principle of historical linguistics is that all languages change over time, and so diverge increasingly from related languages. Thus the more differences there are between two neighbouring languages, the further back in time they must have diverged. But comparative linguistics cannot give us absolute dates: the rate of language change is not constant, and the 'original' splitting off of two languages from one another is always a process – a long-drawn-out one – rather than a single, dateable event. Where the comparison is between a long-dead language and living ones, evidently enough, still further problems supervene (see, for example, Mokhtar 1981: 63).

Attempts at statistical analysis have usually proceeded by drawing up lists of a few hundred basic words, which should be as little culturally loaded as possible and which therefore change only very slowly over time. Diop's lists do not conform to these criteria. He makes no apparent attempt to formulate a systematic 'core' vocabulary, or to distinguish between words with strong cultural, religious or ideological overtones and those without. The percentage of closely similar words from this basic list which two languages share provides an indicator of how closely related the languages are – with an entry on the list counting as positive only if form and sound are *very* similar and the meanings *identical*, and with the whole process having validity only if one *already* has strong reasons to think that the two languages share a common ancestor. Diop's listings, again, fail to meet these criteria.

Two languages can, of course, also have words in common because in one of them they are 'loanwords' taken over from the other language. There *are* techniques for trying to decide whether a given word is a loanword (Vansina 1990: 14–16); but Diop, once again, does not use them. His evidence gives us no means of deciding whether the presence of similar-sounding words in Egyptian and Wolof indicates common ancestry, or later borrowing by one from the other, or the time-scale and routes for either *if* they exist at all, or even if the similarity is mere coincidence. Where Diop sets outs his methodological protocols, they seem somewhat lax: 'kinship between two given languages is of the genetic type if the concordances are numerous and are verified for the complete system: as is the case for personal pronouns in romance languages' (1977: xvii). But of course, we already know that the Romance languages are closely related to one another; there is a large difference between reconfirmation and speculation.

Diop's best-known intellectual disciple is the Congolese historical linguist Théophile Obenga, who has clearly also been the most important of the relatively few African historians who have sought to pursue and extend Diop's line of thought. Obenga, a little younger than Diop, was born in Brazzaville in 1930, from a Mbochi-speaking background: he has sought to trace parallels between Mbochi and ancient Egyptian languages, just as Diop has done with his native Wolof. Obenga's university training was varied: he studied at Pittsburgh University in the USA, and at the École Pratique des Hautes Études, the Collège de France, and the University of Bordeaux. By contrast with Diop's long years as permanent oppositionist in Senegal,

Obenga spent periods in the Congo Republic's corridors of power, serving
as Foreign Minister in 1975–7 under the Marxist government of Marien
Ngouabi. Thereafter he acted as Director of Research at the 'Centre
International des Civilisations Bantu' in Libreville, Gabon; but he has
recently moved to the USA to take up a post at Molefi Asante's Temple
University, Philadelphia department, the main centre of US Afrocentrism.[9]
A prolific author whose publications include poetry as well as historical and
political works, he was far more heavily represented in the pages of *Présence
Africaine* than was his mentor; his ten articles there include two specifically
on the work of Diop and others on African historiography from a devoutly
Diopian perspective. More recently, he has produced an extended tribute
to Diop's influence, seeing the master as having transformed understanding
of the history of Egypt, Africa and, indeed, the world (Obenga 1996).
Obenga also contributed a chapter to the first volume of the *UNESCO
General History of Africa* – one of the weakest and most problematic pieces in
those extremely uneven volumes.

Obenga is, on the whole, less nakedly polemical in approach than Diop,
and more fully prepared to espouse universalist rather than nationalist
conceptions – his *Pour une nouvelle histoire* (1980) spoke in Senghorian terms
of all human groups contributing to a universal cultural inheritance; while
A Lost Tradition (1995), though mainly devoted to familiar Diopian assertions about African cultural unity and uniqueness, seeks to place these in an
ecumenically global context. Yet he, too, could come out with totalizing
claims, especially on behalf of ancient Egypt, which have no apparent
historical warrant, such as that 'there was never slavery in Egyptian society
at the time of the Pharaohs', and that women were fully liberated and had
equal rights there (Obenga 1992: 162–3). His major early work, *L'Afrique
dans l'Antiquité* (1973), follows broadly the same trajectory as Diop's books,
substantially repeating – or, at best, deepening – the line of inquiry, rather
than broadening it or bringing new types of evidence into play. His
discussions of the African biological origins of humanity (1973: 1–16), of
the blackness of the ancient Egyptians (ibid.: 53–90) and of relations
between Egypt and Nubia (91–127) tread almost entirely in the master's
footsteps, though on the last especially, Obenga uses more up-to-date
archaeological evidence than Diop had done. This is true also of the two
major themes on which Obenga did break new ground: in his extensive
discussions of the idea that there must have been a single, ancestral 'Negro-
African language' (221–331), and of African writing systems (355–443). He
shares with Diop, however, a tendency to make judgements which seem to
owe more to nationalism than to academic caution. Thus, in his eagerness
to refute European assumptions that precolonial Africa had been near-
uniformly illiterate, he describes as forms of writing such phenomena as the
Yoruba's 'Aroko' method of sending messages by an elaborate system of
knot-tying (361–79), and the very limited range of signs employed by the
Gicandi of Kenya and the Mum of Cameroon. To regard such forms of

communication as equivalent to writing in, say, French, Arabic or Hausa is to stretch the definition of literacy very far indeed.

Obenga's founding assumption has remained the same as Diop's: that 'from Ancient Egypt's impact on the culture of the rest of the African continent to the unity of all African languages, African history is one continuous, unbroken narrative of a people with a shared consciousness' (1995: v). It seems generally to be accepted that his linguistic researches are more solidly grounded than Diop's, though the essential beliefs are identical. Obenga had more extensive formal training in linguistics, as well as in history, than did his mentor, including immersion in the work of Ferdinand de Saussure, whom he described as an even more important influence on him than Diop himself.[10] He has also, in his more recent work, offered a fuller discussion of ancient Egyptian belief systems and their alleged relationships with those of Sub-Saharan Africa than Diop, or any American Afrocentrist, has done (see Obenga 1989, 1990). He has been no more successful than Diop, though, in gaining widespread acceptance for his views among specialists, most of whom apparently find his classification system for African languages 'reckless' (Gray 1989: 104). Although he, like Diop, produced extensive listings of words allegedly common to ancient Egyptian and various West African languages, his main claims derived from something broader and vaguer: the belief that 'if language is a social fact, an eminently cultural fact, and if all language implies an "ideology"', then everything suggests 'a single cultural universe of pharaonic Egypt and the rest of black Africa' (Obenga 1988: 25).

Apart from Obenga, Diop seems to have had few productive disciples among African historians. As Diouf and Mbodj note, even in Senegal itself there was neither substantial critical discussion of his work nor a Diopian 'school': they cite only P.F. Diagne and A.A. Dieng, both philosophers rather than historians, as exceptions. The small group of Senegalese Egyptologists which emerged in Paris in the 1980s was quite separate from Diop's influence (Diouf and Mbodj 1992: 126, 128–9). In the Anglophone African world, similarly, it is a polemicist on the nature of African philosophy, Henry Olela, rather than historical or anthropological researchers, who stands most obviously in the Diopian mould.[11] Olela's work is more extreme in its claims and far more feebly based in its standards of evidence than that of Diop. It largely repeats the familiar assertions on the African origins of Greek thought, relying on T.R. Clark's *Myth and Symbol in Ancient Egypt* and on such dubious sources as James's *Stolen Legacy*, Yosef Ben-Jochannen and Albert Churchward (Olela 1981, 1984; see also the damning critique in Masolo 1994: 19–21, 41). Olela also 'overtrumps' most Afrocentrists by proclaiming a Central–East African origin for all Egyptian, and hence Mediterranean, civilization: moving the 'cradle of civilization' still further south than Diop had done. Olela, for reasons left unexplained, calls ancient Egypt 'Sais' after a major Nile Delta city which was briefly capital of an independent state in the last days of Pharaonic Egypt, rather than (like most Afrocentrists) naming it 'Kemet' (1984: 79). As another West African scholar, Augustin Holl, laments, appropriation of Diop's ideas has taken place mostly in 'uncritical and oversimplified' forms (Holl 1995: 204).

This lack of a really productive intellectual legacy deriving from Diop makes it hard to dissent from the judgement of Mamadou Diouf and Mohamed Mbodj:

> There is the problem: to question the work of Cheikh Anta Diop, even from a scientific point of view, was for a long time synonymous with African antipatriotism; to refer to it in passing was an obligation one could readily fulfill, especially in academic work; to repeat its great principles, often without any real knowledge of the work itself, was a certificate of nationalism and Pan-Africanism. In any case, a dynamic oeuvre – paradoxically – paralyzed the African intellects or caused them to look elsewhere. (1992: 118–19)

The most popular alternative place to look was Marxism. If, in the sphere of oppositional knowledges of Africa, the great opponent or alternative to Diopian culturalism and radical nationalism is seen to be Marxist-influenced studies of African history, there can be no doubt which has been more productive. Marxism in Africa, however miserable its failure as politics, has been enormously fruitful as historiography. Diopian unanimism, by contrast – even if it might, in the master's own hands, have offered promise as a research agenda – has almost wholly betrayed that promise. His disciples, as Diouf and Mbodj lament, have merely repeated his principles. The result has been intellectual paralysis. There were, as we have noted, significant Marxist influences on Diop's own thought, especially the earlier books (esp. Diop 1987); but his overwhelming emphasis on culture and race as opposed to economic and social structure makes it extremely misleading to describe him as a Marxist. The few attempts to do so (e.g. Masilela 1994: 312–13) seem very forced.

Thus it is not surprising that few historians of Africa have been persuaded by Diop's linguistic or other arguments about the ancient past. We can note only a few, representative instances of their reactions to his work. The leading French radical Africanist Catherine Coquery-Vidrovitch, virtually damning with faint praise, speaks of Diop's 'intuitions' having merit despite his 'demonstrations, which barely escape the shortcut – common to a number of researchers – to want to explain too much' (1992: 64). Perhaps the most eminent, now venerable, modern expert on West African archaeology is Thurstan Shaw. His overview of West African prehistory was fairly dismissive of Diop and his associates:

> Some writers have sought to give dignity and lustre to West African history by trying to show connections with or even actual migrations from ancient Egypt, to enable West Africa to bask in its reflected glory; not only is this not necessary but a rigorous examination of the proffered evidence shows that it is being asked to carry more than it can bear. (Shaw 1976: 61)

He repeated the same argument in his contribution to the UNESCO *General History of Africa*, adding:

> the third millennium before our era, which was the time when metallurgy, writing, monumental building in stone, the use of the wheel and centralized government became firmly established in Egypt, was also the millennium of the final desiccation of the Sahara when people were moving out of it and when it could no longer serve as an indirect link between Egypt and West Africa. (Shaw 1981: 628)

It is difficult to see quite why Valentin Mudimbe should believe that a Diopian vision of history was 'rigorously reworked in two monumental undertakings, the Cambridge and UNESCO histories of Africa' (Mudimbe 1994: 24). In fact contributors to the UNESCO volumes were sharply divided on whether there is any serious merit in Diop's ideas – a matter we shall explore in a moment – while the Cambridge texts (J.D. Clark 1982), produced by a team almost bound to be less sympathetic to such perspectives, dismiss them in silence. Diop's work is not once mentioned or even footnoted in the Cambridge volume on ancient African history.[12]

Some critics felt, indeed, that the influence of Diopian theories had a generally damaging effect on historiographical development, helping, for instance, to make early volumes of the *UNESCO History* a murky battleground of competing, unresolved views. David Phillipson complained of the first that its ideologically diverse chapters 'show relatively little unity of purpose or presentation' (Phillipson 1982: 115). A non-Diopian contributor, Joseph Greenberg, had his views on the Semitic affiliations of the ancient Egyptian language flatly contradicted by an anonymous Diopian editor (Ki-Zerbo 1981: 298 – presumably this is Ki-Zerbo himself). In the second volume, as another reviewer, Michael Brett, complained – Diop's chapter is:

> followed by a long résumé of a symposium on the subject held in 1974, inserted by way of a corrective to this (Diop's) idiosyncratic view. As a result, there is no discussion at all of pre-dynastic Egypt and the settlement of the Nile valley which made possible the subsequent civilization. (Brett 1982: 117)

The Egyptian historians themselves were the fiercest objectors to Diop's ideas at the Cairo symposium, and as the UNESCO volume's rapporteur admits, the argument 'often took the form of successive and mutually contradictory monologues' (Mokhtar 1981: 49). Abdelgadir M. Abdalla scorned the idea that there was any importance in establishing whether ancient Egyptians were black, negroid, or whatever (ibid.: 63). Abu Bakr insisted that 'the Egyptians had never been isolated from other peoples. They had never constituted a pure race and it was impossible to accept the idea that in the Neolithic period the population of Egypt was entirely black' (ibid.: 67–8). On the issue of whether Egypt's early peopling had included substantial immigration or invasion, 'it became clear that there was total disagreement', with Diop, claiming that there had been, very much in the minority (ibid.: 71).[13] As for the nature of the available historical evidence itself, Diop's claims clearly bemused many other participants at Cairo. He insisted that the physical-anthropological views of nineteenth-century European observers were good enough to obviate need for further analysis, as against Jean Vercoutter's view that almost all such testimony from before 1939 was simply unscientific (ibid.: 74). Not surprisingly, 'Professor Diop's forceful affirmation was criticized by many participants' (ibid.: 74).

Almost a decade later, Wyatt MacGaffey echoed Phillipson's and Brett's complaints that dispute over Egypt's ethnicity and influence had become a sterile dialogue of the deaf (MacGaffey 1991). And Peter L. Shinnie, the veteran archaeologist who had directed pathbreaking excavations at Meroë, was yet more caustic. All the Egyptian chapters in the *UNESCO History* volume 'are uncontroversial, orthodox and somewhat old-fashioned', with one exception:

> The one unconventional, though extremely old-fashioned, chapter on Egypt is the opening one by Cheikh Anta Diop. He presents once again his peculiar view about the nature of the ancient Egyptian population and the closeness of the Walaf (Wolof) and Ancient Egyptian languages, relying on out-of-date sources and apparently unaware of the extensive recent research into the human biology of the populations of the Nile Valley.

It was, Shinnie alleged, 'clear that he (Diop) learnt nothing' from the Cairo conference. The summary of that meeting included in the volume not only contradicts, but 'serves as an apology for' his chapter: 'It seems that UNESCO and (volume editor) Mokhtar were embarrassed by the unscholarly and preposterous nature of Diop's views but were unable to reject his contribution' (Shinnie 1981: 540).

Accounts of the Cairo meeting – none of them written by actual participants, apart from the UNESCO report itself and the summary included in the *General History of Africa* – vary greatly, with Diop's disciples trying in slightly slippery fashion to claim a moral victory for him and Obenga there (e.g. Van Sertima 1989: 323–4). Chris Gray even asserts that the conference 'was clearly a triumph' for Diop and Obenga (1989: 14–15).[14] This seems very far from the truth. The participants – who included five Egyptian and five French experts, though only one American and no British Egyptologists – seem, as Shinnie suggests, to have been mainly hostile to Diop's theories ('Annex to Chapter 1' in Mokhtar 1981).

The controversies, and the political tensions they reflected, produced in the eventual UNESCO volumes what Bogumil Jewsiewicki acidly called a

> conformism more suitable to statesmen than to historians. The euphemisms, pleonasms and dialogues of the deaf serve for example to conjure away the prickly question of pharaonic Egypt's black origins. Instead of presenting an

important epistemological debate, there is a discussion by proxy. What can the uninitiated reader make of it? (Jewsiewicki 1981: 547)

Anyone reading the Preface to the series by UNESCO's Director-General, or seeing Diop's essay in position of honour in Volume II, might suppose that his ideas were central to debate on African history. But neither of the two historiographical essays in Volume I, by J.D. Fage and Philip Curtin, so much as mentioned Diop.

Contrasting with this in its turn, a contribution by Obenga on sources and techniques adopted a predictably Diopian perspective. Obenga claimed 'striking analogies' and 'structural affinities' between Egyptian hieroglyphics and the pictograms or ideographs used by some half-dozen Sub-Saharan peoples (the argument is essentially a summary of the one in Obenga 1973: 355–443). In the case of the Vai of Liberia an 'undoubted causal connection' was asserted (Obenga 1981: 79).[15] Since most of these writing systems are thought to be of very recent date, the nature of the connection and the meaning of the claim are obscure, to say the least. Trying to make a silk purse out of a sow's ear, Obenga half-admits the vast chronological gap, but suggests that this shows

> the remarkable longevity of the impact of Egypt. Egyptian writing, which supposedly disappeared in 394 of our era, is seen to have had an unbroken series of revivals between the seventeenth and nineteenth centuries ... the two are linked by an underground stream.' (ibid.: 79)

He admits (as Diop would not) that the search for a common 'cultural macro-structure' between ancient Egypt and the rest of Africa 'is, properly speaking, a matter of guesswork and awaits formal proof' (ibid.: 80–81), and elsewhere that 'it *might* be scientifically possible to reconstruct the common predialectical ancestor of all these ancient and modern languages' (1992: 157; emphasis added), but there can be no doubt what he *wants* to find.

The other Diopian contribution to Volume I is from Pathé Diagne, one of Diop's very few direct disciples among Senegalese scholars. His chapter on 'Historical Linguistics' offers what seems to the non-specialist a fair and competent introduction to the field, but then swoops off into a series of highly contestable assertions. He tries to smooth over the vast gulf between Diop and Joseph Greenberg on Africa's linguistic map by suggesting that in some obscure ways they were 'in perfect agreement' (Diagne 1981: 241). Like Obenga, but perhaps less guardedly, he proclaims the ubiquitous Egyptian influence: there was not just similarity but 'unity' between hieroglyphics and other African writing systems in their 'ideological presuppositions' (whatever that means) and 'the technique of transcription' (ibid.: 251). Diagne's underlying assumptions are those of unanimism, and of a precolonial Africa marked by general social peace and harmony. He appears even to be arguing that, in these idyllic circumstances, Africans made little

use of writing simply because they had less need of it than less fortunate
people. Theirs was:

> an affluent rural society and economy. Its members were not forced by the
> pressures of poverty to consolidate in their own age their material or
> intellectual acquisitions, because these were not continually threatened. An
> ecology providing an easy balance between resources and population gave
> most African civilizations and their cultural features the power to wax and
> wane geographically while always preserving their essence: their principles.
> (Diagne 1981: 254–5)

Diop, then, certainly succeeded in politicizing the issue of ancient Egypt,
if hardly in the way he might have intended. As Jewsiewicki pointed out
elsewhere, Diop 'appropriated history as a battlefield' (1989: 3). In his
circumstances and his time, there were compelling reasons to do so. And
Diop himself fought that battle with usually rational tactics and some respect
– however stretched at points – for the agreed rules of engagement. The
pity is that so few of his followers have had the intellectual will to vary the
combative stance or the tactics, to realize that in the 1990s the battlefield
has changed.

In the view of Kenyan philosopher D.A. Masolo, Diop's contribution must
thus be seen as more political than scholarly: 'despite the controversies and
disagreements regarding his theses ... (he) has contributed to a major
focus of contemporary discourse – the production of knowledge as a source
of power against others' (Masolo 1994: 19). But in Masolo's opinion, Diop
– together with Henry Olela, who has made somewhat similar claims in the
sphere of history of philosophy – engaged in a 'reductive argument' by
propounding a wholly Egyptocentric diffusionist view, as against the prefer-
able, earlier tradition of thought which proposed 'parallel coexistence of
two separate but equal forms of reason' (ibid.: 21).

Masolo extends his critique of Diop to Martin Bernal and others. While
Bernal's 'scholarly purpose deserves separation from the political mud', this
is by no means true of all Afrocentrists, whose

> outbursts ... frequently lack just what is required for discourse in a scholarly
> framework ... the strengths of Afrocentricity, if any, lie in the political rather
> than the scholarly domain, and have so far been presented in a manner that
> is both uninteresting and unproductive. (ibid.: 23)

Non-specialists who have given attention to Diop have also tended to be
thoroughly – even at times unfairly – negative in their assessments. Kwame
Appiah, for his part, has no hesitation in consigning Diop's thought to the
category of 'romantic racialism' (1992: 162). Robert Hughes is equally
blunt: 'Diop was a crank', he snorts (1993: 134). In a standard reference
work on Senegal, Andrew Clark and Lucie Colvin Phillips tersely dismiss

Diop's scholarship thus: 'His historical work, while generally discredited, has been influential' (Clark and Phillips 1994: 111).

By contrast, Diop's presence among Afro-American intellectuals has been massive and increasing.[16] The initial contact, however, was unpromising in the extreme. The young James Baldwin's lengthy and justly celebrated view of the 1956 *Présence Africaine* conference found room for only the briefest and most scathing mention of Diop, who:

> in sum, claimed the ancient Egyptian empire as part of the Negro past. I can only say that this question has never greatly exercised my mind, nor did M. Diop succeed in doing so – at least not in the direction he intended. He quite refused to remain within the twenty-minute limit and, while his claims of the deliberate dishonesty of all Egyptian scholars may be quite well founded for all I know, I cannot say that he convinced me. He was, however, a great success in the hall. (Baldwin 1985: 57 – the piece originally appeared in *Encounter*, January 1957)

Almost certainly, this will have been the first mention Americans (apart, perhaps, from tiny circles of Paris and Dakar residents) heard of Diop, and for many years the only one. A long-winded, tendentious crank, obsessed with an issue which Baldwin, self-consciously a representative black American, thought irrelevant, and accusing all and sundry of fraud – such was the image. It has even been suggested that these few lines of Baldwin's were responsible for the failure to translate any of Diop's work into English before the 1970s (Spady 1986: 90).

As the dates of translation of Diop's work into English suggest, his reception in the Anglophone world was indeed late, and for a long time limited. Few, even among the Afrocentrists who were to adopt him uncritically, were aware of his writings before the 1970s. He knew little English, and few among the African-American enthusiasts for ancient Egypt understood French. His only visit to the USA took place less than a year before his death, in April 1985. Then, though, Van Sertima claimed: 'His coming was like the arrival of an African President and he was received like one' (1989: 328). His views of US racial politics, however, as expressed on that Atlanta trip, can hardly have pleased his separatist and cultural nationalist Afro-American fans, since reportedly he said: 'I subscribe to the teaching of Martin Luther King Jr. wholeheartedly' (ibid.: 329; see also Van Sertima and Williams interviews [1986] 296–9).

Latter-day Afrocentrists, as we shall see, lean heavily on Diop's work – or perhaps rather, in the same way that Diouf and Mbodj had complained of some Senegalese writers doing, they lean on a few general theses drawn from it and repeated, taken as articles of faith, rather than interrogated or developed. The only criticism which appears to be mounted is of Diop's failure to anticipate the preferred terminology of the Afrocentrists; a complaint which is in essence anachronistic. Thus Victor O. Okafor faults Diop's use of the term 'Negro', his referring to the Egyptian *Book of the Dead* rather than the *Book of Coming Forth by Day*, and to the label 'Black Africans', since this last ignores the Afrocentric dogma that *all* Africans are black, and thus 'plays into the hands of the Eurocentric attempt to divorce northern Africa, including Egypt, from the rest of Africa' (Okafor 1991: 267).

Diop's Afro-American acolytes have not been above making claims on his behalf which it is hard to believe he would actually have advanced himself, such as the assertion Van Sertima puts into his mouth that ancient Egypt was democratic (Van Sertima and Williams 1986: 326), or Charles Finch's claim that Diop agreed with him that Moses's real identity *must* have been Osarsiph, an Egyptian priest of Ra (Finch interview 1989: 371). Finch also seeks to establish connections with the idiosyncratic American Afrocentric tradition, asserting that while Diop, as a lonely student in Paris, was beginning his Egyptian researches, he had a chance encounter with a man who, unlike everyone else, encouraged and applauded him – George G.M. James (ibid.: 372)! If this is true, it would be a fascinating footnote to the history of ideas – but Diop himself, in a 1976 interview, insisted that he had no knowledge of James's *Stolen Legacy* in the 1950s, and certainly mentions no meeting with the man (Moore interview 1989: 375–6).

Diop's most prominent British enthusiast, Amon Saba Saakana, also proposed views considerably more obscurantist than those of his mentor. Whereas the Senegalese, as we saw, recognized that the transmission of knowledge only by oral tradition and secret initiation was a major drag on the development of scientific or critical thought, Saakana saw it as indicating ancient Africa's moral superiority over both the Greeks and the modern West:

> Greece became the incubator for Western science, art and philosophy. But a fundamental error was made in this claim: the concomitant *social system was inimical to the development of humanity*. Instead philosophy, like immoral science itself, became attached to tyrannical governments. The fact that the Western educational system did not perceive of the ritual of initiation which would guarantee the moral perfectibility of humanity before admission to the higher phases of scientific knowledge can only be understood from the materialist proclivities of the societies themselves.... The omission and consequences of such ignorance continue to plague the world with wars, nuclear disasters, ecological catastrophes, and the class system.... True philosophy could never have been achieved in a society in which the king/president/prime minister was never anchored in the ethics of cosmic thought. ('Foreword' in Obenga 1992: 15; original emphasis)

There is a fine irony here. Diopian and Afrocentric thought has frequently seen Plato as the greatest villain of all, the father of Eurocentrism, rationalism and materialism (for the most elaborate argument on these lines, see Ani 1994). Yet Saakana, in this passage, thinks that the ills of the world are mainly due to our not being ruled by Platonic philosopher-kings!

Diop's adherents produced – as well as the numerous appreciations and exegeses, some of which have been mentioned – two substantial volumes of tribute after his death. One, edited by Ivan Van Sertima and Larry Williams, is little more than a collection of panegyrics. The other, a special issue of *Présence Africaine*, though also uncritical and somewhat overlapping with the American volume, includes more intellectually interesting material, including serious efforts to expand on Diop's linguistic theories (notably Gilbert Ngom's attempt to demonstrate Egyptian–Douala parallels, resembling Diop's work on Wolof: Ngom 1989) and some substantial, enlightening interviews with Diop himself. This special issue, 'Hommage à Cheikh Anta Diop', included contributions in both French and English; the former being both the more numerous and the more substantial, since the English essays were largely pious meanderings by Diop's rather eccentric band of Afro-American disciples. There was, however, some feverish conjecture from the Francophones too, like J-C. Bahoken's thoughts on Dogon astronomy, which would not have been out of place in the wilder reaches of American Afrocentric 'science' (Bahoken 1989).

In that volume, Bernard Moitt claims – oddly – that criticism of Diop 'is based largely on semantics rather than on concrete historical data'; thus his theses still stand (Moitt 1989: 347). Moitt also urges the crucial relevance of Diop's view to the African diaspora (ibid.: 354–60), though he is notably vague about what 'concrete historical data' might be derived from it for the New World, and takes refuge in a purely politico-psychological claim. Diop is important 'because Blacks in the *diaspora* face a constant identity crisis and must inevitably seek answers and inspiration from their past' (360).

Daniel McCall, in one of the earliest English-language reviews of Diop, drew on Isaiah Berlin's image of thinkers as hedgehogs and foxes: the fox knows many things, but the hedgehog knows one big thing. Diop, McCall suggested, was a hedgehog: 'Diop "knows" only one thing . . . that Negroes invented civilization' (McCall 1969: 134). In so far as Diop's controversial reputation has come almost entirely from this single idea, the judgement is shrewd. But of course Diop knew many things, and perhaps tried to know too many for the sake of his own reception and reputation. That reputation might also have suffered because critics, particularly specialists in the fields he ventured into, had been exposed initially (and perhaps only indirectly, through hostile rumour or brief dismissals like Baldwin's) to his more polemical, often strident early work. From that they 'knew' that Diop knew only one thing, which was not even a true thing. The more cautious, more subtle, wider-ranging and far more interesting – if still deeply flawed – later writings could therefore be ignored. If *Civilization or Barbarism* had been Diop's first or only book, instead of coming near the end of a long, stormy progress, he might have been noted as an idiosyncratic but extremely interesting metahistorian on the lines of Toynbee or Spengler, rather than dismissed as a crank. And he might have escaped the attentions of his American Afrocentric friends, who have proved to be the worst enemies of his wider repute.

There is no doubt that a wider public consciousness of ancient history would be desirable in Africa, for good educational reasons even if not necessarily the political ones Diop so stressed. African contributors to a recent symposium on archaeology in education lamented the ancient past's lack of place in either formal education or general popular awareness in their countries (Nzewunwa 1990: Wandibba 1990). In a companion volume, another archaeologist expresses concern at how Nigeria's historical museums tend to reflect state ambitions and rivalries, highly localized and ethnicized perceptions of the past rather than a wider historical consciousness (Willett 1990). And numerous visitors to Egypt will attest how even there, many ordinary Egyptians have highly attenuated or distorted ideas about their country's past – including, in the present writer's experience, people who will, with equal vehemence, deny any affiliation to *either* African *or* Arab identities! What is to be doubted, however, is whether Diopian mythmaking can help to remedy any of this in future, any more than it has done in the past.

As for the world outside Africa, the story is at least as bleak. In 1973, Diop lamented that 'the conditions for a true scientific dialogue between Africa and Europe do not yet exist in the very delicate domain of the human sciences' (quoted in Gray 1989: 60). He was right, and he would still be right in the 1990s. The sad thing is that his own work – and, even more, the image of it spread by vulgarizers and propagandists for a racialized cultural essentialism – has made that situation worse, not better.

Notes

1. Most astonishingly, he characterized the Laobe, a traditionally lowly Senegalese caste of carvers of wooden utensils, as 'dissolute', promiscuous, inveterate thieves, 'bellicose', 'the noisiest and most socially undisciplined of all the Africans I know' (Diop 1974a: 188). It is a repertoire of negative stereotypes redolent of the most extreme kinds of colonialist scorn.

2. The politically contentious and academically unproductive Leonard Jeffries had for some time announced himself as being at work on an English translation of this, but the one which eventually appeared was by Yaa-Lengi Meema Ngemi. Jeffries none the less continues, in interview, to claim much of the credit for the book's US publication, as well as for other projects with which his name is not usually associated, such as Alex Haley's *Roots* (Person-Lynn 1996: 221–2, 228–9).

3. Other works worthy of notice include Diop's major contribution to the field in which he held his professional appointment, a treatise on radiocarbon dating entitled *Physique nucléaire et chronologie absolue* (1974b), and the pamphlet *Philosophie, Science et Religion* (1985). The latter, evidently almost the last text he composed, indicates his continued involvement with epistemological questions of the most general kind, his fascination with new theories of knowledge, and his aspiration to bring together philosophical, political, scientific and theological discourses into a new synthesis. His *Égypte ancienne et Afrique noire*, the republication in book form of a long 1962 article from the IFAN *Bulletin* (Diop 1962/ 1989), is essentially another condensed version of his doctoral work.

4. See, however, Diop (1977: xxxvii), where he suggests that 'the most ancient prehistoric paintings found in Saudi Arabia, and reproduced in the Riyadh Museum, reveal an African negro type without traces of admixture (*métissage*)'. And in Diop (1974a) he argued that all Arabia had – much earlier – been part of a Kushite empire.

His sole source for this wild claim, apparently, was the fanciful late-Victorian French historian of the Phoenicians, François Lenormant (Diop 1974a: 123–5).

5. Note, by contrast, how Samia Dafa'alla (1993) argues, with far more detailed archaeological evidence, that the royal succession in the Nubian kingdom of Napata was not matrilineal. Nubia, she suggests, may possibly have been a matrilineal society at some earlier stage, but ceased to be so under Egyptian influence. More generally, Diopian claims that African societies were generally or even universally matrilineal and/or matrilocal cannot be sustained by the evidence. Patrilineal traditions, and those tracing ancestry bilaterally, are widespread across Africa.

6. Diop's discussion (1991 and elsewhere) of the Greek debt to Egypt relies primarily on Diodorus of Sicily, and involves a highly selective and forced reading of even the limited evidence put forward, as Mary Lefkowitz (1996a: 16–22) and others have shown. The substantially more elaborate arguments of Martin Bernal on the same theme are debated below in Chapter 15.

7. Diop (1977: 161–384). See Anttila (1989); Ehret and Posnansky (1982) for overviews of historical linguistics; and Vansina (1990) for both explication of general principles and an important, innovative application to African studies. It may be noted that although Diop's and his disciples' views on the origin of African languages – and Martin Bernal's on those of the eastern Mediterranean – have been judged particularly speculative and weakly grounded by specialists, a high degree of speculation remains endemic to the field of historical linguistics. Certainly, to the non-expert, the theories of many more 'mainstream' scholars, such as Colin Renfrew's on Indo-European origins (Renfrew 1987), seem to include much conjecture.

8. Diop specifies in one place that he is *not* saying that Wolof descends directly from Ancient Egyptian, but that 'Egyptian, Wolof and other African languages derive from a common mother language which one can call paleo-African' (1977: xxv). Elsewhere he seems less clear on this point.

9. One US Afrocentric enthusiast, Charles Verharen, peculiarly describes Obenga's presence at Temple as 'a prophetic turn of events' (1997: 487).

10. Gray (1989: 13). Obenga (1973: 223–37) discusses methodological questions in historical linguistics, while Gray (ibid.: 92–104) gives a clear, though uncritical, summary of Obenga's main claims in this sphere.

11. Although there has been increasing awareness of Diop's ideas among Anglophone Africans, especially in Nigeria (see, for instance, Chinweizu [1987], and several articles and comments in the influential magazine *West Africa* since the late 1980s), I know of only one substantial historical monograph by an Anglophone African which acknowledges Diop as its major influence: Amadiume (1987).

12. More recently Bassey Andah, perhaps the leading black African archaeologist, has shown no sign at all of any Diopian influence. Even in the course of what might in a broad sense be called Afrocentric arguments, asserting the need for a more indigenously based understanding of African prehistory, less dependent on European models, he makes no reference to the views of Diop or his disciples (Andah 1995a, b).

13. As we have seen, the more recent evidence from physical anthropology, presented by Keita, Brace, and others, supports the majority Cairo view.

14. See also Hilliard (1994a: 140–42); Ampim (1994: 191–2), which similarly seek to present the debates as ending in total victory for their hero.

15. This, again, is a paraphrase of the claims in Obenga (1973), though in the earlier work Obenga had qualified the assertion: '*In all probability*, there exists a causal connection, that is to say a necessary relation, between the Egyptian hieroglyphs and Vai writing' (1973: 416; emphasis added). In fact the idea of such a connection appears highly implausible. The Vai script was apparently invented in the 1830s by one Duwalu Bekele, whose virtually single-handed development of a quite original form of writing is surely an African intellectual feat far more worthy of celebration than any supposed subterranean influence from ancient Egypt. A few of the signs in Bekele's script, each of them representing a syllable, were hieroglyphs (just *one* of them, apparently, resembling the Ancient Egyptian sign for the same word), but many more were obviously derived from

the Latin alphabet. The first detailed study of the Vai seems to have been by African-American diplomat George W. Ellis in 1914. He emphasizes the novelty and originality of Bekele's script, and makes no suggestion of Egyptian influence (Ellis 1914: 262–5).

16. Some of the many African-American exercises in repeating or – more rarely – developing Diopian ideas are discussed separately below. Others include Jean (1991); Finch (1990); Crawford (1996); Gordon (1991); Karenga (1982); Okafor (1997); Verharen (1997); several contributions to Karenga and Carruthers (1986); and many of the chapters in Van Sertima and Williams (1986) and Van Sertima (ed.) (1989). Substantial critical discussion of Diop's work has, as we have seen, been far rarer: useful, though brief, instances of such discussion are Froment (1991); Holl (1995).

Martin Bernal

The Afrocentric interpretation of history gained more attention than ever before with the publication in 1987 of the first volume of Martin Bernal's *Black Athena*. As one critic quite plausibly suggests, it 'must be the most discussed book on the ancient history of the eastern Mediterranean world since the Bible' (Liverani 1996: 421). There were several reasons for the unprecedented level of interest and controversy. Bernal, unlike most of the publicists who had previously argued on similar lines, was already a well established, even distinguished, figure within the academy – long a Fellow of King's College Cambridge, latterly a professor at Cornell University. His reputation, admittedly, had been acquired not in Egyptology or classical studies but in the study of China and Vietnam (though he recently said that he turned to this only because at Cambridge in the 1950s it was impossible to specialize in Africa, as he would otherwise have wished to do from the start [Bernal 1994: 101–2]). None the less, when he moved from the mid 1970s onwards to ancient history he achieved a command of the literature and of the relevant languages which enabled him, far more than earlier Afrocentrists, to argue with mainstream classical scholars on their own ground – even if some insist on describing him as an 'amateur' (e.g. Lefkowitz and Rogers 1996: ix), and cast implied doubt on his credentials – as Mary Lefkowitz's phraseology does when she says that Bernal 'claims he knows other ancient languages' (1996b: 12). His work appeared in 'established' academic journals, and *Black Athena* itself, originally issued by a small radical independent press, was soon republished in the mass-market Vintage paperback series, an imprint of the multinational conglomerate Random House.

Undoubtedly the drama of the story Bernal tells (and, critics add, the excessive dramatization of his way of presenting it) also help to account for the book's impact. As Molly Myerowitz Levine suggests, *Black Athena* is structured like a detective thriller:

> every element in the enormously complex plot meshed perfectly to create a story with good guys (Herodotus, Egyptians, Semites) and bad guys (Aryans, racist German philologists); in which the hero-author, the indefatigable

neophyte detective, rereads the files and reworks the clues to uncover the
truth that had long been covered up by a contemptibly corrupt and lazy
police department (contemporary classicists). (Levine 1992a: 459–60)

It is a matter of contention, especially among African-American writers, how
much Bernal's fame owes to another factor: unlike almost all previous
Afrocentric historians, he is white. He himself seemed to regard it as
extremely significant:

> [I]f a Black were to say what I am now putting in my books, their reception
> would be very different. They would be assumed to be one-sided and partisan,
> pushing a Black nationalist line, and therefore dismissed. My ideas are still
> so outrageous that I am convinced that if I, as their proposer did not have all
> the cards stacked in my favour, I would not have enjoyed even a first hearing.
> However, being not only white, male, middle-aged, and middle-class but also
> British in America, has given me a tone of universality and authority that is
> completely spurious. (Bernal 1989: 20)

Bernal's argument is, in essence, extremely simple and quite familiar to
anyone who had read Diop or the several generations of earlier Afro-
American romantic antiquarians.[1] Greek civilization was massively indebted
to African and Asian influences, primarily to the Egyptians and the
Phoenicians. It is clear to Bernal, moreover, that not only the culture but
part of the actual populations of ancient Greece derived, through colonization, from Egyptian and Semitic sources. This view of Greek origins, which
Bernal calls the 'Ancient Model', was accepted by all the classical Greek
writers themselves. Until the late eighteenth century, it was also accepted by
almost all European writers on the ancient world. Later rejection – and,
indeed, suppression – of the 'Ancient Model' was the result of racism, which
gave rise to a substitute and entirely false 'Aryan model' of Greek history
which remains dominant even today. It had several strands, but centred on
the romantic, racialized nationalism which took root, above all in Germany,
around the time of the French Revolution. Philhellenism, or a romantic
love of Greece, dictated commitment to the idea that Greek civilization was
original, autonomous, creative, dynamic – and *white*, taking its inspiration
from the north, not the south or east.[2] The simultaneous rise of anti-black
racism led mainstream scholars to deny any Egyptian influence on Greece,
though a Phoenician presence was still admitted: this was the 'Broad Aryan
Model', dominant in the earlier part of the nineteenth century.

The later rise of anti-Semitism, again especially in Germany, led from the
1880s onwards to the 'Extreme Aryan Model' denying Phoenician as well as
Egyptian influences – mostly because the Phoenicians were supposedly a
'Semitic' people, uncomfortably close to the Jews in language and culture.
Bernal, with the melodramatic touch which often marks his writing, calls
this 'The Final Solution of the Phoenician Problem'. The Extreme Aryan
view not only denied what had been universally accepted by ancient Greeks

themselves, their huge cultural debts to Egypt, but imposed massive distortions on the history of language. These racist scholars preserved the purity of Greece's European roots by dreaming up an imaginary language, 'Proto-Aryan', from which Greek supposedly descended: whereas actually, Bernal argues, up to half of all Greek words, as well as most of the Greek myths, came from Egyptian and Phoenician sources.[3]

Today, Bernal believes, there is a partial shift back from the 'Extreme' to the 'Broad' Aryan Model, with Semitic contributions to Greek development once again admitted. This, like the earlier changes, is a consequence of political rather than academic factors: it results from the post-Holocaust discrediting of anti-Semitism and the efforts of Jewish scholars (Bernal's tendency to 'read off' historians' views from their ethnic origins has, as we shall see, been much criticized). Now a further reassessment is overdue: a realization that the 'Ancient Model', with its emphasis on Egyptian roots of classical civilization, was in essence right all along. This requires certain revisions, notably a recognition that Egyptian and Phoenician colonization of Greece started earlier than once thought, and that there were also invasions from the north, though their cultural significance was small – but basically, the wheel of scholarly orthodoxy must turn full circle. The result will be to 'rethink the fundamental bases of "Western Civilization"' (1987: 2), and 'lessen European cultural arrogance' (ibid.: 73). Later Bernal made the political point even more strongly, saying that demonstration of Greek culture's African and Asian roots 'would have a fundamental and to my mind beneficial effect on not merely the peoples of South West Asia and North East Africa but also those of the rest of the world including Europe' (Bernal 1992: 213).[4]

It will be seen that of the two main claims involved in Afrocentric views of the world of Antiquity – that ancient Egypt was a black African civilization, and ancient Greece an ungrateful, derivative legatee of Egypt's achievements – Bernal's focus is overwhelmingly on the latter, whereas Diop and others had mostly been interested in the former. He discusses earlier European views on the relationship between Egypt and Ethiopia, but only briefly and in rather noncommittal fashion (1987: 243–5). He has indeed been criticized by otherwise approving commentators for neglect of Egypt's Africanness: for not noticing that the Aryan Model's African counterpart has also been demolished (see, for instance, Davidson 1987), or simply for failing to say anything substantial about Egypt's relations to the rest of Africa (Baines 1996: 32). Bernal does, however, appear broadly to accept the Diopian perspective on Egypt too, notably through his belief in – indeed, what he himself calls his 'elaborate effort to resuscitate' – the idea that the 'black Pharaohs' Sesostris and Ammenemes undertook far-reaching conquests across much of the then known world (Bernal 1991: 524). (The elaborate effort comprises pp. 187–273 of ibid. Reasons for scepticism about it are rehearsed, *inter alia*, in Yurco [1996: 72–6]; Tritle [1996: 310–13]).

Bernal's work has, of course, been intensely controversial, on both evidential and political grounds.[5] Perhaps the sharpest, as well as most thoughtful, extended critique of *Black Athena*'s political implications came from Molly Myerowitz Levine. Calling it an 'interesting and dangerous book', she identified the danger in Bernal's 'very nineteenth-century focus on origins and race' (Levine 1992a: 450). Bernal's stress on origins, on the ethnicity of the scholars he discusses as well as of the peoples of Antiquity, led to the abuse of history both by Bernal himself and by some readers:

> [H]e seems to take it as given that the ethnic group you were born in – Jewish, WASP, African American – greatly determines both what you claim as 'objective conclusions' and your reception or rejection . . . by the academy. (ibid.: 451)

This tendency in Bernal himself had been taken up by 'Radical Afrocentrists' who have misused his work to renew 'claims for the irredeemable unreliability of "European" historiography', as well as for the 'Blackness' of the ancient Egyptians (453). Such myths of origin are, in Levine's view, 'profoundly ironic, for they painfully recall the zealous excess with which nineteenth-century Europe appropriated and remade ancient Greece in its own "Aryan" image' (456). Such views tend, she thinks, to fuel a new racism which, following Shelby Steele (1990), she sees as a direct response to the 'politics of difference'. Levine's own position, though, seems rather ambivalent. On the one hand she laments Bernal's politicization of scholarship; but on the other, hers is itself clearly and deliberately a political intervention. To invoke Shelby Steele as she does is evidently to take sides – the conservative side – in current US political arguments over race politics, affirmative action, and so on. Her allegation that Bernal's foregrounding of racial issues 'may inhibit many who differ with him from speaking out, lest they, too, be labelled racists' (ibid.: 445) is surely unfair as a *general* accusation; even if, at times, Bernal does seem disconcertingly free with the 'racist' label, as in his astonishing description of Colin Renfrew's ideas as having 'racist overtones', or of Gordon Childe as 'thoroughly convinced of Aryan racial superiority' (Bernal 1991: 67).[6] Elsewhere (Levine 1992b) she urged that contemporary classicists must adopt a more multiculturalist approach, setting Greece and Rome in their Mediterranean context, including Africa and Asia: both because it is a more historically inclusive view, but also because if the professionals don't do it, 'the wrong people' (i.e. the Afrocentrists) will.

If Levine's charge is that Bernal makes too much of the contemporary political implications of his views, Robert Young's case is that he says too little on the matter. *Black Athena*, Young argues, 'insists on maintaining a sphinx-like silence about its own relation to today's contemporary cultural politics' (Young 1994: 158). This is indicated above all in Bernal's reticence about the racial identity of the ancient Egyptians. If they were not black, says Young, then Bernal's entire wider politico-cultural argument collapses (ibid.: 157). Showing that one group of 'whites', the Greeks, were not culturally original but, rather, dependent on two other 'white' peoples, the

Egyptians and the Phoenicians (or pseudo-Jews), would do nothing to 'lessen European cultural arrogance'.[7] Two quite distinct negative arguments were made by Euro-racist scholars about Egypt: that it did not influence Greece, and that its peoples were not 'black', not truly African. Bernal – according to Young – underplays the second, remains ambiguous about its implications, and fails entirely to address the issue of what it might *mean* to call an ancient people 'black' when this label itself is so very much a modern, political term (ibid.: 159–61). In his history of politicized scholarship on classical civilizations, Young points out, Bernal omits to note the major role nineteenth-century American writers played in asserting the whiteness of the Egyptians, and how closely this was tied to justifications for slavery (ibid.: 160–65; Young [1995: 124–33]). Yet Bernal's very title invokes all these arguments, and depends for its force on allusion to them.

Black Athena's title is itself, then, a troubled matter. Bernal has acknowledged that this is a 'critical issue', and asserted that although he did originally suggest it, he then wanted it changed. 'However, my publisher insisted on retaining it, arguing: "Blacks no longer sell. Women no longer sell. But black women still sell"' (Bernal 1989: 32). This sounds engagingly honest, though it is therefore a touch puzzling that Bernal also used the title with which he says he was so unhappy for his 1985 article in the *Journal of African Civilizations* (Bernal 1985), and apparently for a Cornell lecture series he conducted over several years. On the other hand, he has given more attention to the problematic meanings of 'blackness' than Young suggests – albeit mostly in replies to criticism since his first volume appeared, and in rather inconsistent ways. In his first volume, he expressed scepticism about 'the utility of the concept "race" in general' (1987: 241), argued for the mixed character of the Egyptian population (ibid.: 241–2), repeated his insistence that 'Egyptian civilization was fundamentally African' (242), but said that this issue was 'not relevant to our present discussion, which is concerned with the ambiguities in the *perceived* "racial" position of the Egyptians' (ibid.). In his *Arethusa* response to critics, he appeared within a couple of pages both to claim that the ancient Egyptians were 'black' and to assert the inapplicability of racial terminology to the ancient world (Bernal 1989: 30–31). In the second volume of *Black Athena*, he frequently referred to certain Pharaohs, notably Sesostris, and mythic figures possibly associated with them, as 'black', in ways that left it unclear whether this was because *all* Egyptians should be considered so, or because they probably came from the south of Egypt or from Nubia (1991: 259, 261–2, 268, 271, 524, 587 n.95, 590 n.160). Bernal refers, indeed, to the 'Deep Southern origin of the 12th-Dynasty pharaohs' (ibid.: 268), which makes it sound very much as though he has Memphis, Tennessee more than Memphis, Egypt in mind. He associated the putative Egyptian conquests with reports of 'black' populations in Turkey at various times (ibid.: 249–50); while his references to Sesostris's alleged conquering host as a 'civilized African army' (25), 'many of whom were Black and led by a prince who was Black' (268), seemed strangely overinsistent, in the ways we have already noted among historians who evince an insecure and surely unnecessary compulsion to 'prove' that Africans can be historical actors. He noted the complications involved with the identification of 'Blacks' and 'Ethiopians' in the ancient world, without apparently pausing to reflect on the problems of his own language in this sphere (251–7).[8] John Baines puts the general objection very clearly: Bernal's procedure 'seems inappropriate to any society that does not have an overriding obsession with race; it appears thus to suffer in reverse from the defects Bernal sees in classical scholarship' (1996: 32).

The historiographical framework proposed in *Black Athena* has been criticized on numerous grounds. Its view of eighteenth- and nineteenth-century intellectual history may well be thought schematic and Manichaean. Some believe that it is simply naive (e.g. Lefkowitz 1996b: 14). Bernal's first volume entirely omitted the most influential figure of all in archaeology in the early twentieth century, Oscar Montelius: an omission he remedies very perfunctorily in Volume 2 (1991: 66), without admitting how seriously it distorted the entire historiographical picture drawn in Volume 1. Bernal's strong diffusionism has, as we have already noted, been thought excessive and thoroughly old-fashioned. Most specialists consider his claims about the nature and extent of racism in previous scholarly generations simplistic and exaggerated. Arguably, Bernal concentrates too closely on nineteenth-century German scholarship – which he sees as especially heavily imbued with racial assumptions – and too little on the British role in revaluing Greece.[9] The main impetus for the latter was perhaps not so much directly or overtly racial as it was on notions of Athenian democracy: but also of Athens as *imperial* democracy. The multiple strands of argument involved in positive images of Athens retain their variety and their considerable weight today, as is suggested in different ways in writings by Vassilis Lambropolous (1993) and Cornelius Castoriadis (1989), with their particular concern to defend a notion of Greek originality; or by Robert Young's claim that the discourse of Hellenism is one indicator of the continued hold of racialized thinking (Young 1995: esp. chs 3, 5). Bernal's focus, then, is too narrow, and too inclined to see a *directly* racist motivation for intellectual revisions (a tendency reinforced by what Levine rightly sees as Bernal's disconcerting habit of crudely adducing scholars' views from their ethnic background). It might be more important and compelling to trace how, in *in*direct or covert ways, the discourse of Greek origins – and, indeed, of Greek civility and democracy – fed into, was inflected by, and itself shaped racial and colonial ideas of 'the West and the rest'.

I am not qualified to offer judgement on Bernal's reading of the archaeological, linguistic and other evidence, which involves technical skills and a command of ancient languages which I do not possess.[10] Indeed, Levine suggests that the sheer range of *Black Athena*'s concerns means that 'it requires a committee to review Bernal properly' (1992a: 445). In any case, significant parts of this evidence are to be contained in Volumes 3 and 4 of his mammoth project, which have not yet appeared at the time of writing. Much of the debate among classicists, as opposed to the wider political controversies over *Black Athena*, has inevitably revolved around such questions of evidence. Here it seems to the outsider that some aspects of his work have been significantly faulted by experts.[11]

Some classicists' circles simply dismissed *Black Athena*: several major periodicals in the field appear not even to have reviewed it, while *The Classical World* treated it to a brief, savage notice saying that Bernal had clearly formulated his 'strange conclusions' before he had done any research, and that the book was 'only a strident, revisionist, political pamphlet' (Savvas 1989: 469–70). Bernal and his supporters would, of course, respond that this represents at least in part the defensiveness of an enclosed professional guild unwilling to see its ideological assumptions, many of them reflecting disreputable inherited racial ideologies, challenged. Indeed, Bernal had anticipated such defensiveness in the very first pages of his first volume, and built this into the very heart of his argument throughout.

Bernal, though, seemed more concerned at the failure of the *New York Times*, *Time*, *Newsweek*, the London *Times*, *Independent*, or *Times Literary Supplement* to give due attention to the book. He hints heavily at a racially charged conspiracy of silence (1991: xvii–xxii). In fact some of these either devoted feature-page notice to Bernal's views, or reviewed the second volume (and thus Bernal's general thesis) at some length. Certainly the book has been far more widely discussed in the non-specialist media than any other work about ancient history for decades. Its author's complaints verge on the megalomaniac.

Bernal's use of archaeological evidence has been much criticized – not least for his alleged failure to take account of a full range of relevant fieldwork (Morris 1996; Yurco 1996; Vermeule 1992; Tritle 1996; Lefkowitz 1996b). His linguistic arguments and proposed new etymologies suggesting 'massive' infusions of Egyptian and Semitic words into Greek have been subject to perhaps the most ferocious assault of all: 'a model of tendentious confusion ... misguided ... speculations of the most extravagant kind ... an almost complete disregard for phonetic consistency ... simply false' (Jasanoff and Nussbaum 1996: 187, 189–90, 191, 195). His chronological framework, involving earlier dates for various phenomena than those most specialists prefer, has also come under highly sceptical scrutiny (Baines 1996: 36–7; Yurco 1996: 68–72, 86–9). His assertions about the character of ancient Egyptian science and its influence on Greece have been judged almost entirely wrong by one specialist (Palter 1996a); while his observations on the historiography of the same subject are described as based on 'ignorance and superficial understanding' (ibid.: 214).

Almost no one else in the field seems to find Bernal's belief in an Egyptian colonization of Greece plausible. As Baines says, Bernal's model 'requires Aegean societies to have assimilated and retained influences from abroad across changes that would have left those influences without meaning for the actors' (1996: 38). David O'Connor (1996) and Lawrence Tritle (1996), summarizing the evidence – or near-total lack of it – that might support the idea, find the *Black Athena* case for colonialism entirely speculative and unconvincing. There is, ironically, rather more evidence for Greeks visiting Egypt, at the time of the 18th Dynasty, than vice versa (O'Connor 1996: 54–6). Where the Egyptians *did* undoubtedly conquer and colonize, as in Nubia, the archaeological record of their presence and cultural influence is substantial. For the Aegean, nothing comparable exists: though experts seem to agree that there are better reasons for seeing Egyptian influence on the Mycenaeans than on earlier Greek cultures (Yurco 1996: 89–95).

Ungenerously, one might note that some peripheral matters, like even the misspelling of several names in his list of Acknowledgements (1987: xvi–ii), do not inspire total confidence in Bernal's care in handling more central ones. More importantly, one may register what seems, on general principles, a methodological flaw running throughout *Black Athena*: the striking contrast between the vigilant ideological suspiciousness marking his reading of all classical scholarship from the eighteenth century onwards, and the absence of such vigilance in his treatment of the ancient sources themselves. The modern writers are set in their sociopolitical contexts, tirelessly interrogated for ideological bias, and, as we have noted, often have their scholarly dispositions interpreted in terms of their ethnic origins. The ancients are treated – as various critics like John Baines and Tamara Green have complained (Baines 1996; Green 1989) – with what seems, by comparison, like remarkable indulgence or naivety. Texts are read as sources for factual statements, relatively unencumbered by considerations of ideology, interest or narrative strategy – even texts whose status has long been generally recognized as highly problematic in these respects, like that of Herodotus. Valentin Mudimbe, who is in general highly sympathetic to Bernal's aims, thinks him insufficiently critical of Herodotus's pronouncements, and reminds us of the Greek historian's tales of dog-headed men, headless people with eyes on their chests, people with no names, and so on. 'What is the credibility of such a presenter?', asks Mudimbe with suitable scepticism (Mudimbe 1994: 97). It might well be more productive, as the French historian François Hartog argues with particular force, to see the figure of Egypt in Herodotus and other Greek writings not as the subject of empirical statements to be accepted or rejected on evidential grounds, but as a stereotype, a paradigm, a symbolic 'Other' by comparison with which – indeed, *against* which – the Greeks defined their own culture (Hartog 1986, 1988). Yet Bernal, replying to critics, reasserted that we should indeed, as a general rule, always be more sceptical about modern than about ancient authors (Bernal 1992: 209).

Bernal's treatment of Greek myth as historical evidence has come in for particular criticism. Perhaps his most central argument is that the Greeks believed themselves – or at least, important parts of their population, including various ruling families and ancestral heroes – to be descended from Phoenician and Egyptian immigrants; and that they were correct in this belief. Much of his evidence for this comes from Greek myths. Edith

Hall suggests that his 'entire thesis rests ultimately on his argument that the versions of certain myths preserved in some ancient literary sources contain kernels of that nebulous entity, "historical truth", and ought therefore to be believed' (Hall 1992: 184). Hall mounts several lines of attack against this. She claims that Bernal does not distinguish between 'objective' and 'subjective' ethnicity – the Greeks' real origins, and who they *thought* they were. This may not be a wholly fair complaint: Bernal does separate the two, though not always entirely clearly. Replying to Hall, rather oddly, Bernal first insisted that he *was* clear about the distinction, then that it didn't matter because all ethnicity is subjective (Bernal 1992: 204–5)! More telling is Hall's charge that Bernal's handling of the sheer variety of Greek myth is inadequate: 'Ministries of Ideology in every polis defined their subjective ethnicity by tracing their forefathers' genealogies in different ways' (1992: 191); and for Athenians, this included claiming that *they* were indigenous, whereas other Greeks had come from elsewhere. Bernal, then, allegedly uses specifically Athenian claims about others' origins as evidence for what all Greeks supposedly believed about themselves. He has been taken in by Athenian propaganda, because 'he believes in a homogeneous entity called Greek Myth: he is constantly talking about What the Greeks Themselves Believed' (ibid.: 191).

Moreover, Hall thinks, Bernal drastically underrates the sheer fluidity of ethnic claims in myth: the way Greek gods and heroes keep changing their supposed origins (1992: 193–5). Most damagingly of all, he is simply 'unsophisticated' about the multifarious social functions of myth – symbolic, propagandistic, self-defining, ritualistic, and so on. He wants us to accept that myth can be winnowed – the pure grain of literal historical truth can be extracted, and used as decisive evidence about Greek origins. It is an impossible exercise, says Hall, and in Bernal's hands results in an attempt to replace one legend – the Aryan one – by another. Instead we should focus on the 'really important questions' – who did the Greeks *think* they were, why did they think it, and why does the whole issue seem to matter so much to us at the end of the twentieth century (ibid.: 198)?

In reply, Bernal claimed not only that many ancient Greek myths do indeed contain historical truth, but that modern theorizing about the multiple purposes of ancient legends 'has no bearing on the question of their having, or not having any historicity' (1992: 204). This does not seem satisfactory. Can we really give proper recognition to all the ideological, functional and fictive uses of myth, and still say blithely that alongside all these, quite unaffected by them, there exists a clearly separable core of historical truth?

Elsewhere Bernal had appeared less confident about claims to clear-cut historical truth, suggesting instead that he operated according to a model of 'competitive plausibility' (1991: 4) in assessing rival accounts. This gave rise to some caustic responses, with James Muhly saying that Bernal's approach was certainly competitive, but not very plausible (quoted in Levine 1992a: 442), while Robert Pounder snapped that undergraduate term papers are failed every day for indulging in 'competitive plausibility' (Pounder 1992: 461). Bernal, Pounder alleges, wilfully sets aside require- ments on standards of historical evidence which are 'not the twisted constructs of evil German historians' but as old as Thucydides (ibid.: 463). Josine Blok, similarly, finds that Bernal 'has dropped several essential rules of historical inquiry' (Blok 1996: 724).

There is also an important, unresolved tension in Bernal's work between the 'Africanist' and the 'Semiticist' impulses. He has been claimed as an ally by many of those seeking to urge exclusively Egyptian origins – identified in their turn wholly with black African ones – for Greek civilization; and has appeared happy with that association. In this register, his work is linked with African, and more particularly African-American, cultural assertion; and of course it is this vein in his writing which has attracted most attention and controversy. But Bernal himself has seemed almost as interested in uncov- ering Semitic influences on ancient Greece as African ones; and in *this* vein his work is tied to a resurgent Jewish – and especially Israeli – scholarship of recent decades; and even, in directly political fashion, to the successes of political Zionism. He himself has gone out of his way to emphasize this too, as well as the 'scattered Jewish components' of his own ancestry (1987: xiii); even though he has also stressed the importance as intellectual influences on him, and on the revived 'Ancient Model', of non- or anti-Zionist Jewish scholars like Cyrus Gordon and Michael Astour (ibid.: 36, 415–16). In this way Bernal is certainly less single-mindedly Afrocentric than Diop, who had seen the Phoenicians as mere copyists of Egypt (see Diop 1991: 95).

These two impulses – of emphasis on the one hand on Egyptian, on the other on Semitic or, more specifically, Judaic influences on Greece – are naturally by no means incompatible within the logic of historical scholar- ship. But in the contemporary ethno-political arena which, again, Bernal himself is so eager to see as determining scholarly inquiry, they are very much at odds. The ideologies of political Zionism and of Pan-African or Afrocentric assertion, despite (or perhaps in part because of) their substan- tial shared ancestry, have long been bitterly opposed. This is so not only in the politics of the Middle East and Africa themselves – where an association of Pan-Africanism with anti-Zionism, although it achieved its strongest practical expressions three decades ago under Egypt's President Nasser, has a still vigorous emotional life – but perhaps still more in North America, where relations between blacks and Jews have become ever more ideologi- cally fraught.[12] Bernal himself becomes ideologically uncomfortable only when he has to concede that people who were neither African nor Semitic ever achieved anything, as when he finds it 'difficult to admit' that the Hyksos might have included some Indo-Europeans (1991: 359, and several other similar grouches). His view of the character and significance of Hyksos invasions themselves seems to have shifted several times. Frankly, I cannot make clear sense of it.

It is noteworthy, and depressing, that some of Bernal's fiercest critics – especially, but not only, from within the Afrocentric camp – choose to make a point of identifying him as Jewish. (In fact Martin Bernal's immediate ancestry includes Irish Catholics and American Presbyterians; his own recent assertions of the importance to him of having some Jewish ancestry are a touch vague, and leave one wondering just why he should choose to stress them now[13].) Some of the difficulties here may be indicated in the terms of a critique of Bernal launched by Vassilis Lambropoulos, who is concerned to defend Hellenism in modern culture against what he sees as a concerted Hebraist assault.

Lambropoulos asserts, making a rather odd connection with a leading US literary critic, that 'Like Harold Bloom (who meticulously fashions himself on Disraeli's Sidonia), Bernal presents himself as an outsider (non-classicist, British Jew) . . . and seeks exotic alliances' (1993: 356). His is an example of 'positive use of ethnic origin for potentially dangerous race arguments' (ibid.: 357). Lambropoulos's book *The Rise of Eurocentrism* (an utterly misleading title: it *is* in fact about Hebraism versus Hellenism), though hugely erudite, seems to me in effect complicit in what it analyses, having a rather disconcerting subplot alleging a wicked Hebraist (or even Jewish) conspiracy to calumniate the Greeks, which evidently – and ironically, given the complaints Lambropoulos, and I, make against Bernal – owes more than a little to the author's origins.[14] Bernal is seen as part of this trend, or near-conspiracy. He is misrepresented as 'arguing that the Greeks have stolen everything from the Hebrews, or from the Orient in general. To buttress this idea, Bernal resorts to sensationalism: he manipulates his terminology according to audience demands; he plays the role of the pariah; he conjures up enemies; he uses messianic language' (Lambropoulos 1993: 92 – each item on the charge-sheet is supported by extensive endnotes, at pp. 355–7). More soberly, Lambropoulos suggests, with some justice, that Bernal's treatment of the ancient Greeks, also ironically, fails to show due regard for *their* cultural specificity, or its attractions to later scholars:

> [H]e sees every expression of interest in Greece as a position for or against the Ancient Model which he thinks had prevailed until then. It is as if every Western view of Greece has been determined by one's view of a Near Eastern civilization. . . . The possibility that certain Westerners chose to look at Greece because that culture appealed to them (rather than because they were looking for ways of denigrating the others) is never entertained. (ibid.: 93)

Certainly the implication here – that Bernal stereotypes his intellectual opponents, and may wilfully overdramatize their differences in order to present himself as a lonely warrior for truth and decency – has some basis. Writing in his second volume of the Hyksos empire-building which (on apparently questionable evidence) he believes to have occurred, Bernal protests that he does not believe that 'conquest or domination through violence somehow makes a people or linguistic group morally or creatively *better*' (Bernal 1991: 360; original emphasis). Thus he encourages the implication that all those who disagree with him *do* think violent conquerors are morally superior: an implication he immediately reinforces by explicitly – and in my opinion scurrilously – associating such a view, and his 'Aryanist' opponents, with the Nazi *Shoah* (ibid.: 360)! Lambropoulos's other main point, that Bernal fails to show any regard for Greek cultural specificity, and maligns the ancient (and, by implication, the modern) Greeks – also has some force, albeit of a rather ethnocentric kind, and has been echoed by Mary Lefkowitz and others. But, again ironically, it can equally well be said that Bernal's model fails to indicate any interest in Egyptian – let alone other African or Asian – cultures in their own right. He is interested only in their putative impact on Greece, and thus on Europe: his is, in the end, as Eurocentric a view as those he attacks.

In more aggressive – and, indeed, nakedly anti-Semitic – fashion, Tony Martin writes of 'Bernal, a Jew, (who) was precipitously and prematurely adopted by many Afrocentrists' (Martin 1993: 57), and goes on to see Bernal and his antagonist Mary Lefkowitz as co-conspirators against Africanism:

> Lefkowitz and Bernal actually end up endorsing white supremacy, making a pitch for possible 'Semitic'/Jewish origins of Western civilization and denouncing Afrocentrism. When faced with the Lefkowitz challenge, Bernal preferred to abdicate his potentially precarious Afrocentric throne in favour of 'Semitic' solidarity.' (ibid.: 58)

Manu Ampim's objection is not to Bernal's supposed Jewishness, but more simply to his whiteness. Ampim claims to identify a 'Bernal–Davidson school' of white interlopers into Afrocentric study. This 'school' of 'outsiders' (that is, non-Africans), it is asserted, 'undermines' Afrocentric endeavour by identifying ancient Egyptian populations as racially mixed, and must be 'checked' before it does further damage (Ampim 1994: 191, 192).

Other Afrocentric attacks on Bernal and his book's reputation have been more scrupulous, if not necessarily more accurate, than Tony Martin's and Manu Ampim's bigoted tirades. Some have centred mainly on the not unreasonable complaint that *Black Athena* has gained massive international attention, while a host of black writers who had – often much earlier – made similar arguments were entirely ignored. Bernal, of course, makes this point himself, albeit in rather cursory fashion and with apparently only the most limited knowledge of prior Afro-American or African Egyptophile writings. His failure to note Diop's *Civilization or Barbarism*, whose final chapters raise so many of the same issues as his own book, is especially regrettable. Bernal makes vaguely approving reference to George James's book *Stolen Legacy*, and complains bitterly at the difficulty of getting it accepted into the library at Cornell University – but *Black Athena* says nothing whatever about the substance of James's claims. In a later response to critics Bernal explicitly distances himself from them, insisting: 'At no point do I say or even suggest that I accept James's claim that Aristotle "stole" his ideas from the library at Alexandria' (Bernal 1989: 32).

Equally, however, it must be admitted that Bernal's work is considerably more carefully documented and argued than any of the related studies by black Afrocentrists, Diop not excluded. None the less, a racial element in the contrast between the media coverage and academic debate Bernal's book prompted and the obscurity into which many earlier works in similar vein have fallen cannot be ignored. As Jacob Carruthers remarks:

> For at least two hundred years, African champions of ancient Egypt have been asserting what Bernal concludes about Kemet; now that a European scholar has proclaimed it, the dialogue ... has been reopened. (Carruthers 1992: 462)

Carruthers, undoubtedly one of the more scholarly of the extreme Afrocentrists, does not deny that Bernal 'has made a valuable contribution' (1992: 462). His major criticism of *Black Athena*, perhaps surprisingly, is that its case is too overstated. Bernal emphasizes direct Egyptian colonization of Greece, whereas although colonies *may* have been established, they are not enough, in Carruthers's view, to account for Egyptian influence there. Instead: 'the indirect impact of Egyptian civilization on tricontinental world cultures over a sustained period', together with what Greek thinkers learned from various neighbouring peoples, should be understood (ibid.: 465). Bernal, suggests Carruthers, also understates the connections between Egypt, Phoenicia, and the Mediterranean rim of Western Asia more generally. For instance, one finds strong similarities between Mesopotamian and Greek myths, which share elements 'quite foreign' to Egyptian beliefs (466–7). Carruthers's model of cultural influence, then, is a far more ecumenically multilateral one than Bernal's, and would probably find more acceptance in the academic mainstream. Carruthers, indeed, tends to mock Bernal's protestations of academic marginality: he is 'the inside–outsider trying to really get outside' (471). Carruthers also finds Bernal's treatment of race deeply flawed, and is sceptical of his view that either Christian views or the idea of progress should share the blame for nineteenth-century defamation of Egypt. Instead, the new racial 'science' of the era and Romanticism – 'two sides of the same coin', in Carruthers's view – were the culprits. Finally, Carruthers seems to accept that ancient Greek references to people as 'black' by no means necessarily meant that they resembled modern Zambians, any more than the Greeks themselves resembled modern Swedes. Sensibly, Carruthers urges:

> [T]he Kemites were as Black as the Greeks were White. I believe that the ancient Greeks were thoroughly Eurasian ... many were dark complexioned, some olive or bronze ... [O]ur claim about the Blackness of the Kemites is no more outrageous than the European claim that the ancient Greeks were white. Therefore, let us stop quibbling about what Herodotus meant ... or

what percentage of which dynasties were Black; or whether true Africans had
everted lips. How inverted were the lips of the average ancient Greek?
(470–71)

It is only rather a pity that Carruthers, after all this, appears to slip back into
a racial essentialism of his own with complaints that Martin Bernal 'intrudes
into a two-centuries-old dialogue among African thinkers' (474).

Frank Snowden, the veteran Afro-American historian of racial attitudes in
Antiquity, was even more sceptical about Bernal's racial categorizations. His
respectful – if terse – references to Diop, said Snowden, failed to note how
the Senegalese 'distorts his classical sources' and the strong objections his
theses had met at the Cairo conference (Snowden 1989: 89). Bernal's use
of classical authors was also questioned:

> there is in classical sources no justification for equating 'black', as used by
> Herodotus or any other Greek author, with peoples designated in classical
> texts as Ethiopians, (i.e. Negroes) unless there is additional substantial
> evidence to support such an equivalence. (ibid.: 93)

The basis of Clyde Winters's attack is somewhat different, and he evidently
has little time for the subtleties of a Jacob Carruthers or a Frank Snowden.
Not only has Bernal gained far more than his due of publicity, but his case
on the one hand does not go far enough, on the other contains errors on
which critics have fastened to discredit Afrocentrism, with which Bernal
should not really be associated. Bernal, according to Winters, sees the
Hyksos as the founders of Greek civilization (though this is not really an
accurate summary of his view), as opposed to 'Afrocentric scholars who
recognize that the founders of Athens and Attica were Blacks' (Winters
1994: 176).

A quite different kind of complaint against *Black Athena* seems to me
more serious than any of these. Neither Bernal nor any other writer who
can, however broadly, be grouped within the Afrocentric tradition appears
to be interested in the *content* of the ideas with which Pharaonic Egypt is
argued to have influenced the world. Merely asserting the fact of such
influence appears to be enough. In relation to philosophy, which has been
the most contentious area and site of the most extravagant claims, Appiah
is surely right to say that 'Diop – whose work is clearly the best in the field –
offers little evidence that Egyptian philosophy is more than a systematised
but fairly uncritical folk-philosophy' (1992: 162). And Appiah further
questions whether study of the earliest known philosophical thought,
whether it is conceived of as Egyptian or as Greek, is of major value to the
work contemporary philosophers do, for two reasons:

> I think what matters are answers, not histories of answers ... (and) it is
> absurd to argue that because a thought is African, and the prehistory of

European thought lies in Africa, that thought will help us to understand Western Thought. (ibid.: 161)

More significantly and damagingly still, in so far as we are primarily interested in the broad spheres of moral, social, legal and political philosophy – and pretty evidently almost everyone involved in the controversy *is* so concerned, rather than being preoccupied with more abstract ontological or epistemological questions – it is by no means evident that ancient Egyptian thought has anything whatever to tell us. It presupposes an intensely hierarchical society, based on slavery and on certain persons being divine while others are rightless. It has nothing to say about democracy, equality, liberty, individual rights, the distribution of wealth and power; let alone issues of race, gender, class, ethnicity or ecology – any of the questions which mainly preoccupy modern societies and those who seek to philosophize about them.[15] Its presuppositions might be of value only to people who are keen to re-establish theocratic and authoritarian polities: but then, that is precisely what some Afrocentrists so evidently do dream of. When Molefi Asante seeks to summarize what he believes the world owes to ancient Africa, the only specifically political or social entry on his list is 'the concept of monarchies and divine-kingships' (Asante 1988: 38). If, by this logic, we wish to celebrate and revive the Divine Right of Kings, we should emphasize our African heritage. And if not, not.

As Jennifer Tolbert Roberts's intriguing book *Athens on Trial* shows, debate and dispute over ancient Athens have for many decades – the best part of two centuries – been centred on the issues of democracy and freedom (Roberts 1994). More recently, it has finally been recognized that those issues include, centrally, the rights of women; while the most ambitious single recent contribution to those discussions has come from a black Jamaican-born scholar, Orlando Patterson. It is noteworthy that Patterson's monumental *Freedom in the Making of Western Culture* (1991), identifying the birthplace of modern conceptions of freedom as Periclean Athens, makes no mention at all of Egyptian influence – for there is no sign that the early Greek stirrings of freedom and democracy owed anything to Egypt. And it is because of its association with these ideas that Athens, rightly, has been seen as important to all parts of the world and all ages. In so far as Bernal has legitimated a debate which instead focuses entirely on the racial origins of ideas, his is a regressive, reactionary step. Even Michel Foucault's or Kenneth Dover's interests in Athenian sexuality were framed by concern over its relevance to power relations, to ethico-political questions and to rights. Bernal, let alone his black nationalist supporters, has no such agenda. For him, seemingly, race is all.

Martin Bernal has not been alone among recent scholars in questioning the Aryan and 'isolationist' models of Greek cultural development; though few others have bent the stick so far the other way as he does. The Swiss scholar Walter Burkert, in a book first published in 1984, translated into English in 1992 – ignored by Bernal (who reads German) in his first volume, though extensively referred to in his second – makes a related but apparently more balanced case. He, too, believes that a polarity of 'Occident' and 'Orient' became hegemonic among classical scholars largely as a result of late-eighteenth-century German writings: though it has its precursors in Greek thought itself, arising from their conflict with the Persians (Burkert 1992: 1). Even today it remains 'difficult to undertake unprejudiced discussion of connections between classical Greece and the East ... (without) entrenched positions, uneasiness, apology if not resentment' (ibid.: 1). But in tracing Asian influences on Greece through such fields as craftsmanship (ch. 1), medicine and magic (ch. 2) and the parallels between Akkadian and early Greek literature and myth (ch. 3), Burkert does not conclude – as the Afrocentrists do – by presenting Greece as a wholly derivative civilization:

> [A] cultural continuum including literacy was created by the eighth century [BCE] extending over the entire Mediterranean; it involved groups of Greeks who entered into intensive exchange with the high cultures of the Semitic East. Cultural predominance remained for a while with the Orient; but Greeks immediately began to develop their own distinctive forms of culture through an astonishing ability both to adopt and to transform what they had received. Soon Greece was to take over the leading role in Mediterranean civilization. (ibid.: 128)

Sarah Morris, like Burkert, proposes a model of multiple influences across the ancient Near East, tending to stress Levantine more than Egyptian impact on Greek culture, especially in relation to the visual arts (Morris 1989, 1992, 1996). The increasing tendency among analysts of the ancient eastern Mediterranean, southwest Asia and northern Africa is, on Burkert's and Morris's lines, to see multidimensional interaction between peoples – a genuinely 'multicultural' model quite unlike either the largely discredited Eurocentrism which Bernal assails or the Egyptocentric version he seeks to put in its place.

In somewhat more muted vein than Bernal, and without quite his sweeping claims about modern writers' ethnic prejudices, a rather similar message of the ubiquity of race emanates from the work of the Australian political theorist Patricia Springborg. In *Western Republicanism and the Oriental Prince* (1992), a book which has been oddly and unjustly neglected by comparison with the huge attention given to Bernal, Springborg covers much of the same ground as that traversed in *Black Athena*. She, too, is concerned with the ancient history of relations between 'East' and 'West', and sees modern racism – especially anti-Semitism which, Springborg says, 'affects all Semites, Arab and Jew' (ibid.: vii) – as stemming directly from the way ancient writers came to divide the world. Attitudes to race, private property (whose supposed absence in the Orient was the key to despotism's triumph there) and a host of other key social issues were shaped according to the basic antithesis between East and West.

That polarization concealed the huge extent of Greek intellectual debts to Egypt, and the degree to which earlier Greek writers derived not only their ideas about philosophy and history but their theories of government from the Egyptians. Plato's *Republic*, Springborg argues, is based on Egyptian models (ibid.: 94–115). Plato – like Homer, Hesiod, Herodotus and a host of other early Greek writers – accepted that Greece's origins lay east and south, symbolized in the mythical founder-figures of Danaus the Egyptian and Cadmus the Phoenician. But these early beliefs, and images of wise and benevolent non-European political systems, were later denied and concealed in fabricated alternative myths of origin, and in the mythical, demonized figure of the 'Oriental despot' which haunted all modern Western thought and against which Western ideas of freedom and democracy defined themselves. Perhaps the first full crystallization of such antitheses came with Aristotle, whose defence of slavery rested on a racist substratum asserting that while Greeks were and should be free, Asiatics were natural slaves (ibid.: 23–31).

The structure of prejudice was renewed in the Renaissance, this time with the Islamic world as the main enemy and the negative pole of the antithesis. This proves that, as Springborg asserts, racism and its accompanying stereotypes:

> especially in that form of racial discrimination among the least understood and most horrendous of our century, anti-Semitism, go back as far as recorded history. Moreover ... they have involved a tissue of distortions as elaborately crafted, as embroidered with myth and romance, and as overlaid with legal sanctions, as the fabric from which the control of sexuality is cut. (288)

Like Bernal, Edward Said, Michael Astour and others, Springborg sees herself as engaged in an intellectual crusade to unravel that tissue of distortions. The direct line she draws from ancient past to present politics is underscored by her note that her book was 'concluded in the throes of a war (that precipitated by Iraq's invasion of Kuwait) reflecting the outcome of the deep divide between East and West, as old as history itself' (vii). From Socrates to Saddam, it seems, nothing ever really changes.

Notes

1. It should be noted, however, that not only the grand plan of Bernal's multivolume project, but important aspects of the argument, shifted significantly between his first volume (1987) and his second (1991). Compare especially the 'Introduction' to Volume 1 with the 'Preface', 'Introduction' and 'Conclusion' to Volume 2. Some of the changes announced are puzzling – including the one Bernal says is most important of all. In Volume 2 he proclaims that he has 'given up the mask of impartiality' he previously adopted, abandoned the 'impartial competition I mistakenly thought possible when I first set out the scheme of this project' (1991: 3, 61). It is hard to believe that any reader of *Black Athena*'s first volume can have gained the impression that Bernal was 'impartial' as

between his 'Aryan' and 'Ancient' Models. Still further shifts in argument can be found in various subsequent articles and responses to critics.

2. Bernal returns to this theme in his 1994b, arguing that images of a white, uniquely creative Greece as fountainhead of all knowledge and culture played a crucial role in legitimating European colonial expansion. Somewhat similar exercises to Bernal's have begun to emerge in other areas of ancient history, such as Keith Whitelam's ideological critique (1996) of biblical studies and Middle Eastern archaeology, which, he argues, have robbed the Palestinians of their past through near-exclusive focus on the origins of ancient Israel.

3. Some of the evidence for this is presented in *Black Athena*'s second volume (Bernal 1991); more is promised in two further volumes. The parts of it so far available have already been subjected to powerful criticism, notably in Jasanoff and Nussbaum (1996).

4. Since so much argument in this sphere has involved claims or assumptions that the character of classical Greek and Roman civilization has immense emotional resonances for the present, I should perhaps say here that I (as a middle-class white European) have never *consciously* felt engaged by this issue. I yawned my way through school-level Latin, never even considered learning ancient Greek, and the only examination I have ever failed in my life was a Latin translation exercise at Oxford. Latterly I have been frankly bored by teaching Plato and Aristotle in courses on the history of political theory, and (I'm more ashamed to admit) have almost never felt any urge to read classical authors for pleasure. Whoever the Europeans are who are supposed to have a profound ideological investment in the classical inheritance, it ain't me.

5. Much of the most important criticism is collected in Lefkowitz and Rogers (1996), together with some new articles. That volume's Bibliography traces most of the history of the controversy, though it misses some important contributions, like the books by Lambropoulos and Springborg, discussed below. It notes 67 reviews and responses on *Black Athena*'s two volumes so far, many of them lengthy review essays and symposia, while by my reckoning Bernal has at the time of writing published fifteen separate extended responses to criticism, not including published letters or the still-proliferating list of his printed reactions to Lefkowitz and Rogers. Among the more important of these are Bernal (1990b, 1992, 1993a, b.)

6. Bernal has also – if anything more peculiarly – suggested that Renfrew's anti-diffusionism stems from his support for the British Conservative Party, since the latter's enthusiasm for small businesses parallels affection for the idea of numerous independent civilizational pioneers (Bernal 1990b: 128)! He has even suggested that Frank Snowden, a distinguished Afro-American classicist, is a prisoner of the racist Aryan model (1987: 477).

7. Mary Lefkowitz, similarly but more briefly, complains that Bernal 'ducked the issue' of whether Egyptians were black (1992: 35); while Frank Snowden has argued on several occasions that Bernal's statements on this issue are confused and misleading (Snowden 1989, 1996).

8. The profound ambiguity about what might be meant by 'black' in Antiquity appears again in Bernal 1991: 383–9.

9. See, for instance, Turner (1989: 101–9); Palter (1996b: 359–64), which also suggest that Bernal misrepresents the British classicists he does discuss. It might further be noted that in casting the Germans as prime villains, Bernal unfairly overlooks the antiracist tradition which also existed in German scholarship, to which Malgorzata Irek (1994) has recently drawn attention. Irek is herself a Polish, not a German, writer, and thus hardly likely to be ideologically predisposed towards pro-German apologetics. Well-documented arguments that Bernal oversimplifies, mistakes and/or misrepresents the views of eighteenth- and nineteenth-century German scholars, including Herder, Heumann and Blumenbach, may be found in Palter (1996b) and Norton (1996). In relation to another key early German classicist, K.O. Mueller, whom Bernal casts as a vehement racist substantially responsible for discrediting the 'Ancient Model', Josine Blok has shown in detail that the account of his ideas given in *Black Athena* is wildly distorting, 'untenable in the light of a sincere assessment of the source material' (Blok 1996: 719).

10. Thus I have not discussed *Black Athena*'s more purely technical offshoot, *Cadmean*

Letters (Bernal 1990a), a treatment of the origins of the Greek alphabet. Its main structure of argument is identical to that of the main project, relying on 'competitive plausibility' (1990a: 1), castigating the 'Aryan model', and proposing that Greek writing derived from the Levant, from which it spread much earlier than most scholars have believed. Its general case – that the emergence of Greek literacy was earlier than previously thought, and substantially derived from the Near East – seems to be accepted by many scholars, which is to say that it is not particularly iconoclastic or (as several critics have noted) original. On the other hand, there are grave evidential problems with it, notably the absence of any evidence for a Greek script before the eighth century BCE (Tritle 1996: 327).

11. See, for instance, the *Arethusa* special issue of Fall 1989, the *Journal of Mediterranean Archaeology*'s 1990 review symposium, Levine (1992b); Pounder (1992); Donelan (1989), and the various contributions to Lefkowitz and Rogers (1996). Among the relatively few more or less approving classicists' responses are Vickers 1987 – calling it a work of 'very great merit and lasting value': 481); Rendsburg (1989) and Banham (1989). In the Preface to his second volume, Bernal gives an account of critical reactions to the first. Any author is likely to overstate the praise and understate the criticism which her or his own work has received; but Bernal's perception is unusually highly coloured. He seems proud of the fact that professionals in the relevant disciplines even *discussed* the book, sliding silently over the actual content of the discussion (Bernal 1991: xviii–xix). He makes Molly Myerowitz Levine sound like a supporter (ibid.: xviii)! He makes much of the fact that sharp criticism did not appear until 1989, nearly two years after the book's appearance. Such attack, he says, 'which might well have been shattering to the book's academic reputation in 1987 or 1988, has come far too late' (xx). Here Bernal 'forgets' that, in the frustratingly slow rhythms of academic publishing, reviews in scholarly journals *usually* appear only eighteen months or two years after their subject's publication.

12. Amid a vast literature see, for instance, Berman (1994); Gates (1992, 1994); Friedman (1995); Kaufman (1988); West (1993).

13. Guy MacLean Rogers ungenerously suggests that 'it is hard in retrospect not to see the entire enterprise of *Black Athena* as a massive, fundamentally misguided projection upon the second millennium BCE of Martin Bernal's personal struggle to establish an identity' (1996a: 441).

14. The numerous polemical exchanges on ancient Greece and its external relations which have marked contemporary North American academia have, rather typically, failed to note the implications for contending European nationalist claims. The relations between ancient and modern Greek identity have been intensely controversial within the Balkan political arena, though the controversy relates more to the issue of Macedonia than to Egyptian or Levantine links. Scholarly – and very physical – controversies at least as bitter as the US ones over Afrocentrism have raged within the Balkans, centred on rival claims to the ancient Macedonian heritage: see Danforth (1995); Poulton (1995); Ugrinovska (1995). Among contributors to the American skirmishes, only Sarah P. Morris (1996: 172) seems to have noticed the connection.

15. It is arguable, however, that ancient Egypt *did* have a concept of social justice, invoked in one of the meanings of the multipurpose term *ma'at*: see Assmann (1989).

Part Three

Afrocentrism in the Present

Wild Afrocentricity

Having traced a wide range of origins and influences on black – especially African-American – cultural nationalist ideas about Africa, we now turn to their high-profile contemporary manifestations.

Perhaps the most widely acknowledged living inspiration for current Afrocentric ideas in the USA is Maulana Ron Karenga. He looms as a massive presence of influence and stimulus behind Leonard Jeffries, Molefi Asante and other current Afrocentric thinkers. He remains, however, a somewhat mysterious personality. Karenga (Maulana means 'master teacher' in Swahili, while Karenga supposedly means 'the tradition'; so that Ron has immodestly entitled himself the Master Teacher of the Tradition) has written less extensively than Asante. Despite occasional Visiting Professorships and the like, and his more recent elevation to chair of the Black Studies Department at California State University, Long Beach, he has always really belonged to the world of political activism rather than academic Black Studies (although he apparently – in 1995, at a comparatively advanced age – completed a PhD at UCLA, comparing Confucian and ancient Egyptian ethical philosophies). Over the years he has indeed proved adept at playing the role of the hard-headed street activist among academics (see his impressively debunking performance in Karenga 1969), and, deftly reversing himself, playing the *savant* to a less educated audience (Addai-Sebo and Wong 1988). He is a more interesting, in some ways a shadier, but also a more considerable character than most of the latter-day Afrocentric ideologues. An undoubtedly substantial endowment of streetwise wit, and in latter years an infusion of socialism into his eclectic brew of ideas, have helped to make his discourse usually more rational than those of the younger Afrocentrists.

In Karenga's earlier (1960s) days, when he first founded and headed the cultural nationalist organization US – standing either for 'United Slaves' or simply for 'Us' as against 'Them': accounts vary – the rationality was far less in evidence. US was based on a paramilitary system of hierarchy, with members supposed to wear khaki neo-African robes; on unquestioning obedience to Karenga's decrees; and on extreme sexism. The poet Amiri Baraka (LeRoi Jones), a former follower of Karenga, recalled that

'Karenga's doctrine made male chauvinism a revolutionary legitimacy.... When brothers (male members) went by, the women were supposed to "salimu" or "submit", crossing their arms on their breasts and bowing slightly.' Karenga himself, Baraka alleged, was persistently verbally offensive to women and sexually exploitative of US's female members (Baraka 1984a: 275).

Amiri Baraka's judgements on that score may have been coloured by disillusioned hindsight, though the picture he paints is one that could be paralleled for the intensely chauvinist atmosphere in many 1960s black – and white – radical groups, not least the Panthers (see E. Brown 1993; Pearson 1994: *passim*). On the nature of Karenga's doctrines, however, even a glance at the US booklet *The Quotable Karenga* (Halisi 1967; and, for a clear summary, Van Deburg 1992: 171–6), or the Maulana's later writings and speeches, will confirm how accurate is Baraka's assessment: that they were an extraordinary *mélange* of phrases and fragments of ideas lifted from a huge range of sources – with the borrowings from white writers, as Baraka sneered, heavily disguised – and given such coherence as they possess by the force of Karenga's personality and by being rooted in 'an ahistorical unchanging never-never-land Africa' (Baraka 1984a: 253). Karenga's rhetoric at that time also allegedly included direct incitements to kill whites (see Genovese 1972: 217; and Karenga's 1968 Manifesto 'Black Art', in Gates and McKay 1997: 1976, which certainly appears to hint in that direction).

US's activities degenerated into a bloody faction fight with the Black Panthers – a fight encouraged, and some allege in large part created, by FBI covert operations (see O'Reilly 1989). As a result, Baraka alleges, Karenga's behaviour became ever more paranoid and eccentric: he kept a machine gun mounted in his living-room, and developed heavy drug dependence (Baraka 1984a: 280, 289). It is reported that Molefi Asante first emerged to prominence as an attempted peacemaker in these California battles. The organization survived at least in name – one of the few 1960s-vintage black radical bodies to do so, as Karenga boasted in 1986 (Addai-Sebo and Wong 1988: 177); but its only significant success was the popular reception in Afro-America of 'Kwanzaa', a pseudo-African 'traditional' festival Karenga had invented as a substitute Christmas.[1] Karenga himself incorporated more and more Fanonist and socialist elements into his teachings, so that the eventual synthesis was very similar to the ideas of the Black Panthers against whom he had once so bitterly fought, except that Karenga's version lacked the Panthers' insurrectionary fervour. He sought to buttress his Afrocentric neo-traditionalism with Diopian ideas on ancient Egyptian wisdom, expressed in a series of works co-authored with Jacob Carruthers – in which, it must be assumed, the detail was overwhelmingly the work of Carruthers, a genuine, if highly idiosyncratic, Afrocentric scholar.[2] Karenga even began to speak of the need to combat sexism (see Addai-Sebo and Wong: 224–7).

Alongside Karenga, John Henrik Clarke is perhaps the other most widely cited father-figure of Afrocentrism (if, in this familial trope so dear to

Afrocentrists themselves, we visualize Diop as the solitary, revered grand-father). Clarke is now the longest-serving, and apparently among the more moderate, of the Afrocentric historical writers. Back in the 1960s, he was the prime mover in the battles for control of the African Studies Association, which we have sketched above (pp. 60–63). He has produced a large number of popularizing works, marked more by an old-fashioned desire to create pride in black achievements than by the aggressive separatism of many other writers in the genre.

Clarke, who for many years taught history at Hunter College in New York, was evidently experienced as an inspiring teacher by many younger Afrocen-tric writers (see, for instance, the warm tribute in Ani 1994: xxi–ii). He was also a founder-member of the Harlem Writers' Club, a friend of Malcolm X in the latter's last years, and long-serving Associate Editor of *Freedomways* magazine. There, his close association with both black and white leftists, including Communists, seemed to some rather inconsistent with his gener-ally separatist stance, and brought him bitter criticism from fiercely anti-Communist cultural nationalists like Harold Cruse (Cruse 1967/1984: 337–44, 507–11). He has been a widely published short-story writer as well as historical popularizer. In recent years almost no Afrocentric historical publication, new or reprinted, has seemed complete without an Introduc-tion or a Foreword by Clarke. He has also been a prolific contributor to such journals as *Présence Africaine* and *The Black Scholar*, producing wide-ranging, highly coloured and sometimes frankly simplistic articles on a long list of subjects from ancient Egypt to Caribbean slave revolts. He has presented his own gloss on such familiar themes as the African origins of humanity and the supposed southern roots of Egyptian culture (Clarke 1967), sketched the evolution of Pan-Africanism (Clarke 1988), offered an overview of black American writings on Africa which emphasizes the inspirational, agitational polemics of his own intellectual tradition rather than the more solid – if modest – efforts of specialists (Clarke 1985), and edited, among many other anthologies, an important – though almost entirely hagiographic – collection on the life of Marcus Garvey (Clarke 1974).

Clarke fits well Jacob Carruthers's definition of the 'old scrappers' of Afro-American history, who:

> without any special training, but a sincere dedication to ferreting out the truth about the Black past and destroying the big lie of Black historical and cultural inferiority, took whatever data were available and squeezed enough truth from them as circumstances allowed. (quoted in Hill-Lubin 1992: 170)

Clarke places himself firmly in that tradition, citing Willis Huggins, John G. Jackson, J.A. Rogers, Leo Hansberry and his friend Yosef Ben-Jochannen as his inspirations (Clarke 1986: 46–7). Unfortunately, Carruthers's reference to as much truth 'as circumstances allowed' must be read to mean 'as much as an overriding political purpose, and a very hazy idea of what constitutes valid evidence for a claim, allowed'. Clarke evidently has a relaxed view of evidence, seeing his function as mainly propagandist: making wild claims that, for instance, 'university life was fairly common' in precolonial West Africa (Clarke 1985: 162); that in most precolonial African societies there was no social inequality at all (Person-Lynn 1996: 13); or that black Americans 'have always had a positive image of Africa' (ibid.: 157).

The broad-brush historical sketches he gave for London's 1986 Black History Month (Addai-Sebo and Wong 1988: 37–61, 69–86, 105–31) were shot through with inaccurate claims, but these were considerably less extreme than those made during the same event by Yosef Ben-Jochannen or Frances Cress Welsing. Similarly, Clarke's prejudices appear less sweeping than those of some other Afrocentrists; although his reported remarks on those London occasions included several apparently anti-Semitic innuendos (ibid.: 49–50, 117, 127). While he has replayed in interview old accusations that 'mulattos' betray the black cause in places like Haiti and Jamaica (Person-Lynn 1996: 10), and that Arabs are Africa's historic enemies (ibid.: 11–12), these are muted by comparison with the bigotries of Ben-Jochannen or Tony Martin, or those of Louis Farrakhan.

Clarke's attitude is well summed up in the words of Herbert Aptheker which he adopted as his own, in introducing a polemic over William Styron's novel *The Confessions of Nat Turner.* 'History's potency is mighty. The oppressed need it for identity and inspiration' (quoted in Genovese 1972: 201). Politically as well as intellectually, this is very dubious. As Eugene Genovese responded, the oppressed might be thought, rather, to need history:

> for the truth of what the world has made of them and of what they have helped make of the world. This knowledge alone can produce that sense of identity which ought to be sufficient for inspiration; and those who look to history to provide glorious moments or heroes invariably are betrayed into making catastrophic errors in political judgement. (ibid.: 201)

A third important older practitioner of the Afrocentric approach to history was Chancellor Williams, whose *Destruction of Black Civilization* (1971/1987) is praised and drawn upon by writers as diverse as John Henrik Clarke, Molefi Asante, Amiri Baraka, and Howard University's Vice-President, Andrew J. Billingsley. Williams (1905–92), a student of Leo Hansberry and long-serving history professor at Howard, emerges as an oddly ambivalent figure. On the one hand, his dedication to the task of recovering African history cannot be doubted. It carried him from doctoral research on African-American religion (never published, though he drew on it for one of his three novels), through studies at Oxford, extensive African travels and gathering of oral traditions, to sixteen years of research for *Destruction*, and kept him working even when he was nearly blind (Williams 1971/1987: 17–33).[3] He insisted, in the finest tradition of autodidactic scholarship – a tradition to which he evidently belongs despite his formal qualifications, with his solitary, idiosyncratic labours undertaken with little institutional support – on the need for in-depth archival research. And there is no doubt about the breadth of his reading. In a college lecture series, self-published in 1964, he insisted (in sentiments quite at odds with the approach of his own later book on Africa's past) that:

> African history needs no special pleading, no 'inventions', no romantic idealization, no wishful thinking. What is required is the same as the requirement of any and all history, the truth as fully as it can be reasonably determined. (Williams 1964: 6)

Williams's first major book, *The Rebirth of African Civilization* (1961), mainly a study of social mores and educational change in Ghana during its transition to independence, was based on substantial fieldwork and was a serious, if neglected, contribution to the 1960s debate on Africa's future, despite its idiosyncratic forays into comparative ethics and moral exhortation. On the other hand, the more influential *Destruction* is, in many of its aspects, as thoroughly fantastic a piece of historical mythmaking as any of Afrocentrism's more obviously slapdash productions.[4] Above all, Williams presents a view of history more relentlessly racialized than almost anything else in the genre. Racial identity is, for Williams, literally 'the reason for being' (1971/1987: 250). He gives us a picture of Africa as the site of unbroken racial war stretching across fifty centuries: indeed, more, for 'It seems quite clear that this see-saw conflict . . . covered centuries back into prehistory' (Ibid.: 64). It was not, as we might expect, primarily a war between Africans and Europeans, though; Williams's great conflict is between black Africans and Arabs. The 'Asian imperialists' have been trying to take over the continent right from the start of the Egyptian Empire – Williams invents an entirely fanciful story of bitter, centuries-long conflict over Pharaonic Egypt, with black Nubians and Ethiopians resisting the white Arab–Asian takeover and infiltration of their land, which had once formed a single black empire from the Mediterranean to Zimbabwe. He attributes to the 'Arabs' who gradually took over Egypt an insensate hatred of blacks; while the black Africans' 'badge of eternal honor was the blackness of their skin. . . . They were "Children of the Sun" blessed with blackness by the Sun God himself. . . . Their very blackness, therefore, was religious, a blessing and an honor' (122–3).

Arab tactics included infiltration, planned interbreeding in order to create a 'mulatto' (Williams's usual term) fifth column within Africa, religious brainwashing, massive destruction of black artworks, monuments and writings, and of course outright invasion and enslavement. The modern conflict in the Sudan between Muslim, Arabizing north and 'black' south – which evidently had a major impact on Williams's view of the world – is just the continuation of the same long war. The wrecking of black civilization was the work of the Arab imperialists far more – and for far longer – than of European ones.[5] It reduced what had once been a single federal, democratic, highly literate African state imbued with near-supernatural wisdom and goodness – governed by a single 'African Constitution' (161–75) – to a condition of fragmented, hopeless savagery.[6] Williams's picture of the flight of the Nile valley Africans, fleeing Arab devastation, is a masterpiece of pathos:

> Once the paths they made in flight could be followed for days by their bloody footprints in the sand. . . . Later travellers and slave-hunters could determine the various routes of flight by the skeletons found here and there, fallen statues left by those who could not make it on. They were generally disjointed and scattered; sometimes it was a bony arm protruding from the windswept sands, a leg over there or a skull seeming to smile 'peace at last!'. The bones of other thousands who died in flight were never seen. They lay buried forever under the tons of sand and rocks. (191)

The only problem with this mournful tale is that, like almost everything that had gone before in Williams's story, it is sheer fantasy. Travellers' tales from the 1820s and earlier do indeed report sightings of numerous human skeletons along Saharan trade routes, and perhaps it is these that inspired Williams's flight of macabre fancy. The skeletons, however, were undoubtedly recent: relics of the trans-Saharan slave trade.

Just as remarkable is the book's utterly damning view of modern Africa. Basically, Williams accepts all the most absurd and derogatory European myths about colonial-era Africa – ubiquitous savagery, incompetence, illiteracy, superstition, cannibalism, and the rest – and modifies the picture only by claiming that this awful situation was the result of the depredations of outsiders: of the Europeans but, far more, of the Arabs. Their unending war against the blacks reduced the latter to 'the lowest levels of dog-eat-dog existence' (49), and to 'hell on earth' (299). For Williams, as for many other Afrocentrists, glorifying Africa's past appeared to require disparaging its present inhabitants.

Together with Karenga, Clarke, Williams and George James, the most frequently cited Afrocentric figure from the older generation is probably John G. Jackson (1907–93), who published several pamphlets on religious and historical themes in the 1930s, and collaborated with Harlem schoolmaster Willis N. Huggins on *An Introduction to African Civilizations, with Main Currents in Ethiopian History* (Huggins and Jackson 1937). Jackson had apparently been Huggins's school pupil (and was later, in old age, to lecture on various college Black Studies courses), but the book itself described him only as a 'member of the Rationalist Press Association, London, England'. Although it partook of many of the usual romantic and ill-evidenced claims about the racial character of the Egyptians, their debts to Ethiopia and Greece's to them, Huggins's and Jackson's work was on other levels an impressive production for its day. Its lengthy bibliographies, survey of the state of educational provision on African themes in the 1930s USA, and suggestions for the teaching not only of African history but that of the entire diaspora including South America and Europe, constituted a genuinely groundbreaking exercise (Huggins and Jackson 1937: 140–203). It may well be that no one else at that time, anywhere in the world, had compiled so wide-ranging a checklist of resources on African history.

The book's political purposes were evident: both the by then time-honoured general one of vindicating past African greatness, and a more specific aim of arousing admiration for Ethiopia's past. A large part of the text was devoted specifically to Ethiopia, then struggling unsuccessfully to maintain its independence against Mussolini's aggression. The struggle aroused widespread interest and sympathy among black Americans, to which the book was evidently intended to contribute – Huggins himself was apparently active in the 'International Council of Friends of Ethiopia' (see J. Harris 1994).

Jackson's own much later *magnum opus*, carrying the same main title as his and Huggins's predecessor, *Introduction to African Civilizations*, and to a limited degree based on it, appeared in 1970. Jackson's work, like that of Chancellor Williams or J.A. Rogers, is an uneasy mixture of assiduous independent scholarship and wild fantasy; though with far less of the latter than there is in Williams's writing or that of several younger Afrocentrists. Jackson certainly exhibited some of the now familiar faults of this kind of history-writing: an indiscriminate use of sources, including reliance on mystical and global-diffusionist speculation by the likes of Albert Church-ward and Gerald Massey; romantic inflation of the glories of past African kingdoms; a dogmatic and undocumented belief that Egyptian civilization must have come down the Nile from Nubia and Ethiopia; and a general tendency to fill the gaps in his knowledge with brightly coloured reveries. He also occasionally spills over into genuinely bizarre statements, like saying that the Lighthouse of Pharos 'was erected at a cost of about $680,000; and in those days dollars were worth much more than they are at the present time' (1970/1994: 118). But other parts of Jackson's work, especially those which deal with the more recent past, are merely romanticized rather than wholly fantastic. His yet more ambitious *Man, God and Civilization* (1972) similarly mixed lucid and vigorous attacks on targets ranging from organized religion to Eurocentric historiography, with a reliance on sources that were at best dated, at worst (as with Churchward, Godfrey Higgins and Jackson's great hero Gerald Massey) downright eccentric. Still, despite Jackson's wilder flight of fancy, in him one again sees an example of an earlier, obscure, self-taught Afrocentrist producing work superior to that of most of the younger, far more highly educated and publicized exponents.

Considerably more bizarre than Clarke, Jackson or Williams are figures such as Leonard Jeffries, Frances Cress Welsing and Yosef Ben-Jochannen. The best-known advocate of modern Afrocentric approaches is probably Jeffries, of New York's City College. Yet since he has published very little – as opposed to giving many media interviews – it is hard to summarize his views responsibly, or to ascertain how far they may have been misrepresented by sensationalist coverage.[7] Certainly his reported belief that whites are biologically inferior because of their relative lack of melanin and their genes malformed by the Ice Age, as against the innate superiority of black 'Sun People', is not intellectually serious or responsible. Nor is his supposed insistence on the particular guilt of the Jews for the slave trade (see D'Souza 1991: 7; Leslie 1992; Person-Lynn 1996: 215–45).

Leonard Jeffries is clearly both an intellectual authoritarian and a demagogue. In a speech in 1991, he allegedly claimed that the Jews bore the main responsibility for the Atlantic slave trade, while latterly they, through their control of the film industry and in unholy alliance with the Italians (!), were masterminding the oppression and even destruction of Afro-Americans. City College, in reaction, sacked him as chairman of the Black Studies Department. He took them to court, was reinstated and won $400,000 in damages, but this judgement was reversed on appeal by New York's Supreme Court.[8]

Frances Cress Welsing is probably best known as the most prominent advocate of the view that AIDS is the product of a genocidal white conspiracy to exterminate people of colour. This planned genocide in its turn is supposedly motivated by whites' consciousness of their own genetic inferiority, which leads them to fear 'genetic annihilation' by non-whites (Welsing, in Addai-Sebo and Wong 1988: 293). 'I say that skin whiteness is a genetic mutation. Black people can produce white people. White people can only produce white people. Whites are mutants of black people' (Person-Lynn 1996: 72). White persecution and massacre of blacks is thus an inescapable, biologically determined survival strategy. Hitler's attempted destruction of the Jews was an earlier phase in this same process – Jews being:

> the products of the genetic mixture produced when white Greek and Roman soldiers invaded Africa and raped African women, who of course were black, Semite is the same as the word mulatto. Thus they were considered to be half black and half white or genetically coloured people. Thus, a yellow coloured star was placed on their outer clothing by the German government in the Hitler era. (Addai-Sebo and Wong: 294)[9]

It is difficult to convey a full impression of Cress Welsing's texts without being able to reproduce her diagrams, which 'show', for instance, how the Christian cross is a symbol of the black male genitalia, as are the Nazi swastika – and the Christmas tree, the gun, the Washington and Jefferson Memorials in DC, the 1941 New York World's Fair logo, footballs, baseballs, cigars, chocolate bars, the bull in Spanish bullfighting . . . (Cress Welsing 1991: xiv–xv, 47, 62–3, 67, 75–6, 108–9, 112–13, 131–43). Her thoughts on Christmas may, however, gave a faint flavour of the whole book's character:

> The Christmas tree is, in its abstracted form, a cross – the symbol of the Black male genitals. (See Diagram V.) First, the Christmas tree is *chopped down* in the *forest*. Then it is taken home. In the US, when the Christmas tree is

decorated, *colored* 'balls' are hung on the tree. When the tree is taken down and burned, the 'balls' are first *taken off.* Then we can all dream of a 'white Christmas' and a surviving white Christ. (ibid.: 75; original emphasis)

According to Cress Welsing, whites do not fear, hate and feel obsessed by black male members because they are supposedly bigger than white ones (though Cress Welsing believes that too [ibid.: 96–7]). Rather, their obsession is:

because of Blacks' ability to produce the highest levels of melanin and thereby the greatest potential for white genetic annihilation. This basic logic of disgust with the white genetic and genital self drives the brain-computer in the white-male collective to self-negating patterns of behaviour . . .

[W]hite male homosexuality may be viewed as the symbolic attempt to incorporate into the white male body more *male substance* by either sucking the penis of another male and orally ingesting the semen, or by having male ejaculate deposited in the other end of the alimentary canal. Through anal intercourse, the self-debasing white male may fantasize that he can produce a product of color, albeit that the product of color is fecal matter. This fantasy is significant for white males because the males who can produce skin color are viewed as the real men. (47; original emphasis)

That dreadful passage, with its multiple levels of bigotry, is not an isolated aberration. There are many paralleling it in Cress Welsing's work,[10] even if there are more which read like ideas salvaged from Lenny Henry's or Richard Pryor's wastebins. (Whites think that a dog is their best friend, whereas other peoples know that God is theirs [27]; white males at weddings wear 'black tails', symbolizing yet again their penis envy [148]). . . . Enough. But Cress Welsing's idiotic and contemptible book had reportedly sold 40,000 copies within a few months of publication, almost entirely through black-owned outlets (Dyson 1993: 159).

Much the same mixture of incredulity and distaste is induced by some of the ideas of an otherwise far more reputable figure, Yosef Ben-Jochannen (born 1917), who appears to espouse what one might charitably call a more activist conception of the idea of race war than that found in Cress Welsing's work. Addressing a London conference in 1986, Ben-Jochannen several times hinted heavily at his desire for the audience to kill whites, though 'I'm not here to tell you when or where, or how, in public' (Addai-Sebo and Wong 1988: 119). Praising Henry Christophe's massacre of whites in revolutionary Haiti (though Ben-Jochannen has it wrong: Christophe committed no such massacre, and he probably means Dessalines, who did), he burst out: 'Christophe did the right thing. He should have killed off the whole of Santo Domingo' (ibid.: 58). Pontificating about the undesirability of interracial marriage, he asked: 'Can I lay [*sic*] in bed tonight with a white woman, then plan her father's murder and tell her: "I'm going to kill you [*sic*] father tomorrow"?' (ibid.: 48). He went on: 'we are at war, thus I am in a death struggle ... this is a war; and a war is fought on every level' (ibid.: 50–51). Elsewhere, in interview, he urged that the answer to alleged unjust police killings of African-Americans was to 'just kill the policeman, or his family, or somebody in his family in revenge' (Person-Lynn 1996: 61).

Ben-Jochannen has taught, on a part-time or visiting basis, in a wide variety of academic institutions over the years (he more than once boasted, doubtless exaggerating, of having been fired from forty-seven different schools! [Addai-Sebo and Wong 1988: 124; Person-Lynn 1966: 52]), but he is proud of a primary affiliation to the self-taught intellectualism of the street corner and the Garveyite nationalist tradition. Overwhelmingly the most important political influence on his career, he has acknowledged at length, is the Garveyite legacy (1982: 15–23; Person-Lynn 1966: 61). He was apparently for a long time an activist in – and, after 1963, President of – a small Harlem-based nationalist organization called 'African Nationals in America' (1971: 589). At the beginning of one book, he pays 'tribute to the unclaimed heroes who stood on the *Harlem street corners* on their ladder day and night ... preaching *the Black man's heritage* to countless African-Americans who once passed them by as if they had leprosy' (1971: 2).[11] Offering a long list of these activists, he places himself firmly among their number. Elsewhere he reflected on his work:

> I write it for the little man in the street, so to speak ... I write for the masses of the people – which would be around the 7th or 8th grade levels. Whenever I don't use words within that scope, it is because I find no way in which I can explain myself at that level ... I don't care if they never called me a scholar. (1982: 13)

Rejecting any notion of academic objectivity as a deceit, he avows that his central aim is to arouse the emotions of his readers: 'I want you to get mad, I want you to get sad and I want you to get happy when I write' (ibid.: 14–15).

Alongside this populism, however, lies an intense scholasticism typical of the autodidact black vindicationism we have been tracing. Ben-Jochannen's works may be intended for 'the little man in the street', but they are also heavy with bibliographies and references to often obscure texts, allusions to hidden knowledge, long quotations from a wide range of sources. His list of publications, extending over nearly fifty years, is very long: though there is a huge amount of repetition both within and between his main works. There is an obsessional quality about his writing – largely self-published, at least until the Baltimore-based Black Classic Press began reissuing some of it in the late 1980s. He sees himself engaged in a lonely battle for the truth, against powerful and even sinister forces:

> I have purposefully traversed the once most holy grounds of the tabooed, and removed the cover of secrecy surrounding the myth of a '*Semitic, Hamitic*' or '*Caucasian*' east or north Africa; thereby, showing that behind these terms

are the *seeds of racism and religious bigotry*, all of which had their origin as far back as *the Book of Genesis* in the Hebrew (Jewish) *Torah* or Christian *Old Testament* of the Holy Bible (any version). For this I am willing to pay the price that befalls anyone who dares to tread into the *Holy* of *Holies* of Judaeo-Christian Greek-Centric Anglo-Saxon Indo-European Aryan mythological racism and religious bigotry. (1971: xii–iii)

Despite the evident, intense – albeit indiscriminate – study Ben-Jochannen devoted over many years to Egyptology and related fields, his command of African history is as bizarre as every other aspect of his thought. He places the founding of the Monomotapa kingdom in Zimbabwe at 100 CE, and the beginning of the Zulu kingdom at 300: dates respectively at least 1,000 and 1,450 years too early (1972: 17). Elsewhere, yet more haywire, he dates Monomotapa to 'about 1200 to 1700 BCE' (ibid.: 79). He has urged that the Yoruba and the Hutu peoples (the latter of whom he quite wrongly identifies with 'pygmies') derive from ancient Egypt (Person-Lynn 1966: 54–6). He is even capable of telling a black London audience that to discover their Egyptian heritage they should visit: 'Not only the *Museum of Natural History*, but you need to look at the *Egyptian Museum*, located a few blocks from one another' (Addai-Sebo and Wong 1988: 114). This is rather like a man selling coals to Newcastle who doesn't have any coal to sell, tries to tell the buyers his coal is green, and thinks Newcastle is just next door to Brighton.[12]

Ben-Jochannen has thus been a prolific – if extremely repetitive – author, pursuing ideas about the Egyptian, and therefore black origins of civilization, and of a concerted white conspiracy to conceal these, which represent the most elaborated version of the long Afro-American autodidact tradition of Egyptophilia. Ben-Jochannen pays tribute to some significant precursors in that tradition, especially G.G.M. James and John G. Jackson. Otherwise, there are repeated references to the genre's most popular sources on ancient history: Herodotus and Volney, of course, plus a wide range of Egyptologists (mostly very old and largely superseded works like those of J.H. Breasted, E.A. Budge, Gaston Maspero, and Flinders Petrie) and eccentrics like Albert Churchward and Gerald Massey. Ben-Jochannen's preoccupations also offer many parallels to the theories of Cheikh Anta Diop, though clearly Ben-Jochannen developed his ideas without knowledge of Diop's – his best-known works, *Africa: Mother of 'Western Civilization'* (1971) and *Black Man of the Nile and His Family* (1972), which draw on a remarkable and promiscuous range of sources including many mystical and Masonic texts, make no mention of Diop.

Black Man of the Nile is an extraordinarily rambling, seemingly structureless book, full of asides on everything from the blackness of Jesus and the falsity of white Jews' identification with the Hebrews of the Bible to the Egyptian origins of Freemasonry. The earlier book, equally strangely organized, is clearly intended to serve in part as a student text, with essay assignments, passages in question-and-answer form, and interspersed 'Lecture-Essays'.

Major themes of both (and of Ben-Jochannen's other books, which largely repeat the same material) include all the expected *idées fixes*: the blackness of Egypt; the Ethiopian origins of Egyptian culture and the Egyptian roots of Greece, of monotheistic religion, of all art and science; the cultural unity of Africa; the wrongness – indeed, wickedness – of the label 'Negro' (a particular fetish of Ben-Jochannen's, this) et cetera. Summary is near-impossible, and in any case Ben-Jochannen advances no arguments not to be found, more coherently expressed, in the work of Diop and others.

Ben-Jochannen claims to be of Ethiopian Jewish origin. This is apparently false, an impersonation in the grand old tradition of all the pretending Ashanti princes, Yoruba priests, and so on, who have for decades intermit-tently grabbed the attention and sought to lighten the purses of particularly gullible Afro-Americans. In the case of 'Dr. Ben', seemingly in reality of Puerto Rican origin,[13] the identification serves mainly as a stick with which to beat American Jews, and a cover for his oddball but vehement brand of anti-Semitism. He returns time and again to the argument – one with a much older Afro-American history, as we have seen – that the 'white Jews' of the Western world are imposters on a historic scale, falsely claiming a heritage which rightfully belongs to black Africans, and propounding a racist creed dating to the very origins of Judaism (among many such discussions, see Ben-Jochannen 1983: *passim*; 1971: 584–627; 1972: 67–70; Addai-Sebo and Wong 1988: 52, 66). He can assert – ridiculously – that Mussolini exterminated 4.5 million Falashas in his 1930s invasion of Ethiopia (Addai-Sebo and Wong 118). He can 'explain' the Balfour Declaration (the British Government's First World War promise of support for a Jewish national homeland) like this: 'they arranged to double-cross the Arabs with a secret agreement ... signed by Heime Wiseman, an English Jew living in England, Jonah B. Wise, and Stephen Wise and others' (ibid.: 52). It is almost superfluous to point out that the only genuine historical personage among Dr Ben's three wise men is American rabbi Stephen Wise, who had nothing whatever to do with the Balfour Declaration. Ben-Jochannen's speeches and writings are spattered, moreover, with dismissive references to the 'so-called Holocaust', with allegations about the Jews being primarily responsible for the Atlantic slave trade, and so on (e.g. Addai-Sebo and Wong 34, 46–8, 117–18).[14]

This poisonous nonsense would not be worth tarrying over, if echoes of the same views – as well as the same ludicrous vision of history – were not to be heard in more reputable Afrocentric academic circles. It also connects with a wider argument, identifying the original biblical Hebrews as a black nation. This idea has been popular among the various communities of US black Jews (whose beliefs and rituals have tended to be just as widely removed from those of Judaism itself as the Nation of Islam's are from the mainstream of world Islam), and such eccentric groups as the Washington, DC 'Church of God and Saints in Christ', 'Prophet' Cherry's movement in Philadelphia, the 'Original Hebrew Israelite Nation', and the Command-ment Keepers of Harlem, all of which identified themselves as lost tribes of

Israel (Brotz 1970; Moses 1993: ch. 11). Latter-day equivalents have included the Ansaru Allah Community of Brooklyn, formerly the Nubian Islamic Hebrew Mission – as Wilson J. Moses says, a 'singularly eclectic sect' who mix Judaic, Christian and Islamic beliefs (1993: 191; see also Gardell 1996: 225–31) – and the Reverend Albert Cleage's Detroit Shrine of the Black Madonna (Moses 1993: 220–21).

A more coherent, better documented, though little more persuasive version of these arguments than Ben-Jochannen's has recently been presented by another US Afrocentric writer, Jose Malcioln (1996); while California clergyman William LaRue Dillard has argued at length that a vast range of the peoples and characters referred to in the Christian Bible are identifiably black or African (1990). A related idea – which Ben-Jochannen among others, propagates – is that Judaism, and later Christianity and Islam, derived entirely from Egyptian sources. This is argued not only on the basis of the tenuous similarities between some biblical texts and certain Egyptian ones, and the speculation – made famous by Sigmund Freud – that Moses was an Egyptian priest, but on account of allegedly similar religious practices such as circumcision and a taboo on eating pork (the last is an error which goes as far back as Herodotus: in fact there is abundant evidence of pig-keeping in ancient Egypt). Associated beliefs include the insistence, which has been recurrent for well over 150 years, that Jesus was black (see Albert Cleage's *Black Messiah*, 1968[15]) – Marcus Garvey, among many others, identified himself with this claim – and that the Christian image of the Madonna is a mere copy of Egyptian depictions of Isis as mother-goddess.[16]

The Ansars apparently have their own version of the widespread idea that blacks are the original human beings, and whites an accursed, degenerate offshoot. The original whites were lepers, shunned by their black relatives, who retreated in ancient times from Africa to the Caucasus. There 'they (mainly the women) had sexual intercourse with the jackal (the original dog) and, through this intercourse, the offspring that was brought forth was an ape-like man' (Ansar pamphlet quoted in Moses 1993: 192). This has echoes of the earlier theories of mutant or degenerate white origins proposed by the Nation of Islam; while rap group Public Enemy have regularly popularized their own version of it (see Tate 1992: 125); and such Afrocentric pseudo-scholars as Frances Cress Welsing also endorse the idea (Person-Lynn 1996: 85–7). The legend also has some surprising parallels yet further afield: apparently some Chinese believed that the Japanese were descended from the union of monkeys and degenerate Chinese criminals (Dower 1986: 85).

There is less distance than one might think between bizarre beliefs of this kind and much present-day academic Afrocentrism. Indeed, although most of the leading theorists of Afrocentrism hold academic posts, the real aim some seem to pursue is to present not a new scholarly approach, nor even – as critics like Schlesinger and Hughes suggest – a form of compensatory therapy for the disadvantaged, but something more akin to a new religion.

This will become more apparent as we look in some detail at the writings of the most prominent such theorist, Molefi Kete Asante.

Notes

1. On the widespread adoption, commercialization and 'mainstreaming' of Kwanzaa, see Karenga (1988); McClester (1993); plus Wilde (1995).

2. See especially Carruthers (1995), probably the most detailed examination of ancient Egyptian thought yet produced by a US Afrocentrist; though it is by no means clear how far Carruthers's writings on ancient Egypt are based on primary research or knowledge of relevant ancient languages. He writes overwhelmingly in the shadow of Cheikh Anta Diop, whose ideas pervade his work, together with subsidiary influences from less careful authorities like James's *Stolen Legacy* and Ben-Jochannen's works. Carruthers's major purpose is to establish the relevance of ancient Egyptian philosophy for modern Afro-Americans. Like Diop, he wants to see Ancient Egyptian replace Greek and Latin as the 'classical' languages of the education system (Carruthers 1984: 40). He remains wedded to the Diopian view of 'Western' knowledge as inherently alienating and inhumane, as against the spiritual and holistic inclinations of 'African Deep Thought' (Carruthers 1995); and he feels that the 'Wisdom of Governance in Kemet' provides a model for modern statecraft (Carruthers 1986).

3. Brief biographical details and a hagiographic intellectual sketch of Williams's work are given in Rashidi (1994).

4. John Henrik Clarke suggests that the book's unevenness may be attributable to the aged author's poor health while he was completing it (Person-Lynn 1996: 11).

5. It may be noted that these wild claims, unlike so much else in the literature, are *not* prefigured by Diop – whose work Williams does not seem to have known. On the contrary, Diop had insisted that ideas of Arab invasion into Sub-Saharan Africa were 'figments of the imagination' (1987: 102).

6. These emphases are already evident in the earlier, generally far more level-headed, *Problems in African History* (Williams 1964), albeit more moderately expressed. The anti-Islamic prejudices are already aired there, including a peculiar claim that Muslim regions of Africa had less educational provision than any other part (1964: 6), the romantic view of ancient African 'democracy' (54–6) and the overarching schema of belief in cata-strophic continental decline after the fall of medieval African empires.

7. Jeffries has claimed to be at work on a major history of the slave trade, and a ten-volume (!) study of the Jewish role in the enslavement of Africans: Person-Lynn (1966: 229, 243).

8. Jeffries's own version of these events is given in an extended interview with Kwaku Person-Lynn (1996: 229–45).

9. The notion of Jews as products of black–white admixture is far from new, and can be found, for instance, in Diop's writings: see Diop (1991: 65).

10. Indeed, Cress Welsing has repeated these claims almost verbatim in interview, adding the predictable assertion that homosexuality is a natural outgrowth of the white psyche but alien to that of Africans: Person-Lynn (1996: 83–5).

11. Emphases here and in subsequent Ben-Jochannen quotations are original: frequent use of underlinings and block capitals is an integral feature of his distinctive style.

12. To explain, for any reader who does not know London: the Natural History Museum is devoted to dinosaur bones and stuffed animals, containing no Egyptian relics at all; there is no such place as the 'Egyptian Museum'; and the British Museum, which does contain the major Egyptian collections, is several miles from the Natural History Museum.

13. He has spoken in interview of growing up there and of having been active in the New York-based movement for Puerto Rican independence (Ben-Jochannen 1982: 16–17; Addai-Sebo and Wong 1988: 119); while his first recorded publication was a pamphlet in Spanish. If he were indeed born in Gondar, Ethiopia, as he has claimed, it is hard to see

where he might have acquired the middle names Alfredo Antonio. As St Clair Drake rather charitably puts it: 'Ben-Jochannen's books challenge the reader to exercise alert vigilance to distinguish between fact, statements with a high degree of probability, and assertions based merely on a will to believe' (1987: 326).

14. Ben-Jochannen has on occasion, however, written in more conventional vein. A junior high-school textbook on Africa he co-wrote in 1971 (Ben-Jochannen, Brooks and Webb) is a basic, competent, unexceptionable survey of the continent, with almost no trace of Dr Ben's usual biases or obsessions.

15. Although such historical claims are made only sketchily in Cleage's book, whose main purpose is to put forward a kind of Afro-American liberation theology based more on the psychological and political utility of conceiving of Jesus as black than on the historical truth of such assertions. Jesus was, for Cleage, 'the non-white leader of a non-white people struggling for national liberation against the rule of a white nation, Rome' (1968: 3). He was 'trying to rebuild the Black Nation Israel' (ibid.: 72), the original Jews being 'a Black Nation intermingled with all the black peoples of Africa' (243), who also included the Egyptians, the Canaanites, and the Chaldaeans, from whom Abraham came (39–40). Like Ben-Jochannen and others, Cleage argues that white Jews are descendants of much later converts. In any case, it is now African-Americans who are the Chosen People of God (53–4, 59).

16. Ben-Jochannen's *African Origin of the Major Western Religions* (1974) makes these arguments at great and disorganized length. His *Afrikan Origins of the Major World Religions* (with Oduyoye and Finch, 1988) is a more concise version. In this volume Modupe Oduyoye puts forward a more cautious and rational argument, suggesting parallels between Judaeo-Christian and African religious names, but *not* asserting that the former necessarily copied the latter. Oduyoye's and Ben-Jochannen's editor, the British Afrocentrist Amon Saba Saakana, makes his displeasure at Oduyoye's relative good sense plain (ibid.: Preface: pages unnumbered).

17

Molefi Asante:
Godfather of Afrocentrism

Molefi Kete Asante was born in small-town Georgia in 1942, and originally christened Arthur Lee Smith. He claims that his family had strong traceable Asante and Mandinka ancestry, though he also notes a Muskogee Indian great-grandmother (Asante 1993a: 127). He adopted his present name, he informs us, after a visit to Ghana in 1972, when the University of Ghana librarian expressed surprise that someone called Arthur Smith was not an Englishman: 'He could not understand how a person with an African phenotype could have an English name or so it seemed to me ... I vowed then and there that I would change my name' (ibid.: 141). The story sounds odd: a university librarian, in a country whose notable historical and political figures include people with surnames like Brown, Jones, Moore, Williams, Taylor, Timothy, Welbeck, Woode, Dadson, Mercer, Hutton-Mills and a whole dynasty of Casely Hayfords – all of them with unquestionably 'African phenotypes' – unable to understand that a 'Smith' could be black? I take leave not to believe in his disbelief, or in Asante's story.[1]

Be that as it may, it is clear that Asante's upbringing in intensely segregated, racial-violence-haunted Georgia and Tennessee, well before the Civil Rights movement made any serious inroads there, must have shaped his subsequent thought. He insists time and again in a recent autobiographical essay on the absolute divisions of that early environment: 'I knew from a very early age that the world of America was black and white ... two colors, two origins, two destinies' (ibid.: 129). The utter Manichaeism of his later thought comes straight from this mould. He even appears to be grateful for it: 'It might have been another matter if I had gone to school and to church with whites when I was younger. I might have suffered confusion, double-consciousness, but I did not' (ibid.: 137). The only surprise, perhaps, is how far Asante, with his constant invocations of 'centeredness', his avowal that 'One becomes Afrocentric by exploring connections, visiting the quiet places, and remaining connected' (ibid.: 142), has incorporated New Age catchphrases into his language despite being brought up poor in Georgia rather than affluent in California. No doubt his period as a graduate student and lecturer in southern California accounts for this.

Asante is the most influential, widely quoted Afrocentric writer today. He heads the African-American Studies Department at Temple University, Philadelphia, has been a hyperactive consultant on the establishment of Afrocentric school curricula throughout the USA, and is the long-serving editor of the Afrocentric movement's house magazine, the *Journal of Black Studies*. (In the later 1990s he has been joined by a co-editor, Terry Kershaw, also of Temple University.) Unlike Jeffries and most other academics working this vein, he has published prolifically. Scrutiny of his long list of publications soon reveals, however, that they include a considerable amount of repetitive matter. We can therefore reasonably confine ourselves, primarily, to his two most major recent texts: *Afrocentricity*, his widely cited, impassioned statement of position which has gone through three editions (Asante 1988); and *Kemet, Afrocentricity, and Knowledge* which, by contrast, is the most extended attempt to give the movement academic credentials (Asante 1990). We shall also look at the *Journal of Black Studies* which Asante edits, at various Temple University colleagues and disciples of Asante, and at the most extended, heavily documented attempt to formulate an Afrocentric philosophical critique of Eurocentrism, Marimba Ani's *Yurugu* (1994). The far more intellectually substantial output of Cheikh Anta Diop – which provides almost all of what little underpinning the movement has in historical scholarship – has already been discussed (see Chapter 14 above). Diop – an erudite, if clearly sometimes wrong-headed, thinker – does not belong in this company, despite Asante's *chutzpah* in alluding matily to 'Cheikh, as some of us often called him', seeking to pretend an intimate friendship with the Senegalese (1988: ix). We shall also investigate more briefly some other currently active Afrocentric writers, though on the whole they appear to advance few – if any – substantial themes or theses not found in Diop's, Bernal's, Asante's, Ben-Jochannen's or Karenga's writings.

The organizing principle of Molefi Asante's work is, of course, an organicist conception of nationhood, never clearly defined but intended to assert the natural, psychic and spiritual unity of all people of African descent around a set of principles supposedly derived from ancient Egypt. From this core arises a set of propositions which (imposing order on Asante's often chaotic writings rather than discerning order in them) may be summarized as follows:

1. Humanity first developed in Africa, so that Africans have some kind of cosmological as well as chronological priority over other human groups.
2. The first civilization was that of ancient Egypt, or Kemet. This was specifically a black African civilization, whose founders came from the south, but whose intellectual, technological and other developments were autarkic.
3. These Egyptian civilizational developments formed the basis for all African culture and thought across the continent. This therefore forms a unity in all spheres, from shared spiritual values to common technologies.

4. Egyptian ideas and inventions also formed the basis for ancient Greek civilization, and thus of all European development.
5. Process (3) was a result of diffusion, but process (4) was one of theft. Subsequently Europeans have conspired to obscure (1) and (4), while brainwashing Africans into forgetfulness of (2) and (3).
6. The cultural and spiritual unity of Africans, derived from ancient Egyptian sources, extends also – and in undiluted form – to diasporic peoples of African descent. They must return to these deliberately obscured sources, value only that which tends to strengthen them, and eschew all ideas or practices which do not derive from them.
7. All of this makes African-Americans a nation – or, more properly, part of the unitary African nation – with its own civilization, values, belief system, social practices and even language ('Ebonics', defined as the 'language spoken in the United States by African-Americans which uses many English words but is based on African syntactic elements and sense modalities' [Asante 1988: 121][2]). These are superior to those of other groups, and especially to those of European-descended peoples.

Very few, if any, of these claims are original to Asante: as we have seen, almost all of them can be found (more coherently argued for) in Diop's work, and many repeat motifs from successive generations of Afro-American publicists since at least the 1840s. The reasons why little of it can be taken seriously as history are very numerous. That (secondary) aspect of the case which relates to supposed Egyptian origins for Greek thought is discussed elsewhere, in the more challenging context of Diop's and Bernal's ideas. As for the notion – more important for Asante's argument – that all African cultures are based predominantly on Egyptian sources, this rests on three fallacies, which we have also previously noted but may be rapidly summarized. The first is 'unanimism': the belief that Africa is or was culturally homogeneous in the sense that all Africans share a common world-view. The second fallacy is diffusionism: the belief that if human phenomena of any kind are found to be similar in different places, they must necessarily have spread from one to the others. The third is primordialism: a claim that presently observable beliefs, practices or identities derive by long, unbroken continuity from an ancient past. All these are thought by most serious students of African history to be generally untrue: the 'invention of tradition' has been as ubiquitous in Africa as anywhere else. The mass of historical literature tracing the modern making and remaking of 'tribal' identities is an obvious case in point (see, for example, Lonsdale 1977; Spear and Waller 1993; Vail 1989).

If the unanimist, diffusionist and primordialist notions of African identity mythicize the history of the continent itself, this is still more true of African-descended groups in the Americas. There is a rich and complex literature on the question of African cultural 'survivals' in various New World societies, ranging from claims (also now pretty thoroughly discredited) of total deculturation under slavery to assertions of very important continuities.

Some of these debates are surveyed above. We can say, however, that *no* intellectually serious position can support the claims made by Asante and other Afrocentrists, for at least three reasons. First, their arguments here rest once more on unanimism, whereas any substantial case for New World African 'survivals' necessarily depends on demonstrating a relationship between particular Afro-American cultural traits and those of *particular* African peoples. Second, the Afrocentric programme depends on an assertion that *only* African-derived beliefs or practices are (or should be) of significance for people of African descent in the Americas. Again, no serious scholar believes this: all note the historical facts of European, in many places of Amerindian, and of specifically 'colonial' or 'creole' cultural influences, and above all of *hybridity*[3] and *syncretism*. These multiple roots shaped even slave-era African-American cultural forms, let alone the yet more complex and global influences on contemporary, largely urban black America. Third, it is generally agreed that the identifiably African component within these always compound cultures is on the whole smaller in the present United States than in most other parts of the Americas, notably Brazil and the larger Caribbean islands, for evident historical reasons, including greater heterogeneity of slaves' African origins, lower black–white ratios, and the usually small size of plantations. It may be added that neither Asante nor his followers show any sign of close acquaintance with that mass of previous literature on the subject.

In reality, however, Asante's and other Afrocentrists' insistence on the purity, homogeneity and primordiality of African cultural influences among Afro-Americans is not a historical or sociological hypothesis, but a normative assertion masquerading as a methodological imperative. To see different parts of Africa as having different cultural traits 'is to commit a major intellectual crime', says Asante (1990: 56). In parallel with (and in contradiction to) the attempts to establish historical proof for the Afrocentric world-view's claims is a dismissal of the whole notion of proof as Eurocentric, and the substitution for it of an ill-defined concept of 'soul as method' (ibid.: 104–12). Apparently, 'what this means is that history is relative, that ethnography is biography, that definitions are personal because the scholar is engaged with the acquisition of knowledge in a social way' (111).

Apart from the oxymoronic character of the last clause, the general irrationalism here has, of course, many analogues in more academically respectable quarters. In Asante's work and in that of numerous epigones, it is linked to a notion of quite distinctive, culture-bound ways of acquiring knowledge. African-Americans supposedly learn and know reality through emotion, symbolic imagery, and rhythm. For some proponents, this is elevated into the dignity of an 'affective epistemology' (Schiele 1990: 154). It is a view which harks back to some central – if always internally contested – claims of *négritude* and Haitian *noirisme*, though those earlier writers never committed the absurdity of seeking to erect a pseudo-scholarly methodology on its back. It is, equally evidently, a view consonant with many of the classic claims of Euro-American racism about the 'Negro personality'.

Asante's thought also involves a fierce cultural ethnocentrism, a contention that Afrocentrism 'studies every thought, action, behaviour, and value,
and if it cannot be found in our culture or in our history, it is dispensed
with quickly' (1988: 5). As a supposed research strategy, this naturally leads
to wholly circular, self-confirming results:

> Whether the researcher is exploring African American child-rearing prac-
> tices in North Philadelphia or African kinship patterns among the Galla in
> Ethiopia, reconfirmation and delinking are necessary steps in establishing
> the Afrocentric focus of the work ... the process itself asserts the discipline
> in the given project. (Asante 1990: 56)

Asante defines 'reconfirmation' as a process by which 'the scholar pursues
the organic, Diopian unity of African thought, symbols, and ritual concepts
to their classical (i.e. ancient Egyptian) origin'. Delinking, perhaps more
obviously, means dissociation from the 'European intellectual project'
(ibid.).

Molefi Asante repeats often, and at great length, the claim that 'Africalogy
is a discipline': not interdisciplinary inquiry into the Afro-American experience, but 'a separate and distinct field of study' (1990: 140–42). Such an
assertion is evidently useful when it comes to avoiding the standards of
rational inquiry and proof demanded in all established intellectual disciplines, not to mention its value to academic empire-building. But Asante's
thought does depend centrally on claims drawn from specific academic
disciplines – above all, on claims about history, although his writings never
engage with historical evidence as such. His various outline accounts of
African historical development, though they are evidently dependent on
Diopian assumptions, are both confused and mythologizing. In an early
version he first asserts that ancient Egypt owed certain specific culture traits
to the south, to what he loosely calls Nubia: 'The Nubians brought Egypt
the monarchy, a belief in divine kingship, and the worship of Horus and
other ancestors, thus greatly enriching the civilization' (Asante 1985a: 5).
Then, a few lines below, Nubia did not 'enrich' Egypt; rather, Egypt was
wholly a Nubian creation. Egyptian civilization 'sprang up in Nubia's belly
and migrated to Egypt' (ibid.: 5). As for Egypt's all-important influence on
the rest of Africa, this is seen as resulting from the Arab-Islamic invasions,
whose impact on Sub-Saharan Africa is vastly exaggerated and demonized.
The image of Arab incursions causing vast waves of disruption right across
the continent – presumably between the seventh and tenth centuries CE,
though Asante is notably vague about chronology – is pure fantasy: 'The
Arabs, with their *jihads*, or holy wars, were thorough in their destruction of
much of the ancient culture.' This 'total conquest' and 'historic persecution'
led to Egyptian priests spreading, often surreptitiously, right across the
continent, carrying their beliefs with them: 'It is as if small bands keeping
just ahead of the Islamic onslaught managed to preserve certain aspects of
the traditional culture of Egypt' among the Wolof, Yoruba, Asante, and so

on (1985a: 5–6). Asante's source for this peculiar view would seem to be Chancellor Williams's *Destruction of Black Civilization* (1971/1987), which sets out at great length a quite mythical 'history' of centuries-long Arab–black race war. Asante has been repeating the same claims about ancient history, both wild and derivative, for most of his career (see, for instance, Asante 1980b, which at least acknowledges its debts to Williams).

Asante is similarly cavalier about historical linguistics. Thus when he wanted to assert the continuing centrality of African languages to black American expression, he did not engage with any of the complex evidence on identifiable 'Africanisms' in Afro-American speech. Indeed, he showed little sign of having read any of the relevant literature. Actual evidence was an irrelevance to his case: 'I want to contend that Black Americans retained basic components of the African linguistic experience rather than specific artifacts' (1985b: 235–6). Appeal to the notion of 'linguistic experience', intangible, mysterious, independent of any specific linguistic feature, naturally leaves Asante's claims impossible to verify or refute.[4]

Afrocentricity culminates in a kind of catechism, a series of numbered statements forming 'Njia, the Way'. Utterly random in construction, 'The Way' comprises pseudo-historical claims, bits of mysticism, crackerbarrel philosophy ('Consider the racoon who washes before he eats; his example is a piece of gold' [1988: 113]), and advice on personal behaviour all mixed together in no apparent order. Njia makes no small claims for itself: 'The Way is neither poetry nor is it prose, yet it is both' (ibid.: 116). The model is clearly, more or less directly, Garveyite; though without the residue of rationality which Garvey's similarly structured 'African Philosophy' contained. And Asante's call to arms could have come directly from any 1920s Garveyite:

> Up from the intellectual and spiritual pit which has held our mighty people! Let each person take his position in the vanguard of this collective consciousness of Afrocentrism! Teach it! Practice it! And victory will surely come as we carry out the Afrocentric mission to humanise the Universe. (1988: 6)

Asante attempts, both in *Afrocentricity* and in *Kemet*, to provide a sort of ideological genealogy for his stance. This derives above all from Diop who, in *Kemet*, forms the starting point for a lengthy, meandering discussion of ancient Egypt's legacies (43–104). This once more includes a pseudo-religious element, claiming to come from recovery of the principles of the Egyptian goddess Ma'at (80–96). Martin Bernal and, ridiculously, Albert Churchward are also invoked as authorities on Egypt (96–104), as is Karenga (80–81, and in numerous endnotes). Naturally, there are villains as well as heroes, and they are drawn especially from the Arab and Islamic worlds: supposed traducers of Africa like the great medieval North African historian Ibn Khaldun (62, 136); Ali Mazrui, who is alleged to be 'Eurocentric' and a 'cynic' driven wholly by jealousy of Diop, 'a rival for African Islamic intellectual hegemony' (114); even Edward Said, who supposedly 'bought into the

invisibility of Africa and has claimed classical Africa as a part of the Orient'
(123). Prominent Afro-American scholars are rubbished, too – thus Houston
Baker and Henry Louis Gates are damned for attacking that 'brilliant critic
and theorist' Joyce A. Joyce, and 'employing the most vile forms of Eurocentric argumentation' against her (147). There is a quite incoherent critique
of Marxism (169–79), though it is suggested (entirely without evidence) that
Frantz Fanon and Walter Rodney, before their premature deaths, were in
the process of shaking off the Marxist contagion and being 'on the path to
an Afrocentric view of history' (175). Fanon, indeed, 'was clearly writing in
the tradition established by Garvey and Du Bois' (179).[5]

It is that tradition to which Asante claims allegiance, presenting elsewhere
an eclectic lineage of precursors: Booker T. Washington (1988: 7–10);
Marcus Garvey, founder of 'the most perfect, consistent, and brilliant
ideology of liberation in the first half of the twentieth century' (ibid.: 10);
Elijah Muhammed (14–15); Du Bois (15–18); Malcolm X (18–19); and the
culminating figure, the John the Baptist to Asante's Redeemer,[6] Karenga
(19–21). Asante's 'Njia' 'builds upon that foundation'. The stage was being
set for it 'for over 100 years. Each level of awareness predictably led to the
manifestation of Njia' (21). Njia, 'The Way that came to Molefi in America'
(109), quotes extensively from Karenga's 'Kawaida' doctrine.

Asante's notion of what constitutes a source is idiosyncratic to say the
least. Together with the list of politically inspirational figures presented in
Afrocentricity, one may consider the more academic inventory of influences
which Asante and his wife Kariamu put forward in a bibliographical essay
for their *Rhythms of Unity*. The only things it has in common with the other
are its extreme eclecticism, and the fact that every entry on it is male.
Students of the Afrocentric approach are directed towards some fairly
predictable – albeit often unreliable – authorities: Diop and Obenga; J.A.
Rogers; Chancellor Williams; John Henrik Clarke, and the like. But they are
also apprised of the merits of romantic (and indubitably European, not to
say Eurocentric) ethnophilosophers Placide Tempels and Marcel Griaule,
and of the fraudulent Zulu 'witchdoctor' and apartheid apologist Credo
Mutwa (Asante and Welsh Asante 1985: 254–9). Most bizarre is the praise
for Leo Frobenius: the Asantes call his work 'an intellectual triumph. . . .
What is lacking in Frobenius is made up in the works of Diop, Obenga, and
Ki-Zerbo' (ibid.: 255). Frobenius was indeed also a major influence on Diop
and the others. But that just makes the matter more remarkable, given the
entirely outdated and profoundly flawed nature of the German's work.

As Sidney Lemelle points out in a sharp, Marxist-inflected critique, while
Asante purports to reject all European influences his thought actually falls
squarely within a major European – and, says Lemelle, Eurocentric –
philosophical tradition: idealism. He is a latter-day analogue of Hegel or
Carlyle, draped in a borrowed *kente* cloth:

> Thus, at the base of Asante's Afrocentric conceptualization is the primacy of
> ideas over material reality. He claims that by using 'ideas' and 'words' to

critique a society and its ruling ideology, his words will ... alter, indeed create, another reality. (Lemelle 1994: 334)

Lemelle adds further charges: that Asante is an essentialist (undoubtedly true by any understanding of that term), a male chauvinist (ditto), and a utilitarian (ibid.: 334–6). By the last Lemelle seems to mean not a disciple of Jeremy Bentham, but someone who evaluates ideas only according to their usefulness for some specific project. In that sense, the charge sticks. Asante has been prone to such claims as this:

> To say that 'such and such a programme on television is a good programme' means that you have made an Afrocentric analysis.... If the brother makes that statement from an Afrocentric perspective, that is, if he asks if it is in the best interest of Afrocentricity? then it becomes a conscious statement. If not, then he misunderstands the contextual nature of good and evil. (Asante 1988: 86–7)

Comment is probably superfluous, except maybe to wonder what 'the sister' might make of 'the brother['s]' 'conscious statement'.

Asante's ambitions are considerable. Not only does he see himself as on a mission to remodel the whole of the intellectual and academic worlds, but he has entrepreneurial aspirations too. He has established his own publishing business, Asante Imprint Books, which has recently launched 'the first declared Afrocentric series of books for students in our schools' (Asante 1995a: iv). The claims made for the series are Asante's familiar ones. This is to be 'a profoundly Afrocentric endeavour', not to be confused with others' 'watered down version of multiculturalism in textbooks'. For the first time: 'teachers using *Asante Imprint Books* will have materials allowing them to center themselves and their students within the culture, history and experiences of African centeredness. *Asante Imprint Books* puts any reader of any age on-line with the centric idea' (ibid.: iv–v).

Encouragingly, though, the first volume in the intended series, Asante's own *Classical Africa* (1995a), does not partake of the wilder or more mystical elements in Asante's theorizing. Specialists might consider its picture of ancient and precolonial African history romanticizing, often speculative and highly elitist in its emphasis on mighty monarchs and empires; but unlike much of Asante's and his collaborators' work, it makes few historical claims which they would judge to be clearly false. Asante highlights 'six classical civilizations of ancient Africa': Kemet, Nubia, Axum, Mali, Ghana and Songhay. In relation to the first two, it is asserted that the first Nile valley civilization lay 'around the modern city of Khartoum' (1995a: 10) and that 'ancient Egyptians looked more like the present-day Nubians than the present-day Arabs' (ibid.: 23): both highly suppositional affirmations, the latter backed by a statement that 'Egyptians today look much like African Americans', and a photograph of Asante himself with two modern Egyptians, both darker than him. The reader is challenged: 'Can you tell which is Dr.

Asante?' (25). The standard Afrocentric dogma that Nubian civilization preceded and created that of Egypt, however, is merely implied, not stated as fact except by way of a quotation from John G. Jackson (53–70). Descriptions of the glories of Axum (71–92), Ghana (93–110), Mali (111–22) and Songhay (123–41) are all exaggerated, speculative and uncritical, but again they contain little obviously *false* information. The most evidently falsifiable assertions relate to medieval Timbuktu, wildly described as 'the greatest city in Africa and one of the greatest cities in the world in the 13th century CE' (111); and the sweeping judgement, following in the footsteps of Chancellor Williams's myth of decline, that after the fall of Songhay 'there was general instability throughout all of Africa' (123). In fact, as we have seen, there is little doubt that Timbuktu was outstripped in size and significance by numerous other African urban centres, let alone those on other continents; while there is no evidence that Songhay's collapse produced general instability even in its own region, or that it had any impact whatsoever in east, southern or north Africa.

And even in his most ecumenical and emollient moods – as in presenting Afrocentricity as nothing more than a programme of educational reform, one operating in the legacy of the reformer and scholar Carter Woodson rather than that of the separatist, nationalist tradition, and insisting that it 'does not condone ethnocentric valorization at the expense of degrading other groups' perspectives', and is nothing more than a 'stepping stone' towards true multiculturalism (1991/1997: 290–91) – Asante insists on associating that programme with questionable and even unsustainable claims. Even in that context, he urges that children must be taught such 'true and accurate information' as that 'the first philosophers were the Egyptians Kagemni, Khananup, Ptahhotep, Kete, and Seti'; that 'African civilizations predate all other civilizations'; and that 'Africans visited and inhabited North and South America long before European(s)' (ibid.: 293).

Notes

1. Among Asante's many publications is a *Book of African Names* (1991c), designed to offer inspiration to Afrocentric parents seeking appropriate appellations for their off-spring. The suggestions include numerous Arabic names – bizarrely, given Asante's Arabophobia; presumably he includes them under the delusion that they are Swahili. Ann duCille's comment on the whole exercise is apt:

> In many traditional West African societies ... naming is an essential postnatal ritual, a communal cultural event ... christening a child *in utero* – with the aid of a book of 'African names' – is something akin to a sacrilege. Much the same is true of the Afrocentric practice whereby black adults rename themselves ... for many Ghanaians the idea of an adult male born on a Monday inadvertently naming himself Kofi (Friday) rather than Kojo (Monday) is at once laughable and deeply lamentable. (duCille 1994: 28–9)

There is, intriguingly, a character named Asante-Smith (a hypocritical, intellectually corrupt TV executive) in one of the finest and best-known Ghanaian novels, Ayi Kwei Armah's *Fragments*, first published in 1970.

2. The term 'Ebonics' has subsequently gained quite wide currency, especially since the School Board of Oakland, California decided in late 1996 that it should be recognized as a distinct language – which, they unwisely suggested, was genetically transmitted among African-Americans – and thus generated enormous media controversy.

3. This in itself is a controversial term, since its usage can be held to imply (as in the genetic model from which it derives) that originally 'pure' and distinct essences have subsequently become mingled. I intend no such implication.

4. One of Asante's admirers and former students, Dhyana Ziegler, argues explicitly that Asante's work cannot be understood or fairly assessed unless the critics themselves first adopt an Afrocentric world-view (Ziegler 1995b: 64).

5. For a more extensive and thoughtful Afrocentric critique of Marxist and liberal historiography, warmly endorsed by Asante himself, see Jean (1991). Further polemical, highly coloured presentations of Afrocentric historical claims include A. Hilliard (1992) and, with specific reference to school-level education, Hilliard (ed.) (1989).

6. Carolyn Calloway-Thomas (1995) notes Asante's 'penchant for a religious vocabulary' (13), and that *The Afrocentric Idea* 'is an evangelical document' (12), but appears rather to approve of this than otherwise.

18

The Network, the School and the Fellow-Travellers

The twin flagships of Afrocentrism as defined and advocated by Asante are the African-American Studies Department at Temple University, Philadelphia, of which Asante is Chairperson, and the *Journal of Black Studies*, which Asante edits from Temple and whose contributors are very heavily drawn from the department's staff and graduate students. Reading the *Journal*, and especially the contributions from past and present Temple researchers, one gets an overwhelming and disturbing sense of intellectual homogeneity, conformism and, indeed, authoritarianism. Article after article cites the same restricted list of sources, writers closely associated with Asante and the Afrocentric movement, and often *only* they are cited. Article after article begins and ends with a recital of quotations and paraphrases from Asante's work, declarations that his beliefs and methodology will guide the author's thinking, assertions of the truth, comprehensiveness, liberatory potential and superiority to all other approaches of Asante's ideas. The pattern varies little, whatever the specific subject matter of the article. To describe the style as pious and the results as monolithic would be considerable understatements. Almost the only, partial, exceptions are the occasional special issues devoted to themes quite distant from Asante's main concerns and edited by people besides himself. One is entitled to wonder whether the *Journal* would ever consider publishing a contribution whose methodology or conclusions were to any significant degree at variance with Asante's, or which failed to make ritual obeisance to his authority.

Asante is quite unashamed of the intellectual homogeneity he imposes. As he explained to New York *Village Voice* journalist Greg Thomas:

> The only determination of who's Afrocentric or not is the definition of Afrocentricity – which I developed. It's kind of foolish to say, for example, that one is a Marxist and yet does not believe in the principles established by Marx. Or that one is a deconstructionist and doesn't believe in the principles of Derrida. How can one say they are an Afrocentrist if one does not accept the fundamental basis of Afrocentricity as laid out in my works? That seems to me to be a contradiction in terms. (Thomas 1995: 29)

He also described his approach as 'the growing and dominant school of thought in the African American studies field', and remarkably, as if he were President of some authoritarian state, condemned critics like Henry Louis Gates and Kwame Appiah as 'renegades' (ibid.). One might expect Asante to blow his own trumpet as hard as possible. What is more surprising is just how hard, and how monotonously, others puff for him too. Fairly typical examples include Jeffrey Lynn Woodyard's 'Evolution of a Discipline' (1991), which sketches seven stages of development in African-American studies. The earlier stages Woodyard identifies are uncontroversial and, indeed, rather conventional, progressing from individual literary achievements under slavery, through the founding of black colleges and the Harlem Renaissance, to the results of 1960s student militancy. The seventh and latest stage, though, is the 'presence of an exemplar' for African-American studies (ibid.: 241). This exemplar, of course, is one Molefi K. Asante, his 'paradigm' and his department:

> It will suffice to acknowledge that reaction to the Afrocentric paradigm ... suggests that it will function as the leading exemplar in the discipline. Disciplinary status is assured for African American Studies so long as the Temple School of Afrocentrists and others can demonstrate its consistency, durability, and praxis. (250)

Victor O. Okafor, in what purports to be an examination of Cheikh Anta Diop's thought, actually devotes nearly half his space to an entirely uncritical exegesis of Asante's *Kemet*, proclaiming: 'The following analysis applies the protocols of Africalogical inquiry, as delineated' in that work (Okafor 1991: 253). Nilgun Anadolu Okur, also of Temple, proclaims that since Asante invented Afrocentrism 'in his now classic book, *Afrocentricity*, the theory has gained prominence in all academic circles ... the most important contribution to Afrocentric theory is made in the major works of Asante' (Okur 1993: 88–9). Ayele Bekerie, an Assistant Professor at (you guessed it) Temple, effuses:

> The idea of centeredness finds perhaps its most dynamic articulation and movement in the theory and praxis of Afrocentricity. ... This is the guiding principle under which scholars of the Temple School, such as Asante ... and more than 200 graduate students conduct their studies and research. (Bekerie 1994: 131)

Clyde Ahmad Winters – who, for the sake of variety, does not seem to be affiliated to Temple University – says that the field 'has been outlined excellently by Asante' (Winters 1994: 170); and, in case that may not be emphatic enough, entitles his article 'Afrocentrism: A Valid Frame of Reference'. Jerome Schiele, fairly typically, cites Asante's work sixteen times in an article fifteen pages long (Schiele 1990); while Tolagbe Ogunleye quotes Asante three times in his essay's first paragraph alone, then gives the master the last word too (Ogunleye 1997). One could go on for a very long time multiplying instances of this alarmingly conformist and homogenizing mode of academic work. Its intellectual authoritarianism, however, cannot be better illustrated than in the work of Temple's Victor Okafor. After proclaiming that Africalogy 'approves of Herodotus's historiography' – we are not told on what grounds – and that any scepticism about Herodotus's claims can be motivated only by an attempt to deny Africa's real role in history (1991: 258), Okafor proceeds to a list of demands:

> Africalogical research is *expected* to underscore the southern origin of the Nile Valley civilization. It *should* stress the indigenous nature of the Nile Valley achievements. Africalogists are *expected* to uphold the fact that European-Africans never existed in antiquity. (ibid.: 260; emphasis added)

Cheikh Anta Diop, for all his faults, never 'expected' that people would believe things simply because he, or Herodotus, said them.

The most remarkable expression of this hero-worship, however, is a volume issued in 1995 under the editorship of Dhyana Ziegler, entitled *Molefi Kete Asante and Afrocentricity: In Praise and In Criticism.* The title misleads: contributions emit unmixed praise for Asante's work and influence, with no substantive – let alone negative – criticism at all. The nature of the book is extremely unusual in terms of academic habits. When a distinguished scholar retires or (more sadly) is felt to be near death or senility, admirers, former students and specialists in that writer's field often come together to produce a *Festschrift*, a work of tribute which usually includes a few invocations of the great man or woman's influence, but mainly consists of new contributions to the fields in which he or she has worked. To offer a volume of unmixed laudation – which, moreover, includes very few substantive investigations as opposed to celebrations – to a writer still in mid-career, however, is, to put it bluntly, an act of sycophancy almost unprecedented in academic circles.

The volume is topped and tailed by effusions from its editor, Dhyana Ziegler. In the Preface, she urges that Asante has 'unlocked the door to a revolution in disciplinary inquiry, African scholarship, and American education, to say the least' (Ziegler 1995a: ix). She goes on: 'Asante's wisdom has touched the spirit of many who have embraced his wisdom, who have allowed themselves to be challenged by his philosophy, and who have opened their hearts to his energy and spirit' (ibid.: xi). In her Conclusions, redoubling the emphasis, she proclaims that Asante 'has indeed been blessed by his African ancestors with creativity, intelligence, and boldness' (1995c: 275). In between, the guru is praised for 'leaving his stamp of excellence on everything he did ... without doubt one of the most prolific writers and gifted orators of the twentieth century' (1995b: 60–62).

Numerous other contributors follow the same line. For Sandra Van Dyk, *Afrocentricity* is 'a demarcation point signalling the shift from an educational paradigm of European cultural universalism to one of cultural pluralism'

(1995: 2) – as if the critique of Eurocentrism were novel and unique to Asante. Jeffrey Lynn Woodyard and Anita Mooijman both speak of the vast political hopes supposedly opened up by Asante's perspectives: 'the discovery and restructuring of knowledge that will set us – all of us – free!' (Woodyard 1995: 32). Tony Anderson exposes the 'empty' criticism of Afrocentricity; focusing, rather oddly, on Mary Lefkowitz's *New Republic* article 'Not Out of Africa' (1992), which was actually an attack on Martin Bernal rather than on Asante. For Anderson this seems to amount to a kind of sneaky backdoor Eurocentrism, engaging with the white 'Afrocentrist' Bernal rather than the black originators. Deborah F. Atwater, addressing an earlier phase in Asante's career, elucidates his 'brilliant contributions' to communications theory (1995: 45). Alan Jay Zaremba offers more personal acclaim for Asante's qualities as a teacher and colleague. Hpri Geru-Maa (one of several of Asante's disciples to have adopted supposedly Egyptian names) proposes to 'develop' Asante's paradigm for an Afrocentric historical linguistics, but in fact gives only an uncritical exegesis of Diop and Obenga.

Accompanying the creation of an enclosed, self-validating circle of true believers is the necessary complement: a sense that the circle is under attack. Bekerie (1994: 132) claims that 'a low-intensity intellectual warfare is in progress almost on a global scale.... Initial attempts to crush Afrocentricity did not succeed. The strategy of its opponents now is to attempt to wrest control of the movement.' Winters worries that the enemy is focusing its assaults on the dead Pharaoh, Diop: 'To attack Afrocentrism, the resisters are attacking the great research of Cheikh Anta Diop . . . who laid the foundations for the Afrocentric idea in education' (1994: 171).

Occasionally, to be fair, Asante has seemed to evince a more pluralist attitude to inquiry; but one with an odd sting in the tail. Thus the book he co-edited with his wife, Kariamu Welsh Asante, *African Culture* (1985), contained contributions whose arguments were quite at odds with the editors' beliefs. They included one from Wole Soyinka (1985) insisting on very sharp divisions between 'Black Africa' and the Arab north: a distinction contradicting basic Diopian faith. Aguibou Y. Yansane, discussing precolonial West African states, emphasized their cultures' indigeneity, and made no mention of Egyptian origins or influences (Yansane 1985). Maulana Karenga (1985) presented a basically Marxist account of African intellectuals' political choices. The oddity is that Asante, in his editorial comments, sought to present each of these contributions as if they supported his kind of Afrocentrism rather than fundamentally contradicting it.

Such seemingly inherent authoritarianism and pseudo-traditionalism brings Afrocentricity into some odd collusions with the ideas of both colonial rulers and postcolonial African tyrants. Thus Harvey Sindima, a researcher at Colgate University, quotes with entire approval the lament of a 1913 official report from British Central Africa that young people 'have in recent years evinced an inclination to emancipate themselves from the disciplinary responsibilities of village life and obedience to authority'

(Sindima 1990: 192). British colonial administrators and at least some modern Afrocentrists can, it seems, unite – at any rate in their shared detestation of liberalism. Asante has disparaged the idea of freedom of expression and of the press, which allegedly stems from the 'Western conflict view' of society (Asante 1980a: 27). The African ideal of harmony, by contrast, recognizes that such freedoms are 'not objective but relative', and negates 'the overextended concept of freedom of the press' (ibid.: 25). Africans do not understand when news media attack the government: 'when the traditional cultural patterns emphasize harmony and dictate that the propagation of news speak for the royal court' (ibid.: 26).

Yet more nakedly authoritarian is the Afrocentric psychologist Joseph A. Baldwin. His belief that race 'constitutes the most basic and fundamental binding condition underlying human existence, and ultimately transcends all subsequent or secondary bonds' (1980: 98) is 'illustrated' by examples including 'the Jews' false claims to African land' (ibid.: 103).[1] Baldwin goes on:

> Another relevant illustration of this problem involves the furor, primarily in the white community, over the 'moral character' of former President Idi Amin of Uganda . . . it is clear that the European community is committed to creating (in the minds of black people) a conception of Brother Amin as the most evil, destructive and 'dangerous' individual that this universe has ever witnessed.

In Baldwin's eyes, such attack on 'Brother Amin' is simply a racial conspiracy. No European should have the 'audacity to question the moral character of any non-European, given their own immoral and destructive history'. By contrast: 'the masses of our people in Africa appear to hold Brother Amin in the highest esteem' (ibid.: 103). No evidence is given, or could be given, for that assertion. Brother Amin is an African, all Africans are of the same mind, all are virtuous, and all Europeans seek to malign them. Therefore the butcher of Kampala is an honourable man. QED.

Dispiritingly, ideas of this kind also seep into the 'African History' and 'Black Holocaust' volumes of the usually excellent cartoon-strip *Beginner's Guides* series, which provide popular introductions to a wide range of heavyweight subjects. The African volume (Boyd 1991) engages in some fairly wild claims about homogeneous, solidaristic African world-views, and cites Ben-Jochannen and Van Sertima among its recommended authorities. *The Black Holocaust for Beginners* (Anderson 1995) is a questionable work in more various ways. Its very title naturally raises hackles in some circles, seeming as it does to engage in a distasteful kind of African–Jewish competition over the status of historical victimhood. Its opening pages, somewhat irrelevantly to the main theme of the Atlantic slave trade, rehearse vague and grandiose claims about ancient African civilizations long predating Mesopotamian or Egyptian states, their trade with the Americas and Australia, and so on (ibid.: 8–15, 25–8). It is claimed that the Dravidians of

India were Africans (30). The numbers involved (killed or transported) in both Arab and Atlantic slave trades are grotesquely inflated – the former to at least 28 million (41), the latter to anywhere between 100 and 270 million – and it is quite falsely asserted that historians W.E.B. Du Bois, Basil Davidson, Cheikh Anta Diop, Joseph Inikori and Walter Rodney support such wild claims (159).[2] And the book exhibits a sheer carelessness of production quite absent from earlier volumes in its series, with a mass of typographical, literal and factual errors.

The necessarily self-confirming nature of the Afrocentric approach is well demonstrated in a supposedly empirical, even scientific, study of 'Afrocentric Cultural Consciousness and African-American Male–Female Relationships' by three Florida researchers (Bell, Bouie and Baldwin 1990). It starts by counterposing two supposed world-views, a Euro-American one and an African-American one. The former is characterized by individualism and a drive to mastery 'through competition, aggression, materialism, domination and power, oppression, independence, and the transforming and rearranging of objects in nature' (ibid.: 163). All this is naturally reflected in heterosexual relationships, which are governed by 'power, competition, material affluence, and physical gratification' (ibid.). The African world-view, by contrast, emphasizes 'oneness with nature' and 'survival of the group', giving rise to relationships stressing 'spiritual-communal character qualities', where 'each partner provides for the other's physical, intellectual, emotional, and social stimulation'. Such relationships are 'inspirational', 'mutually affirmative', 'visionary', 'committed to goals, accomplishments, and aspirations that are related to the survival and development of the Black family'. Couples 'celebrate themselves, their achievements, aspirations, and developments as African people' (169–71). All the foregoing is 'proved' by citations exclusively from the little band of Afrocentric academics, primarily Asante and the article's co-author Joseph Baldwin.

So much for theory; now for research. A sample of 88 men and 89 women – we are not given a coherent account of how they were selected – was tested against an 'African Self-Consciousness Scale' developed by Baldwin, to see how they measured up to the Afrocentric values previously described. The same group was also tested on their attitudes to heterosexual relations, including such questions as whether respondents agreed or disagreed with the statement: 'In mate selection and/or evaluation, Black men and Black women should consider Black cultural beliefs and values (or cultural consciousness) as a main or primary criterion' (175). They also involved scenarios in which: 'The Afrocentric alternative involved being totally supportive of the mate in hardship, while the Eurocentric alternatives ranged from partial to total withholding/withdrawal of support' (176).

The data were analysed with correlational and chi-square procedures, with the 'Pearson product moment correlation coefficient', and so on (176–80). It sounds impressively professional, until one recalls the basic tenet of all statistical and computing techniques – GIGO: garbage in, garbage out. The results? 'Afrocentric cultural consciousness is positively related to perceptions (values, attitudes) that prioritize an Afrocentric value orientation in Black heterosexual relationships' (185). It is as obvious a tautology as one can well imagine.

Sadly, this kind of writing is not atypical – it stands out only in its unusually energetic effort to appear conventionally scholarly. Overall, the pious judgement of Bayo Oyebade, another researcher in Asante's department, is wildly misplaced:

> Afrocentricity insists that investigation of African phenomena ... must be subjected to proper research. For those who confuse Afrocentricity with Négritude, those who tend to see it as a reincarnation of Négritude, this insistence on meticulous research distinguishes it.... To the extent that Afrocentricity rejects undue glorification of Africa, it goes beyond Négritude. (Oyebade 1990: 237)

The main Afrocentrists have university posts, but their work has little to do with 'meticulous research'. Not infrequently, articles in the *Journal of Black Studies* slip into a mixture of New Age and ethnophilosophical mysticism, as with Adekotunbo Knowles-Borishade's invocation of a supposed classical African oratical mode derived directly from ancient Egyptian sources (1991: 488) and inspired by 'Nommo': 'The metaphysical principle behind the power of Nommo is its vibratory nature, which becomes multiplied in strength by the psychic energy imparted by the Caller' (ibid.: 496). Other recent works mingle Afrocentric and New Age romanticisms to make yet more sweeping claims for the power of ancient African wisdom to heal the troubles of the present. Thus Linda James Myers, in *Understanding an Afrocentric World View*, proclaims a 'reasoned faith (positive belief) in the achievement of everlasting peace and happiness ... based on the teachings of ancient Africans' (Myers 1988: v).

Jerome H. Schiele, in an article claiming to present Afrocentric approaches to organization theory, proposes that such approaches offer a unique framework for 'human-service organizations'. According to this framework, 'organizational and group survival replaces productivity as the overriding concern' (Schiele 1990: 150). There 'would be no need to practice rigid supervision and control' (ibid.: 154); organizations 'would not place so much emphasis on efficiency or rationality' (155). '(T)he strengthening of interpersonal relationships in an organization would be perceived as an end in itself' (156). Or in other words, the 'Afrocentric paradigm', despite the disclaimers Schiele hastily inserts, would sanction – or positively value – a notion of public service organizations as self-perpetuating, cosy, inefficient, irrational and unproductive bureaucracies. Such a stance is beyond parody. In a companion piece suggesting the implications of Afrocentricity for higher education, Schiele proceeds by way of the familiar Diopian antitheses between European individualism, competitiveness, aggression, and so on, and African humanism to propose a model of education 'based on traditional African philosophical assumptions'

(Schiele 1994: 152), among which is apparently that 'there is no perceptual separation of the individual from other people' (ibid.: 154) – which must be a bit confusing when one is trying to eat, or put on one's shoes.[3] The actual implications for education seem to be that tutors and students should be nice to one another, should co-operate, and should be eager to learn (155–8). This is certainly a powerful blow against all those philosophies of education that advocate rudeness and idleness as the ideal pedagogical tools.[4]

The idea that present-day systems of education, philosophy, governance, psychiatric counselling, and so on can and should be drawn from sources in ancient Egypt or 'classical Africa' recurs regularly. Maulana Karenga and his collaborator Jacob Carruthers (Karenga 1985; Karenga and Carruthers 1986) have proposed it in relation to politics and philosophy. Asa Hilliard, like Schiele, thinks educational models can be drawn from Kemitic wisdom (Hilliard 1986, 1989, 1994b). Afrocentric mathematician Deborah Maat Moore has even claimed in interview that the very act of reading Ancient Egyptian hieroglyphs is 'cleansing', morally and spiritually uplifting (Person-Lynn 1996: 146). We shall look later at parallel claims made in relation to science and technology.

Despite Asante's pre-eminence, undoubtedly the most powerfully argued, as well as most extensive, presentation of the essential general features of an Afrocentric world-view is a recent, massive book by Marimba Ani (formerly Dona Richards: her renaming may seem to some a touch immodest, since 'Ani' is an Ancient Egyptian word for a bearer of wisdom!). In *Yurugu* (Ani 1994) she sets out a sweeping, heavily documented critique of the entire structure of Western thought and behaviour. Her title comes from a Dogon legend of a doomed, destructive, incomplete being, the rejected offspring of the Creator. This, of course, is her image of the European: the irony being that her source for the Dogon story is a European writer, Marcel Griaule. Ani's book has the dubious merit of carrying its relentless pursuit of racialized thinking to logical conclusions within its own structure, by having two separate Bibliographies and Indexes – one for 'Africans', one for others. This gross intellectual apartheid has certain logical difficulties, of course; its fencing off of 'Africans' (actually including hardly any African as opposed to Afro-American authors) seems to contradict the book's central claim that the basic division lies between Europeans and everybody else. In fact, though, it is the segregation of the Index which best reflects Ani's preoccupations, for like almost all her fellow Afrocentrists she has not the slightest interest in Asian, Middle Eastern, Oceanic, Australasian or Native American peoples. Her 'Non-African' Bibliography includes just one name from any of these groups: the American Indian writer Vine Deloria. Seventy per cent of the world's people are as irrelevant to her as they allegedly are to Eurocentric thinkers. But her categorization has further, rather predictable problems. W.E.B. Du Bois, among many people of mixed descent, is placed in the 'African' Index and Bibliography, with scant regard for the French and Dutch ancestry of which he was actually rather proud.

Also typically, Marimba Ani appears to be quite uninterested in Africa itself. She makes much of her conceptual scheme and analytical tools being drawn from African thought, using concepts like 'Utamawazo' (roughly, world-view), 'Asili' (cultural essence) and 'Utamahoro' (vital force) – though, confusingly, she also tells us that these three are all the same thing. All three are Swahili words, but Ani shows no sign of knowing that language, still less of being concerned about the sheer variety of peoples who use it, its substantially Arabic origins, or its development in large part as a medium for slave-trading: let alone worrying how far its concepts are translatable into other African languages. Occasionally, she throws in Yoruba, Twi and other terms as well. But beyond some rather routine denunciations of South African policies – already well out of date before the book was published – she has nothing whatever specific to say about Africa, or manifestations of the European 'Utamawazo' there.

None the less, Ani's book has real strengths in comparison with almost all the other literature of Afrocentrism. She has read widely, worked (as she tells us) for at least sixteen years on the manuscript – indeed, the book's major ideas appear in embryo as Richards (1980) – and offers rhetorically powerful – if relentlessly reductionist – readings of aspects of Western thought from Plato onwards. All this is vitiated, however, by indiscriminate indulgence towards the wildest claims and theories, so long as they are sufficiently hostile to the 'Western worldview': the racist ideas of Frances Cress Welsing, Michael Bradley or Richard King; the charge that AIDS is a deliberately created disease, a genocidal plot against Africans (Ani 1994: 437–46) or that the Nazi Holocaust was far less destructive than European colonialism, and arouses condemnation only because the victims were white (ibid.: 418).

Quite apart from the wild totalizations involved in claiming all world history as determined by opposition between a homogeneous European culture which incarnates all evil, and an equally homogeneous 'everyone else' embodying all virtue, Ani's book depends on a quite unsustainable counterposition of the concepts of logic, abstraction, analysis, individualism, materialism and rationalism (all seen as European, and destructive) against those of holism, spirituality, intuition, love, collectivism, and so on, identi-fied with non-European 'majority cultures'.[5] In other words, Ani is an anti-universalist in all three of the senses set out above (pp. 11–12). She sees African world-views as governed by an alternative, superior, non-Aristotelian 'logic':

> The universe is understood through phenomenal interaction, which pro-duces powerful symbols and images, which in turn communicate truths. 'Diunital logic' indicates that in African thought a thing can be both A and not A at the same time ... 'diunital logic' can be understood as the recognition and affirmation of the ambiguity and multidimensionality of phenomenal reality. What is contradictory in Euro-American Aristotelian logic is not contradictory in African thought. (97–8)

Such claims as Ani's could come only from someone who – without philosophical training and, far worse, without having given a moment's serious thought to the question of what 'logic' means – has glibly swallowed postmodernist or extreme cultural relativist claims that the idea of logic is intrinsically culture-bound. The best response to this is in the words of a genuine, and genuinely philosophical, African thinker, Kwasi Wiredu. He deplores:

> the well-intentioned but unwelcome plea, entered on behalf of Africa by some of her friends, that although African thinking does not operate with such principles as Noncontradiction and Excluded Middle, it is none the worse for it, since there are alternative logics . . . a quite simple consideration suffices to demonstrate that no coherent logical system or even logical thinking is possible that dispenses not just with some particular formulation but with the essence of the principle of Noncontradiction. . . . If a given system does not have this principle . . . the notion of valid deduction must consequently be absent. (Wiredu 1992: 304–5)[6]

Does Marimba Ani go shopping, and expect to be able to add up her bill? If she asks someone the time, does she expect to be told 'Ten a.m., *and* three-thirty p.m.', or maybe 'I don't recognize the linear conception of time, Ma'am: go ask somebody European' (see Ani 1994: 59–62)? In her book's Acknowledgements, she is engagingly honest about the limits to her computer literacy; but *presumably* when she hits the 'A' key, she expects her screen to show an 'A', rather than 'both A and not-A'. One might moreover ask: if Ani believes that categories like logic, abstraction and the analytical are inherently Eurocentric, why has she burdened her book with a huge apparatus of (mostly accurate) references, and why does she attempt to argue for the propositions she advances? Why not rest content with a piece of purely affective writing, appealing only to the emotions or, indeed, to the authority of the ancestors?

Another major theme in Afrocentric historical – or pseudo-historical – writing is the supposed African presence in pre-Columbian America. Ivan Van Sertima, in *They Came Before Columbus* (1977), claims two major patterns of voyaging. The ancient Egyptians and Nubians went to the Gulf of Mexico – carrying with them everything from the art of pyramid-building to that of writing (though apparently forgetting to pass on the idea of the wheel either to Americans or to Sub-Saharan Africans). Rather later, the Mande of West Africa travelled to Mexico, Panama, Ecuador, Columbia, Peru and various Caribbean islands. The oddity in their case is that very soon thereafter they not only forgot how to navigate or build ocean-going craft, but (perhaps in irritated self-disgust at this absentmindedness) retreated to live well away from the coast. Van Sertima's grab-bag of evidence for such culture contact amounts mainly to a superficial and highly selective list of alleged similarities between Egyptian and Mesoamerican cosmologies, architectures, and so on, claims that several early European voyagers to the

Americas – including Columbus himself – observed black-skinned people already there, and the observation that some Olmec sculpture depicts people with thick lips. From the African side, the main supposed evidence is a possible tradition (very weakly attested) that two large fleets of ships from the Malian Empire, during the reign of Abubakar II in the early fourteenth century, sailed westward and never returned.

Van Sertima is not by any means the only person advocating ideas of early African voyages to the Americas (almost simultaneously an imaginative amateur historian, Barry Fell, was putting forward similar theories (Fell 1976)), and has indeed sought more conscientiously to argue from evidence than some enthusiasts have done. This generally rational approach was, however, confused or undermined in *They Came Before Columbus* by the dramatizing, even fictionalized, narrative style he adopted there: though a decade later (in Van Sertima 1987) he sought to defend the approach and, with a number of collaborators, to produce new arguments for the original claim. He found support from the veteran German art historian and Mexico City museum curator Alexander von Wuthenau (von Wuthenau 1987), and sought to resurrect the memory of a neglected precursor in the field, Leo Wiener (1862–1939), best known as a translator of Tolstoy and as father of Norbert, the founder of cybernetics. In 1919–22 Wiener produced a massive three-volume attempt at documentation of the alleged African discovery of America (see Muffet 1987).[7] In reviving that tradition, Van Sertima (1987: 15–17) distanced himself from the wilder ideas of amateur historians like Rafique Jairazbhoy, who had argued that the Egyptians *founded* the Olmec culture, whereas Van Sertima only asserted that Africans *influenced* it. None the less, in his later edited volume Van Sertima still found space for sweepingly speculative claims like those of Beatrice Lumpkin about alleged influences of Egyptian pyramid-building on vaguely similar American structures (Lumpkin 1987), or Keith Jordan's sketchy and entirely unscientific arguments from physical anthropology (Jordan 1987). Van Sertima is more cautious and coherent in his procedures than most Afrocentric writers (and is clearly disapproved of by many of them[8]), but the friendly assessment of St Clair Drake greatly exaggerates in suggesting that he 'present[s] a convincing case.... There is little to which his peers in "the academy" could object in his book' (Drake 1987: 312). And as Drake concedes, such a defence could not be mounted in relation to many of Van Sertima's collaborators on the *Journal of African Civilizations*: 'who have used folklore and mythology, along with esoteric types of language analysis, in ways that raise questions about the scholarly character of their intellectual operations' (ibid.).[9]

Of course, the cynic might suspect that the only real question in all this is how the doughty African explorers found room to land, since America's beaches were jostling with so many pre-Columbian visitors: St Brendan and his Irish monks, Prince Madoc on his way to found colonies of Welsh-speaking Indians,[10] Carthaginians and Phoenicians (see Bradley 1992a: 15–20), Vikings – some of them African, too, as a contributor to another book edited by Van Sertima asserts (Rashidi 1985: 258) – and King Arthur's knights. More seriously, it might be concluded that whereas most historians find the evidence for pre-Columbian Viking settlement in the Americas very convincing, the case for African voyages is little – if any – less speculative than the older stories about Brendan or Madoc: lack of scholarly acceptance for it cannot be attributed solely, or even mainly, to racial or Eurocentric prejudice.

Fantasies of this kind have, evidently, an unquenchable polymorphous-ness. In 1978 – to take one of the more bizarre examples – a book was published in Paraguay, endorsed by members of the country's semi-fascist military regime, arguing that Paraguay's Ache Indians were degenerate descendants of the Vikings (Holland 1990). But Van Sertima also has more reputable company than that of Latin American generals. Remarkably, renowned cultural critic bell hooks seems uncritically to accept Van Sertima's claims about African–Amerindian contact. She draws great politi-cal hope from this encounter, since it was supposedly a non-imperialist one, in which the participants did not make 'a site of imperialist/cultural domination' out of their cultural differences (quoted in Gross and Levitt 1994: 211). Nigerian poet and polemicist Chinweizu, too, takes the truth of Van Sertima's flaky claims for granted, and also finds positive political lessons in them: 'I find it somehow inspiring to learn that there was fruitful cultural exchange between Africans and Americans long before the coming of Europeans to both places, and I think we should all know more about it' (1987: 93). In fact Van Sertima's and his co-thinkers' fantasies are not of 'cultural exchange' – they give no sign that they think their African adventurers learned anything from the native Americans – but are simply another aspect of compensatory African-American aggrandizement. Indeed, Bruce Trigger is surely nearer the mark when he says that Van Sertima 'denigrates, we trust unwittingly, native peoples by attributing major ele-ments of their cultural heritage to others' (1989: 407).

Equally surprising, Lerone Bennett, in *Before the Mayflower*, his massively popular history of black America, quotes Van Sertima without demur, accepting his ill-evidenced claim that 'there was extensive pre-Columbian contact between ancient Africa and the Americas' (Bennett 1984: 4). This is a departure from the generally cautious and sober way in which Bennett's work (very much an example of the 'contributionist' strand of historical retrieval) uses others' research on the distant past.

Matching the claims made about African influences in the pre-Columbian Americas are similar assertions of widespread African colonization in Europe.[11] Van Sertima leads the pack here too, with his edited collection *African Presence in Early Europe* (1985). The contributions range from pious little biographical sketches of figures like Alexander Pushkin and the Chevalier de Saint-Georges, through effusions on 'The Moor: Light of Europe's Dark Ages' (illustrated with obviously nineteenth-century drawings claimed to be of much greater age), to arguments asserting the African origins of Europe's early historic populations.

Like most of the other central notions of Afrocentrism, this last, a varied set of ideas about African origins for European peoples and civilizations, has a much older history. The major originators in this instance appear to be two late-Victorian British writers, Gerald Massey and David MacRitchie. Both Massey's and MacRitchie's books have been reissued by African-American enthusiasts, and have become highly influential texts for the Afrocentric movement.[12] Runoko Rashidi (1985: 251–2) tells of his 'intense search' for MacRitchie's 'exceedingly rare' book, and the sacrifices he incurred to find it. It is a touch poignant to note that, by contrast, the copy of MacRitchie in Oxford's Bodleian Library has sat apparently unread for over a century: when I consulted it there, the pages were still uncut.

Gerald Massey (1828–1907) was the son of an impoverished canal boatman from Hertfordshire, England. Deprived of formal education, he became a noted autodidact, a prolific if undistinguished poet, and a campaigner for both Spiritualism and Christian Socialism – often cited as the inspiration for George Eliot's *Felix Holt, the Radical*. He was also yet another of the era's enthusiasts for the Egyptian origins of absolutely everything. His *Book of the Beginnings* (1881) traced at massive length the alleged colonization of prehistoric England by Egyptian settlers, who built Stonehenge and the British Isles' other ancient monuments, provided the religious beliefs and cultural practices of the people – still to be discerned in many surviving customs of evident Egyptian origin – and contributed much to the English language. The longest section of Massey's first volume provided a huge list of English words supposedly derived from Ancient Egyptian, while the second volume 'uncovered' similarly extensive Egyptian influences on Hebrew, Assyrian and – extraordinarily enough – the New Zealand Maori languages.

MacRitchie's *Ancient and Modern Britons* was issued anonymously in 1884. His basic theory was that large parts of the British population had originally been what he called 'Melanochroi', descendants of the interbreeding of white Europeans with black 'Australoids'. These latter had been the first Britons, and were supplemented by later 'black' migrants, notably black Huns, Moors and Danes. Pure-blooded blacks no longer, of course, existed in Britain (ignoring, as MacRitchie did, the migrant and settler enclaves in various Victorian British seaports), but MacRitchie found evidence of their presence all over the place, especially in Scotland – with Galloway the most prolific hunting-ground. They built ancient stone circles, dolmens, and so on. Folktales and customs kept their memory alive. Every place-name and family name with 'black', 'dark', and related words in it, or any hint of them, indicated African descent: thus not only surnames like Black, Brown, Dunn or Gray, but the Celtic Dougal, Carr, Douglas, Donn, Murray (from 'Moor') and many, many more (or Moore) were living witness to African ancestors.

A little later our old friend Albert Churchward, in his *Origin and Evolution of the Human Race*, was not only tracing Egyptian influence in Northern Europe, including claims that the Inuit were black (1921: 416–25), but asserting that the Chinese were descended from Egyptians (ibid.: 367–71), that Piltdown Man was a 'Nilotic Negro' (34–46, 497–9) and that the British Isles were settled first by Pygmies, then by more 'Nilotic Negroes' (462–6). There are some even more eccentric recent footnotes to this view, like Ahmed and Ibrahim Ali's little book *The Black Celts* (1993), which also purports to trace ancient African civilizations in Britain and Ireland.[13] The Alis bring to bear an impressive, if utterly indiscriminate, mass of data – folkloric (ibid.: 14–51), linguistic (104–5, 127–78), plus a mass of 'evidence' from the analysis of skulls (64–5, 69–70, 77–84, 87–103) and blood groups (111–26) – to argue that before the Celts came to the British Isles, the archipelago was inhabited by various African peoples. These diverse groups – allegedly all originating in Ethiopia, though migrating via Spain and various parts of North Africa – have left their traces everywhere from stone circles to round skulls of supposedly distinctively African type. There is the predictable charge that all this has been hushed up: 'Modern archaeoligst (*sic*) and historians ignore the Afro–Iberian colonisation of Britain and Ireland' (57). Perhaps the wildest set of claims, however, is made in a text evidently designed for high-school students, *What They Never Told You in History Class* (1983) by a Bronx (New York) maths teacher writing under the name Indus Khamit Kush. Drawing indiscriminately on the whole pantheon of Afrocentric 'authorities' from Volney, Churchward and Massey, through the 'old scrappers' Jackson, James, Rogers, Clarke and Ben-Jochannen to Diop and Van Sertima, Kush asserts that the original inhabitants and bearers of civilization across the entire globe were black Africans – the first Japanese (ibid.: 207), Vietnamese, Siamese and Malays (209), Greeks (228–9), Romans (232–4), Spanish (234–5), Britons (238–40) and Americans (243–7).

Writings in this vein – dominated today by Ivan Van Sertima and his followers, but with their much older and often highly whimsical ancestry – have a rather different and in some ways less exclusivist focus from those of most Afrocentric currents. Rather than asserting the uniqueness, superiority and self-sufficiency of supposedly African traditions or world-views, they seek traces of ancient African influence everywhere in the world. Thus they might open the way to a more ecumenical, multidirectional vision of world history, one free of the reverse racism of much Afrocentric dogma (and certainly the overt bigotries of many other prominent writers in the genre, like anti-Semitism, are absent from Van Sertima's work). Van Sertima has indeed registered sharp dissent from those – like a contributor to his own edited works, Manu Ampim – who seem to judge ideas by their authors' racial background. Intellectual work 'cannot be subjected to the melanin dosage test', and criticism of white scholars is of value 'only where it pinpoints specific errors of fact, specific conceptual contradictions' (1994a: 11). Van Sertima's *Journal of African Civilizations* has occasionally published the work of white scholars, whereas several other journals and publishing houses in the field appear to operate a *de facto* colour bar on contributors. Van Sertima insists that his Afrocentrism is intended only as a balancing corrective to Eurocentrism in education, not as a counter-myth (Person-Lynn 1996: 32). If all of us are in some measure of African descent – and far more recently so than via 'Lucy' or 'Eve' – and all our cultures include African influence, then racisms of any kind have no historical basis. Unfortunately, though, the cultural model proposed by the *Journal of African Civilizations*, or by Temple University's Afrocentrists, is *not* one of multidirectional influence, but one in which everything radiates from Africa.

However, there are a few straws in the wind to suggest the possibility of an academic Afrocentrism which eschews fantasy and reverse racism. A considerably more coherent, less dogmatic approach to understanding history than Asante's (or those of most of the better-known Afrocentric writers) is provided by his Temple colleague C. Tsehloane Keto. South African-born Keto thus conforms to the general rule that the wilder reaches of identitarian cultural nationalism are rarely to be found occupied by African, as opposed to Afro-American, intellectuals. Keto expounds Asante's pet notion of 'centredness' in relatively muted – albeit still essentialist – fashion: 'researchers should specify, at the level where they apply their chosen methodology on concrete situations, the geographical and cultural location that they adopt as the primordial core from which they extrapolate values and priorities' (Keto 1989: 1). He asserts – as Asante does in his more emollient moods – that Afrocentrism aims to be a balance, rather than a hegemonic alternative, to Eurocentrism (ibid.: 3). For that matter, a *non*-hegemonic Eurocentric historical practice is possible; Keto cites, in a rather arbitrary-sounding list, such names as William Appleman Williams, Harold Cruse and Sande Cohen (11–13). A 'symbiotic' relationship to Marxism, and an alliance with concern for gender issues, rather than Asante's blanket hostility to both, are proposed (21–2, 16–18). Afrocentrists in the USA are suggested – via a metaphor borrowed, unacknowledged, from Du Bois – to be making a constructive contribution to debate on America's future rather than opting out from it (31–2). The final goal is some kind of universal pluralism (40–42), and in what may well be read as a warning to his Afrocentric colleagues, Keto urges:

> The lure of hegemony is not only a temptation to European centred scholarship. The Afrocentric perspective can also carry hegemonic undertones when all claims to progress in all regions of the world are explained in terms of the African presence and the African presence alone. This hegemonic tendency, though ego-boosting to people whose egos have been historically pounced on, should be rejected. (17)

Keto's emphases are a valuable corrective to the dogmatism of much Afrocentric writing. He does not, however, appear to have produced any substantive historical studies exemplifying his perspective, beyond the two slim booklets setting it out in general terms (1989, 1995). More extensive works are beginning to appear by scholars who proclaim themselves as Afrocentrists, share in some of the uncritical fervour for the Diopian tradition, and partake in the insistent racialization of intellectual inquiry, but maintain distinctions between history and myth, between anti-racism and reverse racism. Books like Clinton N. Jean's *Behind the Eurocentric Veils* (1991) and Clovis M. Semmes's *Cultural Hegemony and African American Development* (1992) are in this vein. They may proclaim themselves as Afrocentric; they may, as Jean does, assert that their identification of 'black anteriority' is part of a school that 'elevates blackness' (Jean 1991: 99); they may, like Semmes, offer a vague approval of Cress Welsing's ideas (Semmes 1992: 23–4, 29); but they both extend the field of inquiry and escape the dead hand of unquestioned authority extended by Asante.

It may yet be – and it is certainly to be hoped – that stances like Keto's, Jean's and Semmes's will become more the norm, as Afrocentric inquiry matures and diversifies. Certainly that is the proclaimed belief of Ivan Van Sertima. Introducing and praising the collected essays of Charles S. Finch, Van Sertima suggests that:

> The first crude phase of the struggle to revise our history is passing. Those earlier hollow boasts about the vague and vast achievements have given way to something deeper, more cautious and yet more confident, more danger-ous, closer to the detail of historical truth and therefore more revolutionary. Finch's essays belong to that new revisionist body of work that is so meticulously documented, so reasonably argued, that it does not have to circulate within the closed circle of the converted but can begin to shock and change the climate of thinking in the world at large. ('Foreword', in Finch 1990: 1)

Unfortunately, the nature of the very essays which those remarks preface raises doubt about the judgement. Finch – a medical doctor who has forayed into history and Egyptology – relies almost entirely on the same narrow and often idiosyncratic range of sources as most other contemporary Afrocentr-ists, including an entirely uncritical allegiance to Diop, 'the movement's Erasmus' (1990: 3) possessed of 'fathomless knowledge' (ibid.: 21), and enthusiasm for Gerald Massey's odd theories (Finch 1989). There is no sign that he has conducted any kind of research beyond a reading of such sources. He advocates the view that white people are products of albinoid mutation from the original black human form (1990: 39–45; see also Van Sertima 1985: 17–22), asserts that 'Nile Valley civilizations exercised a cultural hegemony over all of Western Asia in antiquity' (1990: 59), holds the familiar but entirely speculative idea that the original Jews must have been black (ibid.: 64), and the almost certainly false one that the 'Great Queens of Ethiopia' ruled over a matriarchal society (93–120). He makes very sweeping and seemingly unsubstantiated claims about Egyptian and other ancient African medical knowledges (121–40), and buys wholesale the conviction that Christianity was almost entirely derived from Egyptian religion (169–94).

The most assiduous effort toward rehabilitating the old 'vindicationist' tradition of Afro-American historical polemic, and combining it with serious scholarly standards, has come from a slightly surprising source: the then already venerable (since sadly deceased) *doyen* of sociological research on black America, St Clair Drake. In retirement, Drake quite purposefully moved away from the procedures of academic convention to produce in his two-volume *Black Folk Here and There* a synthesis of Afrocentric research in which 'the author consciously and deliberately makes whatever sacrifice of academic "objectivity" is needed to present this subject from a black perspective' (Drake 1990: xi). Arguing that notions of 'objectivity' have in any case come under serious challenge from a wide range of developments in the sociology of knowledge, Drake believes that such developments confer validity on his stance. This is one in which:

> The adoption of a black perspective in history, philosophy, or the social sciences deliberately restricts the frame of reference within which people and events are observed and evaluated. The focus is narrowed so as to concentrate on the Black Experience. (1987: 1)

Drake's model is, evidently, primarily that of Du Bois's exercises in synthesizing global black history – and his title makes allusion to one of these, the elder statesman's 1939 *Black Folk Then and Now*. He also, however, offers a partial rehabilitation of the entire 'vindicationist' tradition, including its often mythologizing views of ancient African history. As he argues:

> Crucial in the Afro-Americans' coping process has been their identification, over a time span of more than two centuries, with ancient Egypt and Ethiopia as symbols of black initiative and success. . . . Great myths are always part of group-coping strategies. (1987: xv)

Yet this does not involve Drake in abandoning critical standards of logic, evidence and plausibility. In his extensive and valuable bibliographical essays, he certainly offers judgements on writers in the vindicationist vein which may strike the more detached observer (one who does not or cannot adopt 'the black perspective' and, indeed, doubts whether such a singular entity really exists) as overly indulgent. But such writers are still evaluated according to the weight and coherence of the evidence they put forward; and where they are found wanting, this is stated clearly – as with Frances Cress Welsing and the melanin theorists, of whom Drake says, rightly: 'no results of controlled experimental research design had been produced to bolster their bold, far-reaching assertions' (1987: 101). And Drake's own historical narrative quite clearly indicates where its assertions are speculative, and seeks to balance evidence drawn from the romantic Afrocentrist, Diopian and vindicationist schools against that from more conventional sources in history, archaeology, anthropology and sociology. Sometimes this exercise may seem to the less sympathetic reader – as it does to this one – a matter of trying to give equal weight to sources which make serious use of evidence and those which do not. However, if bridges *can* be built between Afrocentric scholarship and more orthodox kinds, Drake, more than anyone else, has shown the way to do so.

Notes

1. A formulation which presumably refers to Israel/Palestine, and would be thought equally grotesque by *all* sides of the argument over Israeli occupation of *Arab* land.

2. Of these, only Diop could be said ever to have offered even the most tangential support for such claims. He never wrote in any detail about the slave trade; but in one passing, unsubstantiated reference in an early work, he claimed that it 'has been estimated that the slave trade swallowed up one hundred to three hundred million individuals' (1987: 142).

3. Linda James Myers solves the problem – according to the 'ancient African teachings' she advocates, not only are you what you eat, you *are* your shoes, and everything else: '(the) Self then includes all ancestors, the yet unborn, the entire community, and all of nature' (1988: 19).

4. Other efforts to argue that Afrocentrism offers a total, liberating transformation of educational philosophy include Neter (1995); Dickerson (1995); C. Crawford (1996). In an earlier Asante-edited volume, Thaddeus H. Spratlen presents an equally pretentious and vacuous argument for 'Racial Perspectives in Economics' (Spratlen 1980). The process of asserting a distinctive but contentless 'African approach' evidently could be – and probably will be – extended to every imaginable field of study or activity.

5. The procedure also involves, as critic Michael Blakey (1995: 222–4) has noted, crude misreadings of the history of ideas. Identifying an ideology of progress as a crucial – and undesirable – aspect of all European thought from Plato onwards, Ani completely misunderstands the relative novelty of that ideology, which came to the fore only with the late Renaissance or even the eighteenth-century Enlightenment. Prior to this, most European thought, from Platonic doctrines to Christian theologies, held to a static or cyclical view of history.

6. The principle of Noncontradiction is, straightforwardly, that a thing *cannot* be both A and not-A at the same time. The principle of Excluded Middle, as Wiredu implies, involves more complex arguments, but in essence says merely that any given proposition must be either true or false.

7. Wiener's book was republished by Afrocentric enthusiasts in 1992. Other writers who had earlier proposed the thesis that Africans voyaged to the Americas included Afro-Americans Joel Augustus Rogers, John G. Jackson (1972), and Harold Lawrence (1962), as well as the English esotericists Albert Churchward and Gerald Massey.

8. His and his disciples' writings are rather conspicuous by their absence from the bibliographies or acknowledgements of Molefi Asante and the Temple 'school', as well as those of Karenga, Carruthers and *their* circle – and vice versa.

9. Among the wilder exercises in mythmaking by contributors to Van Sertima's many edited volumes are those of Wayne Chandler, Asa Hilliard, Legrand H. Clegg and Phaon Goldman in *Egypt Revisited* (1989); and Chandler, Lumpkin and Don Luke in *African Presence in Early Europe* (1985), as well as some of the claims about ancient African achievements in *Blacks in Science* (1983).

10. See Gwyn A. Williams (1979), an enormously stimulating book with wide implications for the formation of historical myth, for the history of this remarkably durable legend.

11. And, indeed, Asia: yet another Van Sertima-edited collection (with Rashidi, 1988) traces, more or less fancifully, ancient African colonizations from Sinai to Singapore, Aden to Australia. Runoko Rashidi (1992) focuses on the supposed African origins of Indian populations and cultures, including a claim that the Buddha was an African. Edward Scobie (1994), largely derivative of Van Sertima, claims to trace an African 'global

presence'. For far more scholarly views of African presences in Asia, mainly the result of the Arab slave trade, see Harris (1971); Ali (1996).

12. For instance, Charles Finch devotes a laudatory essay to Massey's life and works in Van Sertima (1989); while John G. Jackson's book *Man, God and Civilization* (1972/1983) is dedicated to Massey's memory. Other such invocations, from a long list, include J.A. Rogers (in Van Deburg [ed.] [1997: 67]), Van Sertima (1994a: 11); Hilliard (1994b: 385); C. Crawford (1996: 5, 102, 105, 120–21, 123).

13. The persistence of these ideas with a certain kind of English romantic antiquarian is noted, for instance, by Patrick Wright (1995: 111–13); while the young James Joyce was attracted to their Irish counterparts (Cheng 1995: 47–8). Martin Bernal's *Black Athena* suggests sympathy with such views in passing, and only in endnotes: Bernal (1991: 563–4 n.37; 611 n.189).

Afrocentrism and Science

Afrocentrism has been an affair mostly of the humanities, of claims about history, culture and mentality. Yet the movement has also achieved significant bridgeheads in the natural sciences, and it is here that many of the most outrageous and disturbing arguments have been advanced.

A major source of the most extreme claims is Ivan Van Sertima's collection *Blacks in Science, Ancient and Modern* (1983), a peculiar mixed bag of piously exaggerated assertions about the importance of various modern black scientists, and absurd affirmations about ancient African science. Among the artifacts illustrated in support of the latter is a small wooden effigy of the Egyptian god Horus, who took the form of a falcon. Khalil Messiha claims that this is a model glider, showing the Pharaohs' command of the principles of aeronautics and their ability to fly (Messiha 1983: the pictures and the claims are reproduced also in Browder [1992: 132–3])! Ancient Egyptians also invented the wet-cell battery, and pioneered most aspects of geometry (Lumpkin 1983a).[1] The Dogon discovered that Sirius had a small companion star centuries before Western astronomers did so, indicating either invention of refracting telescopes, or mystic powers (H. Adams 1983a, b). Tanzanians were using semiconductors in the fifth century (Shore 1983). And so on. Yet the book has been endorsed uncritically and at length by noted feminist philosopher of science Sandra Harding (1991: 223–7).[2] As Robert Hughes comments: 'To plough through the literature of Afrocentrism is to enter a world of claims about technological innovation so absurd that they lie beyond satire, like those made for Russian science in Stalin's time' (Hughes 1993: 136).

Indeed, the connections between Stalinist pseudo-science and the Afrocentric variety are in at least one case quite direct. In *African Systems of Science, Technology and Art: The Nigerian Experience* (Thomas-Emeagwala 1993), F.P.A. Oyedipe draws on the 'technique' of Kirlian photography, which was 'invented' by the Russian Semyon Kirlian in 1939 and is claimed to capture invisible energies radiating from material objects. Oyedipe thinks this is relevant to 'the metaphysical aspects of Yoruba traditional medicine', because the Yoruba traditional healer 'indeed knows much about the unseen aspects of life which Kirlian photography has pointed out' (ibid.:

59). He thinks it is 'pertinent to ask questions about the scientific validity of data collected and collated from this invisible metaphysical realm' (ibid.: 61). As this implies, Oyedipe, like Asante and many other Afrocentrists, has assimilated elements of New Age thought to his cultural nationalist concerns – his sole source for Kirlian photography is apparently *The Encyclopaedia of Alternative Medicine and Self-Help*, though it is noteworthy that Cheikh Anta Diop had drawn attention to Kirlian's ideas rather earlier (Diop 1991: 367).

Oyedipe – in a book whose other contributors, it should be pointed out, mostly offer modest, sensible and scholarly accounts of early Nigerian techniques of dyeing, metalworking, food processing, and so on – also indicates another tendency in efforts to assert the scientific achievements of low-tech cultures: to claim so wide a variety of activities as 'science' that the term is emptied of meaning. For Oyedipe, Yoruba healers were practising 'science' when they – well – looked at things: 'Science at the pre-literate level of social organisation ... can be understood to mean that natural phenomena was (*sic*) observed as much as possible. The five senses saw, tasted, touched, smelled and heard' (Thomas-Emeagwala 1993: 56).

Oyedipe – and most of Van Sertima's contributors – at least write coherently. When Yosef Ben-Jochannen addressed a 1987 London conference, supposedly talking about 'The African Contribution to Technology and Science', his discourse as later published defied all notions of rationality. Essentially repeating the standard stories of how the Greeks and the Jews stole all their ideas from Egypt, Ben-Jochannen said virtually nothing whatever specifically about Egyptian, or other African, science or technologies. He did, however, offer thoughts on race pride in general, urge his listeners always to carry mirrors with them to look at how beautiful they were, and claim that Queen Elizabeth II is descended from 'an Ethiopian woman by the name of Martha' and therefore 'belongs to the family' (Addai-Sebo and Wong 1988: 64–5), that Africans invented the calendar 12,000 years ago, and numerous other *jeux d'esprit*.

Claims for prior or superior African scientific rationality alternate in Afrocentric rhetoric with celebrations of supposed irrationality: an anti-science ideology which harks back to Aimé Césaire's version of *Négritude* ('Heiah for those who never invented anything!', in the words of his famous long poem *Cahiers d'un retour au pays natal*) and looks forward to New Age anti-rationalism. Dorthy L. Pennington, for instance, applauds the superiority of an allegedly non-linear African concept of time:

> The mathematical division of time observed by Westerners has little relevance to Africans ... one year may have 350 days, while another may have 390 days, since the actual number is of secondary importance. ... Time, as continuity, was directed from the perspective of the past, rather than toward a future goal. (1985: 131–7)

Now, it may well be that conceptions of time are radically culture-specific, and that there are quite distinctive African traditions on the subject – the work of Johannes Fabian (1983), John S. Mbiti (1969) and D.A. Masolo (1994: 108–19) offers important theoretical reflections on this point. Pennington, however, is claiming that Africans and those of African descent are inherently inept at tasks requiring accurate measurement, efficiency, goal-directed future planning. Their minds simply don't work that way. No colonialist vapourings about 'the African Mind' could possibly be more disparaging than her supposedly affirmative account.

Extensive, and maybe excessive, publicity has been given to the science section of the Portland African-American Baseline Essays, introduced in 1987 for junior-school teachers in Portland, Oregon; subsequently adopted in several other cities, debated in many more, and subjected to amused or outraged media attention. The science 'Baseline Essay' is by the same Hunter Havelin Adams III who contributed some of the most ridiculous claims to the Van Sertima collection on African science (1983). He supposedly believes, on the basis of the Horus-falcon 'glider' mentioned above, that the ancient Egyptians had made extensive use of full-size gliders. Ancient Egyptians, in his view, also had a wide range of psychic powers and 'a possible understanding of quantum physics and gravitational theory' (Gross and Levitt 1994: 208).

Adams was described as a research scientist, 'advancing the state of the art of proton beam detection and diagnostic equipment' at the Argonne National Laboratory's Atomic Accelerator. It was later revealed that in fact he was an industrial hygiene technician at Argonne, did no research there, and had no formal education beyond a high-school diploma (Gross and Levitt 1994: 209). The tendency to claim or imply grand-sounding academic careers and affiliations seems to be quite widespread among Afrocentrists. One notes Maulana Karenga's former Directorship of the Institute of Pan-African Studies, Los Angeles; that Cress Welsing is Clinical Director, Paul Robeson School for Growth and Development; Clyde Ahmad Winters is founder and head of the Uthman Dan Fodio Institute; Abena Walker, chief consultant (at a reported fee of $250,000) to Washington DC's Afrocentric school programme, directed and awarded herself degrees from her own Pan-African University. Most sonorously of all, Yosef Ben-Jochannen was 'Senior Professor of Egyptology, First World Alliance School of African Thought, Harlem' (Addai-Sebo and Wong 1988: 315). One wonders how many of these institutions exist other than as letterheads.

On the one hand, this inflation of titles testifies to the long exclusion of many highly able African-Americans from more conventionally prestigious appointments and genuine institutions of higher learning. On the other, it partakes of the equally long tradition of charlatanry in American public life, with its endless litany of fake degrees (some available for export, as with 'Dr' Ian Paisley), fake religious ordinations and, among blacks, fake African princes and sages. Perhaps the most splendid piece of such *chutzpah* in the history of American Africanism was the ethnic entrepreneur who, during the 1930s Abyssinian crisis, reportedly sought to raise money by claiming to be an emissary from Abyssinia, while going under the name Wyxzewixard

S.J. Challaoueliziczese (Essien-Udom 1964: 319). It would be tempting, were it not so callous, to say that anyone who believed in a name like that *deserved* to have their money stolen.[3]

The other major tendency in Afrocentric claims about science is an older, less absurd but in its extremes sadder phenomenon than the attribution of any and every discovery to ancient Egyptians or Yoruba: the sometimes desperate search for black contributions to modern science and technology: 'contributory history' at its most extreme. The Van Sertima volume includes several instances of this kind, notably essays by John Henrik Clarke and by Van Sertima himself.

The pioneering figure most often fastened upon is George Washington Carver, a plant biologist who researched at Booker T. Washington's accommodationist Tuskegee Institute. Not only is Carver's actual significance as a scientist routinely overstated, but – as the prominent African-American historian of science Kenneth R. Manning notes – the focus on him has some highly dubious facets:

> Carver ... espoused the traits of humility, diligence and manual dexterity that whites appreciated in blacks.... Carver's work was inventive, rather than scientifically creative; product-oriented, rather than pressing to new theoretical heights; and carried out in the black community with few if any intrusions into the white. Carver, white scientists might have opined, 'knew his place' and accepted it. (K. Manning 1993: 328)

In other words, Carver was a perfect analogue to the political role of his boss, Washington. Men such as William Augustus Hinton, Elmer Imes or Ernest Everett Just, whose creative and theoretical achievements were greater, are relatively neglected – they just don't fit the populist proclivities of Afro-American cultural nationalism.

John Henrik Clarke's enumeration of 'the African-American inventors that we have with good records' includes such utterly marginal figures as Benjamin Banneker, who 'literally, made the first clock in the United States' (Addai-Sebo and Wong 1988: 73–4) – the implication being, presumably, either that no one had ever built a clock on American soil during the colonial period, or that Banneker woke up one day and said 'Hey! They're signing the Declaration of Independence in an hour or two. If I get working on those flywheels right now I'll be in the history books!' Clarke also includes one James Fontaine, who supposedly had the idea of making soldiers' trousers out of tent-cloth so that they would last longer (ibid.: 74). Quite why these feats qualified Banneker or Fontaine as 'inventors' or 'scientists' is impossible to tell. Proclaiming them as such merely devalues the achievements of genuine Afro-American scientists – of the handful of black American men and women who, before the very recent past, surmounted all obstacles to achieve significant, often unrecognized, scientific or technical innovations. Banneker, descended from both African slaves and English indentured servants, was in fact a remarkable figure whose genuine achievements against vast odds are only diminished by his being appropriated to mythographies like Clarke's. He was a town surveyor (one of the original planners of Washington, DC), publicist, fighter for racial justice, and talented self-taught mathematician and astronomer. He was *not*, however, a scientist in any conventionally understood sense of the word.

Such fanciful appropriations are, if anything, even more insulting to the work of the many men and women of African descent who, now that *some* of the old barriers have come down, are working and making major contributions in all scientific fields worldwide. This kind of ethnic-absolutist puffing would have been – and for the living often evidently is – thoroughly distasteful to most practising African-American scientists themselves. As Manning says:

> The degree to which black scientists devoted themselves to this model of 'pure' science, untrammeled by extraneous considerations of race or culture, is quite remarkable. Not always with complete success, they insisted on being called 'scientists', *never* 'Negro scientists'. The racial qualifier was to them an insidious, obfuscating element. (Manning 1993: 328: original emphasis)

Although he notes that the neutrality of the profession was, in American circumstances, often breached in practice, and that black scientists were discriminated against in numerous subtle ways, Manning broadly shares his subjects' views:

> [T]he notion of a Negro writer, dancer, musician, poet, lawyer, or historian carries with it certain connotations or assumptions about the individual's work. Some of these assumptions may be legitimate, others not. A cultural basis, perhaps an ethnic perspective may sometimes be discerned within the work of someone working in any of these fields. But, in the abstract, there can be no such entity as Negro science – no Negro physics, chemistry, or biology, no peculiarly Negro way of gathering and analyzing scientific data or of solving problems. (ibid.: 332–3)

It is this cultural neutrality, and even the aspiration to it, which Afrocentric theories seek to dissipate. In the past, and on the whole, the claims of African-American cultural nationalists have made no inroads into the actual substance, the subject matter, of scientific research – their procedures and interests, not to mention their lack of relevant expertise, made it impossible for them to do so. They could only laud, or exaggerate, the achievements and influence of individual black researchers without saying anything significant, let alone prescriptive, about their work. As Gross and Levitt say, when one reads the nascent literature of Afrocentric science, one is struck by the great quantity of Afrocentrism, and equally by the remarkable paucity of science (1994: 205). An attempt is now being made to change that, in so far as the claims by Asante and others about 'soul as method', 'affective epistemologies', and Afrocentrism as holistic approach to knowledge are

evidently intended to apply to the natural sciences as well as social studies
and humanities. Few, if any, practising scientists, however, are likely to take
such claims seriously, and that is all to the good.

Notes

1. The author of this set of claims, Beatrice Lumpkin, fortified them in a simultaneously
published novel, *Senefar and Hatshepsut*, which she called a tale of 'Egyptian genius'
(Lumpkin 1983b). No very clear boundaries seemed to be observed between the historical
article and the avowedly fictional effusion. See also Lumpkin (1994); and the related
claims in Amen (1993).

2. Harding does not appear to have substantiated her unqualified endorsement of Van
Sertima's book by looking at *any* other writing on ancient Egyptian and African
technologies or knowledges. She seems, moreover, to accept equally uncritically Afrocentric claims about the Pharaonic Egyptian population, referring to 'the period when Egypt
was occupied by "Africans" (before the eleventh-century spread of Islamic culture)' (1991:
223–4), and to Walter Rodney's arguments about colonially induced African degeneration
(ibid.: 227–31). Her further forays into the field (Harding 1994, 1997), though they
provide very extensive lists of sources on the 'sociology of science' and 'science and
colonialism', continue to show a surprising lack of curiosity about the actual substance of
the 'non-Western knowledges' towards whose value she gestures.

3. For further examples, see Gerald Early's pioneering little study of Afro-American
magicians, most of whom seem to have claimed African, and usually royal, birth (Early
1994).

Psychology, Race and Magic Melanin

Many of Afrocentrism's major themes, especially claims about distinctive psychological and emotional characteristics, derive – as we have seen – from 1960s and 1970s cultural nationalism. The 'New Black Psychology' of that era, led by figures like Alvin Poussaint, Charles W. Thomas and Wade Nobles, was heavily influenced by Fanon, and emphasized a need to create positive black self-images and self-esteem. Pride in one's appearance and in black cultural creativity in America was heavily stressed; pride in African history, at this stage, less so. The latter could, however, be seen as a natural corollary of the demand for more positive collective self-perceptions. Together with this appeared the view propounded by some, but not all, 1960s black radical psychologists that there existed a distinctive 'black personality'. It was an idea which was, of course, taken over direct from Senghor's *négritude*, and not really compatible with Fanon's stance; in some Afro-American thought, none the less, the two were combined. All these streams of thinking flowed into later Afrocentric ideas on psychology, which, however, have taken them very much further in the directions of unanimism, essentialism and assertions of inherent black psychic superiority than the earlier theories did – though Wade Nobles, who was already pontificating in the 1970s about the need to revive an 'African philosophical orientation' to fight 'scientific colonialism' (quoted in Van Deburg 1992: 59), and had progressed in the 1980s to expounding the crucial relevance of ancient Egyptian thought to modern black psychology (Nobles 1986a, b), forms a point of contact and continuity.[1]

A quite contrary current of thinking about African-American psychology has also retained some currency in nationalist circles – one which, far from proclaiming black superiority in mental and emotional health, asserts that these are marked by extreme, congenital weaknesses. The intention of such seemingly self-defaming arguments appears to be twofold: to underline, in the sharpest possible way, the damage done by slavery and its legacies; and to argue that such defects can be overcome only by embracing the particular political or religious solutions that the writer advocates. This strategy appears widespread in 'born again' religious circles of all kinds, certainly not only Christian ones: one of its most extreme exponents is the Black

Muslim publicist Na'im Akbar. Adopting the widespread trope of comparing slavery to the Nazi Shoah (a device which has, of course, provoked recurrent hostility and misunderstanding between black and Jewish groups), he argues that the enslavement of Africans was the most traumatizing experience in human history: 'including the Nazi atrocities at Auschwitz which were fleeting and direct, destroying bodies, but essentially leaving the collective mind intact'. And the abolition of chattel slavery was succeeded by a form of mental slavery still worse in its effects (Akbar 1984: 1). Describing its legacies, Akbar proceeds to a quite remarkable list of alleged psychic disabilities among Afro-Americans: laziness (ibid.: 9–12), obsession with status and showy consumption (12–15), disrespect for leadership (16–19), clownish behaviour (20–22), inferiority complexes (23–6), divided communities (26–30), weak families (30–35) and internally divisive colour complexes (35–40). The charge-sheet is remarkably similar to that drawn up against blacks by the classic expressions of white American racism. Akbar is also the author of some of the wildest Afrocentric claims about the wisdom of ancient Egypt, proclaiming, for instance, that it was 'both technologically and spiritually' far in advance of twentieth-century societies (Akbar 1994: 341).

The rise of the 'melanin scholars' can no doubt be attributed partly to reaction against such rhetorics. In the 1980s and 1990s a current thesis attributing extraordinary powers to melanin – the chemical which pigments skin – gained ground.[2] The notion of melanin as crucial to social destiny is not new. Jean Price-Mars, while expressing due scepticism about the concept of human 'races' (1959: 57–9), none the less concluded an address to a *Présence Africaine* conference with a peroration which linked environmental determinism with the notion of Africans as distinguished and privileged by the melanin in their skins:

> To what, then, did Africa owe the enjoyment of such a great privilege millions of years ago if not to the mildness of her sunny climate at a time when the glaciation of other continents rendered them inadequate, if not impossible, as abodes? There is in Africa's past an inclination towards hospitality and creation which the Melano-Africans claim as their heritage. . . .
>
> For the Melanic type . . . which other men have called the scum of humanity, this type has awakened from a long sleep of expectation to demand its rightful place among its brothers by blood and by destiny. (ibid.: 65)

Present-day 'melanin scholars' proclaim significance for that humble substance far beyond anything Price-Mars's rational sensibility could have imagined. Dubois Phillip McGee, in one of the earlier expressions of the melanist view, asserts: 'we are convinced that the absence of melanin is directly linked with the malfunctioning of the central nervous system' (1976: 220), but admits that the supposed relationship is 'poorly understood'. Later protagonists have dropped that residue of caution. Frances Cress

Welsing, probably the most influential, thinks that melanin is 'perhaps the most fantastic stuff on the planet. It allows for the special spiritual qualities and emotional refinements black people have ... melanin is the neuro-chemical basis of what we call "soul" ... sort of like a hydrogen bomb at the genetic level' (Person-Lynn 1996: 81–2). According to one of their sharpest critics, Bernard Ortiz de Montellano:

> They claim that melanin is a superconductor, that it absorbs all frequencies of the electromagnetic spectrum, that it can convert sound energy to light energy reversibly, and that it can function as a minicomputer to process information ... people with high melanin levels have better muscular co-ordination (which makes them better athletes), are mentally superior, have unusual faculties, such as ESP, and are influenced by the magnetic fields of other humans and of the earth. (Montellano 1992: 163)

According to Amos Wilson: 'Black superiority in the areas of mental development, neurological functioning, and psychomotor development ... (are) all related to the possession of a high level of melanin' (quoted in Schlesinger 1991: 64). In Cress Welsing's version, white people's fear of the melanin-rich (quite a rational fear, given the latter's innate superiority) led Europeans to persecute Africans throughout history, culminating in the present, deliberately created 'AIDS Holocaust' (Addai-Sebo and Wong 1988: 289–99; Cress Welsing 1991: 291–301).

As Montellano notes (1992), many of the more extreme 'melanin scholarship' claims are difficult to document in the usual way, for they are rarely committed to print but, rather, circulate in public lecture form and as broadcast talks on independent black radio stations. Much of his evidence comes from the latter source. Such information is also now broadcast on the Internet, where the 'Melanin Library', run by psychologist Richard King and operated as part of 'United Brothers and United Sisters Communi-cations Systems, Inc.', advertises itself as a 'Melanin research center', a 'repository of books, research articles, theses, audio and video tapes and other information' and a 'Speakers Bureau for Guest and Keynote Speakers about information related to Melanin'.[3]

However, some of their material does appear on the bookstalls (apart from the writers discussed here, see Barnes [1988]; Finch [1990]; Moore [1992a]). Richard King has developed the most elaborate published theory on these lines, a theory which combines pseudo-science with mysticism, starting from the latter. The primary substance involved in all life processes, says King, is carbon – which is, of course, black. Blackness, as the origin of life, is thus divine, as ancient African civilizations recognized:

> These original titans found that all life came from a black seed, all life was rooted in blackness, all things possessed a memory of their collective ancestors. Blackness, the universal solvent of all was seen as the one reality from which spun the threads of the loom of life ... black was the color of

carbon, the key atom found in all living matter of our world; carbon atoms linked to form black melanin, the first chemical that could capture light and reproduce itself, the chemical key to life; and the brain itself was found to be centered around black neuromelanin. Inner vision, intuition, creative genius, and spiritual illumination were all found to be dependent upon pineal gland blood borne chemical messengers that controlled skin color and opened the hidden door to the darkness of the collective unconscious mind ... to universal knowledge of the past, present, and future. (King 1990: 13–14)[4]

So – given this literally holy perfection of blackness, which the Ancients well understood, how did pale people come into existence? As some Africans migrated north, they found that in colder climates with less sunlight high-melanin skin prevented the photosynthesis of Vitamin D, which humans need for calcium (ibid.: 57–9). Natural selection thus favoured the occasional lighter-skinned mutants or albinos, who came to prevail in European populations. But they and their descendants, naturally, paid a high price for thus surviving in the icy, sunless north. With less melanin, their pineal glands functioned less actively, which in turn meant that their mental, emotional and spiritual powers atrophied (ibid.: 60–64: one may note again the close congruence with latter-day Euro-racist ideas, as expressed by John Baker or Philippe Rushton). With only the left sides of their brains working, they emphasized rationalist and materialist values to compensate for their loss of intuition, creativity and spirituality. They also became aggressive and competitive. And they could not bear to be reminded of what they had lost, so they came to hate and fear black people. King therefore thinks that whites react to blackness with a sense of trauma, because the sight of black people reminds them of the loss of their culture and spiritual consciousness: they stigmatize as evil those whose superiority they unconsciously know and resent (ibid.: 63–4).

King's theory not only explains white aggression, lack of spirituality, racism, and so on, not only indicates why whites are inferior people, but suggests that they are not proper people at all: they are an aberrant, mutant breed, *Untermenschen* in the fullest sense. Such premises are, of course, ridiculous fantasies which bear no relation to the state of geneticists' knowledge about melanin (for admirable summaries, see Montellano [1993]; Wills [1994]). Skin-colour differences are governed not by different amounts of particular alleles, but by tiny genetic variations in the way the relevant genes are regulated. The brain is not 'centred round' neurome-lanin, which is one of thousands of compounds in the human brain, and scientists still have little idea what its purpose is. They have found suggestive but inconclusive associations between levels of melanin in the brain and such apparently disconnected traits as greater resistance to jet-lag and susceptibility to Parkinson's Disease (Steve Jones 1996: 193, 197). So it is not *impossible* that it has all the mystic powers King and others claim – it is just an extremely unlikely piece of ideologically charged speculation. Moreover, there is little – if any – correlation between levels of skin melanin and levels of neuromelanin, so that whatever further mysterious properties the latter may turn out to have, they will have nothing much to do with concepts of race. Individual melanin granules, by the way, are not even black, but mainly a deep golden-yellow!

The same conclusions are reached by Joseph Baldwin (or, as he has renamed himself, Kobi Kazembe Kalongi Kambon) as by King and Cress Welsing. Baldwin/Kambon – whom we have already encountered praising Idi Amin and directing self-confirming 'research' on Afrocentric values and male–female relationships – apparently believes that the intrinsic abnormality of the melanin-deficient, their awareness of being 'outside of nature', accounts for their pathological behaviour across time. To be white is to be unnatural, to exist in an antagonistic relationship with nature. 'The sense of being "other", "not natural", "apart from", of being born as "disordered" caused overwhelming fear, anxiety, and insecurity' (Ani 1994: 472, citing Kambon's presentation at the First National Conference on Global White Supremacy, Chicago, October 1990).

The magic powers of melanin are also said to account for ancient Egyptian, other African and subsequent black scientific genius. According to Cress Welsing (in papers which, perhaps significantly, she chose not to publish or to republish in her collection *The Isis Papers*), the Dogon people of Mali had been enabled by their mystic melanin to know a huge range of astronomical facts otherwise inaccessible to people without advanced infrared telescopes and other late-twentieth-century technology. They knew that the earth and other planets revolve round the sun, that they do so in elliptical rather than circular orbits, that Jupiter has four satellites, that Sirius has a small faint companion star, and so on. How could they thus leap ahead of all other 'primitive peoples' and of modern science in their knowledge of the heavens? Because the melanin in their pineal glands enabled them to sense it all, says Cress Welsing. She also claims that this companion star, Sirius B, acts as a storehouse of energy and information transmitted from earth: people with high melanin levels can tap into all that information, which helps to account for their superiority over whites (Montellano 1992: 165–6). The same assertions are advanced by Hunter Havelin Adams, author of the much-derided Portland Science Baseline Essay – and the claims about the Dogon's astronomical achievements, though not about their supposed melanic source, are endorsed without demur in a recent major multiculturalist textbook (Shohat and Stam 1994: 58).

In fact none of these ideas about the Dogon's advanced astronomical knowledge is original. The French ethnographer Marcel Griaule had presented them all, drawn from his interviews with the blind Dogon sage Ogotemmeli, in the 1940s (Griaule 1965; Griaule and Dieterlen 1965; see the critical discussions in Masolo 1994: 68–83, Mudimbe 1988: 141–3). Montellano suggests that Cress Welsing and Adams may not have picked them up directly from Griaule, but from R.G. Temple's book *The Sirius Mystery* (1976), which argued that visitors from other planets gave the

Dogon their knowledge; while – as with so much else in the Afrocentric pantheon – Cheikh Anta Diop had given an airing to these ideas (without their more mystical elements) too (1991: 313–23). The beliefs taken over from Griaule did indeed seem to suggest the presence of startlingly advanced ideas about astronomy among a low-tech and non-literate African people – unless, as has been suggested, the Dogon incorporated European astronomical knowledge, gleaned from travellers, into their mythology sometime during the later nineteenth century (see Mudimbe 1988: 13–15 for arguments for and against this hypothesis), or unless there was a deliberate hoax by Griaule's informant. Personally, I find the last idea rather attractive: the notion of an elderly, highly intelligent man, who is being quizzed (and no doubt condescended to) by a colonial researcher about his ancestral 'primitive' knowledge, deciding to fox him by throwing in ideas he has gained from his reading or hearing about modern science.

All that Cress Welsing and the other melanin scholars have added to Griaule is the 'explanation' that melanin in the pineal gland enabled the Dogon to know all this. Actually, when one thinks about it, such an explanation is not particularly flattering to the Dogon. It suggests that if the Dogon did indeed make better sense of the stars than did Europeans before Copernicus and Galileo, or even before our century, this was not because some of them were notably intelligent, observant people. It was just their glands working: they couldn't help it. (And why the Dogon, rather than all or any other Africans? They show no evident sign of having more melanin than their neighbours; while in many scholars' eyes the very existence of a distinct Dogon 'tribe' is largely a product of colonial categorizations.)

Cress Welsing also asserts that George Washington Carver, the pioneering African-American biochemist, knew what plants to experiment on because they 'talked to his melanin and told him what they were good for' as he strolled in the woods near Tuskegee (quoted Montellano in 1992: 165). As Montellano caustically comments, teaching such ideas to African-American schoolchildren could be deeply damaging: it would implant a belief that they do not need to study, but can 'Let my melanin pick up the vibes' (ibid.: 165).

Leonard Jeffries, also associated with the melanin theorists, achieved notoriety by drawing in his lectures and broadcasts on the theory that whites are 'Ice People' and blacks 'Sun People', their collective personalities determined by evolutionary pressures in the distant past. This basic notion has a long history, and has been put to relatively rational uses – as we have seen, for instance, in the writings of Cheikh Anta Diop. Marcus Garvey, too, had clearly picked up this idea from somewhere in the 1920s (Hill and Bair 1987: 269). The particular and far more extreme theory to which Jeffries was alluding, however, had been expounded first in a book called *The Iceman Inheritance: Prehistoric Sources of Western Man's Racism, Sexism and Aggression* (Bradley 1978/1991).

The Iceman Inheritance was written by a white Canadian author – albeit US-born, and boasting of a distant trace of Cherokee ancestry – one Michael

Bradley. Bradley has been a prolific purveyor of arcane historical theories drawing on a wide range of occult and mystical ideas. In *The Columbus Conspiracy*, for instance, he suggests that the real reason for Columbus's voyage to the Americas was to establish a refuge for a secret pan-religious cult associated with the Cathars, with the Holy Grail myth, with direct biological descendants of Jesus Christ, the Knights Templar, and latterly with such unexpected initiates as Franklin D. Roosevelt and Canadian politician T.C. Douglas (Bradley 1992a). Although Bradley does not identify this cult as Masonic, its similarity to the ideas developed by some Masonic writers about their society as a repository of ancient wisdom transcending religious divisions and carrying a mission to establish worldwide peace and harmony will be evident. These ideas, like Bradley's, have had considerable appeal to many present-day Afrocentrists; and in *The Columbus Conspiracy* Bradley also endorsed claims about pre-Columbian African voyages to America.

It is Michael Bradley's theories of prehistory, however, which have had the greatest appeal to Afrocentric publicists. In *The Iceman Inheritance* Bradley argued as follows:

Modern Europeans are descended from Neanderthal man, whereas other human races' ancestors are of quite different stocks.[5] They have inherited psychological and behaviour patterns which first developed to cope with the extreme cold Neanderthals encountered during the Ice Ages. The harsh environment made them unusually aggressive, selfish and territorial. Physically, they became heavy, hairy, short-limbed and 'grotesque' in appearance (Bradley 1978/1991: 90). Incidentally, part of Bradley's evidence for this comes from supposed twentieth-century sightings of surviving Neanderthals in the Caucasus (ibid.: 99–102); a view also advanced by another highly eccentric present-day writer, Myra Shackley (1983). They also developed extreme sexual dimorphism – that is, males and females looked more different from one another than they did in other races. Therefore: 'each tended to regard the other as something of a distinct species. I think that there may have been grave difficulties in each sex recognizing the other to be completely human' (Bradley 1978/1991: 122). This explains why the two sexes among 'Caucasians': 'have never really got used to each other, never really completely trusted each other' (ibid.: 123). This incompatibility also heightened the general xenophobia of the European character.[6]

Neanderthals additionally, according to Bradley, developed an aggressive, territorial conception of time, involving a desperate urge to outdo the achievements of the past and a fear that the future – and thus their own offspring – might outdo them. This made them innovative, but ambivalent about procreation. (Compare Cress Welsing's belief that whites dislike their children because the latter show to them, and perpetuate, their own melanin-deficient and therefore inferior state.) Since whites thus fear both the opposite sex and children – not to mention the fact that the males have shrunken genitals and the females, so Bradley implies, oversized vaginas (108–10) – they are characteristically undersexed. Sexual energy is displaced on to violent aggression against others. The only hope that they could become decent members of the human family lies in their turning more of their energies to sex and sensuality.

Perhaps it hardly needs to be said that almost every element of Bradley's account is fantastic. Although, as we have seen, some scientists continue to believe that modern humanity developed from several distinct population groups in different parts of the Old World, none of the 'multiregionalists' (like Milford Wolpoff: 1989a, b): who propose this claims that modern Europeans are solely, directly or mainly descended from Neanderthals. Moreover, to this non-expert reader at least, the weight of evidence in the argument between the multiregionalists and the 'out of Africa' school seems to lie heavily with the latter. The whole notion of Neanderthals as literal 'Ice People' is clearly erroneous, since the furthest extent of Late Pleistocene glaciation hardly overlaps at all with the known areas of Neanderthal settlement: though that is not to say that some Neanderthal physical traits did not result from adaptation to cold climates (Stringer and Gamble 1993: 10–11). Neanderthal physical appearance probably bore little relation to Bradley's image – as Stringer and Gamble show, the classic picture of the hirsute, beetle-browed, stooped, thuggish 'caveman' is a product of Victorian stereotyping, heavily tinged with racial ideology, rather than of the archaeological evidence (ibid.: 16–33, and Plates 1–18; see also Trinkaus and Shipman 1993: 398–410). Even the wide Neanderthal female hips of which Bradley makes so much, associating them with childbearing and with sexual incompatibilities passed on into the European present, become less significant on closer inspection. *Both* sexes of Neanderthals had wide hips: the trait had nothing to do with 'extreme sexual dimorphism' or with childbearing. Finally, there is simply no evidence whatsoever for Bradley's wild claims about Neanderthal psychology and cultural behaviour.

What is operating in the thought of David Bradley and his Afrocentric fellow-travellers is the kind of environmental–ancestral determinism which was widespread in certain versions of nineteenth-century European racial 'science' – and also, incidentally, in the racial theories proposed by some medieval Arab writers.[7] It had been common for anthropologists, wedded to notions of white superiority, to argue that Africa's environment acted to block social development there. Henry Fairfield Osborn asserted: 'The evolution of man is arrested or retrogressive . . . in tropical and semi-tropical regions, where natural fruits abound and human effort – individual and racial – immediately ceases' (quoted in Lewin 1987: 308). In 1933 Robert Broom echoed this sentiment: 'It seems impossible for the higher types of man even to live for any length of time in the tropics without degenerating. . . . Apparently a steady improvement of the brain was only possible in a temperate climate' (ibid.: 308).[8]

Much more recently, John Baker, Richard Lynn and Carleton Coon have revived similar ideas, while Philippe Rushton, too, has proposed his own renovated version of the climatic-determinist theory. Indeed, there are striking similarities among Cheikh Anta Diop's 'two cradle theory', Michael

Bradley's 'iceman hypothesis', and the racist ideas of Lynn and Rushton (see, for example, Lynn 1991), while Bradley explicitly aligns himself with Coon and with the older polygenicism of Franz Weidenreich (Bradley 1978/1991: ix).

In the contemporary Afrocentric version, however, rather than producing a claim for white or Arab intellectual supremacy, early environment accounts for black moral and spiritual superiority. The founding belief is that Africans maintained a solidaristic, sociable, life-affirming character in their hospitable original environment; whereas in the hostile climate and circumstances of the north – or more specifically, in the Ice Ages during which European 'cavemen' are erroneously thought to have evolved – whites developed a correspondingly individualistic, selfish, aggressive disposition.

As history and science, this is evidently laughable. More significant is that the theories, and underlying assumptions, here are strikingly parallel to those of much nineteenth-century European racial discourse: the similarities between Cress Welsing and Gobineau are especially close. The science – even the popular science – of the late twentieth century has little time for such views. It is true that there is – and will no doubt long continue to be – serious argument between those (like Robert Ardrey) who emphasize aggression and competition as the keys to early human development and those (such as Richard Leakey) who urge instead the paramount importance to evolution of peaceable co-operation. But these are arguments about the origins of humanity *as a whole*; no serious scholar suggests that one or the other bundle of such characteristics marks off 'races' from one another – no serious scholar, that is, unless one regards latter-day Euro-racists like Lynn, Baker and Coon, or certain American Afrocentrists, as deserving that title. We shall see below the assiduity with which some of the latter press such essentialist – if not racist – claims.

Notes

1. St Clair Drake (1987: 107–14) offers a thorough bibliography and literature review of these various currents.

2. The best critical accounts of these ideas I have seen are Montellano (1991, 1992), and especially his longer and more technical (1993). See also Wills (1994); Steve Jones (1996: 184–97).

3. I am indebted to Marek Kohn for this reference.

4. Elsewhere King has sought to underpin his claims about the preternatural wisdom of ancient Africans by way of a quite bizarre 'analysis' of the finds from Tutankhamun's tomb, which, he believes, prove the Egyptians' profound knowledge of the mystic powers radiating from the pineal gland, melatonin, and melanin (King 1994).

5. There is an implicit anti-Semitism in *The Iceman Inheritance*, signalled by Bradley's view that the 'purest' descendants of the Caucasian-Neanderthals are modern Jews. A far more explicit and elaborate statement of Bradley's case for the peculiarly asocial, aggressive and iniquitous influence of the Jews is made in his more recent *Chosen People from the Caucasus* (1992b).

6. For more balanced – though still controversial – views of the Neanderthals, see Shreeve (1995); Stringer and Gamble (1993).

7. As Aziz Al-Azmeh (1992) shows, numerous medieval Arab writers, drawing on a theory of climatic zones which seems originally to have been proposed by the Greeks, saw black Africans as suffering from mental deficiency resulting from life in excessive heat and dryness: 'Negroes therefore tended to be given to erratic behaviour, to levity, to prodigious sexuality, and to be much disposed to dance and rhythm, all because of the afore-mentioned effects of the sun' (1992: 9).

8. This claim refers to a long-running colonial debate about the allegedly damaging effects, physical and moral, of living in tropical climates: see Kennedy (1990); Livingstone (1994).

Polemics and Prejudices: Sex, Race, Religion and Afrocentrism

Much Afrocentric and related writing slips from ethnocentrism and neo-conservatism into full-blown racism, sexism and homophobia. Such distasteful aspects of the movement have already been alluded to at several points, especially in relation to the 'melanin scholars', but it is necessary in conclusion to return to these themes in more detail.

In one sense, the single feature which most starkly marks out Afrocentric writing on history and culture is a single-minded insistence on the centrality of race to all questions about human society. As we have seen, the general tendency of modern scholarship in all fields and almost all parts of the world since 1945 has been to question – if not flatly deny – the reality or relevance of the concept of race. In the West, there have been two main exceptions to this. One is among scholars of the radical right, ranging from the overtly racist 'science' of a Richard Lynn or Roger Pearson to the views of a Charles Murray, with their now substantial presence in the mainstream of intellectual debate. The other is the Afrocentric tradition, whose proponents have often insisted – following Cheikh Anta Diop, although his stance, like that of Du Bois or Jean Price-Mars, cannot fairly be called racist – that denial of the reality of race is merely a Eurocentric obfuscation designed to undermine African pride. The Afrocentrist amateur historian Legrand H. Clegg exemplifies the in-your-face version of that attitude. Attacking 'the new anthropological party line' which refuses the race concept, he proclaims that, by contrast:

> we shall not only include race as an integral part of our historical writings, but we shall prominently focus on it whenever and wherever the truth can be told until sincere men of science return the Black race to its former position of respect and reverence on the earth. (1989: 255)

Such a position may be obscurantist, but it is not in itself a charter for intolerance – even if it might easily open the way to one. Overt racial bigotry is most evident, and most notorious, in Louis Farrakhan's Nation of Islam. Accusations and counter-charges about the anti-white and, more specifically, anti-Jewish sentiments expressed by Farrakhan and his followers have been a media staple for years, and I shall not try even to begin to summarize that media debate. Among the books sold and recommended by the Farrakhan movement are not only such reputable works as Rodney's *How Europe Underdeveloped Africa*, and Carter Woodson's *The Mis-Education of the Negro*, but George James's *Stolen Legacy*, the Nation's own *The Secret Relationship between Blacks and Jews*, billed as 'a true account of Jewish involvement in the 400-year plus Black Holocaust compiled from actual Jewish documents', and Bradley's *The Iceman Inheritance*. This last work, as we have seen, has become a central text for the disreputable 'melanin scholars'.[1] The most publicized facet of this organization's racism is its anti-Semitism, which is indeed vehement.[2] The objects of prejudice, however, do sometimes shift and broaden. A cartoon in the issue of *The Final Call* immediately following the 1992 Los Angeles riots depicted 'Ghetto Merchants', money-laden, fleeing the burning city. Once the stereotypes would doubtless have been Jewish ones: now there is an Arab, a Korean and an Indian (*The Final Call*, 5 June 1992). Despite such occasional evidence of scattergun xenophobia, controversy has centred on an anonymously authored book published by Louis Farrakhan's movement, *The Secret Relationship between Blacks and Jews* (Nation of Islam 1991). The book is credited to the 'Nation of Islam Historical Research Department', an entity which has had no traceable existence or publications apart from this work (see Gardell 1996: 260–61). Under the guise of a scholarly treatise, and utilizing (though often misquoting or otherwise abusing) a very wide range of sources, this is in reality a violently anti-Jewish tract. It massively exaggerates the role of various Atlantic Jewish communities in slavery – a role which was in reality minuscule, with the partial exceptions of Jewish investors in the Dutch West India Company (Jewish investment there having been estimated as at different times between 0.5 per cent and 10 per cent of the total, while the company itself controlled, at its peak, a maximum 16 per cent of the Atlantic slave trade [D. Davis 1994: 15]), a handful of Jewish plantation owners in Surinam (Dutch Guiana), and a not precisely quantifiable number of Portuguese Marranos (Christians of actual, alleged or partial Jewish ancestry, who formed a significant portion of Portugal's and her colonies' populations after the Inquisition).[3]

More revealing still of the book's real nature is the repeated suggestion that Jewish involvement in slavery (no less and no more blameworthy than the far greater Christian and Muslim embroilment, and hugely overstated by mis-citation and innuendo) stems from some uniquely evil racial-religious characteristic, and has subsequently been concealed by the all-too-predictable conspiracy of media and financial power. Yet *The Secret Relationship* is a far cleverer work of propaganda than its critics seem to assume. An impressive amount of research – albeit almost entirely in secondary sources – has gone into its compilation, however egregiously the results are then misused. It does not directly claim, as responses from the Anti-Defamation League and elsewhere asserted, that Jews are 'genetically predisposed' towards the exploitation of blacks; though the unwary reader might easily draw such a conclusion from it, and that, no doubt, was the anonymous author's intention. It draws attention dozens of times to instances across the centuries and the continents when Jews were accused of rapacious and dishonest business dealings. It never *quite* directly says that such accusations were true, or that they reflect a noxious, invariant pattern of Jewish racial behaviour. Nor, of course, does it say that they were *not* true: it just leaves the reader to conclude that such multifarious and insistent charges must be solidly based.

Charges of anti-Semitism in relation to Afrocentrism have been almost as pointed, and as bitterly contested, in the context of the activities of two academics, Leonard Jeffries and Tony Martin. Jeffries, as we have seen, is no scholar. He has published little, and storms over his public statements have related to speeches and media outbursts rather than to writings in even pseudo-academic form. Tony Martin is a somewhat different matter. He has been a prolific author, notably on the life and ideas of Marcus Garvey.

Yet in some respects Martin, who teaches at the elite Wellesley College, must be seen as falling broadly under the same heading as Jeffries – indeed, it would seem, increasingly so. He could, for instance, proclaim that *all* culture and learning in Europe throughout its history came from Africa, whether through early Egyptian influences or the eighth-century 'African invasion' of Spain – a more sweeping assertion than almost any made by Asante:

> To be sure there was learning in some parts of Europe before the Africans invaded Spain – there was learning in Greece and in Rome, and those parts of Europe which were nearest Africa and which historically came under Africa's civilising influence, but it might possibly be stressing (*sic*) a point to say that more distant parts of Europe like England, Scotland, Germany and so on had any learning worth talking about before the Africans brought that learning to Europe. (Addai-Sebo and Wong 1988: 136)

Martin's impressive list of publications on Marcus Garvey and his movement, most substantial of them his *Race First* (1976), have been marked by an uncritical, cheerleading attitude towards their subject; but also by solid research. His embroilment in controversy has resulted from work outside his speciality, and especially from his teaching of an outline course in African-American History at Wellesley. For this, his reading assignments to students apparently included *The Secret Relationship between Blacks and Jews*. It is alleged that he persistently supported and amplified the book's claims in his teaching, and pressed students to do so also. Naturally, no one who was not present in Professor Martin's classroom at the relevant times can truly judge whether his teaching included anti-Semitic themes or remarks, as alleged. However, one can judge what is in the public domain, notably the poisonous little book which Martin issued about the controversy, entitled *The Jewish Onslaught* (Martin 1993). Here he not only engaged in unbroken categorical claims about the vicious and manipulative nature of 'the Jews', but went out of his way to scorn any idea that such claims might be true, if at all, only of 'some Jews': 'all kinds of Jews ... generalize about "the Jews" when it suits them. The "some Jews" business is yet another red herring and attempt at special rules for Jews' (ibid.: 37). The indiscriminate – indeed, ridiculous as well as bigoted – nature of Martin's own critique is well illustrated by his reprinting, under the title 'Jewish Hate Mail', just three letters addressed to him: one racist diatribe from an allegedly Jewish correspondent, one equally racist spiel expressing specifically, explicitly *Christian* views, and one entirely courteous critique of Martin's stance (ibid.: 108–10).

In classic Afrocentric style, Martin wields fantasized ideas about ancient history as if they referred to what happened five minutes ago. Thus, because the idea of a curse on the 'sons of Ham' derives from the Hebrew Torah/ Christian Old Testament, he proclaims: 'Now it is the turn of the Jews to retract, apologize and pay reparations for their invention of the Hamitic Myth, which killed many millions more than all the anti-Jewish pogroms and holocausts in Europe' (ibid.: 35).[4] One could continue indefinitely to detail the bigotries and absurdities of *The Jewish Onslaught*, but it would be too depressing to trace further the degeneration into racist fantasy of a formerly reputable, if one-eyed, scholar.

In the controversy over Martin, Afrocentrists seemed to close ranks in just the fashion some of them accused Jews, whites, Eurocentrists, and so on of doing. Asante, reviewing *The Jewish Onslaught*, lavished quite unstinted praise on this unpleasant outburst. It is, he said, 'a polemic of the highest order' – the finest by an Afro-American since Walker's *Appeal* of 1829 – 'a new literary event', a work of 'incredible power' (Asante 1994: 118). It is, said Asante, 'only by reading *The Jewish Onslaught* that one can fully appreciate the brilliant mind of Tony Martin' (ibid.: 119). By contrast, it should be noted that not only the vast majority of African-American political leaders, but such major black scholars as Henry Louis Gates (1992, 1994) and Cornel West (1993) have sharply repudiated all manifestations of black Judaeophobia.

Tendencies towards racial, gender and other group prejudices are not confined to the pseudo-Islamists or the lunatic fringe of Afrocentrism. Even Molefi Asante has also, it must be said, made disconcertingly bigoted statements. There is no overt sign of his being 'anti-white' in any sense of vulgar prejudice, or of identification with the wild beliefs about white genetic inferiority proposed by some Afrocentrists. He has several times – for instance in *Newsweek*, and in a sharp exchange with critic Diane Ravitch – insisted that Afrocentrism as a movement is entirely free from racism or ethnocentrism of any kind – though one must add that if he doesn't think his own theories are proudly, openly ethnocentric, then the word is meaningless to him (Asante 1991a, b). Asante has also dismissed any suggestion that there could be any trace of anti-white racism in his or any other African-American's thought – not on the widely held, if contestable, ground that the label 'racism' is only by definition applicable to the powerful, but on the odder basis that supposedly: 'racism is based on fantasy; black views of whites are based on fact' (Asante 1988: 32). His published writings eschew the anti-Semitism which disfigures the work of some of his colleagues, even if his gushing praise for Tony Martin's *Jewish Onslaught* must give pause for thought here. Indeed, as we have seen, Asante's works are more marked by anti-Arab and anti-Muslim than by anti-Jewish animus. What is far more overt is their homophobia. Homosexuality, says Asante, 'cannot be condoned or accepted as good for the national development of a strong people'. It is:

a deviation from Afrocentric thought because it makes the person evaluate his own physical needs above the teachings of national consciousness. . . . We can no longer allow our social lives to be controlled by European decadence. The time has come for us to redeem our manhood through planned Afrocentric action. (1988: 57)

Here Asante reflects a much wider anti-feminist as well as anti-gay trend. Afrocentrists see themselves as opposing Western 'decadence', upholding the integrity of the black family and family values. In this they perpetuate a long-standing black nationalist trope (see 'It's a Family Affair', in Gilroy 1993b), but they also echo much of the rhetoric of the New Christian Right. There is therefore fierce opposition to feminism, which is, in classic fashion, associated simply with hostility to men. Victor Okafor summarizes:

a clear need exists for the Africalogist, male or female, to avoid the Western trap of conceptualizing gender relations on the basis of antagonism . . . generally speaking, the African male and his female (!) experience a more harmonious relationship than their Western counterparts, despite the relative affluence of the West. The crumbling state of the family institution in the West testifies to this. In order to save the African family, African families must guard against cultural aggression. Africans must guard against the set of Western values, practices, and sexual habits which negates the family institution. (Okafor 1991: 255)

In related fashion, one of the few original works by British Afrocentrists (Ekwe-Ekwe and Nzegwu 1994) puts forward a wildly idealized and homogeneous picture of the 'traditional' African world-view (actually mostly derived from the Nigerian ethnophilosopher J.A. Sofola [1973]) as the basis for a revision of gender roles. The prescribed positions for women, despite a few ritualistic preliminary allusions to African queens, are as mother, provider and nurturer (Ekwe-Ekwe and Nzegwu 1994: 28–46). For men, the prescriptions are all about fatherhood, leadership and discipline (ibid.: 46–50). The end-goal is the promotion of 'self-worth' and, as usual with this kind of writing, the authors' ideas about what must be done for the future of Afro-British communities include not a word on political or economic change of any kind.

There have been various rather vaguely formulated attempts, some of them noted at various points above, to suggest affinities between Afrocentrism and some strands of feminist thought, in terms of a shared challenge to materialist, rationist values and dominant systems of knowledge, and perhaps a common commitment to holism and spirituality. Attention to women's roles in Afrocentric historiography, however, seems almost never to have gone further than Diopian assertions about African matriarchy or more or less imaginative listings of 'great Nubian queens' (for example, Asante 1995a: 65, 68–9). The very few major efforts I have found which argue for a relationship between Afrocentricity and women's studies – notably D. Williams (1995) and some contributions to C. Sanders (ed.) (1995), present a picture of *parallel* rather than interconnecting discourses. Essayists in the latter volume, black women theologians mainly associated with Howard University's School of Divinity, range from seeing Afrocentrism (almost entirely associated with Asante's writings) and the 'womanism' propounded by writers like Alice Walker as largely compatible (Gilkes 1995) to very sharp critiques of Asante's sexism (C. Sanders 1995b; D. Williams 1995).

Afrocentrism's profound masculinist bias has often been noted and criticized. It is a feature which it shares with the revived iconography of Malcolm X, and with a great deal of rap music and other male manifestations of hip hop culture. Asante's pantheon of heroes and precursors in *Afrocentricity*, as we have already seen, is exclusively male. In his work and throughout the school he heads, as Barbara Ransby and Tracye Matthews complain, an only marginally modified biological determinism is used to underpin assertions of the 'naturalness' of male-headed families and traditional sexual hierarchy: 'Thus, male-headed nuclear families are synonymous with strong functional families. Those who reject or challenge the prescribed gender roles are dismissed as inauthentic and/or Eurocentric' (1993: 59; for some of the most extreme examples of the syndrome they criticize, see Akbar 1991; Shahrazad Ali 1989). The implications are that the problems of black America are essentially behavioural rather than economic; are *internal* to its communities, with barely a nod to wider structural pressures; and are centred on feckless, lazy, welfare-dependent black mothers who raise their children without suitable male role models. This has everything in common with the discourse of the New Right, and with a tradition of scapegoating which goes at least as far back as the 1960s Moynihan report on the 'pathology' of black family structures. As Ransby and Matthews scornfully conclude: 'The solution, of course, is to celebrate and recreate artificially the "greatness" and "authenticity" of a mythical and generically ancient African family' (1993: 60).[5]

In the eyes of some critics the patriarchal bias is closely linked to a class-based one. Ransby and Matthews make this point in passing, seeing Afrocentric rhetoric as implicitly invoking classic stereotypes of the dysfunctional black 'underclass' (ibid.: 59–60). The argument is more central, however, in polemics like that of the prolific black socialist scholar Manning Marable, who sees the real origins of Afrocentrism like this:

> The black-nationalist-oriented intelligentsia, tied to elements of the new African-American upper middle class by income, social position and cultural outlook, began to search for ways of expressing itself through the 'permanent' prism of race, while rationalising its relatively privileged class position. (Marable 1993: 118–19)

Asante's theories, in Marable's view, represent the more scholarly and philosophically coherent version of such elite self-rationalization. More 'vulgar' Afrocentrists – among whom Marable singles out Leonard Jeffries – not only espouse a cruder, more dogmatic racial essentialism shot through with anti-Semitic rhetoric, but express their elitist biases more nakedly:

> Vulgar Afrocentrists deliberately ignored or obscured the historical reality of social class stratification within the African diaspora. They essentially argued that the interests of all black people – from ... Colin Powell ... (and) Clarence Thomas, to the black unemployed, homeless and hungry of America's decaying urban ghettoes – were philosophically, culturally, and racially the same. ... As such, vulgar Afrocentrism was the perfect social theory for the upwardly mobile black petty bourgeoisie. It gave them a vague sense of ethnic superiority and cultural originality, without requiring the hard, critical study of historical realities. ... It was, in short, only the latest theoretical construct of a politics of racial identity, a worldview designed to discuss the world, but never really to change it. (ibid.: 121–2)

Given the evidence of wildly unscholarly statements from writers like Asante that we have documented, one may think that Marable is overstating a distinction between 'scholarly' and 'vulgar' Afrocentrists, but his overall judgement has considerable weight. Many of the same charges have been levelled by radical or feminist Afro-American critics against major recent currents in black US popular culture. The 1990s celebration and near-deification of Malcolm X – or, rather, of a quite mythologized image of that complex, rapidly changing man, above all in Spike Lee's commercially successful film – is a case in point. The return of Malcolm X has coincided and interrelated with the rise of Afrocentrism, and evinces the same intensely elitist and masculinist bias. (The connections are especially explicit in Asante's celebration of Malcolm X as revived 'cultural hero': Asante [ed.] 1993b.) As Ransby and Matthews point out, it has involved a highly selective reconstruction of the recent past, with the dichotomy between Malcolm and Martin Luther King, the whole story of grass-roots Civil Rights organizing, and especially its female component, and Malcolm's own highly problematic attitudes to gender (which he began to subject to autocritique at the very end of his life), all airbrushed out. We are left with:

the disempowering misperception that only larger than life great men can make or change history, and that this process is an individual rather than collective venture. The struggle for Black liberation is thus equated solely with the struggle to redeem Black manhood ... by militant posturing heroes, not by the arduous and often unrewarding task of daily organizing.' (Ransby and Matthews 1993: 62)

The subsequent attempt by the Van Peebles posse cinematically to renovate identification with the Black Panthers, evidently derivative of Lee's paint-job on Malcolm X, has similar effects.

Still worse, in the context of gender roles and images, have been major strands in rap music. Despite the presence of a handful of feminist-orientated women rappers, and of mixed-sex groups like Arrested Development, whose lyrics challenge stereotypes, the mainstream of rap (as of much white rock music: though one must say bluntly that the worst of the rappers are more regressive in this respect than any rock band I have heard) is aggressively sexist. At the extreme – as with Dr Dre, Snoop Doggy Dogg, Ice Cube or Public Enemy (an extreme which, in terms of sales and popularity, *is* a large part of the mainstream) – violent misogyny is the rule. Critics like Tricia Rose, who emphasize female participation and at least proto-feminism within parts of the rap scene, often give the impression of clutching at straws (Rose 1994: esp. 146–82; see, by contrast, the far more sceptical reflections of Paul Gilroy [1994]; as well as Ransby and Matthews; and Lusane [1993: 52–4]).

The anti-Arab and anti-Islamic prejudice we noted in relation to Asante is a pervasive phenomenon, largely ignored in the North Atlantic fixation on purely bipolar 'Africa versus the West' or, more narrowly, 'Blacks versus Jews' paradigms. We have seen how a fantasized picture of the Arabs as relentless enemies of Africa, wreckers and traducers of all its indigenous achievements, across several millennia is purveyed in Chancellor Williams's *Destruction of Black Civilization*, and faithfully copied by Asante and others. Here, too, such otherwise bitter antagonists and ideological polar opposites as the Nigerian writers Wole Soyinka (1985, 1991) and Chinweizu (1978, 1987) share much common ground – both are marked by a deep dislike for Arabs and Islam. For both of them, this hostility evidently owes much to internal Nigerian north–south political schisms, though this is not openly acknowledged. More generally, a perception of Arab imperialism, slave-raiding and attempted conquest – including alleged present-day expansion-ism – in Africa, seen as directly analogous to or even worse than European incursions, is the major motivator of antagonism. It has also found notable literary expressions in Yambo Ouologuem's *Le Devoir de violence* (1968/1971) and Ayi Kwei Armah's *Two Thousand Seasons* (1973). It must be added that the lines of prejudice between some black Africans and some Arabs by no means run only one way. Not only is there a long and relatively neglected tradition of anti-black prejudice in Arab culture – analysed by Al-Azmeh (1992), by Murray Gordon (1989) and, in perhaps a less balanced way, by Bernard Lewis (1986, 1990) – which runs counter to the genuine 'colour-blind' universalism preached by Islam and evident in many modern Arab states. There are also more contemporary manifestations, some of which are noted by Soyinka (1991) and by the American historians Dennis Hickey and Kenneth Wylie (1993: 48–55).[6]

On the other hand, the African scholars most often cited as inspirations by American Afrocentrists rarely appear to share their more prejudiced perspectives. Pushed to endorse Cress Welsing's peculiar views, Cheikh Anta Diop would only admit that yes, he believed that whites developed later than blacks, as a result of depigmentation, and had their social outlook shaped by a harsh environment, but: 'we must be careful because, when we deal in this abstract realm ... a great deal of caution is necessary' (Moore interview 1989: 379). He also refused to commit himself on claims that white racism developed as a result of consciousness of minority status, and thus as a means of self-preservation; or that racism might be 'a biological or other type of instinct' among 'Aryans' (ibid.: 379–80). Elsewhere he more clearly repudiated such views, insisting throughout his major books on environmental and cultural, rather than racial, determinism. He warned repeatedly against reverse racism, and argued that while African civilizational achievements and moral codes were indeed superior to Eurasian ones: 'insofar as one can speak of a race, the civilization that is his (the African's) might have been created by any other human race placed in so favorable and so unique a setting' (1974a: 235).

What is most disturbing is the extent to which claims of the kind made in *The Secret Relationship* have apparently gained fairly wide circulation, especially through certain independent black radio stations (see, for example, Fiske 1993: 273–5), in urban Afro-America. Only a handful of academics among the most extreme Afrocentrists, notably Jeffries and Martin, have publicly endorsed them. But they have taken their place, as a kind of secret, forbidden and therefore all the more compelling knowledge. They circulate alongside such beliefs as those that the Atlantic slave trade actually claimed perhaps a 100 or 150 million victims killed or enslaved, rather than the 10–15 million range within which serious historians' estimates cluster (surely monstrous enough figures in themselves![7]), that the AIDS and crack epidemics are genocidal conspiracies against blacks, the deranged pseudo-scientific claims of a Frances Cress Welsing or Richard King, and so on.

Marimba Ani's book *Yurugu*, which we have already discussed as perhaps the most intellectually impressive single work yet to appear from US Afrocentric circles, is none the less prey to such fantasies. Ani accepts the 'Aryan myth' wholesale, for instance in relation to India and the caste system (1994: 285–6). She relies heavily on a handful of century-old, classically racist – indeed, proto-fascist – works by writers like Winthrop Stoddard, Gobineau, and Madison Grant as supposedly representative examples of 'white nationalism'. When she wants an up-to-date instance, she has to turn to P.W. Botha (ibid.: 288)! Even with Botha, who would surely be thought quite capable of condemning himself out of his own mouth, she resorts to a newspaper report of a newspaper report, involving an American black nationalist student's alleged paraphrase of a South African reporter's paraphrase of what Botha is supposed to have said, but much of which is utterly implausible as a version of the public words of that canny politician. It may seem absurd to complain of an African-American author 'misrepresenting' a political figure as bloodstained as Botha; but surely if truth and accuracy matter at all, they matter in all political situations.

That last sentiment would be not so much disputed as dismissed out of hand by those who insist that there are only local, situation-specific truths. We have already looked at the endorsements of certain less-than-plausible Afrocentric claims by high-profile figures like cultural critic bell hooks, bestselling popular historian Lerone Bennett and philosopher of science Sandra Harding. The basis for their enthusiasm would seem to be different in each case. Bennett gives no sign of adherence to anything other than a straightforward realist (what opponents misname an empiricist) notion of historical truth, and presumably therefore supports claims about ancient African trips to the Americas because, not having looked at the evidence closely, he thinks they are true. In hooks's case, she endorses the same claims because she finds them politically inspiring – and, one takes it, also thinks they are true. Harding adheres to a version of 'standpoint epistemology': that is (crudely), what is true depends substantially on where you're looking from, with the 'where' understood mainly in terms of gender and, secondarily, race.

A far more alarmingly glib and sweeping version of that stance is proposed by Media Studies guru John Fiske. He details, in a tone that veers between the neutral and the approving, a whole series of (in my view) absurd, damaging, paranoid and racist beliefs he has encountered among Afro-Americans, including the theories of Cress Welsing and Leonard Jeffries – notions of whites as devils, as congenitally evil, and so on (Fiske 1993: 227–302 passim[8]). He focuses especially on the 'Cress Theory' of inherent black superiority, which he approves because it gives whites 'deconstructive jolts':

> If the Cress Theory is racist, and to some eyes it will inevitably appear so, it is 'weak' racism, defensive and not imperialist. ... [It] is used not to justify a future Black domination of whites, but to empower the Black refusal of white domination ...
>
> The primary function of these Black insights into whiteness is to strengthen African Americans in their daily lives ... but when glimpsed or overheard by whites they are equally useful in disturbing white knowledge of itself.
>
> I do then endorse the Cress theory and equivalent Black knowledges, not for any essential 'truth', but for their deconstructive counter to white ways of knowing whiteness. (1993: 283–4)

John Fiske, the respected white Australian-born academic who skilfully deploys the fashionable language of deconstruction and extreme relativism, is more wildly and culpably wrong, perhaps, than any other author cited in this book. No one is or can ever possibly be 'empowered' or 'strengthened' by believing in lies and fantasies. No better society, or even better social attitudes, can be built on them. None of the ideas Fiske mentions, and none of those which have been the main subjects of this book, offers any strategies whatsoever for improving the lot of the poor, oppressed and underprivileged, whether in North America, in Europe or in Africa. They need accurate information about their world more than anyone else, if they are ever to change it.

As for such ideas being 'overheard' by whites, the effect is highly unlikely to be that of a productive 'disturbing' of white 'knowledge of itself' (the very use of the singular, abstract term carries a great burden of racial essentialism: what on earth is whiteness itself?). What it would 'disturb' if it were taken seriously, taken as representative or authoritative for black social thought, are the true 'knowledges' that people of African descent are as rational, as capable of constructing coherent social, historical, psychological and political theories as anyone else, and that they are not typically consumed by incoherent fantasies of revenge or compensatory delusions of past and future glory. Extreme Afrocentrism and associated theories are the white racist's dream come true. If Asante or Cress Welsing and the rest did not exist, racists would have had to invent them – but they wouldn't have had the necessary imagination. Only a great novelist could have dreamed up anything as wild as some of the theories we have been examining. In a way, a great novelist already had. Here is Ralph Ellison's *Invisible Man*, back in 1952, caught in a nightmare vision of mad preacher and entranced congregation:

'Brothers and sisters, my text this morning is the "Blackness of Blackness".'
    And a congregation of voices answered: 'That blackness is most black, brother, most black . . .';
    'In the beginning . . .'
    'At the very start', they cried.
    '. . . there was blackness . . .'
    'Preach it . . .' (Ellison 1983: 12)

And so, ever more insanely, on. Ellison's preacher is a bad dream. His Ras the Exhorter, the Garveyite fantasist of racial revenge, is a down-at-heel street agitator. Some of their successors, weaving delusions of black atoms and black Pharaohs at the beginning and end of everything, are university professors and designers of school curricula. Within the group which has been perhaps the most consistently oppressed of all victims of racial thinking, a new structure of such thought has emerged, the mirror-image of that which for so long attacked those for whom it claims to speak. It is all unutterably sad.

Notes

1. See regular full-page advertisements in its newspaper, *The Final Call*. The mail-order booklists advertised by the rival African Islamic Mission include fewer works of this nature, though *The Iceman Inheritance* is sold by them.

2. For a summary of the controversy, perhaps all the more damning in the light of its author's sympathetic attempt to present the Farrakhan movement's side of the story, see Gardell (1996: 245–84).

3. For genuinely scholarly overviews of Jewish participation in the Atlantic slave trade and New World slaveowning, see Drescher (1993); D. Davis (1994). A more polemical response to the Farrakhan's movement's book, not without its own ethnocentric touches, is Brackman (1992).

4. There is, of course, no textual or intrinsic reason whatsoever to identify this biblical story with racial theories: that association came many centuries later. At the very earliest, it can be traced to the Babylonian Talmud of the third century CE: and then only most ambiguously. It is intriguing in this context that in present-day liberal Israeli circles, the vernacular Hebrew term 'Kushim' for black Africans is regarded as politically dubious, because of its associations – tenuous though they are – with such ideas.

5. See also White (1990) on Afrocentric masculinism; and Decker (1994) for its manifestations in rap music. For a more analytical overview of the 'crisis of black manhood' in the USA, see Majors and Gordon (1994); plus – for the predictable claim that Afrocentric education has the answers to it – W. Oliver (1989).

6. St Clair Drake, once more, attempts to bridge the gulfs between rival, ideologically charged views about historical Muslim and Jewish racial attitudes (1990).

7. As we have seen, a recent volume in the formerly reputable *For Beginners* . . . series (Anderson 1995) reproduces such claims; while Louis Farrakhan has also done so (see Gardell 1996: 256). This is yet another area of great uncertainty, but taking a rough midpoint of different modern historians' calculations, it might be suggested that probably about ten million African people were forcibly transported to the New World, while another three million died or were killed in the course of capture and transit. The Arab-dominated slave trades across the Sahara, Red Sea and Indian Ocean abducted possibly another five million. Somewhere between ten and eighteen million more people were enslaved within the African continent over the past four centuries (this is necessarily the most unclear figure of all) by indigenous, colonial, and in a few cases even contemporary postcolonial states. This last point is worth emphasizing: despite their humanitarian and 'civilizing' protestations, all European colonial regimes in Africa retained, compromised with or actively furthered local slave regimes, while human rights organizations at the end of the twentieth century have repeatedly noted the persistence of 'traditional' modes of enslavement in such states as Mauritania. For a succinct overview of the state of knowledge, see Lovejoy (1982); for an indication of the difficulties of quantification, especially for the Atlantic trade's earliest stages, see Elbl (1997).

8. Fiske returns later to the same themes (1994). In 'Blackstream Knowledge' he parades ostentatious agnosticism over whether the AIDS epidemic is indeed the result of a deliberate genocidal plot against blacks, quotes extensively from transcripts of independent black radio talk-shows replete with ridiculous, paranoid claims about whites' devilish plots, nonsensically false AIDS statistics, and so on (inserting not a word of scepticism or demur about any of these), and concludes that since it would be more damaging *not* to believe such stories if they were true than to believe them if they were false, he will choose to believe them. There could be no more pitiable an abdication of the intellectual's responsibility.

Bibliography

Abbott, Elizabeth (1988) *Haiti: The Duvaliers and their Legacy* (New York).

Adam, S. (1981) 'The Importance of Nubia: A Link between Central Africa and the Mediterranean', in Mokhtar (ed.).

Adams, William Y. (1977) *Nubia: Corridor to Africa* (Princeton, NJ).

——(1984) 'The First Colonial Empire: Egypt in Nubia, 3200–1200 BC' *Comparative Studies in Society and History* 26, 1.

——(1985) 'Doubts About the Lost Pharaohs', *Journal of Near Eastern Studies* 44.

Adams, Hunter Havelin III (1983a) 'African Observers of the Universe: The Sirius Question', in Van Sertima (ed.).

——(1983b) 'New Light on the Dogon and Sirius', in Van Sertima (ed.).

Addai-Sebo, Akyaaba and Wong, Ansel (eds 1988) *Our Story: A Handbook of African History and Contemporary Issues* (London).

Ajayi, J.F. Ade and Crowder, Michael (eds 1976) *History of West Africa*, vol. 1 (2nd edn London).

——(eds 1985) *History of West Africa*, vol. 1 (3rd edn London).

Akbar, Na'im (1984) *Chains and Images in Psychological Slavery* (Jersey City, NJ).

——(1991) *Visions for Black Men* (Nashville, TN).

——(1994) 'Nile Valley Origins of the Science of the Mind', in Van Sertima (ed.).

Al-Azmeh, Aziz (1992) 'Barbarians in Arab Eyes', *Past & Present* 134.

Alexander, J.A. (1988) 'The Saharan Divide in the Nile Valley: The Evidence from Qasr Ibrim', *African Archaeological Review* 6, 1.

Ali, Ahmed and Ibrahim (1993) *The Black Celts: An Ancient African Civilisation in Ireland and Britain* (2nd edn Cardiff).

Ali, Shahrazad (1989) *The Blackman's Guide to Understanding the Blackwoman* (Philadelphia, PA).

Ali, Shanti Sadiq (1996) *The African Dispersal in the Deccan* (London).

Allen, Robert L.(1969) *Black Awakening in Capitalist America* (Garden City, NY).

Alleyne, Mervyn (1988) *Roots of Jamaican Culture* (London).

Amadiume, Ifi (1987) *Afrikan Matriarchal Foundations: The Igbo Case* (London).

Amen, Nur Ankh (1993) *The Ankh: African Origin of Electromagnetism* (Jamaica, NY).

Amin, Samir (1989) *Eurocentrism* (London).

Ampim, Manu (1994) 'The Problem of the Bernal–Davidson School', in Van Sertima (ed.).

Andah, Bassey (1993) 'Identifying Early Farming Traditions of West Africa', in Shaw *et al.* (eds).

——(1995a) 'European Encumbrances to the Development of Relevant Theory in African Archaeology', in Ucko (ed.).

——(1995b) 'Studying African Societies in Cultural Context', in Schmidt and Patterson (eds).

Anderson, S.E. (1995) *The Black Holocaust for Beginners* (New York).

Anderson, Tony (1995) 'Blowing Smoke: Exposing Empty Criticism of Afrocentricity', in Ziegler (ed.).

Ani, Marimba (1994) *Yurugu: An African-Centered Critique of European Cultural Thought and Behaviour* (Trenton, NJ). *See also* Richards, Dona.

Anon. (1987) 'Back to the Blackland', *West Africa* 6 July.

Anthony, David H. (1994) 'Max Yergan and South Africa: A Transatlantic Interaction', in Lemelle and Kelley (eds).

Anttila, Raimo (1989) *An Introduction to Historical and Comparative Linguistics* (2nd edn Amsterdam, PA).

Appadurai, Arjun *et al.* (1994) 'Editorial Comment: On Thinking the Black Public Sphere', *Public Culture* 7, 1.

Appiah, Kwame Anthony (1985) 'The Uncompleted Argument: Du Bois and the Illusion of Race', *Critical Inquiry* 12, 1.

——(1992) *In My Father's House: Africa in the Philosophy of Culture* (London).

——(1992/3) 'African-American Philosophy?', *The Philosophical Forum* XXIV, 1–3.

Armah, Ayi Kwei (1973) *Two Thousand Seasons* (London: cited from 1979 pb. edn).

——(1995) *Osiris Rising: A Novel of Africa Past, Present and Future* (Popen-guine, Senegal).

Armelagos, George J. and Mills, James O. (1993) 'Paleopathology as Science: The Contribution of Egyptology', in Davies and Walker (eds).

Arnold, A. James (1981) *Modernism and Négritude: The Poetry and Politics of Aimé Césaire* (Cambridge, MA).

Asante, Molefi K. (1980a) 'The Communication Person in Society' in Asante and Vandi (eds).

——(1980b) 'International/Intercultural Relations', in Asante and Vandi (eds).

——(1985a) 'Afrocentricity and Culture', in Asante and Welsh Asante (eds).

——(1985b) 'The African Essence in African-American Language', in Asante and Welsh Asante (eds).

——(1987) *The Afrocentric Idea* (Philadelphia, PA).

——(1988) *Afrocentricity* (3rd rev. edn Trenton, NJ).
——(1990) *Kemet, Afrocentricity, and Knowledge* (Trenton, NJ).
——(1991a) 'Putting Africa at the Center', *Newsweek*, 23 September.
——(1991b) 'Multiculturalism without Hierarchy: An Afrocentric Reply to Diane Ravitch', *The American Scholar* 60, 25.
——(1991c) *The Book of African Names* (Trenton, NJ).
——(1993a) 'Racism, Consciousness, and Afrocentricity', in Early (ed.).
——(1993b) *Malcolm X as Cultural Hero and Other Afrocentric Essays* (Trenton, NJ).
——(1994) 'Review of Martin: *The Jewish Onslaught*', *Journal of Black Studies* 25, 1.
——(1995a) *Classical Africa* (Maywood, NJ).
——(1995b) *African American History* (Maywood, NJ).
——(1991/1997) 'The Afrocentric Idea in Education'; orig. pub. in *Journal of Negro Education* Spring 1991; cited from Van Deburg (ed.) 1997.
——and Abdulai S. Vandi (eds 1980) *Contemporary Black Thought: Alternative Analyses of Social and Behavioural Science* (Beverly Hills, CA).
——and Kariamu Welsh Asante (eds 1985) *African Culture: The Rhythms of Unity* (Westport, CT).
——and Abu S. Abarry (eds 1996) *African Intellectual Heritage: A Book of Sources* (Philadelphia, PA).
Assmann, Jan (1989) *Ma'at: L'Égypte pharaonique et l'idée de justice sociale* (Paris).
——(1992) *Politische Theologie zwischen Aegypten und Israel* (Munich).
——(1995) *Egyptian Solar Religion in the New Kingdom: Re, Amun and the Crisis of Polytheism* (London).
——(1996) 'The Mosaic Distinction: Israel, Egypt and the Invention of Paganism', *Representations* 56.
Atanda, J.A. (1980) 'The Historian and the Problem of Origins of Peoples in Nigerian Society', *Journal of the Historical Society of Nigeria* X, 3.
Atwater, Deborah F. (1995) 'Asante and the Naming of Names: The Evolution of Rhetorical Concepts', in Ziegler (ed.).
Bahoken, J.-C. (1989) 'Universalité de la pensée philosophique africaine: L'apport de l'Égypte', *Présence Africaine* 149–50.
Baines, John (1991a) 'Was Civilization Made in Africa?', *New York Times Book Review*, 11 August.
——(1991b) 'Egyptian Myth and Discourse: Myth, Gods and the Early Written and Iconographic Record', *Journal of Near Eastern Studies* 50, 2.
——(1996) 'The Aims and Methods of *Black Athena*', in Lefkowitz and Rogers (eds).
and Malek, Jaromir (1980) *Atlas of Ancient Egypt* (Oxford).
Baker, Houston A. Jr (1984) *Blues, Ideology and Afro-American Literature: A Vernacular Theory* (Chicago).
Baker, John R. (1974) *Race* (London).
Baldwin, James (1985) *The Price of the Ticket: Collected Non-Fiction 1948–1985* (London).

Baldwin, Joseph A. (1980) 'The Psychology of Oppression', in Asante and Vandi (eds).

Banham, Bracht (1989) 'Hellenomania', *Liverpool Classical Monthly* 14, 4, April.

Bank, Andrew (1996) 'Of "Native Skulls" and "Noble Caucasians": Phrenology in Colonial South Africa', *Journal of Southern African Studies* 22, 3.

Baraka, Amiri/Leroi Jones (1966) *Home: Social Essays* (New York).

——(1967) *Black Music* (New York).

——(1979) *Selected Plays and Prose* (New York).

——(1984a) *The Autobiography* (New York).

——(1984b) *Daggers and Javelins* (New York).

Barboza, Steven (1994) *American Jihad: Islam after Malcolm X* (New York).

Bard, Kathryn A. (1996) 'Ancient Egyptians and the Issue of Race', in Lefkowitz and Rogers (eds).

Barkan, Elazar (1992) *The Retreat of Scientific Racism: Changing Concepts of Race in Britain and the United States between the World Wars* (Cambridge).

Barnes, Carol (1988) *Melanin: The Chemical Key to Black Greatness* (Houston, TX).

Bartlett, Robert (1993) *The Making of Europe: Conquest, Colonization and Cultural Change 950–1350* (London).

Bauval, Robert and Gilbert, Adrian (1994) *The Orion Mystery* (London).

Beach, D.N. (1980) *The Shona and Zimbabwe 900–1850* (London).

Bekerie, Ayele (1994) 'The Four Corners of a Circle: Afrocentricity as a Model of Synthesis', *Journal of Black Studies* 25, 4.

Bell, Augustus T. (n.d.) *The Woolly Hair Man of the Ancient South and a Digest of Facts from the Original Languages* (New York).

Bell, Bernard W., Grosholz, Emily R. and Stewart, James B. (eds 1996) *W.E.B. Du Bois on Race and Culture* (New York and London).

Bell, Yvonne R., Bouie, Cathy L. and Baldwin, Joseph A. (1990) 'Afrocentric Cultural Consciousness and African-American Male–Female Relationships', *Journal of Black Studies* 21, 2.

Ben-Amos, Paula (1980) *The Art of Benin* (London).

Ben-Jochannen, Yosef (1971) *Africa: Mother of 'Western Civilization'* (New York).

——(1972) *Black Man of the Nile and his Family* (New York; repr. Baltimore, MD 1989).

——(1974) *The African Origin of the Major Western Religions* (New York; repr. Baltimore, MD 1988).

——(1980) *Axioms and Quotations of Yosef Ben-Jochannen* (New York; ed. E. Curtis Alexander).

——(1982) *Dr. Ben Speaks Out* (New York: interview with E. Curtis Alexander).

——(1983) *We the Black Jews: Witness to the 'White Jewish Race' Myth* (New York).

——with Oduyoye, Modupe and Finch, Charles (1988) *The Afrikan Origins of the Major World Religions* (ed. Amon Saba Saakana, London).

——with Brooks, Hugh and Webb, Kempton (1971) *Africa: Lands, Peoples and Cultures of the World* (New York).

Bennett, Lerone Jr (1984) *Before the Mayflower: A History of Black America* (5th edn New York).

Berghahn, Marion (1977) *Images of Africa in Black American Literature* (London and Basingstoke).

Berman, Paul (ed. 1994) *Blacks and Jews: Alliances and Arguments* (New York).

Bernal, Martin (1985) 'Black Athena: The African and Levantine Roots of Greece', in Van Sertima (ed.).

——(1987) *Black Athena: The Afroasiatic Roots of Classical Civilization. I. The Fabrication of Ancient Greece* (London).

——(1989) '*Black Athena* and the APA', *Arethusa* Special Issue, Fall.

——(1990a) *Cadmean Letters: The Transmission of the Alphabet to the Aegean and Further West before 1400 BC* (Winona Lake, IN).

——(1990b) 'Responses to Critical Reviews of *Black Athena*, Volume 1', *Journal of Mediterranean Archaeology* 3, 1.

——(1991) *Black Athena II. The Archaeological and Documentary Evidence* (London).

——(1992) 'Response to Edith Hall', *Arethusa* 25, 1.

——(1993a) 'Response' (to S.O.Y. Keita), *Arethusa* 26, 3.

——(1993b) 'Response: The Debate over *Black Athena*', *Journal of Women's History* 4, 3.

——(1994a) 'Basil Davidson: A Personal Appreciation' *Race & Class* 36, 2.

——(1994b) 'The Image of Ancient Greece as a Tool of Colonialism and European Hegemony', in George C. Bond and Angela Gilliam (eds) *Social Construction of the Past: Representation as Power* (London).

Bernstein, Richard (1994) *Dictatorship of Virtue: Multiculturalism and the Battle for America's Future* (New York).

Berry, Mary F. and Blassingame, John (1982) *Long Memory* (New York).

Birch, Anthony H. (1989) *Nationalism and National Integration* (London).

Bjornson, Richard (1991) *The African Quest for Freedom and Identity: Cameroonian Writing and the National Experience* (Bloomington, IN).

Blackburn, Robin (1997) *The Making of New World Slavery: From the Baroque to the Modern 1492–1800* (London).

Blakey, Michael L. (1995) 'Race, Nationalism, and the Afrocentric Past', in Schmidt and Patterson (eds).

Blassingame, John W. (1979) *The Slave Community: Plantation Life in the Antebellum South* (2nd edn New York).

Blauner, Robert (1972) *Racial Oppression in America* (New York).

Blayechettai, J.E.C. (*c.*1922) *The Pen of an African* (no place of pub. given).

——(*c.*1926) *The Hidden Mystery of Ethiopia* (no place of pub. given).

Blench, Roger (1991) 'Connections between Egypt and Sub-Saharan Africa: The Evidence of Cultivated Plants', in Davies (ed.).

——(1993) 'Recent Developments in African Language Classification', in Shaw *et al.* (eds).

Blok, Josine H. (1996) 'Proof and Persuasion in *Black Athena*: The Case of K.O. Mueller', *Journal of the History of Ideas* 57, 4.

Bloom, Allan (1987) *The Closing of the American Mind* (New York).

Bodunrin, P.O. (1984) 'The Question of African Philosophy', in Richard A. Wright (ed.).

Boggs, James (1970) *Racism and the Class Struggle* (New York).

Bonnet, Charles (1992) 'Excavations at the Nubian Royal Town of Kerma: 1975–91', *Antiquity* 66.

Bowen, J.W.E. (ed. 1896) *Africa and the American Negro: Addresses and Proceedings of the Congress on Africa* (cited from 1969 reprint, Miami, FL).

Boxill, Bernard (1992/3) 'Two Traditions in African American Philosophy', *The Philosophical Forum* XXIV, 1–3.

Boyd, Herb (1991) *African History for Beginners* (New York).

Brace, C. Loring, Tracer, David P., Yaroch, Lucia Allen, Robb, John, Brandt, Kari and Nelson, A. Russell (1993) 'Clines and Clusters Versus "Race": A Test in Ancient Egypt and the Case of a Death on the Nile', *Yearbook of Physical Anthropology* 36. Revised version in Lefkowitz and Rogers (eds) 1996.

Brackman, Harold (1992) *Farrakhan's Reign of Historical Error: The Truth Behind* The Secret Relationship between Blacks and Jews (Los Angeles).

Bradley, Michael (1978/1991) *The Iceman Inheritance: Prehistoric Sources of Western Man's Racism, Sexism and Aggression* (orig. pub. 1978; cited from 1991 New York edn).

——(1992a) *The Columbus Conspiracy* (New York).

——(1992b) *Chosen People from the Caucasus* (Chicago).

Brathwaite, Edward (1973) *The Arrivants: A New World Trilogy* (Oxford).

Braxton, Joanne M. and McLaughlin, Andree Nicola (eds 1990) *Wild Women in the Whirlwind: Afra-American Culture and the Contemporary Literary Renaissance* (New Brunswick, NJ).

Breman, Paul (ed. 1973) *You Better Believe It: Black Verse in English* (Harmondsworth).

Brett, Michael (1982) 'Review of G. Mokhtar (ed.) *General History of Africa vol. 2*', *Journal of African History* 23, 1.

Brooks-Bertram, Peggy (1994) 'The Sixth Napatan Dynasty of Kush', in Van Sertima (ed.).

Brothwell, D.R. and Chiarelli, B.A. (eds 1973) *Population Biology of the Ancient Egyptians* (New York).

Brotz, Howard (1970) *The Black Jews of Harlem* (New York).

Browder, Anthony T. (1992) *Nile Valley Contributions to Civilization* (Washington, DC).

Browder, Atlantis Tye and Browder, Anthony T. (1991) *My First Trip to Africa* (Washington, DC).

Brown, Elaine (1993) *A Taste of Power: A Black Woman's Story* (New York).

Brown, Terence A. and Keri A. (1992) 'Ancient DNA and the Archaeologist', *Antiquity* 66, 250.

Brown, William Wells (1863) *The Black Man: His Antecedents, His Genius, and His Achievements* (Boston, MA).

Bruckner, Pascal (1986) *The Tears of the White Man* (New York).

Brunson, James (1989) 'Ethnic or Symbolic: Blackness and Human Images in Ancient Egyptian Art' in Van Sertima (ed.).

——(1991) *Predynastic Egypt: An African-centric View* (DeKalb, IL).

Bryan, Beverley, Dadzie, Stella and Scafe, Suzanne (1985) *The Hearts of the Race: Black Women's Lives in Britain* (London).

Bryan, Patrick (1991) 'Black Perspectives in Late Nineteenth Century Jamaica: The Case of Dr. Theophilus E.S. Scholes', in Rupert Lewis and Patrick Bryan (eds) *Garvey: His Work and Impact* (Trenton, NJ).

Buhle, Paul (1987) *Marxism in the USA* (London).

Burkert, Walter (1992) *The Orientalizing Revolution: Near Eastern Influence on Greek Culture in the Early Archaic Age* (Cambridge, MA; orig. pub. in German 1984).

Calloway-Thomas, Carolyn (1995) 'Hearing Voices of the Ancestors: Religious Themes in *The Afrocentric Idea*', in Ziegler (ed.).

Calt, Stephen (1994) *I'd Rather be the Devil: Skip James and the Blues* (New York).

Campbell, Horace (1985) *Rasta and Resistance: From Marcus Garvey to Walter Rodney* (London).

Campbell, Jane (1986) *Mythic Black Fiction: The Transformation of History* (Knoxville, TN).

Cambridge, Alrick and Feuchtwang, Stephan (1992) *Where You Belong* (Aldershot).

Cann, Rebecca, Stoneking, Mark and Wilson, Allan (1987) 'Mitochondrial DNA and Human Evolution', *Nature* 325.

Carmichael, Stokely (1968) 'Black Power', in David Cooper (ed.) *The Dialectics of Liberation* (Harmondsworth).

and Hamilton, Charles V (1967/9) *Black Power: The Politics of Liberation in America* (cited from 1969 Penguin edn: orig. pub. USA 1967).

Carruthers, Jacob H. (1984) *Essays in Ancient Egyptian Studies* (Los Angeles).

——(1986) 'The Wisdom of Governance in Kemet', in Karenga and Carruthers (eds).

——(1992) 'Outside Academia: Bernal's Critique of Black Champions of Ancient Egypt', *Journal of Black Studies* 22, 4.

——(1995) *Mdw Ntr: Divine Speech. A Historiographical Reflection on African Deep Thought from the Time of the Pharaohs to the Present* (London).

Castoriadis, Cornelius (1989) 'The End of Philosophy?', *Salmagundi* 82–3.

Caton Thompson, Gertrude (1931) *The Zimbabwe Culture: Ruins and Reactions* (Oxford).

Champion, Timothy C. (ed. 1989) *Centre and Periphery: Comparative Studies in Archaeology* (London).

Chandler, Wayne (1989) 'Of Gods and Men: Egypt's Oldest Kingdom', in Van Sertima (ed.).

——(1994) 'Seven Times Seven: The Seven Hermetic Principles of Ancient Egypt', in Van Sertima (ed.).

Charters, Samuel (1981) *The Roots of the Blues: An African Search* (London).

Cheng, Vincent J. (1995) *Joyce, Race and Empire* (Cambridge).

Chevannes, Barry (1995) *Rastafari: Roots and Ideology* (Syracuse, NY).

Chinweizu (1978) *The West and the Rest of Us* (London and Lagos).

——(1987) *Decolonising the African Mind* (Lagos).

Churchward, Albert (1920) *The Origin and Evolution of Freemasonry Connected with the Origin and Evolution of the Human Race* (London).

——(1921) *Origin and Evolution of the Human Race* (London).

Clark, Andrew F. and Phillips, Lucie Colvin (1994) *Historical Dictionary of Senegal* (2nd edn Metuchan, NJ).

Clark, J.D. (ed. 1982) *The Cambridge History of Africa. vol. 1: From the Earliest Times to c.500 BC* (Cambridge).

Clarke, John Henrik (1967) *A New Approach to African History* (mimeo, no place of pub. given).

——(1970) 'Confrontation in Montreal', *African Studies Newsletter* II, 6–7.

——(ed. 1974) *Marcus Garvey and the Vision of Africa* (New York).

——(1985) 'African-American Historians and the Reclaiming of African History', in Asante and Welsh Asante (eds); orig. pub. in *Présence Africaine* 110 (1979).

——(1986) 'Africa in the Ancient World', in Karenga and Carruthers (eds).

——(1988) 'Pan-Africanism: A Brief History of an Idea', *Présence Africaine* 145.

——(1991) *Notes for an African World Revolution: Africa at the Crossroads* (Trenton, NJ).

——(1992) 'Introduction' to Browder.

Clarke, Sebastian (1980) *Jah Music: The Evolution of the Popular Jamaican Song* (London).

Cleage, Albert B. (1968) *The Black Messiah* (New York).

Cleaver, Eldridge (1970) *Soul on Ice* (London).

——(1971) *Post-Prison Writings and Speeches* (London).

Clegg, Legrand H. III (1989) 'Black Rulers of the Golden Age', in Van Sertima (ed.).

Clifford, James (1988) *The Predicament of Culture: Twentieth-century Ethnography, Literature, and Art* (Cambridge, MA).

Coleman, John E. (1996) 'Did Egypt Share the Glory That Was Greece?', in Lefkowitz and Rogers (eds).

Collier, Peter and Horowitz, David (eds 1997) *The Race Card: White Guilt, Black Resentment and the Assault on Truth and Justice* (Rocklin, CA).

Collins, Robert O. *et al.* (eds 1993) *Problems in African History: The Precolonial Centuries* (Princeton, NJ).

Condit, Celeste Michelle and Lucaites, John Louis (1993) *Crafting Equality: America's Anglo-African Word* (Chicago).

Connah, Graham (1987) *African Civilizations, Precolonial States and Cities in Tropical Africa: An Archaeological Perspective* (Cambridge).

Connor, Walker (1994) *Ethnonationalism: The Quest for Understanding* (Princeton, NJ).

Coombes, Annie E. (1994) *Reinventing Africa: Museums, Material Culture and Popular Imagination* (New Haven, CT).

Coon, Carleton S. (1962) *The Origin of Races* (New York)

Cooper, Frederick (1977) *Plantation Slavery on the East Coast of Africa* (New Haven, CT).

Coquery-Vidrovitch, Catherine (1992) '*Présence Africaine*: History and Historians of Africa', in Mudimbe (ed.).

Corbett, John (1994) *Extended Play: Sounding Off from John Cage to Dr. Funkenstein* (Durham, NC).

Cottrell, Leonard (1955) *The Mountains of Pharaoh* (London).

Councill, W.H. (1898) *Lamp of Wisdom; Or, Race History Illuminated* (Nashville, TN).

Cowan, L. Gray (1970) 'President's Report', *African Studies Review* 13, 3.

Crawford, Clinton (1996) *Recasting Ancient Egypt in the African Context* (Trenton, NJ).

Crawford, Keith W. (1994) 'The Racial Identity of Ancient Egyptian Populations based on the Analysis of Physical Remains', in Van Sertima (ed.).

Creel, Margaret Washington (1988) '*A Peculiar People': Slave Religion and Community-Culture among the Gullahs* (New York).

Crowder, Michael (1967) *Senegal* (London).

Crummell, Alexander (1862) *The Future of Africa: Being Addresses, Sermons, &c. &c. Delivered in the Republic of Liberia* (New York, 2nd edn).

——(1891) *Africa and America: Addresses and Discourses* (Springfield, MA).

Cruse, Harold (1967/1984) *The Crisis of the Negro Intellectual* (New York, 2nd edn).

——(1968) *Rebellion or Revolution* (New York).

Cummins, Eric (1994) *The Rise and Fall of California's Radical Prison Movement* (Stanford, CA).

Curl, James Stevens (1994) *Egyptomania. The Egyptian Revival: A Recurring Theme in the History of Taste* (Manchester).

Dafa'alla, Samia (1993) 'Succession in the Kingdom of Napata, 1300–900 BC', *International Journal of African Historical Studies* 26, 1.

Danforth, Loring M. (1995) *The Macedonian Conflict: Ethnic Nationalism in a Transnational World* (Princeton, NJ).

Dash, J. Michael (1981) *Literature and Ideology in Haiti 1915–1961* (London).

——(1988) *Haiti and the United States: National Stereotypes and the Literary Imagination* (Basingstoke).

Dathorne, O.R. (1989) 'Africa as Ancestor: Diop as Unifier', *Présence Africaine* 149–50.

——(1994) *In Europe's Image: The Need for American Multiculturalism* (Westport, CT).

Davidson, Basil (1959) *Old Africa Rediscovered* (London: US title: *The Lost Cities of Africa*).

——(1964) *The African Past: Chronicles from Antiquity to Modern Times* (Boston, MA and London).

——(1974) *Africa in History* (London).

——(1987) 'The Ancient World and Africa: Whose Roots?', *Race and Class* 29, 2.

Davies, W. Vivian (ed. 1991) *Egypt and Africa: Nubia from Prehistory to Islam* (London).

and Walker, Roxie (eds 1993) *Biological Anthropology and the Study of Ancient Egypt* (London).

Davis, David Brion (1994) 'The Slave Trade and the Jews', *New York Review of Books*, 22 December.

Davis, Mike *et al.* (eds 1987) *The Year Left 2: Toward a Rainbow Socialism* (London).

Davis, Whitney (1990) 'The Study of Rock Art in Africa', in Robertshaw (ed.).

de Barros, Philip (1990) 'Changing Paradigms, Goals and Methods in the Archaeology of French West Africa', in Robertshaw (ed.).

Decker, Jeffrey Louis (1994) 'The State of Rap: Time and Place in Hip Hop Nationalism', in Andrew Ross and Tricia Rose (eds) *Microphone Fiends: Youth Music and Youth Culture* (New York and London).

deGraft-Johnson, J.C. (1954) *African Glory: The Story of Vanished Negro Civilizations* (cited from 1986 Baltimore, MD repr.).

Delany, Martin R. (1880) *Principia of Ethnology: The Origins of Race and Color, with an Archaeological Compendium of Ethiopian and Egyptian Civilization from Years of Careful Examination and Study* (2nd edn Philadelphia, PA; orig. pub. 1878).

Dennis, Denise (1984) *Black History for Beginners* (New York).

Dent, Gina (ed. 1992) *Black Popular Culture* (Seattle, WA).

Diagne, P[athé] (1981) 'History and Linguistics', in Ki-Zerbo (ed.).

Diawara, Manthia (1992) 'Afro-Kitsch', in Dent (ed.).

Diaz-Andreu, Marguerita and Champion, Timothy (eds. 1996) *Nationalism and Archaeology in Europe* (London).

Dickerson, Bette J. (1995) 'Afrocentric Education: A State of Consensus or Confusion? A Case Study', in Ziegler (ed.).

Diederich, Bernard and Burt, Al (1969) *Papa Doc: The Truth About Haiti Today* (New York).

Dikotter, Frank (1992) *The Discourse of Race in Modern China* (London).

Dillard, William LaRue (1990) *Biblical Ancestry Voyage: Revealing Facts of Significant Black Characters* (Monrovia, CA).

Diop, Cheikh Anta (1956) 'The Cultural Contribution and Prospects of Africa', *Présence Africaine* Special Issue, nos. 18–19.

——(1959) 'African Cultural Unity', *Présence Africaine* Special Issue, nos 24–5.

——(1960) *Les Fondements culturels, techniques et industriels d'un état fédéral d'Afrique noire* (Paris).

——(1962/1989) *Égypte ancienne et Afrique noire* (Dakar; orig. pub. in *Bulletin de l'IFAN* 24, B, 2–3 as 'Histoire primitive de l'Humanité: Évolution du monde noir', repr. in book form 1989).

——(1967) *Antériorité des civilisations nègres: mythe ou vérité historique?* (Paris).

——(1973) *'Introduction à l'étude des migrations en Afrique Centrale et Occidentale: Identification du berceau nilotique du peuple sénégalais', Bulletin de l'IFAN* 35, B.

——(1974a) *The African Origin of Civilization: Myth or Reality* (Chicago: abbreviated trans. of works orig. pub. in French, 1955 and 1967).

——(1974b) *Physique nucléaire et chronologie absolue* (Dakar).

——(1975) *L'Antiquité africaine par l'image* (Dakar).

——(1977) *Parenté génétique de l'égyptien pharaonique et des langues négro-africaines: processus de sémitisation* (Dakar).

——(1981) 'Origin of the Ancient Egyptians', in Mokhtar (ed.).

——(1984) *Black Africa: The Economic and Cultural Basis of a Federal State* (Westport, CT; revised edn of 1960).

——(1985) *Philosophie, Science et Religion* (Dakar).

——(1986) 'The Beginnings of Man and Civilization' (lecture at Morehouse College, Atlanta, 6 April 1985), in Van Sertima and Williams (eds).

——(1987) *Precolonial Black Africa* (New York; orig. pub. in French 1960).

——(1988) *Nouvelles recherches sur l'égyptien ancien et les langues négro-africaines modernes* (Paris).

——(1989) *The Cultural Unity of Black Africa* (Chicago; orig. pub. in French 1960, in English 1963).

——(1990) *Alerte sous les Tropiques: articles 1946–1960. Culture et développement en Afrique noire* (Paris).

——(1991) *Civilization or Barbarism: An Authentic Anthropology* (New York; orig. pub. in French 1981).

(Charles S. Finch, 1989) 'Interview with Cheikh Anta Diop' and 'Further Conversations with the Pharaoh', *Présence Africaine* 149–50.

(Ivan Van Sertima and Larry Williams, 1986) 'Two Interviews with Cheikh Anta Diop', in Van Sertima and Williams (eds).

(Carlos Moore, 1989) 'Conversations with Cheikh Anta Diop', *Présence Africaine* 149–50.

Diouf, Mamadou and Mbodj, Mohamed (1986) 'Senegalese Historiography: Present Practices and Future Perspectives', in Jewsiewicki and Newbury (eds).

——(1992) 'The Shadow of Cheikh Anta Diop', in Mudimbe (ed.).

Dols, Michael (1977) *The Black Death in the Middle East* (Princeton, NJ).

Donelan, James (1989) 'The Argument from Noise', *Critical Texts* 6, 3.

Dower, John (1986) *War Without Mercy: Race and Power in the Pacific War* (London).

Drake, St Clair (1970) *The Redemption of Africa and Black Religion* (Chicago).

——(1987, 1990) *Black Folk Here and There: An Essay in History and Anthropology* (2 vols Los Angeles).

and Cayton, Horace R. (1945) *Black Metropolis: A Study of Negro Life in a Northern City* (New York).

Draper, Theodore (1960) *American Communism and Soviet Russia* (New York).

Drescher, Seymour (1993) 'The Role of Jews in the Transatlantic Slave Trade', *Immigrants and Minorities* 12.

D'Souza, Dinesh (1991) *Illiberal Education: The Politics of Race and Sex on Campus* (New York).

——(1995) *The End of Racism* (New York).

Du Bois, W.E.B. (1899) *The Philadelphia Negro* (New York: cited from 1967 Schocken edn).

——(1903/1961) *The Souls of Black Folk* (cited from 1961 Fawcett edn; first pub. New York 1903).

——(1915) *The Negro* (cited from 1916 1st London edn; first pub. New York 1915).

——(1939) *Black Folk Then and Now* (New York).

——(1940) *Dusk of Dawn: An Essay Towards the Autobiography of a Race Concept* (New York).

——(1947) *The World and Africa* (New York).

——(1985) *Creative Writings by W.E.B. Du Bois* (ed. Herbert Aptheker, White Plains, New York).

Dubow, Saul (1995) *Scientific Racism in Modern South Africa* (Cambridge).

duCille, Ann (1994) 'Postcoloniality and Afrocentricity: Discourse and dat course' in Sollors and Diedrich (eds).

Duignan, Peter and Gann, L.H. (1984) *The United States and Africa: A History* (Cambridge).

Dyson, Michael Eric (1993) *Reflecting Black: African-American Cultural Criticism* (Minneapolis, MN).

Early, Gerald (ed. 1993) *Lure and Loathing: Essays on Race, Identity, and the Ambivalence of Assimilation* (New York).

——(1994) '"Black Herman Comes Through only Once Every Seven Years": Black Magic, White Magic, and American Culture', in Sollors and Diedrich (eds).

——(1995) 'Understanding Afrocentrism: Why Blacks Dream of a World without Whites', *Civilization*, July–August.

Easton, Hosea (1837) *A Treatise on the Intellectual Character and the Political Condition of the Colored People of the United States and the Prejudice Exercised towards them* (Boston, MA).

Edgerton, Robert (1992) *Sick Societies: Challenging the Myth of Primitive Harmony*, (New York).

Edwards, David N. (1989) *Archaeology and Settlement in Upper Nubia in the 1st Millennium AD* (Cambridge, Monographs in African Archaeology 36).

——(1996) *The Archaeology of the Meroitic State: New Perspectives on its Social and*

Political Organisation (Cambridge, Monographs in African Archaeology 38).

Ehret, Christopher and Posnansky, Merrick (eds. 1982) *The Archaeological and Linguistic Reconstruction of African History* (Berkeley, CA).

Ekwe-Ekwe, Herbert and Nzegwu, Femi (1994) *Operationalising Afrocentrism* (Reading).

El-Amin, Mustafa (1985) *Al-Islam, Christianity and Freemasonry* (Jersey City, NJ).

Elbl, Ivana (1997) 'The Volume of the Early Atlantic Slave Trade, 1450–1521', *Journal of African History* 38, 1.

Ellis, George W. (1914) *Negro Culture in West Africa* (New York).

Ellison, Ralph (1983) *Invisible Man* (Harmondsworth; orig. pub. 1952).

Eribon, Didier (1992) *Michel Foucault* (London).

Essien-Udom, E.U. (1964) *Black Nationalism: A Search for Identity in America* (2nd edn New York).

Evans, William McKee (1980) 'From the Land of Canaan to the Land of Guinea: The Strange Odyssey of the Sons of Ham', *American Historical Review*, 85, 1.

Evans-Pritchard, E.E., Firth, Raymond, Malinowski, Bronislaw, and Schapera, Isaac (eds 1934) *Essays Presented to C.G. Seligman* (London).

Eze, Emmanuel Chukwudi (ed. 1996) *Race and the Enlightenment: A Reader* (Oxford).

——(ed. 1997) *Postcolonial African Philosophy: A Critical Reader* (Oxford).

Fabian, Johannes (1983) *Time and the Other: How Anthropology Makes its Object* (New York).

Fagan, Brian M. (1977) *The Rape of the Nile: Tomb Robbers, Tourists and Archaeologists in Egypt* (London).

Fage, J.D. (1981) 'The Development of African Historiography', in Ki-Zerbo (ed.).

Fagg, William, Pemberton, John III and Holcombe, Bryce (1982) *Yoruba Sculpture of West Africa* (New York).

Falola, Toyin (ed. 1991) *Yoruba Historiography* (Madison, WI).

Fanon, Frantz (1952/1970) *Black Skin, White Masks* (orig. pub. Paris 1952; cited from 1970 London edn).

——(1959/1965) *A Dying Colonialism* (orig. pub. Paris 1959; cited from 1965 New York edn).

——(1961/1967) *The Wretched of the Earth* (orig. pub. Paris 1961; cited from 1967 Harmondsworth edn).

——(1964/1970) *Toward the African Revolution* (orig. pub. Paris 1964; cited from 1970 Harmondsworth edn).

Faulkner, R.O. (trans. and ed. 1985) *The Ancient Egyptian Book of the Dead* (London).

Feierman, Steven (1974) *The Shambaa Kingdom: A History* (Madison, WI).

Fell, Barry (1976) *America BC: Ancient Settlers in the New World* (New York).

Ferguson, James (1987) *Papa Doc, Baby Doc: Haiti and the Duvaliers* (Oxford).

Ferris, William H. (1913, 2 vols) *The African Abroad or, His Evolution in*

Western Civilization. Tracing His Development under Caucasian Milieu (New Haven, CT).

Finch, Charles (1988) 'The Kamitic Genesis of Christianity', in Ben-Jochannen *et al.*

——(1989) 'The Works of Gerald Massey: Studies in Kamite Origins', in Van Sertima (ed.).

——(1990) *The African Background to Medical Science: Essays in African History, Science and Civilizations* (London).

——(1994) 'Nile Genesis: Continuity of Culture from the Great Lakes to the Delta', in Van Sertima (ed.).

Finkielkraut, Alain (1988) *The Undoing of Thought* (London).

Finn, Julio (1986) *The Bluesman* (London).

Fiske, John (1993) *Power Plays, Power Works* (London).

——(1994) 'Blackstream Knowledge: Genocide', in *Media Matters* (Minneapolis).

Fitzgerald, Mary Anne (1995) 'Rift Valley', *The Sunday Times*, 19 March.

Floyd, Samuel A. Jr (1995) *The Power of Black Music: Interpreting its History from Africa to the United States* (New York and Oxford).

Forbes, Ella (1990) 'African-American Resistance to Colonization', *Journal of Black Studies* 21, 2.

Forman, James (1981) *Self-Determination and the African-American People* (Seattle, WA).

Fox-Genovese, Elizabeth (1988) *Within the Plantation Household: Black and White Women of the Old South* (Chapel Hill, NC).

France, Peter (1991) *The Rape of Egypt: How the Europeans Stripped Egypt of its Heritage* (London).

Franklin, John Hope (1985) *George Washington Williams: A Biography* (Chicago).

——(1988) 'George Washington Williams and Africa', in Genna Rae McNeil and Michael R. Winston (eds) *Historical Judgements Reconsidered* (Washington, DC).

Franklin, Vincent P. (1992a) *Black Self-Determination: A Cultural History of African-American Resistance* (2nd edn New York).

——(1992b) 'Caribbean Intellectual Influences on Afro-Americans in the United States', in Alistair Hennessy (ed.) *Intellectuals in the Twentieth-Century Caribbean. vol. 1: Spectre of the New Class: the Commonwealth Caribbean* (London).

Fredrickson, George M. (1995) *Black Liberation: A Comparative History of Black Ideologies in the United States and South Africa* (New York and Oxford).

Frederikse, Julie (1983) *None But Ourselves: Masses vs. Media in the Making of Zimbabwe* (London).

Friedman, Murray (1995) *What Went Wrong? The Creation and Collapse of the Black–Jewish Alliance* (New York).

Frobenius, Leo (1913) *The Voice of Africa: Being an Account of the Travels of the German Inner African Expedition in the Years 1910–1912* (2 vols, London).

——(1933) *Kulturgeschichte Afrikas: Prolegomena zu einer historischen Gestaltlehre* (Zurich).

Froment, Alain (1991) 'Origine et évolution de l'homme dans la penseé de Cheikh Anta Diop: une analyse critique', *Cahiers d'Études Africaines* 31, 1/2.

Fryer, Peter (1984) *Staying Power: The History of Black People in Britain* (London).

Gaines, Kevin (1993) 'Black Americans' Racial Uplift Ideology as "Civilizing Mission": Pauline E. Hopkins on Race and Imperialism', in Amy Kaplan and Donald E. Pease (eds) *Cultures of United States Imperialism* (Durham, NC).

Gardell, Mattias (1996) *Countdown to Armageddon: Louis Farrakhan and the Nation of Islam* (London: pub. in USA as *In the Name of Elijah Muhammad*, Durham, NC).

Gardner, Brian (1968) *The Quest for Timbuctoo* (London).

Garlake, Peter S. (1973) *Great Zimbabwe* (London).

——(1982) 'Prehistory and Ideology in Zimbabwe', *Africa* 52, 3.

——(1995a) 'The African Past', in Phillips (ed.).

——(1995b) *The Hunter's Vision: The Prehistoric Art of Zimbabwe* (London).

Garland, Sonja D. (1995) 'Afrocentricity: Know the Truth of the Past for a Successful Future', in Ziegler (ed.).

Garnet, Henry Highland (1848) *The Past and Present Condition, and the Destiny of the Colored Race: A Discourse Delivered at . . . Troy NY, February 14, 1848* (New York).

Garvey, Marcus (1923/1925/1986) *Philosophy and Opinions of Marcus Garvey* (orig. pub. in 2 vols 1923 and 1925; repub. in 1 vol. New York 1986; ed. Amy Jacques Garvey).

Gates, Henry Louis Jr (1988) *The Signifying Monkey* (Oxford).

——(1991) 'Critical Fanonism', *Critical Inquiry* 17, 3.

——(1992) 'Black Demagogues and Pseudo-Scholars', *New York Times*, 20 July.

——(1994) 'I'm Tired of "Yes, but . . ."', *Times Higher Educational Supplement*, 20 May.

and McKay, Nellie Y. (eds 1997) *The Norton Anthology of African American Literature* (New York and London).

Gathercole, Peter and Lowenthal, David (eds 1990) *The Politics of the Past* (London).

Geiss, Imanuel (1974) *The Pan-African Movement* (London; orig. pub. in German 1968).

Genovese, Eugene (1972) *In Red and Black: Marxian Explorations in Southern and Afro-American History* (New York).

——(1981) *From Rebellion to Revolution: Afro-American Slave Revolts in the Making of the New World* (New York).

George, Lynell (1992) *No Crystal Stair: African-Americans in the City of Angels* (New York).

Ghosh, Amitav (1992) *In an Antique Land* (London).

Gilkes, Cheryl Townsend (1995) 'We Have A Beautiful Mother: Womanist Musings on the Afrocentric Idea', in Sanders (ed).

Gilroy, Paul (1982) 'Steppin' Out of Babylon – Race, Class and Autonomy', in Centre for Contemporary Cultural Studies: *The Empire Strikes Back* (London).

——(1987) *There Ain't No Black in the Union Jack* (London).

——(1992) 'Cultural Studies and Ethnic Absolutism', in Lawrence Grossberg, Cary Nelson and Paula Treichler (eds) *Cultural Studies* (London).

——(1993a) *The Black Atlantic: Modernity and Double Consciousness* (London).

——(1993b) *Small Acts: Thoughts on the Politics of Black Cultures* (London).

——(1994) 'After the Love Has Gone: Bio-politics and etho-poetics in the Black Public Sphere', *Public Culture* 15.

Ginzburg, Carlo (1980) *The Cheese and the Worms: The Cosmos of a Sixteenth-century Miller* (London; orig. pub. in Italian 1976).

——(1983) *The Night Battles: Witchcraft and Agrarian Cults in the Sixteenth and Seventeenth Centuries* (London; orig. pub. in Italian 1966).

——(1990) *Ecstasies: Deciphering the Witches' Sabbath* (London; orig. pub. in Italian 1989).

Glazer, Nathan (1997) *We Are All Multiculturalists Now* (Cambridge, MA).

Glazier, Stephen D. (ed. 1993) 'The Spiritual Baptists, Shango and Others: African-derived Religions in the Caribbean', *Caribbean Quarterly* Special Issue, 39, 3/4.

Gomez, Michael A. (1990) 'Timbuktu under Imperial Songhay: A Reconsideration of Autonomy', *Journal of African History* 31, 1.

Goonatilake, Susantha (1989) 'The Son, the Father, and the Holy Ghost', *Economic and Political Weekly*, 5 August.

Gordon, Lewis R., Sharpley-Whiting, T. Denean and White, Renee T. (eds 1996) *Fanon: A Critical Reader* (Oxford).

Gordon, Murray (1989) *Slavery in the Arab World* (New York).

Gordon, Vivian Verdell (1991) *Kemet and Other Ancient African Civilizations* (Chicago).

Gould, Stephen Jay (1981) *The Mismeasure of Man* (New York).

Gray, Chris (1989) *Conceptions of History in the Works of Cheikh Anta Diop and Théophile Obenga* (London).

Green, Tamara M. (1989) '*Black Athena* and Classical Historiography: Other Approaches, Other Views', *Arethusa* Special Issue, Fall.

Griaule, Marcel (1965) *Conversations with Ogotemmeli* (London; orig. pub. in French 1948).

and Dieterlen, Germaine (1965) *Le Renard pâle* (Paris).

Griffin, Jasper (1989) 'Who Are These Coming for the Sacrifice?', *New York Review of Books*, 15 June.

——(1996) 'Anxieties of Influence', *New York Review of Books*, 20 June.

Grimal, Nicolas (1992) *A History of Ancient Egypt* (Oxford; orig. pub. in French 1988).

Gross, Paul R. and Levitt, Norman (1994) *Higher Superstition: The Academic Left and its Quarrels with Science* (Baltimore, MD).

Gugelberger, George M. (1991) 'Decolonizing the Canon: Considerations on Third World Literature', *New Literary History* 22, 3.

Gurr, Ted Robert (ed. 1989) *Violence in America: vol. 2: Protest, Rebellion, Reform* (Newbury Park, CA).

Guthrie, Paul Lawrence (1992) *Making of the Whiteman: History, Tradition and the Teachings of Elijah Muhammad* (San Diego, CA).

Gutmann, Amy (ed. 1994) *Multiculturalism: Examining the Politics of Recognition* (Princeton, NJ).

Gutzmore, Cecil (1988) 'The Image of Marcus Garvey in Reggae Orature', in Kwesi Owusu (ed.) *Storms of the Heart: An Anthology of Black Arts and Culture* (London).

Gyekye, Kwame (1987) *An Essay on African Philosophy* (Cambridge).

Hacker, Andrew (1992) *Two Nations: Black and White, Separate, Hostile, Unequal* (New York).

Hakem, A.A. (1981) 'The Civilization of Napata and Meroë', in Mokhtar (ed.).

Haley, Alex (1976) *Roots* (Garden City, NJ).

Haley, Shelley P. (1993) 'Black Feminist Thought and the Classics: Remembering, Re-claiming, Re-empowering', in Nancy Sorkin Rabinowitz and Amy Richlin (eds) *Feminist Theory and the Classics* (London).

Halisi, Clyde (ed. 1967) *The Quotable Karenga* (Los Angeles).

Hall, Edith (1989) *Inventing the Barbarian: Greek Self-Definition through Tragedy* (Oxford).

——(1992) 'When Is a Myth Not a Myth?: Bernal's "Ancient Model"', *Arethusa* 25, 1.

——(1996) Revised version of 1992, in Lefkowitz and Rogers (eds).

Hall, Jonathan (1990) '*Black Athena*: A Sheep in Wolf's Clothing?', *Journal of Mediterranean Archaeology* 3.

Hall, Martin (1990) '"Hidden History": Iron Age Archaeology in Southern Africa', in Robertshaw (ed.).

——(1995) 'Great Zimbabwe and the Lost City: The Cultural Colonization of the South African Past', in Ucko (ed.).

Hall, Raymond L. (1978) *Black Separatism in the United States* (Hanover, NH).

Hall, Stuart (1995) 'Negotiating Caribbean Identities', *New Left Review* 209.

Hancock, Graham (1995) *Fingerprints of the Gods* (London).

Hannaford, Ivan (1996) *Race: The History of an Idea in the West* (London).

Hansberry, William Leo (1974) *Pillars in Ethiopian History* (ed. Joseph E. Harris, Washington DC).

——(1977) *Africa and Africans as Seen by Classical Writers* (ed. Joseph E. Harris, Washington DC).

Harding, Sandra (1991) *Whose Science, Whose Knowledge? Thinking from Women's Lives* (Milton Keynes).

——(1994) 'Is Science Multicultural? Challenges, Resources, Opportunities, Uncertainties', in David Theo Goldberg (ed.) *Multiculturalism: A Reader* (Oxford).

——(1997) 'Is Modern Science an Ethnoscience? Rethinking Epistemological Assumptions', in Eze (ed.).

Harding, Vincent (1981) *There Is a River: The Black Struggle for Freedom in America* (New York).

Harlan, Louis R. (1972) *Booker T. Washington: The Making of a Black Leader, 1856–1901* (New York and Oxford).

——(1983) *Booker T. Washington: The Wizard of Tuskegee, 1901–1915* (New York and Oxford).

Harper, Phillip Brian (1993) 'Nationalism and Social Division in Black Arts Poetry of the 1960s', *Critical Inquiry* 19, 2.

Harris, Eddy L. (1992) *Native Stranger: A Black American's Journey into the Heart of Africa* (New York).

Harris, Joseph E.(1971) *The African Presence in Asia: Consequences of the East African Slave Trade* (Evanston, IL).

——(1994) *African-American Reactions to War in Ethiopia 1936–1941* (Baton Rouge, LA and London).

Hartog, François (1986) 'Les Grecs égyptologues', *Annales* 41, 5.

——(1988) *The Mirror of Herodotus: The Representation of the Other in the Writing of History* (Berkeley, CA).

Hasan, Yusuf F. (1967) *The Arabs and the Sudan, from the Seventh to the Early Sixteenth Century* (Edinburgh).

Hassan, F.A. (1993) 'Town and Village in Ancient Egypt: Ecology, Society and Urbanization', in Shaw *et al.* (eds).

Haydon, Geoffrey (1985) 'Introduction', in Haydon, Geoffrey and Marks, Dennis (eds) *Repercussions: A Celebration of African-American Music* (London).

Hayne, Joseph E. (1894) *The Black Man; or, the Natural History of the Hamitic Race* (Raleigh, NC).

Haywood, Harry (1978) *Black Bolshevik* (Chicago).

Hechter, Michael (1975) *Internal Colonialism: The Celtic Fringe in British National Development, 1536–1966* (London).

Hedges, R.E.M. and Sykes, B.A. (1993) 'The Extraction and Isolation of DNA from Archaeological Bone', in Davies and Walker (eds).

Herskovits, Melville J. (1941/1958) *The Myth of the Negro Past* (orig. pub. 1941; cited from 1958 edn, Boston, MA).

Hickey, Dennis and Wylie, Kenneth C. (1993) *An Enchanting Darkness: The American Vision of Africa in the Twentieth Century* (East Lansing, MI).

Hill, Christopher (1972) *The World Turned Upside Down* (London; cited from 1984 Penguin edn).

——(1977) *Milton and the English Revolution* (London).

Hill, Robert A. (1981) 'Dread History: Leonard P. Howell and Millenarian Vision in Early Rastafarian Religions in Jamaica', *Epoche: Journal of the History of Religions* 9, 1.

——(ed. with Barbara Bair, 1987) *Marcus Garvey: Life and Lessons: A Centennial Companion to the Marcus Garvey and Universal Negro Improvement Association Papers* (Berkeley, CA).

Hilliard, Asa G. (1986) 'Pedagogy in Ancient Egypt', in Karenga and Carruthers (eds).

——(ed. 1989): *Infusion of African and African American Content in the School Curriculum* (Morristown, NJ).

——(1992) 'The Meaning of KMT (Ancient Egyptian) History for Contemporary African American Experience', *Phylon* 49, 1–2.

——(1994a) 'Bringing Maat, Destroying Isfet: The African and African Diasporic Presence in the Study of Ancient KMT', in Van Sertima (ed.).

——(1994b) 'Kemetic Concepts in Education', in Van Sertima (ed.).

Hilliard, David and Cole, Lewis (1993) *This Side of Glory: The Autobiography of David Hilliard and the Story of the Black Panther Party* (Boston, MA).

Hill-Lubin, Mildred A. (1992) '*Présence Africaine*: A Voice in the Wilderness, a Record of Black Kinship', in Mudimbe (ed.).

Hine, Darlene Clark (ed. 1986) *The State of Afro-American History* (Baton Rouge, LA).

Hiskett, Mervyn (1984) *The Development of Islam in West Africa* (London).

Hodgson, Marshall G.S. (1993) *Rethinking World History: Essays on Europe, Islam, and World History* (ed. Edmund Burke III, Cambridge).

Hoffman, Michael (1991) *Egypt Before the Pharaohs* (2nd edn, Austin, TX).

Holl, Augustin (1990) 'West African Archaeology: Colonialism and Nationalism', in Robertshaw (ed.).

——(1995) 'African History: Past, Present and Future. The Unending Quest for Alternatives', in Schmidt and Patterson (eds).

Holland, Luke (1990) 'Whispers from the Forest: The Excluded Past of the Ache Indians of Paraguay', in Stone and MacKenzie (eds).

Holloway, Joseph E. (1990) *Africanisms in American Culture* (Bloomington, IN).

Hopkins, Pauline E. (1905) *A Primer of Facts Pertaining to the Early Greatness of the African Race and the Possibility of Restoration by its Descendants* (Cambridge, MA).

Horton, James Africanus B. (1868) *West African Countries and Peoples, British and Native . . . and a Vindication of the African Race* (London).

Horton, Mark (1991) 'Africa in Egypt: New Evidence from Qasr Ibrim', in Davies (ed.)

Hoskins, Linus A. (1992) 'Eurocentrism vs. Afrocentrism: A Geopolitical Linkage Analysis', *Journal of Black Studies* 23, 2.

Hountondji, Paulin J. (1983) *African Philosophy: Myth and Reality* (London).

Hourani, Albert (1991) *A History of the Arab Peoples* (London).

Houston, Drusilla Dunjee (1926/1985) *Wonderful Ethiopians of the Ancient Cushite Empire* (Baltimore, MD; orig. pub. Oklahoma City, 1926).

Huggins, Nathan I. (1986) 'Integrating Afro-American History into American History', in Hine (ed.).

——(1990) *Black Odyssey: The African-American Ordeal in Slavery* (New York, 2nd edn).

Huggins, Willis N. and Jackson, John G. (1937) *An Introduction to African Civilizations, with Main Currents in Ethiopian History* (New York).

Hughes, Robert (1993) *Culture of Complaint: The Fraying of America* (New York).

Hunwick, John (1985) 'Songhay, Borno and the Hausa States, 1450–1600', in Ajayi and Crowder (eds).

——(1996) 'Secular Power and Religious Authority in Muslim Society: The Case of Songhay', *Journal of African History* 37, 2.

Iliffe, John (1995) *Africans: The History of a Continent* (Cambridge).

Irek, Malgorzata (1994) 'From Berlin to Harlem: Felix von Luschan, Alain Locke, and the New Negro', in Sollors and Diedrich (eds).

Isaac, Ephraim (1985) 'Genesis, Judaism and the Sons of Ham', in J.R. Willis (ed.) *Slaves and Slavery in Muslim Africa* (London).

Isaacs, Harold R. (1963) *The New World of Negro Americans* (London).

Isichei, Elizabeth (1976) *A History of the Igbo People* (London).

——(1997) *A History of African Societies to 1870* (Cambridge).

Jackson, George (1971) *Soledad Brother: The Prison Letters of George Jackson* (London).

——(1972) *Blood in My Eye* (London).

Jackson, John G. (1970/1994) *Introduction to African Civilizations* (New York: orig. pub. 1970).

——(1972/1993) *Man, God and Civilization* (New York).

Jacoby, Russell and Glauberman, Naomi (eds 1995) *The Bell Curve Debate: History, Documents, Opinions* (New York).

Jahn, Janheinz (1961) *Muntu: An Outline of Neo-African Culture* (London; orig. pub. in German 1958).

——(1974) *Leo Frobenius: The Demonic Child* (Austin, TX).

James, George G.M (1954/1992) *Stolen Legacy* (Trenton, NJ; orig. pub. San Francisco).

Jameson, Fredric (1986) 'Third World Literature in the Era of Multinational Capitalism', *Social Text* 67.

Jansen, J.J. (1978) 'The Early State in Ancient Egypt', in H.J.M. Claessen and P. Skalnik (eds) *The Early State* (The Hague).

Jasanoff, Jay H. and Nussbaum, Alan (1996) 'Word Games: The Linguistic Evidence in *Black Athena*', in Lefkowitz and Rogers (eds).

Jean, Clinton M. (1991) *Behind the Eurocentric Veils* (Amherst, MA).

Jenkyns, Richard (1996) 'Bernal and the Nineteenth Century', in Lefkowitz and Rogers (eds).

Jewsiewicki, Bogumil (1981) 'L'Histoire-monument ou l'histoire-conscience', *Canadian Journal of African Studies* 15, 3.

——(1989) 'African Historical Studies: Academic Knowledge as 'Usable Past' and Radical Scholarship' *African Studies Review* 32, 3.

——(1992) '*Présence Africaine* as Historiography: Historicity of Societies and Specificity of Black African Culture', in Mudimbe (ed.).

and Newbury, David (eds 1986) *African Historiographies: Which History for Which Africa?* (London).

Johnson, Charles (1988) *Being and Race: Black Writing since 1970* (London).

Johnson, Edward A. (1931) *Adam versus Ape-Man and Ethiopia* (New York).

Johnson, Harvey (1903) *The Nations from a New Point of View* (Nashville, TN).

Johnson, Janet H. (ed. 1992) *Life in a Multi-Cultural Society: Egypt from Cambyses to Constantine and Beyond* (Chicago).

Johnson, Samuel (1921) *The History of the Yorubas* (London – written 1897).

Johnson-Odim, Cheryl (1990) 'The Debate over *Black Athena*', *Journal of Women's History* 4, 3.

Jones, Simon (1988) *Black Culture, White Youth* (London).

Jones, Steve (1996) *In the Blood: God, Genes and Destiny* (London).

——Martin, Robert and Pilbeam, David (eds. 1992) *The Cambridge Encyclopaedia of Human Evolution* (Cambridge).

Jordan, Keith (1987) 'The African Presence in Ancient America: Evidence from Physical Anthropology', in Van Sertima (ed.).

Joseph, George Gheverghese (1991) *The Crest of the Peacock: Non-European Roots of Mathematics* (London).

Joseph, Gloria I. (1990) 'Sojourner Truth: Archetypal Black Feminist', in Braxton and McLaughlin (eds).

Joyce, Joyce A. (1987a) 'The Black Canon: Reconstructing Black American Literary Criticism', *New Literary History* 18, 2.

——(1987b) "Who the Cap Fit": Unconsciousness and Unconscionableness in the Criticism of Houston A. Baker Jr. and Henry L. Gates Jr.' *New Literary History* 18, 2.

——(1991) 'Black Woman Scholar, Critic and Teacher: The Inextricable Relationship between Race, Sex and Class', *New Literary History* 22, 3.

——(1994) *Warriors, Conjurers and Priests: Defining Africa-Centered Literary Criticism* (Chicago).

Karenga, Maulana (1969) 'The Black Community and the University: A Community Organizer's Perspective', in Robinson, Foster and Ogilvie (eds).

——(1978) *Essays on Struggle: Position and Analysis* (San Diego, CA).

——(1982) *Introduction to Black Studies* (Inglewood, CA).

——(1985) 'The African Intellectual and the Problem of Class Suicide: Ideological and Political Dimensions', in Asante and Welsh Asante (eds).

——(1988) *The African American Holiday of Kwanzaa* (Los Angeles).

——(ed. 1990) *Reconstructing Kemetic Culture: Papers, Perspectives, Projects* (Los Angeles).

——and Carruthers, Jacob (eds 1986) *Kemet and the African Worldview: Research, Rescue and Restoration* (Los Angeles).

Kaufman, Jonathan (1988) *Broken Alliance: The Turbulent Times between Blacks and Jews in America* (New York).

Keeley, Lawrence H. (1996) *War Before Civilization: The Myth of the Peaceful Savage* (New York and Oxford).

Keita, S.O.Y. (1990) 'Studies of Ancient Crania from Northern Africa', *American Journal of Physical Anthropology* 83, 1.

——(1992) 'Further Studies of Crania from Ancient Northern Africa: An Analysis of Crania from First Dynasty Tombs, Using Multiple Discriminant Functions', *American Journal of Physical Anthropology* 87, 3.

——(1993) '*Black Athena*: "Race", Bernal and Snowden' and 'Response to Bernal and Snowden', both *Arethusa* 26, 3.

Kellner, Bruce (ed. 1984) *The Harlem Renaissance: A Historical Dictionary of the Era* (New York).

Kelly, David H. (1991) 'Egyptians and Ethiopians: Color, Race and Racism', *Classical Outlook* 68.

Kemp, Barry J. (1989) *Ancient Egypt: Anatomy of a Civilization* (London).

Kennedy, Dane (1990) 'The Perils of the Midday Sun: Climatic Anxieties in the Colonial Tropics', in John MacKenzie (ed.) *Imperialism and the Natural World* (Manchester).

Keto, C. Tsehloane (1989) *The Africa Centered Perspective of History and Social Sciences in the Twenty-first Century* (Blackwood, NJ).

——(1995) *Identity and Time: An Afrocentric Paradigm and the Study of the Past* (Blackwood, NJ).

King, Lewis M., Dixon, Vernon J. and Nobles, Wade W. (eds 1976) *African Philosophy: Assumptions and Paradigms for Research on Black Persons* (Los Angeles).

King, Richard D. (1990) *African Origins of Biological Psychiatry* (Germantown, TN).

——(1994) 'The Symbolism of the Crown in Ancient Egypt', in Van Sertima (ed.).

Kingdon, Jonathan (1993) *Self-Made Man and His Undoing* (London).

Kitchen, K.A. (1982) *Pharaoh Triumphant: The Life and Times of Ramesses II, King of Egypt* (Warminster).

——(1993) 'The Land of Punt', in Shaw *et al.* (eds).

Ki-Zerbo, J[oseph] (ed. 1981) *UNESCO General History of Africa vol. 1: Methodology and Pre-history* (Paris).

——(1981b) 'African Prehistoric Art', in ibid.

Klehr, Harvey (1984) *The Heyday of American Communism: The Depression Decade* (New York).

Klein, Martin (1986) 'The Development of Senegalese Historiography', in Jewsiewicki and Newbury (eds).

Knowles-Borishade, Adekotunbo F. (1991) 'Paradigm for Classical African Orature: Instrument for a Scientific Revolution?', *Journal of Black Studies* 21, 4.

Kofsky, Frank (1970) *Black Nationalism and the Revolution in Music* (New York).

Kohn, Marek (1995) *The Race Gallery: The Return of Racial Science* (London).

Kolchin, Peter (1993) *American Slavery 1619–1877* (New York).

Krzyzaniak, Lech (1991) 'Early Farming in the Middle Nile Basin: Recent Discoveries at Kadero (Central Sudan)', *Antiquity* 65.

Kuhl, Stefan (1994) *The Nazi Connection: Eugenics, American Racism, and German National Socialism* (New York).

Kush, Indus Khamit (1983) *What They Never Told You in History Class* (no place of pub. given).

Kymlicka, Will (1995) *Multicultural Citizenship* (Oxford).

——(ed. 1995) *The Rights of Minority Cultures* (Oxford).

Lahr, Marta Mirazon and Foley, Robert (1994) 'Multiple Dispersals and Modern Human Origins', *Evolutionary Anthropology* 3, 2.

Lambropoulos, Vassilis (1993) *The Rise of Eurocentrism: Anatomy of Interpretation* (Princeton, NJ).

Lateiner, Donald (1989) *The Historical Method of Herodotus* (Toronto).

Lawrence, Harold (1962) *African Explorers to the New World* (Los Angeles).

Layton, Robert (ed. 1994) *Conflict in the Archaeology of Living Traditions* (2nd edn London).

Leadbeater, C.W. (1986) *Ancient Mystic Rites* (Wheaton, IL; orig. pub. 1926 as *Glimpses of Masonic History*).

Leclant, J. (1981) 'The Empire of Kush: Napata and Meroë' in Mohktar (ed.).

Lee, Martha F. (1988) *The Nation of Islam, An American Millenarian Movement* (Lewiston, New York, Queenstown and Lampeter).

Leerssen, Joep T. (1986) 'On the Edge of Europe: Ireland in Search of Oriental Roots, 1650–1850', *Comparative Criticism* 8.

——(1988) *Mere Irish and Fíor-Ghael: Studies in the Idea of Irish Nationality, its Development and Literary Expression Prior to the Nineteenth Century* (Amsterdam).

——(1996) *Remembrance and Imagination: Patterns in the Historical and Literary Representation of Ireland in the Nineteenth Century* (Cork).

Lefkowitz, Mary (1992) 'Not Out of Africa', *The New Republic*, 10 February.

——(1996a) *Not Out of Africa: How Afrocentrism Became an Excuse to Teach Myth as History* (New York).

——(1996b) 'Ancient History, Modern Myths', in Lefkowitz and Rogers (eds).

——and Rogers, Guy MacLean (eds 1996) *Black Athena Revisited* (Chapel Hill, NC).

Lemelle, Sidney J. (1994) 'The Politics of Cultural Existence: Pan-Africanism, Historical Materialism and Afrocentricity', in Lemelle and Robin D.G. Kelley (eds) *Imagining Home: Class, Culture and Nationalism in the African Diaspora* (London).

Leslie, Ann (1992) 'The New Thought Police', *Daily Mail*, 14–17 September.

Levine, Lawrence W. (1977) *Black Culture and Black Consciousness: Afro-American Folk Thought from Slavery to Freedom* (New York).

Levine, Molly Myerowitz (1992a) 'The Use and Abuse of Black Athena', *American Historical Review* 97, 2.

——(1992b) 'Multiculturalism and the Classics', *Arethusa* 25, 1.

——(ed. 1989) 'The Challenge of Black Athena', *Arethusa* Special Issue, Fall.

Levtzion, Nehemia (1973) *Ancient Ghana and Mali* (London).

——(1985) 'The Early States of the Western Sudan to 1500', in Ajayi and Crowder (eds).

Lewin, Roger (1987) *Bones of Contention: Controversies in the Search for Human Origins* (New York; cited from 1991 Penguin edn).

Lewis, Bernard (1986) 'The Crows of the Arabs', in Henry Louis Gates Jr (ed.) *Race, Writing, and Difference* (Chicago).

——(1990) *Race and Slavery in the Middle East: An Historical Enquiry* (New York).

Lewis, David Levering (1993) *W.E.B. Du Bois: Biography of a Race. vol. 1: 1868–1919* (New York).

Lewis, Rupert (1987) *Marcus Garvey: Anti-Colonial Champion* (London).

——(1994) 'Walter Rodney: 1968 Revisited', *Social and Economic Studies* 43, 3.

Lincoln, C. Eric (1961) *The Black Muslims in America* (Boston, MA).

Lipsitz, George (1994) *Dangerous Crossroads: Popular Music, Postmodernism and the Poetics of Place* (London).

Liverani, Mario (1990) *Prestige and Interest: International Relations in the Near East c.1600–1100 BC* (Padua).

——(1996) 'The Bathwater and the Baby', in Lefkowitz and Rogers (eds).

Livingstone, David N. (1994) 'Climate's Moral Economy: Science, Race and Place in Post-Darwinian British and American Geography', in Anne Godlewska and Neil Smith (eds) *Geography and Empire* (Oxford).

Livingstone, Frank B. (1962) 'On the Non-Existence of Human Races', *Current Anthropology* 3, 3.

Lock, Grahame (1988) *Forces in Motion: The Music and Thoughts of Anthony Braxton* (New York).

Lonsdale, John (1977) 'When did the Gusii (or any other group) Become a "Tribe"?', *Kenya Historical Review* 5.

Lott, Tommy L. (1992/3) 'Du Bois on the Invention of Race', *The Philosophical Forum* XXIV, 1–3.

Lovejoy, Paul E. (1982) 'The Volume of the Atlantic Slave Trade: A Synthesis', *Journal of African History* 23.

——(1983) *Transformations in Slavery: A History of Slavery in Africa* (Cambridge).

Lowenthal, David (1985) *The Past is a Foreign Country* (Cambridge).

Luke, Don (1985) 'African Presence in the Early History of the British Isles and Scandinavia', in Van Sertima (ed.).

Lumpkin, Beatrice (1983a) 'Africa in the Mainstream of Mathematics History' in Van Sertima (ed.).

——(1983b) *Senefar and Hatshepsut: A Novel of Egyptian Genius* (Chicago).

——(1987) 'Pyramids – American and African: A Comparison', in Van Sertima (ed.).

——(1994) 'Mathematics and Engineering in the Nile Valley', in Van Sertima (ed.).

Lusane, Clarence (1993) 'Rap, Race and Politics', *Race and Class* 35, 1.

Lynch, Hollis R. (1967) *Edward Wilmot Blyden: Pan-Negro Patriot* (London).

——(1978) *Black American Radicals and the Liberation of Africa: The Council on African Affairs, 1937–1955* (Ithaca, New York).

Lynn, Richard (1991) 'The Evolution of Racial Differences in Intelligence', *Mankind Quarterly* XXXII, 1–2.

McAlister, Melani (1996) '"The Common Heritage of Mankind": Race, Nation and Masculinity in the King Tut Exhibit', *Representations* 54.

McCall, Daniel (1969) Review of Diop (1967), *International Journal of African Historical Studies*, 1, 1.

McClellan, Woodford (1993) 'Africans and Black Americans in the Comintern Schools, 1925–1934', *International Journal of African Historical Studies* 26, 2.

McClester, Cedric (1993) *Kwanzaa* (New York).

McCloud, Aminah Beverly (1995) *African American Islam* (New York).

McDougall, Hugh A. (1982) *Racial Myth in English History: Trojans, Teutons, and Anglo-Saxons* (Hanover, NJ).

MacGaffey, Wyatt (1966) 'Conceptions of Race in the Prehistory of Northeast Africa', *Journal of African History* 7, 1.

——(1991) 'Who Owns Ancient Egypt?', *Journal of African History* 32.

McGee, Dubois Phillip (1976) 'Psychology: Melanin, the Physiological Basis for Psychological Wholeness', in King *et al.* (eds).

McIntosh, Susan Leech and McIntosh, Roderick J. (1984) 'The Early City in West African Prehistory', *Annual Review of Anthropology* 12.

——(1993) 'Cities Without Citadels: Understanding Urban Origins along the Middle Niger', in Shaw *et al.* (eds).

McLaughlin, Andree Nicola (1990) 'Black Women, Identity and the Quest for Humanhood and Wholeness: Wild Women in the Whirlwind', in Braxton and McLaughlin (eds).

MacRitchie, David (1884) *Ancient and Modern Britons: A Retrospect* (2 vols London).

Mackey, Liz (1987) *The Great Marcus Garvey* (London).

Mackey, Nathaniel (1992) 'Other: From Noun to Verb', *Representations* 39.

——(1993) *Discrepant Engagement: Dissonance, Cross-culturality, and Experimental Writing* (Cambridge).

Magubane, Bernard Makhosezwe (1987) *The Ties That Bind: African-American Consciousness of Africa* (Trenton, NJ).

Majors, Richard and Gordon, Jacob (eds 1994) *The American Black Male* (Chicago).

Malcioln, Jose V (1996) *The African Origins of Modern Judaism: From Hebrews to Jews* (Trenton, NJ).

Mallows, Wilfrid (1984) *The Mystery of the Great Zimbabwe: The Key to a Major Archeological Enigma* (London).

Mann, Michael (1986) *The Sources of Social Power. vol. 1: A History of Power from the Beginning to AD 1760* (Cambridge).

Manning, Kenneth R. (1993) 'Race, Science and Identity' in Early (ed.).

Manning, Patrick (1990) *Slavery and African Life: Occidental, Oriental, and African Slave Trades* (Cambridge).

Marable, Manning (1983) *How Capitalism Underdeveloped Black America* (London).

——(1984) *Race, Reform and Rebellion: The Second Reconstruction in Black America, 1945–1982* (London).

——(1993) 'Beyond Racial Identity Politics: Towards a Liberation Theory for multicultural democracy', *Race and Class* 35, 1.

——(1995) *Beyond Black and White: Transforming African-American Politics* (London).

Marchand, Suzanne (1997) 'Leo Frobenius and the Revolt against the West' *Journal of Contemporary History* 32, 2.

Martin, Tony (1976) *Race First* (Dover, MA).

——(1983) *The Pan-African Connection: From Slavery to Garvey and Beyond* (Dover, MA).

——(1993) *The Jewish Onslaught: Despatches from the Wellesley Battlefront* (Dover, MA).

Masilela, Ntongela (1994) 'Pan-Africanism or Classical African Marxism?', in Lemelle and Kelley (eds).

Masolo, D.A. (1994) *African Philosophy in Search of Identity* (Bloomington, IN and Edinburgh).

Massey, Douglas S. and Denton, Nancy A. (1993) *American Apartheid: Segregation and the Making of the Underclass* (Cambridge, MA).

Massey, Gerald (1881) *A Book of the Beginnings. vol. 1: Egyptian Origines in the British Isles; vol. 2: Egyptian Origines in the Hebrew, Akkado-Assyrian and Maori* (London).

——(1907) *Ancient Egypt: The Light of the World* (2 vols, London; repr. Baltimore, MD 1992).

Mbiti, John S. (1969) *African Religions and Philosophy* (London).

Mecca, Andrew M., Smelser, Neil J. and Vasconcillos, John (eds 1989) *The Social Importance of Self-Esteem* (Berkeley, CA).

Mee, Jon (1992) *Dangerous Enthusiasm: William Blake and the Culture of Radicalism in the 1790s* (Oxford).

Meier, August (1966) *Negro Thought in America 1880–1915* (Ann Arbor, MI).

——and Rudwick, Elliott (1986) *Black History and the Historical Profession 1915–1980* (Urbana, IL).

Mendelsohn, Oliver and Baxi, Upendra (eds 1994) *The Rights of Subordinated Peoples* (Delhi).

Merelman, Richard M. (1995) *Representing Black Culture: Racial Conflicts and Cultural Politics in the United States* (New York).

Messiha, Khalil *et al.* (1983) 'African Experimental Aeronautics: A 2000-Year-Old Glider', in Van Sertima (ed.).

Mihill, Chris (1997) 'We're African, No Bones About It', *The Guardian*, 11 July.

Miller, John (ed. 1994) *Alternatives to Afrocentrism* (Washington, DC).

Miller, Joseph C. (1980) *Kings and Kinsmen: Early Mbundu States in Angola* (Oxford).

Mintz, Sidney W. and Price, Richard (1992) *The Birth of African American Culture* (Boston, MA).

Moitt, Bernard (1989) 'Cheikh Anta Diop and the African Diaspora:

Historical Continuity and Socio-Cultural Symbolism', *Présence Africaine* 149–50.

Mokhtar, G (amal). (ed. 1981) *UNESCO General History of Africa, vol. 2: Ancient Civilisations of Africa* (Paris).

Momigliano, Arnoldo (1990) *The Classical Foundations of Modern Historiography* (Berkeley, CA).

Montellano, Bernard Ortiz de (1991) 'Multicultural Pseudoscience', *Skeptical Inquirer* 16, Fall.

——(1992) 'Magic Melanin', *Skeptical Inquirer* 16, Winter.

——(1993) 'Melanin, Afrocentricity and Pseudoscience', *Yearbook of Physical Anthropology* 36.

Mooijman, Anita (1995) 'Molefi Asante's Drinking Well: The Woodson Factor in Africalogy', in Ziegler (ed.).

Moore, Deborah Maat (1992a) *The Pineal Gland and Melatonin: Their Relationship to Blacks* (Detroit, MI).

——(1992b) *The African Roots of Mathematics* (Detroit, MI).

Morell, Virginia (1995) *Ancestral Passions: The Leakey Family and the Quest for Humankind's Beginnings* (New York).

Morris, Sarah P. (1989) 'Diadalos and Kadmos: Classicism and Orientalism', *Arethusa* Special Issue, Fall.

——(1992) *Diadalos and the Origins of Greek Art* (Princeton, NJ).

——(1996) 'The Legacy of *Black Athena*', in Lefkowitz and Morris (eds).

Morrison, Toni (ed. 1992) *Race-ing Justice, En-gendering Power: Essays on Anita Hill, Clarence Thomas, and the Construction of Social Reality* (New York).

Moses, Wilson Jeremiah (1978) *The Golden Age of Black Nationalism, 1850–1925* (Hamden, CT).

——(1989) *Alexander Crummell: A Study of Civilization and Discontent* (New York and Oxford).

——(1993) *Black Messiahs and Uncle Toms: Social and Literary Manipulations of a Religious Myth* (2nd edn Pennsylvania).

——(1996) 'Culture, Civilization, and Decline of the West: The Afrocentrism of W.E.B. DuBois', in Bell, Grosholz and Stewart (eds).

Mottahedeh, Roy (1985) *The Mantle of the Prophet: Religion and Politics in Iran* (London).

Mudenge, S.I.G. (1988) *A Political History of Munhumutapa, c.1400–1902* (Harare).

Mudimbe, V.Y. (1988) *The Invention of Africa: Gnosis, Philosophy, and the Order of Knowledge* (Bloomington, IN).

——(1991) *Parables and Fables: Exegesis, Textuality, and Politics in Central Africa* (Madison, WI).

——(ed. 1992) *The Surreptitious Speech: Presence Africaine and the Politics of Otherness 1947–87* (Chicago).

——(1994) *The Idea of Africa* (Bloomington, IN and London).

Muffett, David J.M. (1987) 'Leo Wiener – a plea for re-examination', in Van Sertima (ed.).

Muhly, James (1990) '*Black Athena* versus Traditional Scholarship', *Journal of Mediterranean Archaeology* 3, 1.

Mulford, Carlo (1987) 'Radicalism in Joel Barlow's *The Conspiracy of Kings* (1792)', in Lemay, J.A. Leo (ed.) *Deism, Masonry, and the Enlightenment: Essays Honoring Alfred Owen Aldridge* (Cranbury, NJ).

Mullin, Michael (1992) *Africa in America: Slave Acculturation and Resistance in the American South and the British Caribbean, 1736–1831* (Urbana and Chicago, IL).

Munro-Hay, Stuart C. (1991) *Aksum* (Edinburgh).

Muraskin, William A. (1975) *Middle-Class Blacks in a White Society: Prince Hall Freemasonry in America* (Berkeley, CA).

Murray, Charles and Herrnstein, Richard (1994) *The Bell Curve* (New York).

Muzzolini, A. (1993) 'The Emergence of a Food-Producing Economy in the Sahara', in Shaw *et al.* (eds).

Myers, Linda James (1988) *Understanding an Afrocentric World View: Introduction to an Optimal Psychology* (Dubuque, IA).

Nation of Islam, Historical Research Department (1991) *The Secret Relationship between Blacks and Jews* (Chicago). (This is described on the cover and title page as 'Volume One', but no further volumes seem to have been issued.)

Neter, Tchet Sesh Am (1995) 'Paradigms in Afrocentric Education Theory: Asante's Cultural Conception', in Ziegler (ed.).

Newman, James L. (1995) *The Peopling of Africa: A Geographic Interpretation* (New Haven, CT).

Ngom, Gilbert (1989) 'L'égyptien et les langues bantu: Le cas de Duala', *Présence Africaine* 149–50.

Nicholls, David (1979) *From Dessalines to Duvalier: Race, Colour and National Independence in Haiti* (Cambridge).

——(1985) *Haiti in Caribbean Context: Ethnicity, Economy and Revolt* (London).

Nitecki, Matthew H. and Doris V. (eds 1994) *Origins of Anatomically Modern Humans* (New York).

Nixon, Rob (1994) *Homelands, Harlem and Hollywood: South African Culture and the World Beyond* (London).

Njeri, Itabari (1993) 'Sushi and Grits', in Early (ed.).

Nobles, Wade (1986a) 'Ancient Egyptian Thought and the Development of African (Black) Psychology' in Karenga and Carruthers (eds).

——(1986b) *African Psychology: Toward its Reclamation, Reascension and Revitalization* (Oakland, CA).

Norris, John William (1916) *The Ethiopian's Place in History and His Contribution to the World's Civilization* (Baltimore, MD).

Norton, Robert E. (1996) 'The Tyranny of Germany over Greece?: Bernal, Herder, and the German Appropriation of Greece', in Lefkowitz and Rogers (eds).

Novick, Peter (1988) *That Noble Dream: The 'Objectivity Question' and the American Historical Profession* (Cambridge).

Nzewunwa, Nwanna (1990) 'Archaeology in Nigerian Education', in Stone and MacKenzie (eds).

O'Connor, David (1990) 'Egyptology and Archaeology: An African Perspective', in Robertshaw (ed.).

——(1991) 'Early States along the Nubian Nile' in Davies (ed.).

——(1993a) *Ancient Nubia: Egypt's Rival in Africa* (Philadelphia, PA).

——(1993b) 'Urbanism in Bronze Age Egypt and North-east Africa', in Shaw *et al.* (eds).

——(1996) 'Egypt and Greece: The Bronze Age Evidence', in Lefkowitz and Rogers (eds).

O'Fahey, Rex and Spaulding, Jay (1974) *Kingdoms of the Sudan* (London).

O'Reilly, Kenneth (1989) *Racial Matters: The FBI's Secret File on Black America* (New York).

Obenga, Théophile (1973) *L'Afrique dans l'Antiquité: Égypte pharaonique – Afrique noire* (Paris).

——(1980) *Pour une nouvelle histoire* (Paris).

——(1981) 'Sources and Specific Techniques Used in African History: General Outline', in Ki-Zerbo (ed.).

——(1988) 'Esquisse d'une histoire culturelle de l'Afrique par la lexicologie', *Présence Africaine* 145, 1.

——(1989) 'African Philosophy in Pharaonic Times', in Van Sertima (ed.).

——(1990) *La Philosophie africaine de la période pharaonique: 2780–330 avant notre ère* (Paris).

——(1992) *Ancient Egypt and Black Africa* (London).

——(1995) *A Lost Tradition: African Philosophy in World History* (Philadelphia, PA).

——(1996) *Cheikh Anta Diop, Volney et le Sphinx: contribution de Cheikh Anta Diop à l'historiographie mondiale* (Paris).

Ogunleye, Tolagbe (1997) 'African American Folklore: Its Role in Reconstructing African American History', *Journal of Black Studies* 27, 4.

Okafor, Victor O. (1991) 'Diop and the Origin of Civilization: An Afrocentric Analysis', *Journal of Black Studies* 22, 2.

——(1993) 'An Afrocentric Critique of Appiah's *In My Father's House*', *Journal of Black Studies* 24, 2.

——(1997) 'Toward an Africological Pedagogical Approach to African Civilization', *Journal of Black Studies* 27, 3.

Okpewho, Isidore (1994) 'The Cousins of Uncle Remus', in Sollors and Diedrich (eds).

Okur, Nilgun Anadolu (1993) 'Afrocentricity as a Generative Idea in the Study of African American Drama', *Journal of Black Studies* 24, 1.

Olela, Henry (1981) *From Ancient Africa to Ancient Greece* (Atlanta, GA).

——(1984) 'The African Foundations of Greek Philosophy', in Richard A. Wright (ed.).

Oliver, Paul (1970) *Savannah Syncopators: African Retentions in the Blues* (London).

Oliver, Roland (1991) *The African Experience* (London).

Oliver, William (1989) 'Black Males and Social Problems: Prevention through Afrocentric Socialization', *Journal of Black Studies* 20, 1.

Ouologuem, Yambo (1968) *Le Devoir de violence* (Paris; trans. as *Bound to Violence* London 1971).

Owens, Leslie H. (1986) 'The African in the Garden: Reflections about New World Slavery and its Lifelines', in Hine (ed.).

Oyebade, Bayo (1990) 'African Studies and the Afrocentric Paradigm: A Critique', *Journal of Black Studies* 21, 2.

Painter, Nell Irvin (1977) *Exodusters: Black Migration to Kansas after Reconstruction* (New York).

——(1986) 'Comment', in Hine (ed.).

——(1996) *Sojourner Truth: A Life, A Symbol* (New York).

Palter, Robert (1996a) '*Black Athena*, Afrocentrism, and the History of Science', in Lefkowitz & Rogers (eds).

——(1996b) 'Eighteenth-century Historiography in *Black Athena*', in Lefkowitz and Rogers (eds).

Parker, George Wells (1917) 'The African Origin of the Grecian Civilization', *Journal of Negro History* 2, 1.

Patterson, Orlando (1977) *Ethnic Chauvinism: The Reactionary Impulse* (New York).

——(1982) *Slavery and Social Death: A Comparative Study* (Cambridge, MA).

——(1991) *Freedom in the Making of Western Culture* (London).

Pearson, Hugh (1994) *The Shadow of the Panther: Huey Newton and the Price of Black Power in America* (Reading, MA).

Pennington, Dorthy L. (1985) 'Time in African Culture', in Asante and Welsh Asante (eds).

Pennington, James W.C. (1841) *A Text Book of the Origin and History, &c. &c., of the Colored People* (Hartford, CT).

Perham, Margery (1960) *Lugard: The Years of Authority 1898–1945* (London).

Perry, Bruce (1992) *Malcolm: The Life of a Man Who Changed Black America* (New York).

Perry, W.J. (1923) *Children of the Sun* (London).

Person-Lynn, Kwaku (1996) *First Word: Black Scholars, Thinkers, Warriors* (New York).

Peters, Erskine (1991) *Afrocentricity: Problems of Method and Nomenclature* (Working Papers in African American Studies, Notre Dame University 3, 15).

Phillips, Tom (ed. 1995) *Africa: The Art of a Continent* (London).

Phillipson, David W. (1982) 'Review of J. Ki-Zerbo: *General History of Africa vol. 1*' *Journal of African History* 23, 1.

——(1993) *African Archaeology* (2nd edn London).

Pinkney, Alphonso (1976) *Red, Black, and Green: Black Nationalism in the United States* (Cambridge).

Porter, Bernard (1988) *Gibbon* (London).

Post, Ken (1978) *Arise Ye Starvelings: The Jamaican Labour Rebellion of 1938 and its Aftermath* (The Hague).

Poulton, Hugh (1995) *Who Are the Macedonians?* (London).

Pounder, Robert L. (1992) '*Black Athena II*: History without Rules', *American Historical Review* 97, 2.

Price, Richard (1983) *First-Time: The Historical Vision of an Afro-American People* (Baltimore, MD).

Price-Mars, Jean (1928/1983) *So Spoke the Uncle* (Washington, DC; orig. pub. in French as *Ainsi Parla L'Oncle* 1928).

——(1959) 'Palaeontology, Prehistory and Archaeology', *Présence Africaine* Special Issue 24–5.

Raboteau, Albert J. (1978) *Slave Religion: The 'Invisible Institution' in the Antebellum South* (New York).

Radano, Ronald M. (1993) *New Musical Figurations: Anthony Braxton's Cultural Critique* (Chicago).

Ram, Uri (1993) 'The Colonization Perspective in Israeli Sociology: Internal and External Comparisons', *Journal of Historical Sociology* 6, 3.

Rampersad, Arnold (1988) *The Life of Langston Hughes. vol. II: 1941–1967. I Dream a World* (New York and Oxford).

Ranger, T.O. (1970) *The African Voice in Southern Rhodesia, 1898–1930* (London).

Ransby, Barbara and Matthews, Tracye (1993) 'Black Popular Culture and the Transcendence of Patriarchal Illusions', *Race & Class* 35, 1.

Rashidi, Runoko (1985) 'Ancient and Modern Britons: A Review Essay', in Van Sertima (ed.).

——(1992) *Introduction to the Study of Classical African Civilizations* (London).

——(1994) 'Tribute to a Departed Scholar (In Memory of Chancellor Williams)', in Van Sertima (ed.).

Ray, Benjamin C. (1991) *Myth, Ritual and Kingship in Buganda* (Oxford).

Ray, John (1990) 'An Egyptian Perspective', *Journal of Mediterreanean Archaeology*, 3, 1.

Read, Alan (ed. 1996) *The Fact of Blackness: Frantz Fanon and Visual Representation* (London and Seattle, WA).

Redkey, Edwin S. (1969) *Black Exodus: Black Nationalist Movements 1890–1910* (New Haven, CT).

Reed, Ishmael (1972) *Mumbo Jumbo* (New York).

Rendsburg, Gary (1989) '*Black Athena*: An Etymological Response', *Arethusa* Special Issue, Fall.

Renfrew, Colin (1987) *Archaeology and Language: The Puzzle of Indo-European Origins* (London).

Resnick, Idrian N. (1970) 'Report of the Radical Caucus', *African Studies Newsletter* II, 6–7.

Reynolds-Marniche, Dana (1994) 'The Myth of the Mediterranean Race', in Van Sertima (ed.).

Rice, Michael (1991) *Egypt's Making* (London).

Richards, Dona (1980) 'European Mythology: The Ideology of "Progress"', in Asante and Vandi (eds).

——(1985) 'The Implications of Afro-American Spirituality', in Asante and Welsh Asante (eds). *See also* Ani, Marimba.

Robb, Peter (ed. 1995) *The Concept of Race in South Asia* (New Delhi).

Roberts, Jennifer Tolbert (1994) *Athens on Trial: The Antidemocratic Tradition in Western Thought* (Princeton, NJ).

Robertshaw, Peter (ed. 1990) *A History of African Archaeology* (London).

Robinson, Armstead L, Foster, Craig C. and Ogilvie, Donald H. (eds 1969) *Black Studies in the University* (New York).

Robinson, Cedric J. (1983) *Black Marxism: The Making of the Black Radical Tradition* (London).

——(1993) 'The Appropriation of Frantz Fanon', *Race & Class* 35, 1.

Robinson, John G. (1989) *Born in Blood: The Lost Secrets of Freemasonry* (London).

Rodney, Walter (1972) *How Europe Underdeveloped Africa* (London).

Rogers, Guy MacLean (1996a) 'Multiculturalism and the Foundations of Western Civilization', in Lefkowitz and Rogers (eds).

——(1996b) 'Quo Vadis?', in Lefkowitz and Rogers (eds).

Rogers, J.A. (1927) *This Mongrel World: A Study of Negro-Caucasian Mixing Throughout the Ages, and in all Countries* (New York).

——(1940) *Your History from the Beginning of Time to the Present* (Pittsburgh, PA; repr. 1983).

——(1940–44) *Sex and Race* (3 vols New York).

——(1947/1972) *World's Great Men of Color* (2 vols New York; cited from 1972 edn ed. and intro. by John Henrik Clarke).

——(1952) *Nature Knows No Color-line: Research into the Negro Ancestry of the White Race* (New York, 3rd edn).

——(1957) *100 Amazing Facts About the Negro, with Complete Proof: A Short-cut to the World History of the Negro* (New York, 23rd edn).

Rose, Tricia (1994) *Black Noise: Rap Music and Black Culture in Contemporary America* (Hanover, NJ).

Saad el Din, Muri and Cromer, John (1991) *Under Egypt's Spell: The Influence of Egypt on Writers in English from the Eighteenth Century* (London).

Saad, Elias N. (1983) *The Social History of Timbuktu: The Role of Muslim Scholars and Notables, 1400–1900* (Cambridge).

Said, Edward W. (1988) 'Michael Walzer's *Exodus and Revolution*: A Canaanite Reading', in Said and Christopher Hitchens (eds) *Blaming the Victims* (London).

——(1993) *Culture and Imperialism* (London).

Sall, Babacar (1986) 'Obituary of Cheikh Anta Diop', *West Africa* 2, June.

Sanders, Cheryl J. (1995a) 'Black Women in Biblical Perspective: Resistance, Affirmation, and Empowerment', in Sanders (ed.).

——(1995b) 'Afrocentric and Womanist Approaches to Theological Education', in Sanders (ed.).

——(ed. 1995) *Living the Intersection: Womanism and Afrocentrism in Theology*, (Minneapolis, MN).

Sanders, Edith (1969) 'The Hamitic Hypothesis', *Journal of African History* 10, 4.

Savage, Elizabeth (1992) 'Berbers and Blacks: Ibadi Slave Traffic in Eighteenth-century North Africa', *Journal of African History* 33, 3.

Save-Soderbergh, Torgny (1991) 'The Cultural and Sociopolitical Structure of a Nubian Princedom in Tuthmoside Times', in Davies (ed.).

Savvas, Minas (1989) 'Review of Bernal: *Black Athena*', *The Classical World* 82, 6.

Schiele, Jerome H. (1990) 'Organizational Theory from an Afrocentric Perspective', *Journal of Black Studies* 21, 2.

——(1994) 'Afrocentricity: Implications for Higher Education' *Journal of Black Studies* 25, 2.

Schlesinger, Arthur M. (1992) *The Disuniting of America: Reflections on a Multicultural Society* (New York).

Schmidt, Peter R. and Petterson, Thomas C. (eds 1995) *Making Alternative Histories: The Practice of Archaeology and History in Non-Western Settings* (Santa Fe, NM).

Scholes, Theophilus E.S. (1899) *The British Empire and Alliances: Or Britain's Duty to the Colonies and Subject Races* (London).

——(1905 2 vols) *Glimpses of the Ages: Or the 'Superior' and 'Inferior' Races, so-called, Discussed in the Light of Science and History* (London).

Schor, Joel (1977) *Henry Highland Garnet: A Voice of Black Radicalism in the Nineteenth Century* (Wesport, CT).

Scobie, Edward (1994) *Global African Presence* (Brooklyn, New York).

Seale, Bobby (1970) *Seize the Time: The Story of the Black Panther Party* (London).

Seifert, Charles C. (1938) *The Negro's or Ethiopian's Contribution to Art* (New York).

——(n.d. but 1946) *The True Story of Aesop 'The Negro'* (New York).

Sekyi-Otu, Ato (1996) *Fanon's Dialectic of Experience* (Cambridge, MA).

Seligman, C.G. (1930) *The Races of Africa* (London).

——(1934) *Egypt and Negro Africa: A Study in Divine Kingship* (London).

Semmes, Clovis E. (1992) *Cultural Hegemony and African American Development* (Westport, CT).

Senghor, Léopold Sédar (1964) *On African Socialism* (London).

Serequeberham, Tsenay (ed. 1991) *African Philosophy: The Essential Readings* (New York).

Sergi, Giuseppe (1901) *The Mediterranean Race: A Study of the Origin of European Peoples* (London).

Sewell, Tony (1990) *Garvey's Children: The Legacy of Marcus Garvey* (London).

Shackley, Myra (1983) *Still Living? Yeti, Sasquatch and the Neanderthal Enigma* (New York).

Shafir, Gerson (1989) *Land, Labour and the Origins of the Israeli–Palestinian Conflict, 1882–1914* (Cambridge).

Shakur, Sanyika AKA Monster Kody Scott (1993) *Monster: The Autobiography of an L.A. Gang Member* (New York).

Shannon, Magdaline W. (1996) *Jean Price-Mars, the Haitian Elite and the American Occupation, 1915–35* (Basingstoke).

Shaw, Thurston (1970) *Igbo Ukwu* (London, 2 vols).

——(1976) 'The Prehistory of West Africa' in Ajayi and Crowder (eds).

——(1978) *Nigeria: Its Archaeology and Early History* (London).

——(1981) 'The Prehistory of West Africa', in Ki-Zerbo (ed.).

Sinclair, Paul, Andah, Bassey and Okpoko, Alex (eds 1993) *The Archaeology of Africa: Food, Metals and Towns* (London).

Sherif, N.M. (1981) 'Nubia before Napata (*c.* −3100 – −750)' in Mokhtar (ed.).

Sheriff, Abdul (1987) *Slaves, Spices and Ivory in Zanzibar: Integration of an East African Commercial Empire into the World Economy, 1770–1873* (London).

Shinnie, Peter L. (1967) *Meroë: A Civilization of the Sudan* (London).

——(1971) 'The Legacy of Egypt', in J. Rendell Harris (ed.) *The Legacy of Egypt* (Oxford; 2nd edn).

——(1981) 'The UNESCO History Project', *Canadian Journal of African Studies* 15, 3.

——(1996) *Ancient Nubia* (London and New York).

Shohat, Ella and Stam, Robert (1994) *Unthinking Eurocentrism: Multiculturalism and the Media* (New York).

Shore, Debra (1983) 'Steel Making in Ancient Africa', in Van Sertima (ed.).

Shreeve, James (1995) *The Neandertal Enigma: Solving the Mystery of Modern Human Origins* (New York).

Sindima, Harvey (1990) 'Liberalism and African Culture', *Journal of Black Studies* 21, 2.

Skinner, Elliott P. (1983) 'Afro-Americans in Search of Africa: The Scholars' Dilemma' in E. Skinner and Pearl T. Robinson (eds) *Transformation and Resiliency in Africa as Seen by Afro-American Scholars* (Washington, DC).

Small, Christopher (1987) *Music of the Common Tongue: Survival and Celebration in Afro-American Music* (London).

Smith, Abdullahi (1976) 'The Early States of the Central Sudan', in Ajayi and Crowder (eds).

Smith, Grafton Elliot (1923) *The Ancient Egyptians and the Origins of Civilization* (London).

Smith, H.S. (1991) 'The Development of the "A-Group" Culture in Northern Lower Nubia', in Davies (ed.).

Snowden, Frank M. (1970) *Blacks in Antiquity* (Cambridge, MA).

——(1976) 'Iconographical Evidence on the Black Populations in Greco-Roman Antiquity', in Vercoutter *et al.* (eds).

——(1983) *Before Color Prejudice: The Ancient View of Blacks* (Cambridge, MA).

——(1989) 'Bernal's "Blacks", Herodotus, and other Classical Evidence', *Arethusa* Special Issue, Fall.

——(1996) 'Bernal's "Blacks" and Afrocentrism', in Lefkowitz and Rogers (eds).

Sobell, Michal (1987) *The World They Made Together: Black and White Values in Eighteenth-century Virginia* (Princeton, NJ).

Sofola, J.A. (1973) *African Culture and the African Personality* (Ibadan).

Sollors, Werner and Diedrich, Maria (eds 1994) *The Black Columbiad* (Cambridge, MA).

Soyinka, Wole (1985) 'The African World and the Ethnocultural Debate', in Asante and Welsh Asante (eds).

——(1991) 'Triple Tropes of Trickery', *Transition* 54.

Spady, James G. (1986) 'The Changing Perception of C.A. Diop: The Preeminence of a Scientific Spirit', in Van Sertima and Williams (eds).

——(1989) 'Dr. Cheikh Anta Diop and the Background of Scholarship on Black Interest in Egyptology and Nile Valley Civilizations', *Présence Africaine* 149–50.

Spear, Thomas and Waller, Richard (eds 1993) *Being Maasai* (London).

Spencer, A.J. (1993) *Early Egypt: The Rise of Civilisation in the Nile Valley* (London).

Spitzer, Leo (1972) 'The Sierra Leone Creoles, 1870–1900', in Philip D. Curtin (ed.) *Africa and the West: Intellectual Responses to European Culture* (Madison, WI).

Spratlen, Thaddeus H. (1980) 'Racial Perspectives in Economics', in Asante and Vandi (eds).

Springborg, Patricia (1992) *Western Republicanism and the Oriental Prince* (Cambridge).

Staniland, Martin (1991) *American Intellectuals and African Nationalists, 1955–1970* (New Haven, CT).

Stavenhagen, Rodolfo (1965) 'Classes, Colonialism and Acculturation', *Studies in Comparative International Development* 1, 6.

——(1973) 'The Plural Society in Latin America', *Plural Societies* 4, 4.

——(1975) *Social Classes in Agrarian Societies* (New York).

Steele, Shelby (1990) *The Content of Our Character: A New Vision of Race in America* (New York).

Stein, Judith (1986) *The World of Marcus Garvey: Race and Class in Modern Society* (Baton Rouge, LA).

Stepan, Nancy (1982) *The Idea of Race in Science: Great Britain, 1800–1960* (London).

Stevenson, David (1988) *The Origins of Freemasonry: Scotland's Century 1590–1710* (Cambridge).

Stone, Peter and MacKenzie, Robert (eds 1990) *The Excluded Past: Archaeology in Education* (London).

Stringer, Christopher and Gamble, Clive (1993) *In Search of the Neanderthals* (London).

——and McKie, Robin (1996) *African Exodus: The Origins of Modern Humanity* (London).

Strouhal, Eugen (1971) 'Evidence of the Early Penetration of Negroes into Prehistoric Egypt', *Journal of African History* 12, 1.

Stuckey, Sterling (1987) *Slave Culture: Nationalist Theory and the Foundations of Black America* (New York).

Sutton, J.E.G. (1974) 'The Aquatic Civilization of Middle Africa', *Journal of African History* 15, 4.

Szwed, John F. (1997) *Space Is the Place: The Lives and Times of Sun Ra* (New York).

Tate, Greg (1992) *Flyboy in the Buttermilk: Essays on Contemporary America* (New York).

Taylor, Patrick (1989) *The Narrative of Liberation: Perspectives on Afro-Caribbean Literature, Popular Culture and Politics* (Ithaca, New York).

Tempels, Placide (1959) *Bantu Philosophy* (Paris; orig. pub. in Flemish 1945 and French 1949).

Temple, R.G. (1976) *The Sirius Mystery* (London).

Thomas, Greg (1995) 'The Black Studies War', *Village Voice*, 17 January.

Thomas, Keith (1971) *Religion and the Decline of Magic* (London; cited from 1984 Peregrine edn).

Thomas-Emeagwala, Gloria (1993) *African Systems of Science, Technology and Art: The Nigerian Experience* (London).

Thompson, E.P. (1993) *Witness Against the Beast: William Blake and the Moral Law* (London).

Thompson, Robert Farris (1969) 'African Influence on the Art of the United States', in Robinson, Foster and Ogilvie (eds).

——(1983) *Flash of the Spirit: African and Afro-American Art and Philosophy* (New York).

Thornton, John (1992) *Africa and Africans in the Making of the Atlantic World, 1400–1680* (Cambridge).

Toop, David (1984) *The Rap Attack: African Jive to New York Hip Hop* (London).

Torok, Laszlo (1991) 'Iconography and Mentality: Three Remarks on the Kushite Way of Thinking', in Davies (ed.).

——(1995) 'Nubia', in Phillips (ed.).

Trautmann, Thomas R. (1997) *Aryans and British India* (Berkeley, CA).

Trigger, Bruce G. (1976) *Nubia Under the Pharaohs* (London).

——(1978) 'Nubian, Negro, Black, Nilotic?', in S. Hochfield and E. Riefstahl (eds) *Africa in Antiquity: The Arts of Ancient Nubia and the Sudan* vol. 1 (New York).

——(1989) *A History of Archaeological Thought* (Cambridge).

——(1994) 'Paradigms in Sudan Archaeology', *International Journal of African Historical Studies* 27, 2.

——Kemp, Barry J., O'Connor, David and Lloyd, Allan (1983) *Ancient Egypt: A Social History* (Cambridge).

Trinkaus, Erik and Shipman, Pat (1993) *The Neanderthals: Changing the Image of Mankind* (London; cited from 1994 Pimlico edn).

Tritle, Lawrence A. (1996) '*Black Athena*: Vision or Dream of Greek Origins?', in Lefkowitz and Rogers (eds).

Trouillot, Michel-Rolph (1990) *Haiti: State Against Nation* (New York).

Turner, Frank M. (1989) 'Martin Bernal's *Black Athena*: A Dissent', *Arethusa* Special Issue, Fall.

Turner, Lorenzo (1973) *Africanisms in the Gullah Dialect* (Ann Arbor, MI).

Ucko, Peter J. (ed. 1995) *Theory in Archaeology: A World Perspective* (London).

Ugrinovska, Liljana (ed. n.d. but 1995) *Macedonia: Cultural Heritage* (Skopje).

Uya, O.E. (1982) 'Conceptualizing Afro-American/African Realities', in J.E. Harris (ed.) *Global Dimensions of the African Diaspora* (Washington, DC).

Vail, Charles H. (1909) *The Ancient Mysteries and Modern Masonry* (New York).

Vail, Leroy (ed. 1989) *The Creation of Tribalism in Southern Africa* (London).

Vaillant, Janet G. (1990) *Black, French, and African: A Life of Léopold Sédar Senghor* (Cambridge, MA).

Van Beek, W.E.A. (1991) 'Dogon Restudied: A Field Evaluation of the Work of Marcel Griaule', *Current Anthropology* 32, 2.

Van Deburg, William L. (1992) *New Day in Babylon: The Black Power Movement and American Culture, 1965–1975* (Chicago).

——(ed. 1997) *Modern Black Nationalism: From Marcus Garvey to Louis Farrakhan* (New York and London).

Van den Berghe, Pierre L. (1970) 'Research in Africa: Knowledge for What?', *African Studies Review* 13, 2.

——(1986) 'Ethnicity and the Sociobiology Debate', in John Rex and David Mason (eds): *Theories of Race and Ethnic Relations* (Cambridge).

——(1995) 'Does Race Matter?', *Nations & Nationalism* 1, 3.

Van Dyk, Sandra (1995) 'Towards an Afrocentric Perspective: The Significance of Afrocentricity', in Ziegler (ed.).

Van Sertima, Ivan (1977) *They Came Before Columbus: The African Presence in Ancient America* (New York).

——(ed. 1983) *Blacks in Science, Ancient and Modern,* (New Brunswick, NJ).

——(ed. 1985) *African Presence in Early Europe* (New Brunswick, NJ).

——(ed. 1987) *African Presence in Early America* (New Brunswick, NJ).

——(ed. 1989) *Egypt Revisited* (New Brunswick, NJ; 2nd expanded edn).

——(1989) 'Death Shall not Find Us Thinking That We Die', *Présence Africaine* 149–50 (also in Van Sertima and Williams eds 1986).

——(1994a) 'Editorial: African Origin of Ancient Egyptian Civilization', in Van Sertima (ed.).

——(1994b) 'Egypt is in Africa but was Ancient Egypt African?', in Van Sertima (ed.).

——(ed. 1994) *Egypt: Child of Africa* (New Brunswick, NJ).

——and Williams, Larry (eds 1986) *Great African Thinkers. vol. 1: Cheikh Anta Diop* (New Brunswick, NJ).

——and Rashidi, Runoko (eds 1988) *African Presence in Early Asia* (New Brunswick, NJ; 2nd edn).

Vansina, Jan (1978) *The Children of Woot: A History of the Kuba Peoples* (Madison, WI).

——(1990) *Paths in the Rainforests: Toward a History of Political Tradition in Equatorial Africa* (London).

——(1995) 'New Linguistic Evidence and "The Bantu Expansion"' *Journal of African History* 36, 2.

Vercoutter, Jean (1976) 'The Iconography of the Black in Ancient Egypt', in J. Vercoutter, J. Leclant, F. Snowden and J. Desanges (eds) *The Image of the Black in Western Art.* vol. 1 (Cambridge, MA).

——(1992) *The Search for Ancient Egypt* (London).

Verharen, Charles C. (1997) '"The New World and the Dreams to Which it May Give Rise": An African and American Response to Hegel's Challenge', *Journal of Black Studies* 27, 4.

Vermeule, Emily (1992) 'The World Turned Upside Down', *New York Review of Books*, 26 March. Repr. in Lefkowitz and Rogers (eds 1996).

Vickers, Michael (1987) 'Review of Bernal: *Black Athena I' Antiquity* 61, 233.

Vlach, John (1978) *The Afro-American Tradition in Decorative Arts* (Cleveland, OH).

Walker, Charles Thomas (1900) *An Appeal to Caesar: Sermon on the Race Question* (New York).

Walker, Clarence Earl (1991) *Deromanticizing Black History: Critical Essays and Reappraisals* (Knoxville, TN).

Walters, Ronald (1993) *Pan Africanism in the African Diaspora: An Analysis of Modern Afrocentric Political Movements* (Detroit, MI).

Wandibba, Simiya (1990) 'Archaeology and Education in Kenya', in Stone and MacKenzie (eds).

Waters, Anita. M. (1985) *Race, Class, and Political Symbols: Rastafari and Reggae in Jamaican Politics* (New Brunswick, NJ).

Weinstein, Norman C. (1992) *A Night in Tunisia: Imaginings of Africa in Jazz* (New York).

Weisbord, Robert G. (1973) *Ebony Kinship: Africa, Africans and the Afro-American* (Westport, CT).

Welsing, Frances Cress (1991) *The Isis Papers: The Keys to the Colors* (Chicago).

West, Cornel (1988) 'Marxist Theory and the Specificity of Afro-American Oppression', in Cary Nelson and Lawrence Grossberg (eds) *Marxism and the Interpretation of Culture* (Urbana and Chicago, IL).

——(1993) 'On Black–Jewish Relations' in *Race Matters* (Boston, MA).

Wetterstrom, W. (1993) 'Foraging and Farming in Egypt: The Transition from Hunting and Gathering to Horticulture in the Nile Valley', in Shaw *et al.* (eds).

White, E. Francis (1990) 'Africa on my Mind: Gender, Counter-discourse and African-American Nationalism', *Journal of Women's History* 2, 1.

Whitelam, Keith W. (1996) *The Invention of Ancient Israel: The Silencing of Palestinian History* (London).

Wicker, Tom (1978) *A Time to Die: The Attica Prison Revolt* (Harmondsworth).

Wiener, Leo (1919–22) *Africa and the Discovery of America* (3 vols: Philadelphia, PA).

Wilde, Anna Day (1995) 'Mainstreaming Kwanzaa', *The Public Interest* 119, Spring.

Wildung, Dietrich (ed. 1997) *Sudan: Ancient Kingdoms of the Nile* (Paris and New York).

Wilkinson, David (1993) 'Civilizations, Cores, World Economies, and Oikumenes', in André Gunder Frank and Barry K. Gills (eds) *The World System: 500 Years or 5,000?* (London).

Willett, Frank (1990) 'Museums: Two Case Studies of Reaction to Colonialism', in Gathercole and Lowenthal (eds).

Williams, Bruce (1980) 'The Lost Pharaohs of Nubia', *Archaeology* 33, 5.

——(1987) 'Forebears of Menes in Nubia: Myth or Reality?', *Journal of Near Eastern Studies* 46, 1.

Williams, Chancellor (1961) *The Rebirth of African Civilization* (Washington, DC).

——(1964) *Problems in African History: A College Lecture Series* (no place of pub. given, but evidently Washington, DC).

——(1971/1987) *The Destruction of Black Civilization: Great Issues of a Race from 4500 BC to 2000 AD* (orig. pub. 1971; cited from 1987 Chicago edn).

Williams, Delores S. (1995) 'Afrocentrism and Male–Female Relations in Church and Society', in Sanders (ed.).

Williams, George Washington (1882) *History of the Negro Race in America, from 1619 to 1880* (New York).

Williams, Gwyn A. (1979) *Madoc: The Making of a Myth* (London).

Williams, Loretta J. (1980) *Black Freemasonry and Middle-Class Realities* (Columbia, MS).

Williams, Niama Leslie JoAnn (1995) 'Asante's Africalogical Sense and Women's Studies: Selective Encounters', in Ziegler (ed.).

Wills, Christopher (1994) 'The Skin We're In', *Discover*, November.

Wilmer, Valerie (1980) *As Serious As Your Life: The Story of the New Jazz* (Westport, CT).

Wilson, John A. (1964) *Signs and Wonders Upon Pharaoh: A History of American Egyptology* (Chicago).

Winters, Clyde Ahmad (1994) 'Afrocentrism: A Valid Frame of Reference' *Journal of Black Studies* 25, 2.

Wiredu, Kwasi (1979) 'How Not to Compare African Thought with Western Thought', in Richard A. Wright (ed.).

——(1980) *Philosophy and an African Culture* (Cambridge).

——(1992) 'Formulating Modern Thought in African Languages: Some Theoretical Considerations', in Mudimbe (ed.).

Wolpe, Harold (1988) *Race, Class and the Apartheid State* (London).

Wolpoff, Milford H. (1989a) 'Multiregional Evolution: The Fossil Alternative to Eden', in F.H. Smith and F. Spencer (eds) *The Origin of Modern Humans: A World Survey of the Fossil Evidence* (New York).

——(1989b) 'The Place of the Neanderthals in Human Evolution', in Erik Trinkaus (ed.) *The Emergence of Modern Humans* (Cambridge).

——and Caspari, Rachel (1997) *Race and Human Evolution: A Fatal Attraction* (New York).

Woodson, Carter G. (1922) *The Negro in Our History* (cited from 1962 Washington, DC edn).

——(1933) *The Mis-Education of the Negro* (Washington, DC).

——(1936) *The African Background Outlined: Or, Handbook for the Study of the Negro* (Washington, DC).

Woodyard, Jeffrey Lynn (1991) 'Evolution of a Discipline: Intellectual Antecedents of African American Studies', *Journal of Black Studies* 22, 2.

——(1995) 'Locating Asante: Making Use of *The Afrocentric Idea*', in Ziegler (ed.).

Wright, Patrick (1995) *The Village that Died for England: The Strange Story of Tyneham* (London).

Wright, Richard (1954) *Black Power: A Record of Reactions in a Land of Pathos* (New York).

Wright, Richard A. (ed. 1984) *African Philosophy: An Introduction* (3rd edn; first pub. 1979. Lanham, MD).

Wuthenau, Alexander von (1987) 'Unexpected African Faces in pre-Columbian America', in Van Sertima (ed.).

X, Malcolm and Haley, Alex (1965) *The Autobiography of Malcolm X* (New York: cited from 1968 Penguin edn).

Yansane, Aguibou Y. (1985) 'Cultural, Political and Economic Universals in West Africa', in Asante and Welsh Asante (eds).

Yates, Frances (1964) *Giordano Bruno and the Hermetic Tradition* (London).

——(1972) *The Rosicrucian Enlightenment* (London).

Young, Robert J.C. (1994) 'Egypt in America: *Black Athena*, Racism and Colonial Discourse', in Ali Rattansi and Sallie Westwood (eds) Racism, Modernity and Identity (Cambridge).

——(1995) *Colonial Desire: Hybridity in Theory, Culture and Race* (London).

Yurco, Frank (1989) 'Were the Ancient Egyptians Black or White?' *Biblical Archaeological Review* 15.

——(1996) '*Black Athena*: An Egyptological Review', in Lefkowitz and Rogers (eds).

Zachernuk, Philip S. (1994) 'Of Origins and Colonial Order: Southern Nigerian Historians and the "Hamitic Hypothesis", c.1870–1970', *Journal of African History* 35, 3.

Zack-Williams, Alfred (1995) 'Development and Diaspora: Separate Concerns?', *Review of African Political Economy* 65.

Zaremba, Alan Jay (1995) 'Asante. Indeed.', in Ziegler (ed.).

Ziegler, Dhyana (1995a) 'Preface', in Ziegler (ed.).

——(1995b) 'Molefi Kete Asante: Undefined by the Mass Media', in Ziegler (ed.).

——(1995c) 'Conclusion: A Beginning', in Ziegler (ed.).

——(ed. 1995) *Molefi Kete Asante and Afrocentricity: In Praise and in Criticism* (Nashville, TN).

Zouber, M.A. (1977) *Ahmad Baba de Toumbouctou: sa vie et son œuvre* (Paris).

Zureik, Elia T. (1979) *The Palestinians in Israel: A Study in Internal Colonialism* (London).

Index

Abraham, Alton 63
Adams, William Y. 138, 139–40, 141, 142–3, 146
Adams, Hunter Havelin III 258, 261, 268, 269
African Heritage Studies Association 60, 61, 62
African Islamic Mission (USA) 72, 286
African Liberation Support Committee (USA) 13, 27
African Studies Association (USA) 6, 60–63, 217
AIDS 222, 250, 267, 283, 286
Akbar, Na'im 266
Akhnaten, Pharoah 123, 127, 176
Al-Arabi, Ibn 152
Al-Azmeh, Aziz 273
Algeria 78, 81, 132
Ali, Ahmed and Ibrahim 253
Ali, Noble Drew 49, 72
Allen, Robert L. 91
Althusser, Louis 158, 161
Amenhotep III, Pharoah 45
American Negro Leadership Conference on Africa 13
Amin, Idi 243
Amin, Samir 12
Andah, Bassey 191
Ani, Marimba 11, 188, 247–9, 257, 283–4
Ansaru Allah Community 227

Anti-Defamation League 276
anti-Semitism 8, 91, 176, 194, 195, 204, 208–9, 218, 226, 253, 273, 276, 277–8, 281
apartheid 13, 88, 120, 147, 236, 247
Appiah, Kwame Anthony 16, 52, 112, 160, 161, 186, 206, 207
Aquinas, Thomas 152
Arabs, Arabia 15, 46, 54, 80, 118, 119, 120, 135, 137, 140, 144, 147–9, 150, 152, 154, 172, 177, 181, 190, 208, 218, 219–20, 226, 228, 234–5, 237, 238, 243, 245, 248, 257, 258, 272, 273, 274, 276, 279, 282–3, 286
Aristotle 126, 127, 128, 205, 209, 210
Armah, Ayi Kwei 57, 238, 282
Arrested Development (rap group) 282
'Aryans'/'Aryan myth' 15, 47, 115, 171, 177, 193, 194–5, 196, 201, 204, 207, 210, 211, 225, 283
Asante, Molefi K. 11, 15, 16, 57, 67, 72, 79, 86, 130, 147, 148, 153, 180, 207, 215, 216, 218, 228, 230–39, 240–44, 246, 247, 254, 255, 257, 260, 263, 277, 278–9, 280, 281, 285
Asante, Kariamu Welsh 236, 243
Ashanti/Asante people 40, 148, 226, 230, 234
Askia, Mohammed 46

327

Assmann, Jan 128, 135, 211
Association for the Study of Classical
    African Civilisations 124
Astour, Michael 202, 209
Athens 38, 44, 198, 201, 206, 207
Attica prison revolt 95
Augustine of Hippo 38
Axum kingdom 138, 141, 144, 237,
    238

Baba, Ahmed 46, 150, 151, 154
Bachofen, J.J. 168, 175
Baines, John 11, 154, 195, 198, 199,
    200
Baker, Houston A. Jr. 236
Baker, John R. 166, 268, 272, 273
Baldwin, James 187, 189
Baldwin, Joseph A. (AKA Kobi K. K.
    Kambon) 244, 245–6, 269
Balfour Declaration 226
Baltimore 3, 35, 42, 43, 224
Banneker, Benjamin 39, 262
Bantu languages 103, 148, 154,
    156–7, 158, 173, 180
Banu Hilal people 148–9
Baraka, Amiri/Leroi Jones 93, 96–7,
    106, 215–6, 218
Barlow, Joel 123
Beethoven, Ludwig van 38, 53, 56,
    63
Bekerie, Ayele 241, 243
Bell, Augustus T. 36, 63
Bello, Muhammad, Sultan of Sokoto
    121, 152
Benin 40, 105, 115, 159
Ben-Jochannan, Yosef ix, 11, 15, 63,
    66, 67, 69, 72, 77, 124, 127, 147,
    152, 181, 217, 218, 223–6, 227,
    228–9, 231, 244, 253, 259, 261
Bennett, Lerone 21, 284
Bent, J. Theodore 117–8
Bentham, Jeremy 237
Ber, Sunni Ali 151
Berber people 42, 132, 149, 150
Bernal, Martin 4, 8, 11, 67, 117, 123,

124, 132, 133, 134, 135, 186, 191,
    193–211, 231, 232, 235, 243, 258
Bernstein, Richard 7
Berry, Mary F. 59
Biko, Steve 82
Biobaku, S.O. 120
Black Aesthetic movement 27, 144
Black Panthers 77, 78, 97, 216, 282
Blackman, Peter 105
Blake, William 64, 123
Blassingame, John W. 59
Blauner, Robert 91, 92–3
Blavatsky, Helena 65
Blayechettai, J.E.C. 35, 47–8
Bloom, Allan 8
Blumenbach, J.F. 43, 210
Blyden, Edward W. 23, 24, 25, 39, 56,
    75
Boas, Franz 46, 51
Bornu kingdom 143
Botha, P.W. 283–4
Brace, C. Loring 11, 132–3, 134–5,
    145, 191
Bradley, Michael 248, 250, 270–72,
    272–3, 276
Brathwaite, Edward 106, 107
Brazil 101, 102, 104, 111, 233
Brendan, St., legend of 250–1
Britain/British 2, 7, 8, 15, 42, 57, 67,
    69, 73, 82, 88, 98, 109, 110, 112,
    115–6, 117, 118, 142, 169, 184,
    188, 194, 198, 203, 210, 226, 229,
    244, 252–3, 254–5
British Museum 142, 154, 228
Brooks, Alison 34
Browder, Anthony T. 70, 124, 135,
    136
Browder, Atlantis Tye 124
Browder, Earl 90
Brown, E. Ethelred 75
Brown, George W. 59
Brown, William Wells 35, 39
Browning, Robert 38, 53, 56
Bruce, John E. 70, 75
Brunson, James 133–4

Buganda 173
Burkert, Walter 207–8

Cain 37
Cairo 125, 151, 183, 184, 191, 206
Cambridge, Alrick 109–10
Canaanite people 40, 109, 229
Canada 2, 89
Cann, Rebecca 29, 30
Caribbean 1, 12–13, 24, 26, 73–86,
    88, 101, 102, 104, 106, 109, 110,
    111, 217, 233, 249
Carlyle, Thomas 45, 55, 60, 236
Carmichael, Stokely 78, 91–2, 94
Carruthers, Jacob H. 124, 205–6,
    216, 217, 228, 247, 257
Carthage, Carthaginians 36, 37, 43,
    250
Carver, George Washington 262, 270
Castoriadis, Cornelius 198
Caton Thompson, Gertrude 118
Césaire, Aimé 24, 27, 107, 164, 260
Challaoueliziczese, Wyxzewixard S.J.
    261–2
Cheops, Pharoah 173
Chicago 21, 63, 64, 70, 80, 269
Childe, V. Gordon 117, 196
China/Chinese 12, 15, 32, 45, 119,
    193, 227, 253
Chinweizu 251, 282
Christianity/Christians 26, 38, 41, 47,
    48, 55, 65, 66, 67, 71, 74, 101,
    102, 105, 122, 123, 127, 134, 139,
    146, 152, 156–7, 158, 176, 205,
    222–3, 225, 226–7, 252, 255, 257,
    265, 276, 278, 279
Christophe, Henry 223
Churchward, Albert 65, 67–9, 71, 72,
    181, 221, 225, 235, 252–3, 257
Clark, Kenneth 91
Clarke, John Henrik 32, 57, 60–62,
    64, 124, 140, 152, 216–8, 220,
    228, 236, 253, 262–3
Clarke, Sebastian 56–7
Cleage, Albert B. 227, 229
Cleaver, Eldridge 78, 93, 94

Clegg, Legrand H. III 257, 275
Cleopatra 10, 38, 122, 123, 130, 136
Cole, J. Augustus 42
Communism/Communists 52, 53,
    88–90, 91, 92, 94, 95, 217
Connah, Graham 146, 153
Connor, Walker 1
Coon, Carleton 29, 30, 177, 272, 273
Coquery-Vidrovitch, Catherine 182
Coulanges, Fustel de 164
Councill, W.H. 35, 42, 56
Cowan, L. Gray 62–3
Crawford, Clinton 15
Cress Welsing, Frances 218, 221,
    222–3, 227, 228, 248, 255, 256,
    261, 266–7, 268, 269–70, 271,
    283, 284, 285
Crowder, Michael 169
Crummell, Alexander 37, 39, 40, 55,
    56, 75, 76
Cruse, Harold 90, 91, 217, 254
Cuba 73, 102
Cullen, Countee 105

Dafa'alla, Samia 191
Dahomey kingdom 40
Dakar, University of 164, 165, 177
Damas, Leon 24
Darfur kingdom 143
Darwin, Charles/Darwinism 30, 43,
    44
Dathorne, O.R. 110, 112
Davidson, Basil 116, 124–5, 129, 133,
    195, 204, 245
Davis, Anthony 1
deGraft-Johnson, J.C. 57
Dejezer, Pharoah 173
Delafosse, Maurice 116
Delany, Martin 24, 25, 47
Derrida, Jacques 157, 240
Dessalines, Jean-Jacques 223
Detroit 3, 227
Dewey, John 15
Diagne, Pathe 185–6
Diawara, Manthia 110
diffusionism 28, 31–2, 48, 117, 130,

140, 145, 153, 177–8, 186, 198, 210, 221, 232
Diodorus of Sicily 140, 155, 191
Diop, Cheikh Anta x, 4, 8, 10, 11, 31, 33, 47, 49, 57, 80, 103, 110, 116, 119, 121, 125, 130, 132, 133, 134, 135, 136, 147, 150–51, 153, 154, 161, 163–92, 194, 195, 202, 204, 205, 206, 217, 225, 226, 228, 231, 232, 235, 236, 241, 242, 243, 245, 253, 255, 257, 260, 270, 272, 275, 280, 283
Diouf, Mamadou & Mbodj, Mohamed 166, 169, 181, 182, 187
DNA 29–30, 134–5, 137, 144
Dogon people 157–8, 172, 189, 247, 259, 269–70
Dorsainvil, Justin 83
Douglass, Frederick 3
Dover, Kenneth 207
Drake, St.Clair 4, 53–4, 64, 70, 136, 229, 250, 255–7, 286
Dr. Dre 282
D'Souza, Dinesh 3, 7–8, 9
Du Bois, W.E.B. 25, 45, 48, 50–53, 54, 55, 57, 58, 69–70, 75, 77, 83, 84, 106, 236, 245, 247, 254, 256, 275
Dumas, Alexandre (Pere) 38
Durkheim, Emile 26
Dutch West India Company 276
Duvalier, François 84–5

Early, Gerald 6
Easton, Hosea 35, 36–7
Edwards, David N. 143–4
Egypt ix–x, 2, 4, 7, 9–10, 14, 15, 21, 22, 32, 33–58 passim, 64, 66–72, 73, 108, 109, 110, 115, 116, 118, 119–20, 122–37, 138–50, 152, 153, 154–5, 158, 159, 163, 164, 165, 166, 167, 168, 169, 170, 172, 173–4, 175, 176, 177, 178, 179, 180, 181, 182–5, 186, 187–8, 189, 190–92, 193, 194–8, 199–200,

202, 204–5, 206, 207, 208–9, 216, 217, 219, 220, 221, 225–6, 227, 228, 231–2, 234, 235, 237–8, 243, 244, 246, 247, 249, 252–3, 255, 259, 260, 261, 262, 264, 265, 266, 269, 273, 277
Ekwe-Ekwe, Herbert 112, 279
El-Amin, Mustafa 71
Ellis, George W. 46–7, 192
Ellison, Ralph 104, 285
Emerson, R.W. 45
England/English 4, 47, 49, 63, 67, 88, 93, 104, 123, 161, 220, 226, 230, 252, 257, 258, 262, 277
Enlightenment, European 7, 20, 64, 124, 257
Equiano, Olaudah 50
Esan people 120
Ethiopia (state) 28, 29, 32–3, 35, 45, 47–8, 49, 56, 73, 104, 111, 138, 144, 154, 175, 195, 219, 220–21, 226, 228, 234, 253, 255, 256, 260
'Ethiopians' (nineteenth -century synonym for 'Negro') ix, 32, 35, 36, 37, 40, 42, 43, 46, 47–8, 55, 73, 119, 120, 134, 147, 198, 206.
ethnophilosophy 24, 158–62, 167, 170, 236, 246, 279
Euclid 38, 152
Eurocentrism 1, 2, 16, 20, 58, 107, 116, 145, 160, 161, 170, 188, 203, 205, 208, 221, 231, 233, 235, 236, 243, 245, 247, 249, 251, 254, 275, 278, 280
'Eve' 28, 30, 254

Fanon, Frantz 24, 26, 77–81, 94, 216, 236, 265
Farrakhan, Louis 50, 55, 71, 73, 77, 86, 108, 112, 218, 275–6, 286
Fell, Barry 250
feminism 11, 20, 29, 98, 110, 175, 259, 279, 280, 281, 282
Ferris, William H. 45–6, 56, 75
Feyerabend, Paul 20
Finch, Charles 188, 255

Fiske, John 284, 286
Fontaine, James 262
Foucault, Michel 81, 160, 168, 207
France/French 2, 16, 24, 26, 27, 38,
    49, 80, 83, 102, 104, 116, 123,
    156, 157, 163, 164, 166, 168, 182,
    184, 191, 194, 200, 247, 269
Frankfort, Henri 10, 130
Freeman, Reverend F. 38
Freemasonry, Masonic orders and
    beliefs 7, 10, 64, 66–72, 122, 123,
    225, 271
Freud, Sigmund 227
Frobenius, Leo 48, 116, 120, 167–8,
    177, 236

Gambia 110, 149, 173
Gao 151, 173
Garlake, Peter S. 117, 147
Garnet, Henry Highland 35, 37, 39,
    40, 50
Garvey, Marcus/Garveyism 10, 24,
    36, 50–51, 54, 55, 63, 70, 73,
    74–7, 77, 85, 90, 94, 217, 224,
    227, 235, 236, 270, 277, 285
Gates, Henry Louis 78, 104, 236, 241,
    278
Genovese, Eugene 218
Germany/Germans 2, 20, 36, 44, 52,
    83, 103, 116, 117, 131, 167, 172,
    175, 193, 194, 198, 202, 208, 210,
    222, 236, 250, 277
Ghana (medieval kingdom) 46, 143,
    149, 237, 238
Ghana (modern) 52, 57, 61, 106,
    134, 159, 160, 219, 230, 238
Ghosh, Amitav ix
Gibbon, Edward 124
Gilroy, Paul 3, 101, 107, 108–9, 110,
    112, 279, 282
Gobineau, Arthur 273, 283
Gould, Stephen Jay 9
Grant, Madison 283
Great Zimbabwe 117–9
Greece/Greeks 2, 9–10, 32, 35, 36,
    37, 38, 39, 40, 43, 44, 45, 46, 47,

48, 66, 68, 73, 116, 123–4,
    127–9, 130, 131, 134, 136, 152–3,
    155, 158, 159, 164, 165, 167, 169,
    174, 175, 176, 177, 181, 188, 191,
    194–5, 196–7, 198–201, 202,
    203–11, 220, 222, 225, 226, 232,
    253, 260, 274, 277
Greenberg, Joseph 167, 183, 185
Greenblatt, Stephen 10
Griaule, Marcel 157–8, 162, 172,
    236, 247, 269–70
Guyana 81, 82

Habermas, Jürgen 16
Haggard, H. Rider 117, 123
Haiti 24, 25, 39, 51, 83–5, 102, 104,
    111, 218, 223
Haley, Alex 108, 152, 190
Hall, Edith 155, 200–201
Hall, Richard Nicklin 118
Hall, Stuart 12, 13
Ham (Biblical figure), 'Sons of Ham'
    36, 37, 38, 42, 56, 278
Hamilton, Alexander 53
Hamilton, Charles 91–2
Hamites 32, 35, 43–4, 46, 47, 50, 51,
    115–17, 118, 119–20, 132, 153,
    177, 224
Hansberry, William Leo 49, 57, 217,
    218
Harding, Sandra 259, 284
Harding, Vincent 15, 59
Harding, Warren 53
Harlem 31, 64, 90, 154, 217, 220,
    224, 226, 241, 261
Hartog, François 153, 200
Hayne, Joseph E. 35, 47, 75
Hegel, G.W.F. 45, 164, 236
Heraclitus 129
Herodotus 38, 40, 46, 48, 119,
    152–3, 155, 193, 200, 205, 206,
    209, 225, 227, 242
Hermeticism 67, 68, 76, 123
Herrnstein, Richard 20
Herskovits, Melville J. 101, 102–3,
    116

Higgins, Godfrey 64, 65, 221
Hill, Anita 111
Hill, Christopher 64, 123
Hilliard, Asa G. 124, 247
Hilliard, David 78
Holocaust/Shoah, Nazi 195, 204, 226, 244, 248, 266, 278
homophobia, Afrocentrists' 223, 228, 278
hooks, bell 98–9, 251, 284
Hopkins, Pauline 35, 55
Horton, James 'Africanus' 25, 35, 38, 42, 50
Horus (Egyptian god) 68, 234, 259, 261
Howard University 8, 218, 280
Hountondji, Paulin J. 159, 160, 161
Houston, Drusilla Dunjee 35, 48–9
Huggins, Nathan 15, 59
Huggins, Willis N. 35, 217, 220–21
Hughes, Langston 105, 106
Hughes, Robert 3, 8, 11, 186, 259
Huiswood, Otto 89, 91
Hurston, Zora Neale 104
Hutu people 225
Hyksos 202, 203, 206

Ice Cube 282
Igbo people 50, 148
Igbo Ukwu burial site 173
India, Indians (of Asia) 15, 21, 38, 40, 48, 82, 124, 133, 244, 257, 276, 283
'Indians' (of the Americas) 21, 53, 172, 230, 233, 247, 250, 251
Inuit people 172, 252
Ireland/Irish 7, 15, 68, 88, 99, 203, 250, 253, 257
Islam/Muslims 12, 39, 46, 49, 70, 71, 72, 85, 94, 95, 108, 120, 121, 135, 138, 149, 150–52, 154, 163, 172, 175, 176, 209, 226, 227, 228, 234, 235, 275, 276, 277–8, 282
Israel 50, 88, 109, 176–7, 207, 210, 257, 236

Jackson, Andrew 53
Jackson, George 78, 95, 97
Jackson, John G. 11, 35, 57, 67, 130, 135, 217, 220–21, 225, 238, 253, 257, 258
Jahn, Janheinz 103
Jamaica 44, 53, 73, 74, 77, 81, 85, 101, 102, 207, 218
James, C.L.R. 25, 77
James, G.G.M. 11, 15, 63, 66, 69, 70, 72, 73, 128, 181, 188, 204–5, 220, 225, 228, 253, 276
Japan/Japanese 40, 227, 253
Jaspers, Karl 103
Jefferson, Thomas 53
Jeffries, Leonard 61, 64, 124, 190, 215, 221–2, 228, 231, 270, 277, 281, 283, 284
Jesus of Nazareth 38, 43, 73, 141, 223, 271
Jews/Judaism 7, 39, 44, 68, 73, 91, 112, 116, 120, 124, 127, 194, 195, 196, 202–4, 209, 222, 225, 226, 228, 229, 244, 255, 260, 266, 273, 275–7, 278, 282, 286
Johansen, Donald 28, 29
Johnson, Charles 24, 106,
Johnson, Edward A. 71, 95, 107
Johnson, Harvey 35, 42–3
Johnson, John H. 49
Johnson, Samuel 120, 169
Johnston, Harry 52, 115
Joseph, Gloria I. 110–11
Joyce, James 258
Just, Ernest Everett 262

Kagame, Alexis 158, 160, 161
Kanem kingdom 143
Karenga, Ron 'Maulana' 11, 27, 78, 94, 124, 128, 215–16, 220, 231, 235, 236, 243, 247, 275, 261
Keita, S.O.Y. 132, 133, 136
Kenya 29, 180
Kerma 141, 143
Keto, C. Tsehloane 254
Khaldun, Ibn 149, 235

Khartoum 237
Khoi peoples 148
Kikuyu people 148
Kilson, Martin 60, 63
King, Martin Luther 77, 187, 281
King, Richard D. 267–8, 283
Kirlian, Semoyn 259
Ki-Zerbo, Joseph 168, 183
Knowles-Borishade, Adekotunbo F. 246
Koreans 276
Ku Klux Klan 69
Kuhn, Thomas 20
Kush/Kushites (or 'Cushites') 32, 35, 36, 37, 40, 42, 48, 141, 143, 144, 190, 286
Kush, Indus Khamit 253

Lambropoulos, Vassilis 198, 203
Leadbeater, C.W. 69
League of Struggle for Negro Rights 90
Leakey, Richard 29, 273
Lee, Spike 281, 282
Lefkowitz, Mary 9–11, 15, 72, 135, 193, 204, 210, 243
Lemelle, Sidney J. 236–7
Lenin, V.I., Leninism 78, 96, 97, 164
Lepsius, K.R. 138
Levine, Molly Myerowitz 193–4, 196, 198, 211
Levy-Bruhl, Lucien 156
Lewis, Robert B. 35, 37–8, 59
Liberia 41, 46, 59, 74, 76, 105–6, 185
Libya/Libyans 131, 136, 144, 175
Lincoln, Abraham 53
L'Ouverture, Toussaint 39
Lucas, J. Olumide 120
'Lucy' 29, 31, 254
Luke, Don 120, 257
Lumpkin, Beatrice 250, 264
Luxor 150
Lynn, Richard 30, 136, 272, 273, 275

McLaughlin, Andree Nicola 98
MacRitchie, David 252

Macedonia 211
Mackey, Nathaniel 107
Madoc legend 250, 257
Maghreb 148–9
Malcolm X 51, 70, 71, 77, 93, 94, 97, 112, 217, 236, 280, 281, 282
Mali 110, 143, 149, 157, 173, 237, 238, 250, 269
Malinowski, Bronislaw 103, 116
Mande people 249
Mandinka people 230
Manning, Kenneth R. 262, 263
Mantle, L.F.C. 73–4
Mao/Maoism 27, 78, 96, 97
Maori people 98, 252
Marable, Manning 3, 8–9, 59, 94, 98, 281
Marranos 276
Marshall, Paule 106
Martin, Tony 10, 33, 204, 218, 277–8, 279, 283
Marx, Karl/Marxism 20, 25, 26, 38, 56, 78, 82, 84, 88, 90, 96, 97, 117, 159, 160, 164, 166, 167, 176, 180, 182, 236, 239, 243, 254
Masai people 148
Masolo, D. A. 158, 160, 161, 186, 261
Massey, Gerald 65, 71, 72, 72, 221, 225, 252, 253, 255, 257, 258
Matthews, Tracye 280
Mauny, Raymond 165, 171, 177
Mauritania 286
Mazrui, Ali 235
Mbiti, John S. 158, 261
Mbochi people and language 179
M'Bow, Amadou-Mahtar 125
Mecca 71, 120, 121, 152
melanin 2, 222, 223, 253, 256, 266–70, 271, 273, 275, 276
Meroe 40, 120, 138, 141, 143–4, 146, 169, 184
Merriman-Labor, A.B.C. 42
Mesopotamia 32, 43, 48, 130, 204, 244
Messiha, Khalil 259
Mexico 68, 172, 249, 250

Milton, John 64
Milwaukee 3
Mohammed (Prophet of Islam) 54, 138, 172
Monomotapa/Munhumutapa kingdom 119, 225
Montelius, Oscar 196
Montellano, Bernard Ortiz de 267, 269, 270
Moorish Science Temple 49, 70, 72
Moors, Morocco 49, 251, 252
Morgan, Lewis Henry 168, 175
Morrison, Toni 106
Moses (Biblical figure) 123, 127, 188, 227
Moses, Wilson J. 5, 6, 55, 58, 105, 228
Moynihan, Daniel Patrick 280
Mozart, W.A. 10, 123
Mudimbe, V.Y. 24–5, 111, 160, 161, 183, 200
Muhammad, Elijah 71, 72, 94
Muhammad, Wali Fard 49
Muhammad, Warith Deen (Wallace) 71
Muhly, James x
Muntu, concept of 156
Murray, Charles 20, 22, 275
Museum of Natural History, New York 142, 154
Mussolini, Benito 75, 84, 221, 226
Mutwa, Credo 236
Mycenaeans 200
Myers, Linda James 246

Napata 138, 141, 191
Nation of Islam 8, 49, 70–71, 85, 94, 95, 108, 135, 226, 227, 275–7
Neanderthals 30, 120, 271–2, 273
negritude 24, 25, 26–7, 80, 83, 85, 157, 158, 160, 170, 233, 246, 260, 265
Newark, NJ 96
Newton, Huey 78
New York 3, 36, 60, 61, 110, 142, 199, 217, 221, 222, 228, 240, 253

Ngugi Wa Thiong'o 14
Niebuhr, Barthold 36
Niger–Congo languages 148
Nigeria 44, 80, 116, 119–20, 148, 154, 173, 190, 191, 251, 259, 260, 279, 282
Nilo–Saharan languages 148
Njia, doctrine of 235
Nkrumah, Kwame 77, 93
Noah (Biblical figure) 37, 54, 55, 116
Nobles, Wade 265
Norris, John William 35, 43–4, 63
Nubia, Nubians 35, 40, 46, 49, 50, 105, 120, 125, 130, 131, 134, 136, 138–45, 146, 147, 148, 149, 154, 180, 191, 197, 200, 219, 21, 234, 237–8, 249, 280
Numa, Frederick 120

Obenga, Theophile 135, 179–81, 184, 185, 191, 236, 243
Ogotemmeli 157–8, 269–70
Okafor, Victor 241, 242, 279
Okur, Nilgun Anadolu 241
Olela, Henry ix, 67, 181, 186
Olmec people 250
Onwuachi, Chike 61
Ouologuem, Yambo 168, 282

Padmore, George 25, 77
Painter, Nell Irvin 61, 62, 64
Palestine/Palestinians 73, 88, 130, 210, 257
Palter, Robert 11, 129, 210, 257
Parker, George Wells 48, 57, 65
Patterson, Orlando 14, 149, 207
Pearson, Roger 136, 275
Pennington, Dorthy 260–61
Pennington, James 35, 36, 37, 48
Perry, W.J. 57
Peters, Erskine 15
Petrie, W. Flinders 134, 225
Phoenicia/Phoenicians 38, 43, 46, 117, 118–19, 191, 194, 195, 197, 200, 202, 205, 209, 250

Piazzi Smyth, Charles 122, 135
Piltdown Man forgery 120, 168, 253
Plato 116, 124, 126, 188, 209, 210,
    248, 257
Portugal/Portuguese 102, 104, 117,
    121, 276
Powell, Adam Clayton 35
Powell, Colin 281
Presence Africaine 27, 80, 110, 164, 165,
    180, 187, 189, 217, 266
Price-Mars, Jean 51, 83–4, 266, 275
Prince Hall Freemasonry 69, 70
Public Enemy (rap group) 108, 227,
    282
Pushkin, Alexander 38, 251
Pygmy peoples 125, 225, 253
Pyramids 36, 39, 41, 43–4, 55, 63, 66,
    73, 122, 129, 135, 136, 173, 249,
    250
Pythagoras 124

Qustul 140

Ransby, Barbara 280
rap music 3, 6, 108, 227, 280, 282
Rashidi, Runoko 252, 257
Rastafarianism 47, 56–7, 73, 85,
    109–10
Ratzel, Friedrich 116
Ravitch, Diane 16, 278
Ray, Benjamin C. 173
Reed, Ishmael 104, 123
Renfrew, Colin 191, 196, 210
Republic of New Africa 95–6
Richards, Dona 247 see also Ani,
    Marimba
Roberts, Jennifer Tolbert 207
Robinson, John G. 69
Rodney, Walter 81–3, 86, 98, 236,
    245, 264, 276
Rogers, J.A. 11, 35, 54–5, 59, 63, 73,
    75, 106, 217, 221, 236, 253, 257,
    258
Rohmer, Sax 72
Rome/Romans 36, 37, 38, 39, 40, 42,
    43, 44, 47, 48, 68, 73, 123, 131,
    134, 135, 144, 169, 171, 196, 210,
    222, 228, 253, 277
Roosevelt, Franklin D. 271
Roosevelt, Theodore 36
Rose, Tricia 282
Rosicrucianism 66, 67
Rushton, Philippe 30, 268, 272, 273

Saakana, Amon Saba 57, 188, 229
Sadi, Abderrahman 46
Sahara 125, 130, 132, 141, 146–7,
    148, 149, 150, 151, 168, 174, 183,
    220, 286
Said, Edward 4, 12, 112, 209, 235
San peoples 148
Sankore, mosque and 'university' of
    106, 150
Sarich, Vincent 31
Sartre, Jean-Paul 24, 26, 79, 164
Scarr, Sandra 9
Schiele, Jerome H. 241, 246–7
Schlesinger, Arthur 3, 8, 11, 103, 227
Scholes, Theophilus E.S. 44–5, 75
Scotland/Scots 67, 88, 89, 252, 277
Scythian people 153
Seale, Bobby 78
Segou kingdom 149
Seifert, Charles C. 35
Seligman, C.G. 115, 130, 172
Senegal 26, 125, 149, 163, 164, 167,
    169, 173, 174, 177, 179, 181, 185,
    186, 190
Senghor, Leopold Sedar 24, 26–7,
    158, 168, 170, 180, 265
Sergi, Guiseppe 32, 34, 46, 56
Sesostris, Pharoah 124, 195, 197
Shakespeare, William 10
Shakur, Sanyika AKA Monster Kody
    Scott 96
Shaw, Florence 52
Shaw, Thurstan 182–3
Shinnie, Peter 140, 146, 184
Sierra Leone 26, 41–2, 149
slavery, slave trades 14, 36, 37, 41, 43,
    52, 53, 54, 55, 56, 80, 82, 93, 96,
    102, 104–5, 109, 116, 119, 126,

131, 133, 145, 149–50, 151, 152, 154, 180, 197, 207, 209, 217, 219, 220, 222, 226, 228, 232–3, 241, 244–5, 248, 257, 258, 262, 265–6, 266–7, 282, 283, 286
Smith, Grafton Elliot 48, 57, 115, 120
Snoop Doggy Dogg 282
Snowden, Frank 11, 57, 134, 206, 210
Socrates 38, 124, 209
Sofola, J.A. 279
Songhay kingdom 143, 149, 151, 155, 237, 238
South Africa 2, 16, 25, 28, 82, 88, 91, 98, 119, 120, 123, 136, 147, 177, 248, 254, 283–4
Soyinka, Wole 14, 243, 282, 283
Spain/Spanish 102, 104, 152, 222, 253, 277
Sphinx 48, 123, 133, 136, 173
Springborg, Patricia 208–9
Stalin, J.V./Stalinism 89, 90, 96, 164, 259
Steele, Shelby 196
Stoddard, Lothrop 283
Stone, I.F. 91
Stringer, Chris 28, 272
Stuckey, Sterling 59
Sudan 120, 132, 138, 139, 141, 142, 143, 144, 149, 151, 154, 219
Sun Ra 63, 64–5, 107
Suriname 101–2, 276
Sutton, J.E.G. 146
Swahili 94, 117, 152, 215, 238, 248
Swedenborg, Emmanuel 65, 123

Taharka, Pharoah 144
Tanzania 29, 81, 259
Tempels, Placide 103, 156–7, 158, 160, 161, 172, 175, 236
Temple University 180, 191, 231, 240–2, 254, 257
Terrasson, Jean 72, 142
Thackeray, William 155
Theosophism 7, 66, 69
Thomas, Clarence 281

Thompson, E.P. 64, 123
Thompson, Robert Farris 3, 101
Thoth (Egyptian god) 67
Thothmes I, Pharoah 45
Thucydides 153, 202
Timbuktu 46, 150–52, 154, 155, 238
Tolson, Melvin B. 105–6
Towa, Marcien 159, 160, 161
Trigger, Bruce G. 138, 142, 143, 251
Truth, Sojourner 110
Turner, Nat 39, 218
Tutankhamun, Pharoah 22, 67, 125, 273
Twain, Mark 7

Ughulu, Emmanuel 120
unanimism 57, 153, 159, 182, 185, 232, 233, 265
UNESCO History of Africa 125, 165, 168, 180, 183–5
United Nations 12, 19
Universal Negro Improvement Association 74
Urhobo people 120

Vai people and language 46, 185, 191–2
Vail, Charles H. 66, 69, 72
Van den Berghe, Pierre 6, 15, 62
Van Sertima, Ivan 11, 32, 73, 136, 173, 187, 188, 189, 244, 247–51, 253, 255, 257, 259, 260, 261, 262
Vansina, Jan 154, 167, 178, 191
Vikings 120, 250
Volney, Constantin 38, 40, 46, 48, 56, 65, 123, 225, 253

Waldron, Jeremy 16
Walker, Abena 261
Walker, Alice 106, 280
Walker, Charles T. 35
Walker, Clarence Earl 15, 85
Walker, David 24, 36, 278
Warsaw 142
Washington, Booker T. 55, 56, 70, 236, 262

Washington, DC 3, 61, 77, 124, 222, 226, 261, 263
Webb, James M. 35
Weber, Max 26
Weidenreich, Franz 30, 34
Wiener, Leo 250, 257
Wellesley College 10, 277
Welsing, Frances Cress 218, 221, 222–3, 227, 228, 248, 255, 256, 261, 266–7, 269, 270, 271, 273, 283, 284, 285
West, Cornel 97, 99, 102, 278
Wheatley, Phillis 39
White, Timothy 28, 29
Williams, Bruce 140
Williams, Chancellor 11, 51, 57, 72, 133, 147, 148, 150, 151, 218–19, 221, 228, 235, 236, 238, 282
Williams, George Washington 40–41, 56
Winters, Clyde 206
Wiredu, Kwasi 159–60, 161, 249
Wise, Stephen 226

Wolof people and language 163, 172, 178–9, 184, 189, 191, 234
Wolpoff, Milford 28, 30, 34, 272
Woodson, Carter G. 50, 57, 238, 276
Wright, Richard 112
Wuthenau, Alexander von 136, 250

Yellen, John 34
Yergan, Max 13
Yoruba people 40, 104, 111, 115, 116, 119, 120, 121, 146, 149, 154, 169, 180, 225, 226, 234, 248, 259–60, 262
Young, Robert J.C. 196–7
Yurco, Frank 11, 21

Zachernuk, Philip 119
Zaire/Congo 33, 44, 56, 64, 104, 156, 180
Ziegler, Dhyana 239, 242–3
Zimbabwe/Rhodesia 91, 117–19, 219, 225
Zionism 202
Zulu people 145, 147, 225, 236